DATE DUE

DEMCO 38-296

THE JEWS AND THE NATION

THE JEWS *and the* NATION

REVOLUTION, EMANCIPATION, STATE FORMATION, AND THE LIBERAL PARADIGM IN AMERICA AND FRANCE

FREDERIC COPLE JAHER

PRINCETON UNIVERSITY PRESS
PRINCETON AND OXFORD

Copyright © 2002 by Princeton University Press

Published by Princeton University Press, 41 William Street,
Princeton, New Jersey 08540

In the United Kingdom: Princeton University Press,
3 Market Place, Woodstock, Oxfordshire OX20 1SY

Library of Congress Cataloging-in-Publication Data

Jaher, Frederic Cople
The Jews and the nation : revolution, emancipation, state formation, and
the liberal paradigm in America and France / Frederic Cople Jaher.
p.cm.
Includes bibliographical references (p.) and index.
ISBN 0-691-09649-X
1. Jews—France—History—18th century. 2. Jews—Emancipation—France. 3. Minorities—
Legal status, laws, etc.—France—History. 4. France—Politics and government—
18th century. 5. France—Social conditions—18th century. 6. France—Ethnic relations.
7. France—History—Philosophy. 8. National characteristics, French. 9. Jews—United
States—History—18th century. 10. Liberalism—United States—History. 11. Minorities—
Legal status, laws, etc.—United States—History. 12. United States—Politics and government—18th century. 13. United States—Social conditions—To 1865. 14. United States—
History—Philosophy. 15. Multiculturalism. I. Title.
DS135.F82 J34 2003
944'.004924—dc21   2002029339

British Library Cataloging-in-Publication Data is available.

This book has been composed in Sabon

Printed on acid-free paper.∞

www.pupress.princeton.edu

Printed in the United States of America

10 9 8 7 6 5 4 3 2 1

For Irma Margrill
Everyone Should Have an Aunt like Her

CONTENTS

PREFACE   ix

PART I
Introduction   1

CHAPTER 1
The Prospect   3

CHAPTER 2
The Nation   33

PART II
The Account   57

CHAPTER 3
The French Experience I: The Revolution and Its Republic   59

CHAPTER 4
The French Experience II: Napoleon and the First Empire   103

CHAPTER 5
The American Experience   138

PART III
Conclusion   173

CHAPTER 6
The Argument   175

CHAPTER 7
The Outcome   220

NOTES   239

INDEX   285

The Jews and the Nation in many respects continues an inquiry initiated in *A Scapegoat in the New Wilderness*, my examination of the origins and rise of anti-Semitism in America. In both books I explore the impact of the Jews on nations in which they dwelled through a holistic perspective that combines comparative, political, economic, social, intellectual and cultural dimensions. In *Scapegoat*, I emphasized the psychological and cultural facets of my subject and, given the nature of the topic, the negative aspects of the interaction between Jews and the gentile community. Here I give precedence to how the Jews relate to and reflect upon the political culture of France and the United States. I also devote more attention to the response of the Jewish communities in these nations to the challenges and opportunities afforded by national citizenship. Finally, in *The Jews and the Nation* I attempt to resurrect grand theory in historical study by interpreting the Jewish experience through the liberal paradigm as formulated by Alexis de Tocqueville and Louis Hartz. I further analyze the validity of this hypothesis by applying it to other marginalized groups.

It is with great pleasure and appreciation that I acknowledge the venues in which I gave preliminary versions of this study and the assistance I received in its composition. As a "work in progress," *The Jews and the Nation* was presented at the conference "The Jews and the Expansion of Europe to the West: 1450 to the Political Independence of the Americas" organized by the John Carter Brown Library, June 1997, at The Twelfth World Congress of Jewish Studies, Jerusalem, Israel, July–August, 1997, and at a 1997 session of the History Workshop of the History Department of the University of Illinois at Champaign-Urbana. In these meetings I received invaluable critical responses. On an individual basis, I am profoundly grateful for Sudhir Hazareesingh's insightful reading of the manuscript, especially with regard to historically oriented French political theory. Friends and colleagues took time from their own endeavors to read this work in its entirety and to my great benefit: Lillian Handlin's advice was particularly useful on the application of the liberal paradigm to African-Americans and women. Leonard Dinnerstein's reading helped me to improve the chapter on American Jews. Kevin Doak, a student of Japanese nationalism, provided excellent insights on the theory of national culture. John Lynn, a historian of the French Revolution, has a passion for anonymity, but I hope that he will forgive my thanking him publicly for invaluable contributions to the chapters on the Jews and related matters in the sections on the French Revolution and the First Empire. Seymour Drescher twice read the completed manuscript; his readings enriched all aspects of it and he played an indispensable role in its publication. Thomas LeBien, my editor at Princeton University Press, believed in the book, arranged for insightful outside readers, and his unerring judgment enhanced its quality and enabled its publication. Other members of the Press, Timothy Sullivan, Maura Roessner, and Jonathan Munk, my copy editor, were gracious and superb in assisting in the publication of this book. John Katz, my research assistant, did most of the translations and the secretarial staff of the history department, particularly Aprel Orwick, was helpful far beyond their official obligations. I dedicate this book to my Aunt, Irma Margrill who, among other things, taught me how to dance and roller skate and introduced me to Chinese food.

Frederic Cople Jaher
Champaign-Urbana, Illinois

PART I

INTRODUCTION

CHAPTER 1

THE PROSPECT

The Jews and the Nation is a multilayered meditation on the early national history of France and the United States. The exploration features an account of the experience of each country's Jews respectively during the War for Independence and the early Republic and the French Revolution and the First Empire. Since treatment of the Jews always reflects broader conditions and circumstances, this inquiry further ramifies into analytical perspectives on both French and American civic culture and society. In expanding from group to nation—"contextualization" in current jargon—the exploration moves from narrative to interpretation and from account to theory.

The history of the Jews in these epochs and places and its amplification into, and illumination of, state and society is starkly revealed by the resonance of the "Jewish Question," especially those aspects of it that involved emancipation and citizenship in revolutionary France. According to the latest and best study of the *cahiers de doléances*, in frequency of subjects mentioned the lowest ranked subject for the Parish cahiers (primary documents from preliminary rural peasant assemblies of the Third Estate) listed 1088. In the general cahiers (those brought to Versailles in 1789) from the Third Estate and the Nobility, the least-mentioned subjects ranked 1197 and 1125, respectively. In those listings, Jews placed 367, 492.5, and 470, again respectively; nearly in the top third for the Parish documents and high in the top half for the general cahiers. Nevertheless, at least for the cahiers that reached the Estates General, Jews were not a major source of grievance. Only 337 called attention to problems associated with Jews. Compared to Protestants, a much larger, more volatile, and important group, however, Jews were a veritable obsession. The Protestants, who in recent times had waged momentous and bloody struggles with Catholic France, scored 743 in the Parish *Cahiers*, 824.5 in the general cahiers of the Third Estate, and 955.5 in those of the Nobility.[1]

During the short life of the National Constituent Assembly, the status of Jews was discussed at thirty sessions between August 1789 and September 1791. This issue preoccupied the nation's legislature and was frequently raised in meetings of municipal bodies and Jacobin clubs at a time when the 40,000 Jews in France comprised but .16 percent of the national population. In these debates, lifting economic, occupational, and residential restrictions and special taxes imposed upon Jews was rarely and weakly disputed. The primary points of contention were whether Jews should be citizens and the relationship between their emancipation and rights, revolution, republicanism, political culture, civic morality, and the nation-state. As Gary Kates and Ronald Schecter observe, in the debates of the National Assembly the Jews were less substantive than representative. Emancipation and the Jews were markers of greater national concerns like liberty, virtue, and citizenship. Jews compelled attention not only in civic matters and bodies. The ARTFL database of French literature shows for the eighteenth century 2,346 listings for Jews, compared to 1,755 references to the English.[2] Conversely, in America Jews were a minor consideration in deliberations about the Revolution, citizenship, and other matters of freedom and state formation.

For most of their history as nation-states, or at least since their seminal Revolutions, France and the United States have been Republics. They have also tended toward liberal immigration policies and their nationalisms have been territorial rather than *völkisch*, as in Germany. Such differences in national culture have meant that Jews in France and, still more, in America have been likelier than those in Germany to be perceived as a religious rather than an ethnic group. In the intersection of religion, ethnicity and nationhood, Jews were less of a threat to the modern nation-state as another creed than as another blood.

Commitments to democracy, newcomers, and inclusive nationalism (at least for white males) are prevalences rather than absolutes. Xenophobia, organic nationalism, and antirepublicanism have existed in both countries, especially France. Yet the presence of overlapping attitudes toward individual freedom, popular sovereignty, immigrants, and national identity in America and France suggests that variances in these civic sensibilities cannot alone account for differences in each country's treatment of the Jews. Revolutionary and republican France have largely associated religion with a discredited and repudiated past, whereas revolutionary and republican America have prevalently identified their history and community as connected to, and even fulfilled by, religion. Besides showing that nationalism, secularization, and modernism are not necessarily sequential phenomena, this divergence also contributes to the dissimilar trajectories of Jews in France and the United States.

National variances in multiculturalism, state structure and governance, republicanism, and liberalism produced different types of emancipation, particularly since treatment of Jews was emblematic of these larger forces. Since Jews were granted political equality in France during a time of revolution and the formation of a nation-state, what were the interconnections among these developments? Did a similar convergence take place in America during the War for Independence and the early

Republic? And, if so, did revolution, emancipation, and state formation interact in the same way? In a related, but slightly different, analytic mode, was emancipation a sudden, seismic eruption or a gradual emergence?

What is the relationship between multiculturalism and emancipation? The United States is a federated polity and a pluralistic society; France is a centralized state and, compared to America, a monocultural society: Would a more mediated and privatized society give Jews greater autonomy in the sense that citizenship and Judaism would not be presented as conflicting alternatives? Were Jews in this kind of nation less likely to face mutually exclusive choices of withdrawal in closed, pariah communities, participation in the civic community, or emigration to avoid the dilemma of ethnocide or rejection?

Did divisions over emancipation exist within the Jewish national communities? What, if any, dissimilarities on this matter existed between French and American Jewry? Were Jews the primary procurers of their rights? If not, who was and why? Did national variances distinguish liberalizers in France and the United States?

What were the repercussions of emancipation? How did Jews respond to their new political status? What was the reaction of non-Jews to Jews as fellow citizens? Did the responses of Jews and Gentiles to emancipation differ within France and America? Did the degree and results of civic equality vary between these countries? Was emancipation permanent or reversible?

Of particular relevance to this study, which links the Jewish predicament to state creation and national culture, what were the forces that transcended this predicament while simultaneously shaping it? In this category of concerns are the cultural dynamics of spiritual (especially Christian) and secular commitment, of authority and autonomy, of inclusion and exclusion, of diversity and homogeneity, and of rigidity and adaptation to social change. Associated with these phenomenological exigencies are equally insistent imperatives of revolution, nation building, war, conquest, economic development and crisis, and the multitudinous complexities of politics and governance.

Like all complex social phenomena, emancipation was multidimensional: ideological (Enlightenment principles, liberalism, pluralism, republicanism, nationalism, egalitarianism, communitarianism); cultural (national culture as inclusive or exclusive, xenophobia versus tolerance, historical and contemporary attitudes toward Jews in particular and outsiders in general, as well as to Judaism in particular and religion in general); and structural (citizenship in the nation-state, revolutionary transitions, republican rule). Subsumed in yet another analytic rubric is the issue of whether the controversy over Jewish liberation arose primarily from national or transnational forces and whether it had a master (transnational) or differentiated (national) typology.[3]

These and other issues concerning Jews are developed in chapters 3–5. The discussion of theory, however, cannot be wholly postponed or preempted by referral to subsequent examination. Here it is relevant to address the historiographical role of theory and which paradigm has been selected or rejected and why. A conceptual framework is also the subject of chapter 2. Nationalism and national culture and identity are discussed in the abstract and as they generally apply to France, the United States, and Jews. Chapter 6 elaborates on the coherence of the chosen construct by testing its applicability to other marginalized groups, particularly women and blacks, the national context of France and America from 1775 to 1815 and, beyond that, to the respective social structures and values of these countries. Chapter 7 refocuses on the Jewish experience in France and America by bringing it up to date. As usual, these post-1815 developments are integrated into the national cultures of these countries, especially as they touch on issues relevant to liberalism, pluralism, and consensus.

It is well to begin this discussion of historiography and paradigms by reviewing a current dispute and paradox. As noted by Daniel T. Rodgers in 1992 in *The Journal of American History*, from the 1930s to the 1980s several successive "reigning paradigms" have emerged in U.S. history. The Beardian-Progressive construct dominated in the 1930s and 1940s and was followed, in the 1950s and 1960s, by the Tocqueville-Hartz model of liberalism. Starting in the mid-1960s, events and consequent ideological changes radicalized the country and the profession and increasingly discredited the liberal thesis. But fragmentation did not endure. By the mid-1970s, another theory, republicanism, emerged to bring order to American historical studies. This model, however, never dispensed with Hartzian ideas and, by the late 1980s, had lost conceptual sovereignty.[4]

Where Rodgers depicted a current conceptual wasteland, Keith Windschuttle, in *The Killing of History* (1996), found a conceptual overgrowth that threatened to divert, defile, and degenerate historical scholarship. Borrowed from other disciplines, paradigms formulated by structuralism, poststructuralism, postmodernism, and critical theory endangered the historical enterprise. Particularly perilous was the deconstructionist thrust of the latter three discourses. By asserting that truth and reality had no validity independent of time, place, and personal bias, deconstructionism struck at the heart of historical endeavor. For Windschuttle, historians were embracing theories that privileged text over context, language (signs, signifiers, discourses, metaphors) over events, movements, circumstances, and conditions, and heremeneutics over history. The new order of priorities erased distinctions between the subjective and the ob-

jective and between fiction and truth. Thus were negated the basic principles, procedures, and aspirations of the profession—narrative structure,
empirical research, and inductive reasoning employed to authenticate a
palpable past.[5]

One trend transcends the contention of whether too little or too much
theory best describes the present state of the field. Historians of all schools
of thought, with varying reservations and degrees of resistance, agree that
minihistory is the mode of scholarship presently predominant. Small subjects are tentatively treated, which may or may not reveal an uncontested
actuality or clarify larger contexts and developments. This long and hotly
debated historiographical turn has been attributed to a changed disciplinary cynosure. Since the 1960s, previously peripheral groups, among them
women, Indians, blacks, and gays and lesbians, have become central concerns of scholarship. Rather than leading to more comprehensive interpretations, these new studies have been centrifugal analytic forces. Instead
of promoting synthesis, they have fragmented American history into a
mosaic of independent forces, enclaves, and cultures, each marching
under its own banner of agency and autonomy and displaying its own
noble wounds of contested oppression.

The rise of transnational and global studies and their putative displacement of national history is another explanation for the current
trends toward difference and relativity. The nation as an organizing and
determinative category has been weakened. Its increasing displacement
by other modes of analysis has further reduced the possibility of an accept-
able synthesis of the particular experiences of the multivariate genders,
races, ethnicities, classes, and religions that constitute U.S. history and
society. Finally, it has been contended that the discrediting of earlier comprehensive grand theories—Progressive history, Marxism, and liberal consensus—as reliable accounts of the American experience has discouraged
the search for definitive paradigms.[6]

Windschuttle's philippic against recent developments in the humanities and social sciences particularly excoriated the French. Semiotics,
structuralism, and deconstruction were French concoctions that imperiled
not only historical studies but truth itself. This defender of a beleaguered
status quo arraigned the usual culprits—Jacques Derrida, Jacques Lacan,
and Claude Levi-Strauss. Windschuttle's harshest critique was reserved
for Michel Foucault, possibly because he was a historian, and thus a trai-
tor in the service of the postmodern conspiracy against research, relevance, and reality.[7]

Another prime Windschuttle target, Hayden White's *Metahistory:
The Historical Imagination in Nineteenth-Century Europe* (1973), the
historiographical bible of the new methodology, exasperated the doughty
defender of traditional history. The offensive words in the title were "Meta-

history" and "Imagination," which in Windshuttle's view convey the outrageous notion that "histories . . . contain a deep structural content which is generally poetic, and specifically linguistic." The template "serves as the precritically accepted paradigm of what a distinctively 'historical' explanation should be. This paradigm functions as the 'metahistorical' element in all [comprehensive] historical works." History is poetry, its explanatory process is "prefiguration," and its truth is a matter of "linguistic protocol." What White defined as historical inquiry, Windschuttle recoiled from as "a depressing omen" of what "theorists of cultural studies" can inflict upon the historical endeavor.[8]

More polemical than prudent, Windschuttle did at least correctly identify the trends. Since before World War II, French historians have differed from their American counterparts in taking Marx more seriously and being more open to new topics and methodologies and more inclined to social theory. Starting in the 1960s, however, American scholars in a variety of fields have looked to France, and especially to the *Annales* school, for conceptual and methodological leadership. From that turbulent decade to this day historiographical trajectories in these nations have more closely corresponded. French scholars have shown a higher regard for Marxism, but its discourse never dominated historical studies in that country. Historians from France persisted longer in undertaking grand topics, as in the works of Philippe Ariès and Foucault in the 1970s, but they also, as with the *Annales* school, led the downsizing movement that influenced American historians to particularize their own efforts. Finally, the dispersion of subject, theme, and method, which Rodgers reported in American historical studies, took place about the same time and drew the same notice in France.[9]

John Demos's *The Unredeemed Captive* (1994), winner of the Francis Parkman and Ray Allen Billington Prizes of the Organization of American Historians and a National Book Award finalist, epitomizes the regnant genre of history. It's subtitle, "A Family Story From Early America," suggests (perhaps articulates) the microtopicality and contingent view of reality and truth that, depending upon the historian's viewpoint, defy or challenge the profession. In addition, *The Unredeemed Captive* focuses on how an oppressed group (Indians) exercised autonomy and agency.[10]

Minihistory has fragmented the discipline and currently no grand theories integrate the specialized research that threatens to engulf historical studies and stifle generalization or synthesis. Paradigms appropriated from such disciplines as literary, cultural, and linguistic studies, communications, and anthropology intensify disunity because they contradict the traditional premises and purposes of historical inquiry.

Diffusion, however, may be an incentive to seek a unifying theory, even if that quest is incomplete. An abstract model of limited explanatory scope and power may be better than the current state of paradigmatic absence or anarchy. A good place to initiate the search for such a construct is the current mantra of the profession—race, class, and gender. Race and gender are basic components in American society and in modes of social analysis. Yet it would be an aggrandizement to essentialize them in a grand interpretation of French or U.S. history. Among the subjects examined in this study, the Revolutions of 1775 and 1789 for example, crucial features would be lost or distorted by channeling explanations of these events primarily through racial or gender categories.

The current unfashionable Marxian construct of class, by dint of its claim of comprehensiveness, is deceptively more promising. But its core doctrines have thus far proved remote from, and even contradictory to, the development of American capitalism. American historical reality is inaccurately interpreted by applying to this nation Marxist doctrines of immiseration of the masses, leading to a downward mobility that results in a shrinking upper and middle class and a swelling lower class, classes as conflict categories, and a growing class consciousness that erodes ties to distractive (nonclass) groups and identities, ending in a triumphal proletarian revolution.

The liberal consensus propounded by Alexis de Tocqueville in *Democracy in America* (1835, 1840) and Louis Hartz in *The Liberal Tradition in America* (1955), is a more appropriate analytic system for examining the American experience. A modified version of this paradigm is the theoretic motif that undergirds this study. Seemingly suited to the tenor and history of the national culture, these books were well-received as characterizations of American society and civilization. *Democracy in America*, in its eighth edition by 1840, was adopted as a public school text in France, and was also popular in America. The French Academy awarded it a prize and Tocqueville became one of the forty "Immortals" of that august body in 1841. *The Liberal Tradition in America* also received plaudits, among them the Woodrow Wilson Foundation award of the American Political Science Association. High esteem, however, did not last. Although Tocqueville perceived the danger of an aggrieved South and a racially divided community to the future of the country, between 1860 and the end of the 1930s *Democracy in America* languished as a guide to national developments.[11] The liberal consensus model seemed remote from the reality of civil and world war, industrial triumphs and tensions, and the Great Depression.

Starting in the late 1930s, and especially after World War II, the course of history rejuvenated the liberal paradigm, resurrected Tocqueville as an interpreter of American society, and elevated Hartz to a premier place among the postwar generation of political theorists of America. The reversal of fortune was partly due to epistemological changes, perhaps better described as disciplinary modifications in history and political science. For twenty years after the late 1940s, intellectual history was the most fashionable subject in historical studies. At the same time, political theory assumed greater eminence in political science. Additionally, Tocqueville was regarded as an originator of mass society theory (better known in America as "populism") then considered to be a primary explanation for the emergence of fascism abroad and populism, McCarthyism, and the southern rights movement at home. These developments facilitated the revival of Tocqueville and the rise of Hartz.

But the renewal of liberal consensus theory derived mainly from interlocked domestic and global political developments. America's struggle and victory over Nazism, the return of prosperity, the confrontation with Marxism in the Soviet Union and China, and the conservatism of the Eisenhower years made the ideas of Tocqueville and Hartz an ideological haven and propagandistic catapult for what was then called "the American way of life." American equality, freedom, and stability, conflated with an effective absence of radical ideologies and movements, revolutionary impulses, and class conflicts, became the essence of "American exceptionalism." Advocates of this doctrine believed the nation to be moderate, harmonious, and committed to liberty. They saw in these attributes the sources of national success and greatness, as well as the traits of a free republic that contrasted so favorably with despotic communism. From such beliefs came the entitlement notion of an "American century"—the United States was divinely, or at least by dint of its virtue and enlightenment, destined to lead the world. Most significantly, for the purposes of this study, consensus liberals looked upon Tocqueville and Hartz as key formulators of what then seemed like an unassailable hypothesis and profound interpreters of America past, present, and future.

By the 1950s, components of Cold War historicism had fused into a widely held theory of the American past. Freedom, democracy, abundance, stability, civic virtue, national innocence, consensus, and exceptionalism were conjoined neither by mandates of logic or history nor by the nature of these essentialized American traits, but they coalesced in the reigning interpretation of the times. A conservative celebration of the American experience, consensus exceptionalism, displaced the progressive historians' perspective of conflicting interests and groups and, in its own time, would be discredited by another radical revisitation of U.S. history.

Ushered in by the radicalization of the civil rights movement, a new era of civil strife rapidly expanded into face-offs over Vietnam, social justice, and women's and gay rights, creating a counterculture, and engendering mistrust between the generations. By the late 1960s, this crescendo of conflict had discredited the liberal consensus. Friction, diversity, fragmentation, and the struggles of marginalized groups to achieve agency and fend off oppression seemed a more palpable presentation of the nation's past. The exceptionalistic synthesis was now labeled a conservative and conformist denial of long-standing grievances of race, class, and gender. For the new generation of historians, as John Higham observes, America, far from being unique, was just another racist and imperialistic power. Its reality, past and present, was coercive and alienating, as opposed to liberal and unifying, hierarchical rather than egalitarian. Younger scholars thought the country in a state of decline and increasingly unable to address domestic or global predicaments. Hence, they focused on smaller enclaves, usually the downtrodden, instead of larger units like the nation. They constructed narratives of these oppressed peoples and looked upon the larger themes of their predecessors as bromides for the nation's painful, and often ugly, record.[12]

The master narrative of postwar U.S. history is now nearly extinct and its luminaries have been dimmed. Richard Hofstadter, Daniel Boorstin, David Potter, and Oscar Handlin go unmentioned and Louis Hartz has but one entry in *Telling the Truth About History*, a recent and popular historiographical survey. Tocqueville has retained, and even regained, some esteem as a theorist of modern political liberalism, an anticipator of mass society theory, and particularly as an early formulator of the currently popular concept of civil society. Hartz, however, has faded into virtual anonymity. Nine years after *The Liberal Tradition in America*, he collaborated with other scholars in a study of Lockian liberalism in the United States and other fragments of European settlement. *The Founding of New Societies*, however, won no prizes. Themes fresh and dramatic in 1955 were unexciting by 1964. That the provocative had turned prosaic was not the sole factor in the slight impact of the later volume. America had moved on to an era where consensus liberalism seemed less like an epiphany than a rationalization. Oblivion beckoned; Hartz stopped publishing and students in a recent graduate colloquium in U.S. history at a major university knew nothing of *The Liberal Tradition in America* or *The Founding of New Societies*.[13]

The history wars of the 1950s–1970s, with their myths and countermyths and colliding narratives, have long subsided. Nevertheless, it is still useful to remember that not all claimants of consensus exceptionalism extolled their construct of national culture and society. Louis Hartz, balefully contemplating the illiberal consequences of his country's continuous, total, and obsessive embrace of Lockian liberalism, was the pessimistic exception to the exceptionalist school of American history.

Any grand theory conceptualized around a particular nation necessarily posits exceptionalism, and Tocqueville and Hartz proceeded from this premise. According to Seymour Martin Lipset, Tocqueville actually invented the term in addition to advancing the concept. "The position of America is therefore quite exceptional," he wrote in *Democracy in America*, "and it may be believed that no democratic people will ever be placed in a similar one." The uniqueness of the United States proceeds from making the nation the organizing category of social analysis: "Let us cease, then, to view all democratic nations under the example of the American people, and attempt to survey them at length with their own features."[14]

For Hartz, the defining difference between the United States and other countries was the absence of feudalism. Contrasting Europe and America in this respect, "affirm[ed] . . . our national uniqueness." Lacking a feudal past, America was the quintessence of Lockian liberalism, a natural and inherent condition that distinguished it from all other national societies.[15]

No more compelling argument was advanced for the discordance between liberal America and its totalitarian adversaries or, for that matter, between stable America and some of its more volatile allies, than the differences between their revolutions. Analyses of these insurgencies took on ontological dimensions as the variances perceived between the American and other upheavals became signifiers of the essence of, and disharmony between, their systems. The American Revolution was deemed a merited and moderate action for a justified and inevitable transition to independence. According to pundits writing in the Eisenhower era, not the least of the virtues of the rebellion, and a primary cause of its restraint and success in shaping the enduring republic, was the absence of class conflict and its peaceful transfer of power. Indeed, they thought the latter was a consequence of the former. Thus did the American Revolution become a key component of American exceptionalism. Other insurgencies were confrontations between feudalism and modernity, monarchies and republics, capitalists and workers, radicals and reactionaries. America's alleged classless society and conservative battle for independence was favorably contrasted with the strife and agony of the Russian and Chinese Revolutions and their aftermaths. Those making this comparison felt validated by the ideas of Tocqueville and Hartz.

In the course of their exploration of society and polity in France and America, Tocqueville and Hartz commented on the uprisings in these countries that would establish their nationhood. The intellectual engagement of Tocqueville's later life was to undertake a comprehensive account of the French Revolution. On the other hand, even in *Democracy in America*, he devoted little attention to the American struggle for self-government. The index of a standard edition of this book had only one entry on the American Revolution. Joshua Mitchell correctly notes that, although it was mentioned a few more times in the text, the event was largely ignored by Tocqueville, who apparently considered it unimportant.[16]

For Tocqueville, the American Revolution was mild, ordered, and limited. It fostered democracy by contributing to the eradication of the slight (compared to Europe) "aristocratic influence" in colonial times. But equal partition of land, he thought, was in fact more responsible for eliminating the concentration of wealth that fortified the provincial patriciate. After the Revolution, the franchise was broadened, thus removing the other source of support for the landed elite. Overthrow of British rule was relatively uncomplicated and necessitated only minor disturbance: "The Revolution of the United States was the result of a mature and reflecting preference for freedom, and not of a vague or ill-defined craving for independence. It contracted no alliance with the turbulent passions of anarchy, but its course was marked, on the contrary, by a love of order and law."[17] The unstated comparison, of course, was to the French Revolution: "Although I rarely spoke of France in my book [Democracy in America], I did not write one page of it without thinking about her and without having her, so to speak, before my eyes," he told a friend. "And what above all I have sought to put in relief in relation to the United States was less the complete picture of that foreign society than its contrasts and resemblances to our own."[18]

The basic cause for the ordered and moderate insurgency had, however, little to do with voting rights or land distribution. As Tocqueville wrote in an eloquent and celebrated passage from Democracy in America, "The great advantage of the Americans is that they arrived at a state of democracy without having to endure a democratic revolution and that they are born equal instead of becoming so."[19] Here, again, the implicit contrast is with France.

"When Tocqueville wrote that the 'great advantage' of the American lay in the fact that he did not have 'to endure a democratic revolution,'" Hartz said in The Liberal Tradition in America, "he advanced what was surely one of his most fundamental insights into American life." In agreement with his historical mentor that democracy was endemic to the nation and that 1776 therefore entailed no dismantling of a preexisting social system as in 1789 in France or 1917 in Russia, Hartz similarly noted the relative blandness of the American upheaval: "For the great point of departure of great revolutionary thought everywhere else in the world has been the effort to build a new society on the ruins of the old one, and this is an experience America has never had. We are reminded again of Tocqueville's statement: the Americans are 'born equal.' "[20]

This phrase enthralled Hartz. He used the passage in which it appears as the epigraph of the Liberal Tradition in America and the phrase is quoted and approvingly attributed to Tocqueville three other times in the book.[21] Hartz associated parity of origin and circumstances with American submission to Lockian liberal absolutism, thus divorcing autonomy from equality and democracy. Born equal did not mean born free.

Although Tocqueville, like Hartz, argued that equality and republican government could endanger liberty, the tutor was, nonetheless, misrepresented by his disciple. The notion of being born equal is essentialized in *The Liberal Tradition in America*, whereas that of being born free takes precedence in *Democracy in America*.

Tocqueville established the premise on which liberty is privileged in volume I, chapter 2 ("Origin Of The Anglo-Americans, And Importance Of This Origin In Relation To Their Future Condition."). Despite disputing the racialist views of his former acolyte and private secretary Arthur de Gobineau, Tocqueville came near to adopting genetic explanations of national character.[22] Underscoring the implications of its title, Tocqueville in this chapter declared: "America is the only country . . . where the influence exercised on the future condition of states by their origin is clearly distinguishable."[23] This version of organic nationalism was ventured because Tocqueville felt that the American character was essentially unformed at the time of its founding, when European settlers arrived from established countries with entrenched traits and customs.

Love of liberty was one of the values and conventions that British settlers brought on their journey across the Atlantic. Devotion to freedom antedates the American commitment to equality, which resulted from conditions in the New World. In volume II, Tocqueville bluntly states the priority of liberty over equality: "The English . . . carried with them to America" a number of "free institutions and manly customs." They "were conversant with trial by jury; they were accustomed to liberty of speech and of the press, to personal freedom, to the notion of rights and the practice of asserting them." These inherited "institutions preserved them against the encroachments of the state." In fact, "among the Americans it is freedom that is old; equality is of comparatively modern date."[24]

Although parity is more easily and completely achieved in the United States, it is "in Europe, where equality, introduced by absolute power and under the rule of kings, was already infused into the habits of nations long before freedom had entered their thoughts." According to Tocqueville, the propensity for equality in Europe is the "reverse" of the inclination toward liberty in America.[25]

The idea that all are born equal, for Hartz, precluded class formation. With the provincial aristocracy—patroons and planters—dependent upon capitalism or, at best, "feudal relics" long displaced by mainstream Lockian liberalism, America had no class confrontations. Indeed, such conflict could not exist because all Americans were middle class. A "frontal attack against feudalism," as in the overthrow of the Bourbons, "involves a rejection of the past, [whereas] a mopping up campaign against feudal relics in a liberal society involves fulfillment of it. While the one creates deep social scars, the other leads to a comfortable sense of fuller integration." In " 'a nation born equal' . . . history had already accomplished the ending of the old European order in America due to the fact that its 'social revolution', instead of tearing the soul of the nation apart, integrated it further."[26]

Defined thus by Hartz, the "spirit of 1776" had "a sober temper" and "looked forward to the future . . . but worshipped the past as well." Having "inherited the freest society in the world," the "revolutionaries of 1776" were "conservative" in outlook. The unified, bourgeois Americans, however, were an ideal type whose tranquility was not replicated elsewhere. With "no challenge of an aristocratic feudalism," they "lacked the passionate middle-class consciousness" of European liberal thought.[27] Or, to posit the situation in Hegelian and Marxian terms, no thesis meant no antithesis and, therefore, no dialectical conflict of opposites.

Hartz's view about the absence of "aristocratic feudalism" and its consequential absence of class conflict approached more closely than did Tocqueville's formulation of liberty and equality the ingrained national ideology. Americans generally did not perceive a threat to liberty in inequalities of wealth or social standing, but rather in privilege, which was considered the grave danger to democracy. Denial of equal opportunity through law, birth, custom, or other entitlement challenged the cherished American belief (some have called it myth) that government exercised power by consent of the governed. Such prerogatives, usually and negatively associated with European nobility and monarchy, ensured that the state belonged to the elite and not the people and that the few would use their power to tyrannize the many.[28]

Linked to the liberal victory over feudalism and absolutism was the liberal triumph of religious freedom. "The revolution would be led in part by fierce Dissenting ministers," claimed Hartz; consequently, in America no Christian reactionary, antirevolutionary force developed. "Thus the American liberal[s] instead of being forced to pull the Christian heaven down to earth," as the French did in 1793–94, "were glad to let it remain where it was. They did not need to make a religion out of the revolution"—no republic of reason here—"because religion was already revolutionary."[29] In the body of Christ, as in the body politic, the American Revolution, contrary to European insurgencies in harboring no dialectical divisions, united liberalism with stability.

A theorist of American politics and society, Hartz focused more extensively on the American Revolution than on its French counterpart. Chapters 2 and 3 of *The Liberal Tradition* are devoted to the former, whereas the latter has only two index entries in the book as a whole. Although references to the French Revolution are rare, Hartz's discussion of the confrontations between the old order and its deposers clearly indicates that he thought the American upheaval less dialectical, radical, and ideological and, therefore, not as intense, disruptive of communal consensus, or prone to recurrence as were the French Revolution and other European uprisings.

Since Tocqueville's primary concern was with his own country, the French Revolution preoccupied him. This subject had seven entries in the index to a popular edition of *Democracy in America*, and *The Old Regime and the French Revolution* (1856) was projected as the opening volume of a mammoth study of that crisis and its consequences. Regardless of their different priorities and perspectives, Tocqueville and Hartz agreed as much in their interpretations of the French Revolution as they had over the meaning of its American predecessor.

While Tocqueville approved of some aspects of the French insurrection, he regarded it both on its own terms and as measured against its American equivalent, as a failure. According to Tocqueville, the ruin of what had begun so promisingly in 1789 was signified by the interminable turmoil of the rebellion, its inability to resolve the conflicts it initiated or intensified. If a revolution never really occurred in America, it never really ended in France. In America "the great social revolution," wrote Tocqueville earlier in *Democracy in America*, anticipating the memorable phrase quoted above, "has been effected with ease and simplicity; say rather that this country is reaping the fruits of the democratic revolution which we are undergoing, without having had the revolution itself." Only in the United States was it "possible to witness the natural and tranquil growth of society."[30]

France was not so fortunate. Instead of being a catharsis, insurrection was a "chronic complaint . . . we are destined to oscillate for a long time between despotism and liberty, without being able to support either."[31] Reviewing the succession of regimes since 1789—the Constitutional Monarchy, the First Republic, the First Empire, the Bourbon Restoration, the July Monarchy—Tocqueville declared, "After each of these successive changes it was said that the French Revolution, having achieved what was presumptuously called its work, was finished." Yet "here [1848] was the French Revolution starting again, for it was always the same."[32]

Intractable turbulence had a Marxian resonance. "The French Revolution from 1789 to 1830," Tocqueville asserted in 1847, "seems but one long and violent struggle between the old feudal aristocracy and the middle class. Between these two classes there was a long-standing separation of status memories, interests, passions, and ideas." In France, unlike America, the thesis generated an antithesis. The troubles of 1848 confirmed his vision of recurrent class antagonism.[33]

Tocqueville and Hartz perceived the events of 1789 and their aftermath as a continuing clash between the old regime and the new order, the nobility and the bourgeoisie, and the individual and the state. For them, the French Revolution was a profound and prolonged social convulsion, while its American counterpart was primarily a political confrontation. The "real object of the [French] Revolution was less a new form of government than a new form of society," claimed Tocqueville, "less the achievement of political rights than the destruction of privileges." Hartz similarly concluded that American opposition to British rule was not as total or acute as the war among the French: "And one of the main reasons it was less fervent and fanatical was that America, never having a feudal past, was not shattering a social structure." The "social questions of France did not exist and the absolutism they engendered was quite unthinkable."[34]

The radicalism and passion that Tocqueville and Hartz essentialized in the French Revolution was not due solely to intransigent class struggle. In their opinion, factors ranging from property holding to national character also fomented the vehemence, extremism, and, ultimately, the dire consequences of that cataclysm. As with the class conflict brought about by feudalism, these other exacerbations were absent or muted in America. The French Revolution was a spectacle of perpetual polarization, one prolonged battleground whose dissonance resounded down through the ages. Notwithstanding some moderate friction, its counterpart across the Atlantic brought conflicts to closure, thus cultivating the concordances that integrated American society.

For Tocqueville and Hartz, the American and French convulsions and the nations that emerged from these upheavals are, in fundamental respects, counterposed. The Revolution of 1789 was the product and agent of social change. Cataclysmic and continuous, it dealt the final blow to feudalism and accelerated the decline of aristocratic society (a mode of life agreeable to Tocqueville). The War for Independence and the republic it gestated affirmed the democratic and egalitarian predisposition of American society. Unlike the first French Revolution and the formation of the First Republic, the American upheaval and the formation of the United States constituted a triumph, not a tragedy, and definitely not a transformation. The American Revolution marked the rise of democracy, not, as did the French Revolution, the fall of aristocracy, and thus heralded the arrival of an inevitable world force rather than sounding the final retreat of the more distinguished, but nonetheless defeated, age of nobility. Changing nothing fundamental, it reflected and reinforced everything prefigured in the provincial era.[35]

Tocqueville and Hartz concurred that not only were Americans "born equal" and middle-class because concentrations of property had never existed in America, but that they were born prosperous as well. "In

America, the most democratic of nations," remarked Tocqueville in *Democracy in America*, "those complaints against property in general, which are so frequent in Europe, are never heard, because in America there are no paupers." Widespread ownership and acquisitiveness, characteristic of the market revolution then engulfing the nation, discouraged America from rebellious ventures. "I know of nothing more opposite to revolutionary attitudes than commercial ones," he noted. "Thus nations are less disposed to make revolution in proportion as personal property is . . . distributed among them and as the number of those possessing it is increased." Americans "dread a revolution as the worst of misfortunes" because "[i]n no country in the world is love of property more active and more anxious than in the United States." Equality of condition promotes democracy as well as civic tranquility: In "America men have the opinions and passions of democracy; in Europe, we have still the passions and opinions of revolution."[36]

Tocqueville and Hartz were in concord on the nature of revolution and republicanism, as on most matters of civic society. "The Americans," declared the latter, are "a kind of national embodiment of the concept of the bourgeoisie." Even "the American radical" is shaped by "the nonfeudal world from which he derived his strength." Whether artisan or agrarian he is, unlike his French cohorts, a "small capitalist" tilling a backwoods farm or toiling in an urban shop.[37] Hartz, too, was an avid witness to the market revolution.

Religion was another force with contrary influences in France and America—moderating the American and enflaming the French Revolutions. As seen earlier, Hartz reported that the Dissenting clergy supported the Continental cause, a response which he felt removed creedal fervor and its diametric, antireligious frenzy, from the War for Independence and thus reduced zealotry in that struggle. Tocqueville agreed that religion in America fortified liberty, democracy, and social harmony: "American religion has, as it were, laid down its own limits. Religious institutions have remained wholly distinct from political institutions. . . . In the United States Christian sects are infinitely diversified and perpetually modified." The "American clergy stands aloof from secular affairs" and respects majority opinion and rule. "It may be asserted, then, that in the United States no religious doctrine displays the slightest hostility to democratic and republican institutions."[38]

Restraint, diversity, and even democratic impulses, are not, however, the chief service that Christianity renders to the republican community. Morality and spirituality constitute its most significant dispensation to democracy. These qualities curb restlessness, materialism, and individualism and correspondingly strengthen public order and civil society.[39]

Tocqueville argued that in democracies religion should be divided from "political institutions." Unfortunately, such was not the case in the Revolution of 1789: "One of the earliest enterprises of the revolutionary movement was a concerted attack on the Church, and among the many passions inflamed by it the first to be kindled and last to be extinguished was of an anti-religious nature." Religion thus presented another dimension in the dialectic of the French insurrection. A staunch defender of individual liberty, he rued that: "Anti-religious fanaticism," the "most vivid and also the most persistent of the revolutionary passions" was "a principal mark of the Revolution." Not until the fall of Napoleon would believers cease to be censored, persecuted, and in other ways repressed by the state.[40] For the next two centuries, religion differentiated French and American national development in ways set at their emergence as modern nations. The convergence of secularism, republicanism, and religion in France convulsed political culture and the state. In the United States, these forces combined to calm civic life.

Property distribution, the relationship of religion and revolution, and even class conflict, however, do not fully explain the divergent developments of the two rebellions. Tocqueville looked to culture rather than structure to explain the endless disharmonies of one and the relatively equable resolution of the other. "*Moeurs*" (mores, habits, customs, or norms) determined national character, and thus an event like the French Revolution signified the nature of the nation both for its own time and thereafter. Enunciating the guiding principles of *The Old Régime*, Tocqueville "accord[ed] institutions only a secondary influence on the destiny of men . . . . political societies are not what their laws make them, but what sentiments, beliefs, ideas, habits of the heart, and the spirit of men who form them, prepare them in advance to be, as well as what nature and education have made them."[41]

National mores thrust France into "[t]he Terror. Very typically French. . . . Born of our habits, of our character, of our custom." Again and again Tocqueville described the Revolution as unleashing obsessions that verged on fanaticism and created mass society, or in the currently favored term, populism, that destroyed freedom. He discovered "two ruling passions" in the French people in 1789. Regrettably, for this aristocratic and conservative liberal, the "less deeply rooted, was a desire to live . . . as free men." The "more deeply rooted and long-standing was an intense, indomitable hatred of inequality," which led to "the destruction of feudalism." Relentless pursuit of equality launched the mass society movement that overwhelmed Tocqueville's most ardent civic aspiration, civil society: "True we have seen issuing from the French Revolution a new kind of revolutionary, a turbulent and destructive type, always ready to demolish and unable to construct." This new type "scorns individual rights and persecutes minorities. . . . The idea is that there are no individual rights, but only a mass of people to whom everything is permitted is now elevated to a doctrine." The French, who may have "loved . . . liberty in 1789, loved her no longer in 1799." The "Republic had been nothing but agitated despotism" and "tyranny" never "enter[ed] so deeply into the details of private life."[42]

Revolutionary passion synergized with "the ideological character of the French Revolution, its principal *characteristic* though a *transitory* one" [emphasis Tocqueville].[43] Here, too, French and American national culture parted ways. " The Americans show a less decided taste for general ideas than the French. This is especially true in politics."[44]

Hartz also emphasized this difference in orientation and aspiration. America and its Revolution were instrumental and concrete in outlook, dispassionate in feeling, restrained in action, and moderate in objective. "Pragmatism," Hartz wrote, was "America's great contribution to the philosophic tradition" and "feeds itself on the Lockian settlement." The liberal consensus—widespread agreement on basic issues—enabled Americans to take "for granted that all problems emerge as problems of technique."[45]

If Tocqueville and Hartz commonly characterized these national cultures and Revolutions as respectively theoretical and utilitarian, abstract and concrete, they disagreed over the signification of these traits. Tocqueville attributed this difference between the Americans and the French" to different political circumstances in the two countries:

> The Americans are a democratic people who have always directed public affairs themselves. The French are a democratic people who for a long time could only speculate on the best manner of conducting them. The social condition of the French led them to conceive very general ideas on the subject of government, while their political constitution prevented them from correcting those ideas by experiment and from gradually detecting their insufficiency; whereas in America the two things constantly balance and correct each other.[46]

Practicality took on a darker hue in Hartz's scheme. "American pragmatism has always been deceptive because, glacier-like, it has rested on miles of submerged conviction, and the conformitarian ethos which that conviction generates." Instead of promoting balance and freedom, as in Tocqueville's conceptualization, it coincides with "American absolutism." Lockian liberalism is so hegemonic, "so sure of itself that it hardly needed to become articulate, so secure that it could actually support a pragmatism which seemed on the surface to belie it."[47]

As indicated by Tocqueville's and Hartz's shared view of the American and French uprisings and their ramifications, these revolutions both derived from and activated their national cultures. They exemplified the *mentalités* of their countries and, at least as representations, united past and future. Emblematically unbounded by era, they were emphatically bounded by place. In the same respect that they transcended history, each revolution epitomized its national culture. Thus Tocqueville claimed that many of the chief features of the French upheaval—dismantling feudalism, centralizing government—had been underway in the Bourbon regime.[48] And the civil wars pitting Republicans against monarchists and Catholics he regarded as a legacy of the Revolution. Another inheritance was the advent of despotism, which overcame individual rights in 1792, peaked in the First Empire, and thereafter persistently rumbled against the Republic. Living under another Napoleon who ended republican rule, he wrote in 1858: "we now enjoy the [authoritarian] institutions that those who made the Revolution desired."[49]

A historical continuity, albeit of a different sort, also ruled America. The "social condition and the Constitution of the Americans are democratic," stated Tocqueville, "but they have not had a democratic revolution. They arrived on the soil they occupy in nearly the condition in which we see them at the present day."[50] The successive constitutions of the French Revolution usually signaled extreme and violent shifts in power, ideology, and the meaning of the Revolution. But the constitutional era in the United States continued the "calm" feelings of the transition to independence. The Constitution created a nation-state "without it costing a tear or a drop of blood from mankind."[51]

Hartz felt the same way. The American uprising was "liberal America's fulfillment of" the past. Political restraint in 1776 was "a fairly good sign that they [Americans] were going to remain that way during the modern age." The U.S. Constitution exemplified this sustained moderation. "But why has it survived so long? "Why did it not go the way, for example, of the Restoration Charter in France?" Hartz queried, echoing Tocqueville's view of France's history of disruptive governance. Political stability prevailed "precisely because fundamental value struggles have not been characteristic of the United States. . . . The Founding Fathers devised a scheme to deal with conflict that could only survive in a land of solidarity."[52] What, indeed, is *The Liberal Tradition in America*, if not a sustained and impassioned argument that Lockian liberalism is the core and consensual value in the national political culture and has so reigned since colonial times?

Religion is a particularly striking and (for this study) apt contextualization of revolution as a representation of national culture. For Tocqueville, creedal conflict and zeal was an abiding passion of the upheaval of 1789 and its recurrent aftershocks. American sects, on the other hand, were moderate and supported the republic. In 1831, he generalized the civic role of religions in the United States into a national cultural trait. American creedal "tolerance . . . is nothing but indifference." People freely shift denominations and sects and churches "speak of dogma not a word, nothing that could in any way shock a neighbor, nothing that could reveal a hint of dissidence." Pluralism of faiths—"the infinite subdivisions into which the sects have been divided in America"—actually derives from the condition that "religion does not move people deeply." France is more profound and intense in religion as in revolution: "[T}hose who believe demonstrate their belief by sacrifices of time and effort and wealth. One senses that they are acting under the sway of a passion that dominates them and for which they become agents."[53]

This assessment of American religion surfaced early in Tocqueville's travels in the United States and was subsequently revised. "In the United States the sovereign authority is religious," he asserted in *Democracy in America*, adding that "there is no country in the world where the Christian religion retains a greater influence over the souls of men than in America." Tocqueville now argued that sectarian tolerance and diversity was not the residue of apathy. They were basic aspects of an American Christianity that was not only compatible with, but inspired, republican liberty: "[T]here can be no greater proof of its [Christianity] utility and of its conformity to human nature than that its influence is powerfully felt over the most enlightened and free nation of the earth." Discovery of this relationship, however, did not entirely obliterate Tocqueville's early opinion: "In America religion is perhaps less powerful than it has been at certain periods and among certain nations; but its influence is more lasting." What American Christianity lacked in force and supremacy it compensated for in stamina and respect. No epic battle would ensue for mastery and survival between the Church and the Republic as in revolutionary France. But the moderate and enduring balance in the United States resulted from sectarian self-circumscription: "It [religion] restricts itself to its own resources, but of these none can deprive it; its circle is limited, but it pervades it and holds it under undisputed control."[54]

While Tocqueville did not oppose religious ardor as such, zealotry usually repelled him. An aristocratic liberal, he was dismayed that the French Revolution unleashed demons that assaulted the personal and civic values he most esteemed. Individual freedom was now jeopardized by mass society's mania for equality, the elimination of intervening institutions between the citizen and the state, and the tyranny of the majority. One of Tocqueville's subtlest renderings of the threat posed by the revolution and the modern state to freedom surfaced in *The Old Régime*. Contrasting the pre-1789 French and British bourgeois, he argued that the latter had more formal [legal] rights, but the former better resisted government encroachment because the Bourbons more avidly sought middle-class support. "So wrong it is to confound independence with liberty," Tocqueville concluded. "No one is less independent than a citizen of a free state." Interrelated democratic hazards imperiled liberty in France and the United States alike, and, since Tocqueville felt that democracy was an inexorable global development, other nations, as well.[55]

Hartz was not concerned with the dangers of equality, democracy and centralization, but he and Tocqueville similarly feared the despotism of public opinion. "I know of no country in which there is so little independence of mind and real freedom of discussion as in America," said Tocqueville. "I do not know of any European nation . . . that does not present less uniformity . . . than the American people."[56] Hartz agreed that uniformity of thought, the uncontested domain of Lockian liberalism, menaced freedom. The paradox, for him, is that "here is a doctrine which everywhere in the West has been a glorious symbol of individual liberty, but in America its compulsive power has been so great that it has posed a threat to liberty itself." *The Liberal Tradition in America* regularly referred to this belief as "the danger of unanimity", a "tyrannical compulsion," a "conformitarian spirit," "American liberal dogmatism," and "American liberal absolutism."[57]

Although Tocqueville felt that conformity to the majority and uniformity of thought proceeded further in America because of its greater equality and devotion to democracy, by the second volume of *Democracy in America* he had deemed centralization the surest route to despotism. Here France was at greater risk than America. France "centralized the administration [government] more than perhaps has ever been done in a great country," he lamented in 1853. "Whence it results that . . . corruption and intimidation can be made use of only by the government."[58]

The connection between conformity and centralization could, however, have been more clearly established by Tocqueville, a prodigy in spotting ramifications, sequences, and interrelationships. As conceived by him, centralization and conformity are modern developments and mutually derive from, as well as promote, the modern malaise of anomie. They are, however, symbiotic as well as coexistent and Tocqueville never fully traced their mutuality. Both he and Hartz realized that conformance consensus engenders neither individual liberty nor communal trust—an insight that applies also to centralization and reveals the common effect of conformity and centralization that postulates their interdependence.

Tocqueville was more sensitive to the threats of centralization and conformity than to those of restrictive participation. His "democracy," his "majority," was, in fact, a white, adult, male minority. This inconsistency was, at best, indirectly recognized when Tocqueville examined the suppression of Native- and African-Americans.

Regarding Tocqueville's own priorities, America, he felt, had thus far escaped the danger of democratic despotism prompted by centralization. Unlike France, federalism and the absence of a single colossal metropolis has the effect of diffusing power.[59] For Tocqueville, however, institutions and laws were always secondary considerations. The United States balanced freedom and democracy because of values and habits, not arrangements or constitutions. Tocqueville might here have used the American Revolution as an example. The events of 1776 were a revolt against centralization and uniformity, against London as the cockpit of imperial aggrandizement and the monarch as the embodiment of the British imperium.

The institutional incarnation of these liberal instincts is the voluntary association. It is the structural form of civil society, which preserves individual rights by resisting mass society, whose structural form is the centralized state and whose binding force is the tyranny of the majority. "The power of the [voluntary] association has reached its highest degree in America" because only here do "citizens enjoy unlimited freedom of association." Such an "association . . . is a powerful and enlightened member of the community . . . which, by defending its own rights against the encroachments of the government, saves the common liberties of the country." Healthy communities balance authority and autonomy. Too much of the former results in despotism, too much of the latter in atomization. Voluntary organizations, including those devoted to "religious interests," provide order while preserving autonomy and thus prevent "citizens" from being "powerless."[60]

Tocqueville examined the synergy of voluntary association, diversity, and freedom, a convergence that Hartz, the propounder of American democratic absolutism, ignores. Hence, as Richard Vernon notes, the guardian of American liberty is structural pluralism (voluntary association and sovereignty divided among local, state and federal jurisdictions) rather than cultural pluralism (variety of opinion or belief).[61]

In America, religious association is a matter of choice, but race and gender are determined. This distinction persisted after the mid-nineteenth century, when racialism differentiated Caucasian enclaves and fostered racial anti-Semitism. The new form of Jew hatred was comparatively weak on this side of the Atlantic and even at its height, at least in America, Jews could convert to Christianity, but blacks could not turn white or women become men. Given such divergence between creed and race and gender could the Tocquevillian assessment of the United States explain its unprecedented emancipatory, and in other ways uniquely favorable, treatment of Jews while being contradicted by the constraints imposed on women and blacks?

Alarmed by the perils of centralization, Tocqueville seized upon diversity and volition as barriers to the despotic state that he felt had engulfed France and threatened the United States. With an enthusiasm born out of anxiety for the preservation of liberty and despair over the route France was taking, the great liberal abandoned his usual moderation and analytic caution. He did not consider that multiculturalism might present the danger of multipolarism. Group loyalty, whether rooted in class or creed, or ethnic, racial, or regional identity, could generate a centrifugal momentum against the common culture of the nation-state. Groupism could undermine nationhood.

Endemic to American pluralism is the notion that this is a nation of immigrants—of various racial, ethnic, nationality and religious groups. "From many, one" (*e pluribus unum*) is a founding principle of the American creed and countervails difference with consensus. Conceiving America as a political monolith, Hartz omitted immigration and ethnic heterogeneity and other signs of pluralism in *The Liberal Tradition in America*. This manifestation of variety and inclusiveness, however, left Tocqueville surprisingly ambivalent. In 1831, he sounded like an orator on the Fourth of July:

> The Americans in coming to America, brought with them all that was most democratic in Europe. When they arrived, they left behind on the other side of the Atlantic the greater part of the national prejudices in which they had been brought up. They became a new nation which adopted customs and new morals, and something of a national character. The new emigrants bring to their adopted country principles of democracy even more disengaged from any ties, habits even less stamped by convention and minds even freer than the former ones.

In *Democracy in America*, Tocqueville depicted a future where Americans will be "equal in condition, all belonging to one family . . . and preserving the same civilization, the same language, the same religion, the same habits, the same manners, and imbued with the same opinions."[62] Here he echoed a belief common in the early nineteenth century that American vitality would refashion newcomers in the land of freedom.

Exultation of inclusive and assimilative nationalism was not consistent. A few months before heralding immigrants who divested themselves of old "ties" and formed "something of a national character," Tocqueville declared that "American society is composed of a thousand different elements recently assembled," who "are still English, French, German or Dutch. They have neither religion, morals nor ideas in common," and, as a result, no distinctive "American character" had yet emerged. "There is no common memory, no national attachments here."[63]

While *Democracy in America* announced the oneness of all Americans, "Anglo-Americans" were decidedly first among so-called equals. The "sovereignty of the people was the fundamental principle of most of the British colonies in America." In this respect, though not in others, Tocqueville's doctrine of the intrinsic importance of template mores resonated with the organic nationalism that in Europe was excluding Jews from the national community: "The Americans had the chances of birth in their favor; and their forefathers imported that equality of condition and of intellect into the country whence the democratic republic has very naturally taken its rise."[64] Twenty years later—perhaps influenced by the wave of nativism then cresting in the United States—he "confirmed my old opinion that the rapid introduction into the United States of men not of the Anglo-Saxon race is the great danger to be feared in America—a danger which renders the final success of democratic institutions a problem as yet unsolved."[65]

Whatever problems Tocqueville saw in the United States, he felt that nation, when compared with France, had a stronger civil society, better-protected individual rights, and thus came closer to fulfilling his civic ideals. For Tocqueville, America was the land of stable democracy and France of revolution. The latter in its intensity and continuity had the most revolutionary of revolutions and the former the most democratic of democracies. Conversely, the United States never went through a real revolution and French democracy is not a custom, but rather an abstraction imposed by an insurrection. Therefore, France is naturally drawn to civic convulsion and America to stability.

Various factors accounted for America's serenity and defense of liberty and France's recurrent rebelliousness and inclination toward despotism, but for Tocqueville national temperament was the basic determinant. He postulated "two sorts of instability" in "political institutions." The "one affects secondary laws which change with . . . the will of the legislator." Such modulations "can exist in an orderly and well established society." But deeper transformations touch "the very bases of society and the *generating principles* of the laws. That cannot be without troubles and upheavals. The nation that suffers from that is in a state of violence and transition" (italics in original). For Tocqueville, "America provides an instance of the first. For the last forty years we have been tormented by the second."[66]

Differences in national behavior were due to differences in national character. "It hardly seems possible that there can ever have existed any other people so full of contrasts and so extreme in all their doings, so much guided by their emotions and so little by fixed principles," wrote Tocqueville in *The Old Régime*. "Undisciplined by temperament, the

Frenchman is always readier to put up with arbitrary rule, however harsh, of an autocrat than with a free, well-ordered government by his fellow citizens, however worthy of respect they may be." This disposition creates "restlessness, chronic instability, and a permanent inclination to fall back into revolutionary habits."[67]

The motif of *Democracy in America* is that democracy is the political form that comports with equality and centralization; equality, in turn, promotes the rule of the majority. Since America is the most egalitarian, atomized, democratic, materialistic, and conformist society, it would ordinarily be under the gravest threat of despotism. But the United States has an antidictatorial resilience. Unlike France, where the postrevolutionary Republic ushered in the autocrat Napoleon, America maintained liberty while embracing democracy. If republicanism is deeply and historically embedded in American mores (early settlers transplanted "the democratic principle"), so is liberty (these same "Anglo-Americans" also instilled "the *spirit of liberty*" [italics Tocqueville]).[68] Voluntary association embodies that spirit and springs from and stimulates self-reliant disdain for government interference. People coming together, whether out of self– or group–interest, in combination with their free will also curb illiberalism spawned by isolated individuals who, feeling impotent, succumb to populistic programs and leaders.

Much of what Tocqueville asserted about America in the 1830s Hartz claimed for the United States in the 1950s. *The Liberal Tradition in America* focuses on political culture rather than social mores, but arrives at many of the same conclusions. What Tocqueville believed about democracy in the United States, Hartz argued for American liberalism when he called it a "natural phenomenon." Devoted to democratic capitalism, Americans have no alternative ideologies or historical experience and hence have absolutized Lockian liberalism. "The psychic heritage of a nation 'born equal' is, as we have abundantly seen, a colossal illiberal absolutism, the death by atrophy of the philosophical impulse."[69]

Tocqueville and Hartz had considerable conceptual congruence, and, for prolonged periods and in significant ways, each felt like an outsider. A patrician liberal, Tocqueville's paramount concern, however, was individual independence; therefore, he might have felt most personally fulfilled when in the liberal stance of reminding insiders of the perils of power, whereas Hartz, neither well-born nor elegant of expression, seemed to seek identity in passionate criticism of the system in which he achieved so much and was highly honored. At once insider and outsider, perhaps he felt most authentic and publicly valuable when warning that American exceptionalism had turned dangerously messianic.

While their observations share much in the way of thought, if not in tone, their theories differ in one important respect. For Tocqueville, democratic consensus is the defining paradigm of American society. For Hartz, that construct is liberal consensus. Since both consensuses essentialize republican government, conformity to the majority, and entrepreneurial capitalism, the significance of this distinction is debatable. The prior concern of this study is, however, with the application rather than the explication of the Tocqueville-Hartz model. The concepts of Tocqueville and Hartz, and the assessment of the French Revolution and its consequences by the former, will therefore be employed to clarify the examination of the treatment of Jews in France and America and the discussion of the national cultures of these countries: Where are their insights relevant to these and other issues discussed below and where do they provide minimal, or untrustworthy, explanations? Do their analyses, for example, work for certain aspects of the two revolutions and for the treatment of Jews, but not for other marginalized enclaves in these nations? The scope and power of Tocqueville's and Hartz's insights will determine whether their interpretation offers a viable grand theory of the American experience and of the differences between civic society and national culture in France and the United States.

Scope, relevance, and logical consistency, as with all theories, are prime tests of the validity of the liberal consensus as an interpretation of American political culture and an explanation that differentiates the civic cultures of France and the United States. If France was unexpectedly liberal and not as statist or America was decidedly less democratic than their respective national myths would suggest, then the ideas of Tocqueville and Hartz have questionable applicability. Accordingly, the account here rendered of French and American Jewry from 1775 to 1815 derives from, and seeks to illuminate, larger perspectives of revolution, rights, republicanism, and state formation in these countries.

Great systems of thought issue from great thinkers; rarely do they founder on contradictions or other errors of reasoning. The most formidable challenge to consensus liberalism, as usual with grand theories, concerns pertinence and comprehensiveness: What is included and what is left out? Are these conclusions as consequential as what is omitted? If the latter is more determinative, then we must turn from the conceptualizations of Tocqueville and Hartz to new theories.

Critiques of the claims of American liberalism have disputed its inclusiveness by demonstrating that basic freedoms were long denied to African–, Native–, and Asian–Americans and women—a majority of the population. They have additionally argued that economic and political power in the United States is disproportionately concentrated in the hands of an elite few. By both measures they conclude that America is at best a democracy restricted to white males. Findings on dissemination of power are contentious, controversial, and inconclusive, but widespread agreement and unassailable data validate the disqualification by race and gender from equal participation the liberal polity.[70]

Focusing on its exclusionary aspect, political scientists Desmond King and Rogers Smith recently have written commentaries on American liberalism. Indeed, their critique reflects, for their discipline, renewed interest in Tocqueville and Hartz. The latter may have vanished from current American historiography, but has eleven entries in the index to Smith's *Civic Ideals* (1997).[71] The revival does not, however, always derive from negation. Robert D. Putnam, professor of public policy at Harvard University, in his influential and popular *Bowling Alone* (2000), refers to "Alexander Tocqueville, patron saint of contemporary social capitalists" and "American communitarians."[72] *Bowling Alone* investigates America's declining social capital, which he defines as community relations and social networks—a version of Tocqueville's voluntary association. In this context Putnam's mention of Tocqueville's importance to his working concept is indeed a generous acknowledgment of the latter's foundational relevance. The work of Smith, Putnam, and King will hopefully situate my own study as something of a bridge between history and political science.

My main concern here, however, is not with the plaudits of Putnam, but rather with the doubts of King and Smith. Desmond King argues that in liberal democracy the constitutive elements of citizenship are universal rights, equal civic participation, personal autonomy, freedom of opinion and expression, human rationality, and responsive government. Yet he finds programs and policies, such as eugenics, immigration restriction, and "workfare," coercive, repressive, particularistic, discriminatory, and, therefore, illiberal.[73]

Rogers Smith's appraisal of American liberalism more directly confronts matters examined in the present study. In several articles and in *Civic Ideals*, Smith articulates a critique of American liberalism that coincides with my own.[74] We associate Tocqueville with Hartz as core conceptualizers of American liberalism and find their theories to be of considerable merit. Yet we assert that exclusion of marginalized groups from full participation in liberal republican society and the failure of these thinkers to fully acknowledge these exceptions to American exceptionalism undermine their arguments.

With so much agreement, where are our differences? Perhaps because Smith is a political scientist, a discipline more attuned to theory, he finds an ongoing influence of Tocqueville and Hartz that I, as a historian, a discipline less inclined to theory, do not perceive, at least not in my profession. My colleagues currently seem devoted to microtopics and the struggle for autonomy. They are absorbed by ceaseless and discrete historical confrontations between agency and empowerment, and oppression of outsiders like African-Americans, women, workers, gays and lesbians, immigrants and Indians. In my field, therefore, the grand narrative of consensus liberalism seems beleaguered instead of a reigning paradigm whose misguided, even if partially true, assumptions need contestation. Indeed, Smith finds few historians to tilt a lance at.[75]

Where Smith contemplates a triumphal construct in need of challenge, I would rehabilitate a hypothesis that I contend has enough viability to reinvigorate larger historical conceptualizations. It may be that these different outlooks lead me to recommend the republican liberalism of Tocqueville and Hartz as a potential means by which to partly join together the separate excursions of American historians, while Smith judges the system too privileged and too flawed for this purpose.

Purpose and perspective, however, do not fully, or even primarily, explain the divergences in our interpretations. Smith endorses pluralistic liberalism (Hartz, of course, argued that American liberalism was monolithic) and feels that particularistic and ascriptive violations should be overcome so that the Tocquevillian vision can be fully realized. He recognizes, as well, that "material and moral attractions of liberal democratic ideals and institutions have often checked the sway of ascriptive doctrines" and even concedes that "reforms of the second half of the twentieth century have been momentous enough to support beliefs that, in the long run, Tocqueville's view of history's democratic trajectory may prove right."[76]

While I concur, I believe that Smith's view of republican liberalism is fundamentally static and, partly for this reason, underestimates the influence of this ideology over American civic ideals and practices. If American liberalism is viewed as dynamic—expanding and shrinking according to the times and social group—developments that considerably antedate the last fifty years substantiate its influence. Universalism, equal rights, inclusion in the civic body—the essentials of democratic liberalism and Tocqueville's doctrines about America—were operative during the War for Independence and the early national period. It was in this era that significant steps were taken to remove religious and property barriers to civic participation by white males. Women's control over their property and entry into public and higher education began in the 1830s and 1840s. In the 1860s, slavery was abolished and African-Americans obtained citizenship and the vote. Through these times, long-standing unqualified admission of immigrants and undemanding standards of naturalization went unchanged.

A sympathetic reader of *Democracy in America*, surveying the nation in the late 1860s, would find much accomplished in the name of liberalism. Religious and property restrictions on voting and holding office had been virtually removed. Ex-slaves were by law full citizens and African-Americans served in high state offices in the former citadel of slavery and secession and represented the old Confederacy in Congress. Xenophobic movements had been beaten back and in any case had not changed immigration and naturalization policy. Women had started to secure property rights. Ascriptive, hierarchical, and inegalitarian elements of illiberalism had by no means vanished, but the nation seemed to be suppressing them. Women continued to make progress in acquiring equal rights. During the late nineteenth century, they started to appear in professions hitherto the exclusive domain of men and to vote in local elections, and in 1919 achieved total enfranchisement.

Momentum, however, did not always flow in the direction of liberalism. Immigration restrictions in the 1880s began to constrict America's virtually unqualified admission of newcomers and during the 1920s choked off the influx from vast areas of Europe. Civil rights of African-Americans, too, were abridged. Advances during the 1860s were reversed in the next decade and not until the 1930s did African-Americans discernibly begin to reacquire civic rights. Mistreatment of Asian-Americans and Indians similarly exemplified breaches in the American claim of freedom and equality for all.

Herein lies another problem in Smith's analysis: insufficient consideration of the Tocqueville-Hartz critique of American liberalism. No blind booster of the American liberal democracy, Tocqueville disapprovingly notes that Native- and African-Americans were denied civic presence. Like Smith, he knew the limits of humanistic universalism in the young Republic and even asserted that aristocracy in certain respects better preserved personal independence than did democracy.[77]

Hartz, as well, was painfully aware of illiberal tendencies in the land of Lockian Liberalism. Although *The Liberal Tradition* virtually ignored racial oppression, he noted this inconsistency in *The Founding of New Societies* (1964). If Hartz was less sensitive than Tocqueville to the contradiction of racial selectivity in consensus liberalism, he may have surpassed his predecessor in complaints about the tyranny of majority opinion. For both thinkers, democratic conformity curtailed freedom and thus desecrated the universalism, individual rights, and pluralism avowed by American democratic liberalism.

The findings for liberalism are decidedly mixed, but indicate that for the majority of Americans (white men and women) the trend, well before the 1940s, expanded political participation. Notwithstanding significant, tragic, and huge exceptions, painful and slow progress, and injustices yet to be completely erased in the attainment of full citizenship, liberalism has been a vital force for most of the nation's history. It is precisely this vitality that Smith underrates. The index of *Civic Ideals*, for example, contains no entries for civil society and voluntary association, yet these are basic concepts for Tocqueville's confidence in American democracy and individual freedom.

It is one thing to set the agenda; it is a far more immense task to reconstruct the record and configure its interpretation. Having concluded the prospect, I proceed to contemplate the nation and render the account and the argument. Before moving to these weightier matters, however, a final word about the approach. Comparative historical studies involve a number of organizational problems and suggest several solutions. In this study it might be possible to juxtapose the Jewish experience in France and the United States and separate this narrative from the examination, of the respective national cultural contexts. I have chosen both juxtaposition and separation but not in that order. Instead, the Jewish experience in each nation is considered conjointly with its broader national context, thus the exploration in chapters 3–5 is divided not by Jew and nation, but by one nation from another. This seems a more viable alternative because American and French Jewry are here explored as reflections as well as shapers of larger entities and forces—civic society, political culture, and state formation. When, however, liberalism or the nation as an analytic category is explored (chapters 2 and 6) French and American civic behavior are investigated together and compared by topic and theme. Juxtaposition here seemed a better strategy to test the Tocqueville-Hartz thesis. Another pattern might be to isolate certain themes and to consider each binationally, but this strategy militates against showing how a national political culture, and its interaction with Jews as well, is constituted of, and further integrates, interrelated themes. Consequently, I did not in this manner organize chapters 3–5, however, the subjects of chapters 2 and 6 are thematically and binationally analyzed. This strategy was also followed in chapter 7. Although it focuses on Jews, such juxtaposition seemed preferable in an update summary of American and French Jewry.

CHAPTER 2

THE NATION

The French and American nations were born in the advent of nationalism. Identification of nationalism with the French Revolution is pervasive enough to prompt long- standing attempts to quantify nationalist public opinion in that uprising. Until recently, the most systematic of these investigations was Beatrice Fry Hyslop's 1934 monograph, *French Nationalism in 1798 According to The General Cahiers*. Hyslop's results, however, are questionable because she conflated loyalty to the king with loyalty to the nation, a conjunction that the Revolution itself disproved.[1]

Sixty-five years later, Gilbert Shapiro and John Markoff, in *Revolutionary Demands: A Content Analysis of the Cahiers De Doléances of 1789*, explored this source with greater sophistication. By introducing parish and preliminary cahiers they better probed popular opinion than did Hyslop's more restricted examination of general cahiers. In excluding clergy cahiers and comparing cahiers from different levels of representation, however, *Revolutionary Demands* has its own problems. Drawbacks notwithstanding, its findings are insightful.

Shapiro and Markoff tabulated "Special Action Codes," percentages respectively of Parish, Noble, and Third Estate cahiers with at least one grievance. Nationalistic laments were included in the 185 complaints listed. "Let us unite for the common good" recorded percentages of 4.154, 14.141, and 22.892 in the Parish, Third Estate, and Noble cahiers, respectively. These percentages led to placements of seventh (Parish), twenty-first (Third Estate) and tenth (Nobility) in the 185 grievances. When patriotic sentiments were more precisely and firmly formulated, however, the percentages and standings decreased. "We wish everyone to be filled with *amour pour la patrie* [love for country]" drew percentages of 2.889 (Parish), 3.030 (Third Estate) and 6.627 (Nobility). The rankings for this subject were sixteenth (Parish), seventy-sixth with five ties (Third Estate), and thirty-third with three ties (Nobility). If an opinion called for action, the percentages and standings fell even lower. "Deputies are to be representatives of the entire nation" scored: 0.000 (Parish); 4.545 (Third Estate); and 6.627 (Nobility). The placements were: last with many ties (Parish); fifty-eighth and four ties (Third Estate); and thirty-third and three ties (Nobility).[2]

The placements were nonetheless fairly high: The Parish response to deputies being representative of the nation stood last. The next lowest, the Third Estate response to "Love for country," ranked in the top half. Placing in the top third was the Third Estate's response to the plea that deputies should represent the whole country. All other nationalist complaints reached the top fifth or higher. But the placement record is mitigated by the relatively low percentages. The highest was 22 percent for the Nobility in the "common good" subject. Only one other nationalistic grievance reached double digits (the Third Estate response to the same subject). Compare this to several non-nationalistic issues commented upon by over a third to over half of the cahiers of Third Estate and the Nobility. These documents, however, were formulated before many future citizens realized that they had embarked upon a revolution. If the cahiers were preoccupied with non-nationalistic matters, their nonpatriotic priorities heighten the revolutionary transformation from the *ancien régime* to the nation-state.

E. J. Hobsbawm and other students of nationalism postulate that, in the same manner as different groups within a nation may be in different stages of capitalism, even in premarket phases in an otherwise capitalist economy, national consciousness "develops unevenly" within a country; "popular masses—workers, servants, peasants—are the last to be affected by it."[3] This finding is belied by the nationalist responses in the cahiers. On the eve of the Revolution, the Parish cahiers (originating in assemblies mainly consisting of peasants) ranked first in percentage responses to "unite for the common good" and "amour la patrie." Conversely, urban bourgeoisie (Third Estate cahiers), the historically revolutionary class, ranked last in these two special action issues, and behind the Nobility in wanting deputies to represent the nation.

Nor did the standing of these groups, as measured by their respective cahiers, prefigure their subsequent support for the Revolution. City-dwellers of the elite and middling sorts played a prominent role in the Revolution. Numerically, they dominated the department councils and the national legislature.[4] On the other hand, attachment to the Church and revolutionary transgressions against religion, especially against Catholicism, helped turn many rural folk against the First Republic. Similarly, revolutionary egalitarianism and regicide drove many aristocrats into exile and enlistment in foreign war against the Republic.

Graphic evidence of the emergence of nationalism during the Revolution is the frequent display of the slogan "*République Française Une Et Indivisible*" on official and unofficial documents. This phrase appeared on the seal of the Army of the Coast of Brest and on a 1793 print possibly commissioned by the Committee of Public Safety. The latter caricatured the Pope and the European monarchs planning the invasion of France. In front of them is a map of that country with a Phrygian cap. Below this symbol of the Republic is engraved the indivisibility motto. A variation of the shibboleth surfaced on a "*Certificat De Civisime Épuré*" in the First Battalion of Cambral. Such certificates were granted to obtain office or military promotion. Here inscribed was: "*République Francaise, Une Indivisible Et Imperissable* ("French Republic, one indivisible and imperishable"). Under the Directory the slogan lived on. Decrees issued in 1797 on August 28 and September 15, to abolish the Jewish ghetto in French-conquered Padua and destroy its walls bore the inscription: "In the Name of the French Republic One and Indivisible."[5]

Indivisibility, like "*citoyen*," another verbal icon of the Revolution, testified to the rhetorical triumvirate of the Revolution, "*Liberté, égalité, fraternité,*" and to the universalistic vision of this uprising and the nation it gestated. France was a republic, not a monarchy, hence "liberté" and égalité"; a nation (a one and indivisible people), not a state (the political structure), hence "fraternité" (the brotherhood or bonding of the French people as citizens). As Hobsbawm suggests, one nation indivisible fuses the nation and the people. According to the French and American Revolutions, class, religious, linguistic, or ethnic differences could not disrupt nationhood. These various distinctions among citizens were subordinate to the national community generated by common loyalties and historical experiences and defined as the unity of people, civic society, and territory.[6] In these countries and according to their revolutions, the respective nationalisms would thus be inclusive rather than exclusive. French and American revolutionary declarations and aspirations proclaimed universality in rights and citizenship. Their revolutionary and postrevolutionary constitutions and other formative codes ordained this principle. In reality, however, universality was circumscribed by the particularistic, territorial entity of the nation and further specified by race and gender.

The American Revolution had no equivalent to the French slogan of "one indivisible." The Declaration of Independence, however, referred to the necessity "for one people to dissolve the political bands which have connected them with another." A nation could not exist without the consent of the people and this contract between the state and those who assented to it was the union that had been dissolved by the Continental Congress. Four years after the War for Independence ended, the former colonists, who had severed one union, were prepared to forge another between the people and the nation. "WE THE PEOPLE OF THE UNITED STATES, in Order to form a more perfect Union . . . do ordain and establish this Constitution for the United States of America," is the opening sentence of the U.S. Constitution drafted in 1787.

In some respects the iconography of nationalism had a similar trajectory in the French and American rebellions. National symbols emerged early in these insurrections. The Tricolor was adopted as a national emblem in July 1789 and in August became the badge of the National Guard.

In June 1777, the Continental Congress "resolved that the flag of the thirteen United States" have a constellation of thirteen stars on a blue field and thirteen alternating red and white stripes. The official American flag was to replace a variety of banners under which the Continentals marched.[7] The phrase introducing this resolution indicates that the issue of whether the states or the nation took precedence in sovereignty was not yet settled. It would remain unsettled until 1865. France did not face divided and contested federalism as an obstacle to nationalism.

As indicated by structural and cultural divergences with respect to sovereignty, parallels between the nations can be misleading. Preeminent among the predecessors of the Stars and Stripes was a standard variously called the Great or Grand Union Flag, the Cambridge Flag, or the Continental Colours. This flag had the Union Jack in its first canton juxtaposed to thirteen alternating red and white stripes. It was unfurled on January 1, 1776, over the Continental troops assembled in Cambridge, Massachusetts. An expression of America's provincial status and thus incongruous and hesitant commitment to independence, it still sometimes waved after the congressional resolution.[8]

A similar ambivalence about autonomy and nationhood can be detected in the Declaration of Independence written and adopted by the Continental Congress later that year. After an extended and spirited explanation of their departure from the British Empire, heralding the future the concluding paragraph of this document referred to its drafters as "Representatives of the UNITED STATES OF AMERICA, in General Congress." Two sentences later, however, the congressmen are acting "in the Name and by Authority of the good People of these Colonies." A little further these "UNITED STATES" and United "Colonies" have become, through dissolution of bonds with Britain, "Free and Independent States." Like the flags, the rhetoric wavered between colony and country, between united nation and separate states.

Unlike the Tricolor in France and despite its official status, the Stars and Stripes never became the banner of the Revolution. Although General Washington called for a uniform, official flag to which his soldiers could rally, Congress did not send the Stars and Stripes to his army until the last days of the war. The official American flag was chiefly a maritime pennant, flying intermittently over ships of the Continental Navy, apparently at the captain's discretion.[9]

The French revolutionary phrase "one nation indivisible" finally crossed the ocean in 1892, when the Pledge of Allegiance appeared. Since the Pledge is usually made to the Stars and Stripes, the slogan of the French Revolution is now associated with the American flag. Congress did not officially recognize the Pledge until 1942.[10]

Patriotic songs, like patriotic flags, are symbols that augment national identity. The national anthems of France and the United States related to each other the way the national flags did and, consequently, became comparative indicators of the earlier development of nationalism in France. A French army officer composed the words and music of "*La Marseillaise*" on April 25–26, 1792, a few days after the government declared war on Austria. Originally written as a marching song for the Army of the Rhine, the fervor of a nation in battle spread it throughout the country by the summer of 1792. The song became known as "La Marseillaise" when volunteers from Marseille sang it as they stormed the Tuileries on August 10, 1792, to depose Louis XVI. Thus it became identified with the republican phase of the Revolution. "La Marseillaise" was widely popular at ceremonial occasions, although it was not the official national anthem until March 14, 1879, after the Third Republic was consolidated.[11]

Like the Stars and Stripes, the "Star Spangled Banner" had British sources—a sign of the shakier nationalism across the Atlantic. A Washington attorney, Francis Scott Key, wrote the words to the American anthem on September 13, 1814, during the British bombardment of Fort McHenry in Baltimore. The music of what congress adopted as the national anthem in 1931, however, was originally a British drinking song composed in 1780. The tune became popular in America in the 1790s and in that decade and the next provided the music for several patriotic American songs. The British melody and Key's poem came together shortly after his patriotic paean was published and soon became the unofficial national anthem. By the 1890s, the U.S. Army and Navy designated that it be played at public ceremonies by military bands.[12] Nonetheless, France had an official anthem a half century before the United States. Moreover, the "Star Spangled Banner" had its roots in the regime America fought against and in the nation from which America had won independence and was now at war. "La Marseillaise" had no such blemishes as a patriotic symbol.

Another popular national air, "Yankee Doodle," also has a British provenance and, hence, similarly reflects the tenuous American nationalism. Possibly introduced to the colonies about 1750 by a British fife-major in the Grenadier Guards, it was played by English bands in the provinces during the 1760s and 1770s. The words to the tune or march were written about 1775, probably by a Briton or a Tory. Before and at the outset of the War for Independence, "Yankee Doodle" was sung in derision of the American colonials. Legend has it that Colonel Hugh Percy's troops marched to Lexington and Concord to the strains of "Yankee Doodle." After the British soldiers were routed at Concord, Continentals, now singing this air, pursued them. Whether this story is myth or fact, at about this time it became an American patriotic tune.[13]

Although recent scholarship posits the origins of nationalism in the Renaissance, in addition to the events of 1776 and 1789, historians of nationalism cite the partition of Poland (1772) and Johann Gottlieb Fichte's *Addresses to the German Nation*, given in Berlin in 1806, as early signifiers of modern national identity. According to etymological dictionaries, "nationalism" and "*national/nationale*" were introduced at this time. "Nationalism," defined in *The Oxford English Dictionary* as "attachment to one's country or nation; national feeling," first appeared in English with that meaning in 1772 and then in 1785. "National/nationale" defined by *Dictionairre de la Langue Française* as "that which concerns the nation, that which is of the nation. National honor. National holiday. National interests," surfaced in France in 1781. The next citation is Abbé Emmanuel-Joseph Sièyes's suggestion in 1789 that the Estates General reconvene itself as the National Assembly.[14]

Another French association of "nation" with revolution, and this time with republicanism as well, came in September 1792 when the soldiers of Valmy, crying "*Vive la Nation!*" and inspired by the optimistic strains of *Ça Ira* (which cannot be precisely translated but means "it will happen," "it will work out," "it will succeed") drove the Prussians from the fray. The revolutionary slogans and songs at this battle seemed to reverberate the concurrent proclamation of the First Republic. In this context, as Michel Winock notes, nation became identified not only with patriotism against foreign and émigré invasion, but also with liberty, equality, and the sovereignty of the general will against a dynastic and hierarchical foe and past.[15]

"*Vive la Nation*," "*Vive la République*," and "*Vive la France*" replaced the old regime cry of "*Vive le Roi*." Instead of the monarchical past, with its particularistic and hierarchical statuses and loyalties, the revolutionary and republican commitment to universalistic values and the nation was proclaimed instead. Revolutionary France and the United States expressed universalistic ideals, but embodied a particularistic outlook, as well. Universalistic and particularistic imperatives intertwine especially in national crises, perhaps above all during war. At this time, countries whose cultures feature belief in God (the preeminent universal) particularistically declare that the Deity is on their side and entreat Him/Her to support their cause. War, of course, was inseparable from the birth and early years of the United States and modern France. The American Revolution was alternatively called the War for Independence; the young Republic engaged in naval battles against France and England in the 1790s and early 1800s and repelled a British invasion (the War of 1812), which reaffirmed the nation's sovereignty. France was an even more incessant belligerent; from 1793 until Napoleon's defeat at Waterloo in 1815, it was in virtually continuous strife. While America and France battled to spread, defend, or at least exemplify their visions of liberty and equality, they also fought for more concrete aims, such as trade, territory, or simply for the equally particularistic cause of triumphal nationalism.[16]

War also helped bring other nations, or modern versions of them, into the world. Germany achieved unification through armed conflict with Denmark and Austria in the 1860s and France in 1870–71. While the emergence of the modern German state was unrevolutionary and particularistic, the formation of the Soviet Union in 1917 was every bit as revolutionary and utopian as those of America in 1776 and France in the 1790s. America's Revolution might not have occurred without the war with England, and the First Republic might have been a different polity and encountered another fate without the wars of the 1790s. Similarly, the Soviet Union might not have come about without World War I and its regime might have taken a different course without the civil war and the conflict with Poland that almost immediately followed the Armistice.

Previous remarks notwithstanding, universalism and particularism are not in Manichaean combat, with the former invariably the discourse of virtue and the latter the vulgate of vice. In the name of revered absolutes—God, Christianity, salvation, civilization, and freedom—particularisms of the utmost magnitude and danger—ethnocentrism, racism, colonialism, hierarchy, and nationalism—have been practiced.[17] Those who felt they were redeeming, liberating, or civilizing the world were certain that they acted according to the most sublime imperatives. Those who doubted the transcendence of what these visionaries brought, often the recipients themselves, regarded these would-be saviors as imperialistic, nationalistic, hierarchical, hypocritical, self-serving, aggrandizing, and thus contaminated with the ultimate impairments of particularism.

Universalism thus risks the categorical impositions that may erode diversity.[18] Starting with their revolutions, France and America experienced episodes where variety was stifled by the absolute prescription of universalisms. No one was more aware of this paradox than Hartz, who made it the pivotal irony of *The Liberal Tradition in America*. In France, where centralism and homogeneity have historically been privileged over heterogeneity, this pitfall of univeralism seemed less problematic than in America, where diversity and multiculturalism—or, as it was called in Hartz's day, pluralism—are still essentialized in the national culture.

Universalism can, under certain circumstances, encourage or coerce conformity; likewise, particularism is not an inevitable defender of difference. Organic nationalists who would distinguish the truly French or American from citizens of other races, religions, ethnicities, or national origins, and subsequently exclude the latter from the national community, had their own titles and battle cries. To the various "Vives" avowing the Revolution and the republic it birthed, blood and soil antirepublican nationalists responded with *"La France aux Française."* This xenophobic slogan was popularized by Édouard Drumont and perpetuated by Charles Maurras and Jean-Marie Le Pen's National Front.[19] Integral nationalists on the other side of the Atlantic likewise appropriated the name of their country and (unlike their French analogues, who loathed 1789 and its consequences) its Revolution. The anti-Catholic and anti-immigrant American Party was a powerful political force in the 1850s and its ideological descendant, the American Protective Association, flourished in the 1890s. The ancestral-patriotic Sons and Daughters of the American Revolution appeared in the 1890s, the jingoistic American Legion in 1919, and the America First Committee (1940) fortified its isolationism with pronouncements against Jewish-Americans.

The experience of Jews in the emergent modern nations of France and the United States touches on essential elements of state creation and modern civic society: the tensions between rights and obligations, state and society, minority and majority groups, and pluralism and nationalism; the meaning of citizenship; the limits and promise of liberty; the convergence and (real or potential) conflict among ethnicity, religion, and nationalism; and, finally, the meaning and texture of nationalism and variations in that phenomenon in different cultures.

Particular events—calling the Estates General (1788), storming the Bastille (1789), the Declaration of the Rights of Man (1789), the fall of the monarchy (1792) and the formation of the First Empire (1804); or, in the United States, the battles at Lexington and Concord (1775), the Declaration of Independence (1776), the Treaty of Paris (1783), adopting and ratifying the Constitution (1787–88) and the Bill of Rights (1789)— are keystones in nation building. Nationalism, however, is basically a cultural process, the crystallizing of a group loyalty, rather than the construct of signal historical episodes. Patriotic sentiment and culture validate these events.

Almost by definition, nationalisms essentialize this collective consciousness. They also commonly consist of rational and emotional elements, individual and group rights and responsibilities, and past, present, and future foci. Nationalisms nonetheless vary in important respects and a major factor in these differences is the emphasis given to these constituent elements. The organic nationalism of Germany features emotion, ancestral heritage, and obligation to the fatherland (*Vaterland*) over personal rights, reason, and an orientation to the present and future. The Lockian liberal nationalism of the United States tends to reverse these priorities and France seems somewhere in-between. As ideal types, these different nationalisms have been called ethnic versus civic. The former is a biocultural connection predetermined by blood, heritage, language, and so forth. The latter derives from the Enlightenment theory of the social contract and is consequently a freely chosen political connection based on shared ideas and values. Citizenship in the ethnic state is *jus sanguinis* (the law of blood), in civic nations *jus soli* (the law of place). Therefore, membership in the American and, again to a lesser degree, French communities is defined more by territorial citizenship than ancestry, ethnicity, historical memory, and language, as in the German nation.[20] America's unsurpassed current and forward commitment is reflected in its three primary proclamations. The Constitution and the Bill of Rights appeal to no historical figures or events for legitimacy and the Declaration of Independence explains the Revolution as a response to contemporary grievances and foes.

French and American nationalism, accordingly, is less totalistic and more balanced than the organic allegiance characteristic of Germany. National identity in Germany has been based on bonding impulses of blood, religion, and soil. In contrast, America and France are nations of values, ideas, and principles. This difference has also prevented the rise of a totalitarian system like the Third Reich in France and the United States, although France has shown stronger propensities in this direction than has America. Nevertheless, even in the United States state and society have not been separate. Unless imposed by foreign conquest, they are in fact intertwined. As Gérard Noiriel observes, the republican concept of the state deriving from the consent of the governed means that state and society are present in each other. Moreover, republics, France more so than America, help construct society by officially codifying and structuring personal identity through birth, death, and marriage statistics, passport, voting, draft and social security cards, and the like.[21] State formation is also society formation.

In France and the United States, as well as in other countries, liberal or contractual nationalism and organic or integral nationalism blend together, although the balance of this mixture varies from nation to nation. As Tzvetan Todorov notes, political culture amalgamates organic and liberal elements. Like the former, culture exists before the individual and is difficult to change or acquire, unlike citizenship, which can be abruptly obtained by an act of naturalization. Conversely, culture is not innate but acquired; it is attained by willful participation in the national society (i.e., free choice), and therefore is not biologically predetermined.[22]

Republican nations like France and the United States are neither empowered by the absolute obedience, nor legitimized by the absolute autonomy, of their citizens. Total submissiveness contradicts republicanism; total freedom contradicts membership in a nation state. A national republican order, therefore, recognizes that citizens have both rights and obligations. Conversely, citizens recognize their responsibilities to the national community because they believe in the legitimacy of a national order for its own sake or because they feel that their interests and values coincide with those of the nation. Citizenship reconciles dualities of freedom and responsibility, the personal and the communal, civil society and civic society, and the nation and the individual. These dichotomies, rights, and duties are melded in the crucible of citizenship into coalescent facets of nationalism.[23]

Above all other surging nationalisms, the United States had the most individualism and diversity. America may be composed of many ethnic, religious, and racial groups, but what Jewish-Americans, German-Americans, African-Americans, and all of the other hyphenates share is the latter half of the designation, which denotes their unification as members of the American community. Politically defined, their citizenship is the relation between individuals and the state.

Unlike their European progenitors, the colonies, either by origin or adaptation, early embraced entrepreneurial capitalism. By the eighteenth century, pursuit of personal gain in a market unmediated by guilds, communes, and other corporate structures gave rise to unmitigated individualism. The profit motive was behind the founding of most of the colonies and attempts to recreate medieval corporatist arrangements in Maryland and South Carolina foundered upon the bedrocks of American individualism and pragmatism.

America's individualistic nationalism derived from the example of its primary progenitor, England, as well as from its peculiar conditions of settlement. Bourbon France, along with the rest of pre–nineteenth-century Western Europe outside of Britain and Holland, was a corporatist state and society. The sovereignty of the state and its social legitimacy in significant part derived from these medieval structures. In America, allegiance to, and the legitimacy of, the state—or, more properly, the states—derived from a national consciousness that conceived of civic society as implementing the will of the people, who consent to join together to protect their individual rights of life, liberty, and property. Two of the three fundamental American civic documents are devoted to these rights. The Declaration of Independence addresses their assault by a consequently illegitimate power and the natural, protective, and imperative resort to independence. The Bill of Rights would shield individual freedoms of religion, press, speech, and so forth against encroachment from the federal government.

Although American and French nationalism favors individual rights more than does German nationalism, the great republican communities were paradoxically less particularistic than the imperial or Nazi Reich. Born of revolutionary republicanism, they were more committed to universal principles, as expressed in the American Declaration of Independence, The American Bill of Rights, and the French Declaration of the

Rights of Man, than to conceptions of allegiance based on blood, soil, and a shared past. American and French identities, therefore, tended to be assimilationist rather than organically exclusive.

A prime contention in this book is that America, above all other countries, though with significant and prolonged exceptions of race, ethnicity, and gender, has fused in its political culture individualism and inclusion. Federal and state constitutions established rational-legal systems of government, in which public and private sectors are distinguished and the authority of the state is sanctioned only in the former sphere. Expression, conscience, and, to a lesser extent, property are rights constitutionally reserved from government interference. To protect these personal freedoms, as well as to create a national community, there must be universal and equal participation in civil society.

As evinced in the American, French, and Russian Revolutions, equality meant secularization of the state. Whatever claims Christianity made for universalism, denominationally linked political preference particularistically precluded civic equality. American nationalism has identified with Christianity less intensely, consistently, or exclusively than the nationalism of any other Western country and, unique among these nations, has proclaimed its civic religion as Judaeo-Christianity. Such syncretism is remarkable given the history of conflict between these creeds and of Christian triumphalism. As with all salvationist-monotheistic religions, Christianity combated and missionized other faiths, and, when dominant, sought to exclude or suppress them.

Religious diversity in the United States—without established creed, where multisectarian Protestantism, Catholicism, and Judaism coexist, and freedom and equality of worship are protected—underlies the pluralistic values and voluntary associations that resisted what Michael Walzer calls the "intolerant universalism" of monolithic creeds. An alternative label would be the oxymoron "exclusive universalism." Since centralized, authoritarian states, whether secular or religious, typically incorporate spiritual life in their quest for dominance, denominational pluralism is essential in the defense of civil society against the political, as well as the religious, dimension of despotism. In multicultural societies like the United States, citizenship, that is, membership in the national community, does not depend upon kinships of religion, tongue, or ethnocultural roots. These aspects of organic nationalism do not have to be shared in pluralistic nationalism. But common civic and cultural bonds that transcend, without destroying, diversity, must exist in these national communities." "E Pluribus Unum" accordingly merges particularism and universalism.[24]

Universalism, as in universal rights or universal citizenship, is an elemental urge of bourgeois insurgencies, and the French and American uprisings were quintessentially middle-class. Thus defined, citizenship acts as an emancipatory agency. In the French Revolution, it was an ideological instrument wielded against feudalism and aristocratic and monarchical rule. Since feudalism never took root in America, natural rights in the War for Independence legitimized the antimonarchical movement. Universal citizenship, however, not only uprooted the past by displacing the corporate or regal state, but shaped the future by putting national loyalty ahead of other group ties, whether class (nobility), religious, or ethnic. In pursuit of these principles, a fully realized universalism entailed equal application of laws to all citizens regardless of class, creed, gender, race, or ethnicity.[25]

From the time of their revolutions, universalism in France and America has evinced divergent, as well as convergent, emphases and meanings. In both countries, it has been associated with natural, individual rights inherent in human beings. These rights, in fact, defined them as human. Conversely, in both nations, whether directed at corporate or some other differentiating structure of society, universalism has fortified national homogeneity against individual or group diversity. France and America, however, divide over whether to associate universalism primarily with individual liberty or with national solidarity. The priority of universalism in America has historically been the preservation of individual rights; in France it has been the vehicle for collective rights embodied in the nation; that is, the general will.

The liberal paradigm that Tocqueville and Hartz regarded as regnant in America is the fundamental interpretive challenge of this study. As defined by them, its conceptual components include: the lack of a past (feudal and early modern with its religious and class conflicts); equality of status, if not of condition (no legal orders of nobility or other seigniorial privileges, no established church); and individual rights and voluntary association as civic virtues (personal choice and responsibility, and diversity, pluralism, and federalism precluding corporate communities and centralized concentration of power).

Yet there was no absolute line dividing a Lockian America from a Rousseauian France, with personal freedom driving one revolution and the general will the other. Between 1789 and the fall of the constitutional monarchy in 1792, individual rights and free enterprise were an important part of the revolutionary agenda, as evinced in the Declaration of the Rights of Man (1789), the Constitution of 1791, and National Assembly legislation that advanced religious liberty and free enterprise and dismantled the feudal hierarchy and corporate enclaves of Bourbon France. Although deposition of Louis XVI and the Jacobin triumph (1793–94) ushered in widespread oppression and persecution, the triumph of authoritarian centralism did not entirely stifle free enterprise and individual rights. Political and economic liberalism were subsequently rejuvenated by Thermidorian reversals (July 1794–October 1795) of the compulsions induced by the Terror. Thermidor gave way to the Directory (1795–99), a bourgeois regime that fostered economic liberalism and, less successfully, tried to preserve the rule of law against the zealotry, driven by vengeance and idealism, of insurgent Jacobins and White Terrorists. Even under Napoleon, whose imperial dreams and endless wars encouraged economic regulation and political control, free trade continued.[26]

Conversely, as manifested in conducting the War for Independence and the War of 1812, the union of the thirteen states, Alexander Hamilton's financial program (1790–92), the suppressions of Shays's Rebellion (1787) and the Whiskey Insurrection (1794), The Alien and Sedition Acts (1798), Thomas Jefferson's foreign trade embargo (1807–8), the Louisiana Purchase (1803), various Indian campaigns, and African-American slavery, America was no stranger to the exercise of national power and curtailment of civil rights and commercial freedom.

On balance, however, a plausible comparison may be made between an America of diverse ethnicity and religion, divided sovereignty, and laissez-faire liberalism and an interventionist, and at times imperious, French state that sought, with varying degrees of success, to regulate the economy and ensure social solidarity by government diktat. Americans fought each other in their Revolution, but no such conflict enflamed the passions or was enveloped in the repression and violence of the Red and White Terrors or the rebellion and counterreprisals in the Vendée. Further, no American era of republican turbulence ended in an imperial coup. When America engaged in its most bitter and bloody war, with the nation's survival at stake, it could not duplicate the levée en masse of August 1793. Compare the pathetic draft during the Civil War with the Montagnard total mobilization of the French people to face invading armies and internal insurrection: A nation stood at arms. With no substitutions allowed, young, unmarried men were conscripted into the military, married and older men were ordered to forge and transport arms, and women made tents, sewed uniforms, and served in hospitals. Despite some resistance in rural areas and some medical exemptions bought by the rich, the Jacobins and sans culottes raised and equipped 300,000 additional soldiers.[27]

Specific events, or even specific eras, however, are not the strongest basis for this type of contrast between France and the United States. Reviewing French and American history since their Revolutions shows that France repeatedly succumbed to antirepublicanism. Instability and authoritarianism in the civic culture linked The Terror, the two Napoleons, monarchical restoration, and Vichy. Democracy in America for a long time was excessively—perhaps "pathologically" is a better description—narrow, but it eventually broadened without fundamental upheavals. Dismantling Reconstruction in the South dramatically deprived African-

Americans of newly received civic rights, but did not reach the scope or intensity of the coups and insurgencies that periodically disrupted France. The one conflict that imperiled the republic ended in defeat for the rebels, eventuated in the rapid return of national harmony and enlarged, though still shamefully scanted, freedom for a formerly enslaved enclave.

These differences in the civic societies of France and the United States were prefigured in the fundamental markers of their self-creation as nation-states. The Declaration of Independence avows "that all men are created equal; that they are endowed by their Creator with certain unalienable rights; that among these are life, liberty, and the pursuit of happiness . . . . that to secure these rights, governments are instituted among men." The Declaration of the Rights of Man initially affirms the same principles. Article I: "Men are born and remain free and equal in rights." Article II: "The aim of every political association is the preservation of the natural and imprescriptable rights of man. These rights are liberty, property, security, and resistance to oppression." The French Declaration, however, then diverges not only from the American Declaration, but also from its previous definition of human rights. Written at the height of the momentum toward individual liberty during the Revolution, Article III nonetheless claims that "the source of all sovereignty resides essentially in the nation. No body, no individual can exercise authority that does not explicitly proceed from it." Authority no longer ultimately derives from individuals, as in Articles I and II, it now inheres in the nation. Article VI defines the nation: "The law is the expression of the general will; all citizens have the right to work toward its creation; it must be the same for all." Articles I and II speak of natural rights inalienable in individuals because they are innate in human nature. Thus these rights are universally held. In fact, as we shall see later, they may be gendered (both declarations refer to the rights and equality of men). But even if they belong only to males, they inhere in them because of their humanity, not their nationality. By extension, the power of the nation is legitimated by its protection of these rights; the sovereignty of the nation derives from the authority of the individual. According to Articles III and VI, however, these rights are national, not universal or gendered. They are secured by resort to the nation, not to nature, are expressed in the general will, and equality is an equality of all citizens, not of all humans or all men.[28]

The Declaration of Independence, on the other hand, places power in "the people." It "is the right of the people to alter or abolish" governments that are "destructive" of their "rights." In the American declaration, reference to the nation or to citizens is absent. Although "the people" may mean the "nation," its "citizens," or the "general will," it may also signify individual, gendered, or universal rights.

Individual rights had a strong presence in the French and American Revolutions, but differed in conception and in emphasis. As expressed in the Declaration of Independence, people join a political community to protect their individual rights. When that community threatens these rights, its members are obliged to dissolve what they had created. The Declaration of the Rights of Man conceived of the interaction between the individual and the nation in a way that privileged the latter. Unlike the Declaration of Independence, where ultimate sovereignty lay with the people acting as individuals, in the Declaration of the Rights of Man ultimate sovereignty inheres in the people as a general will acting collectively through the nation. Whether as individuals or members of voluntary associations, in America political identity is primarily private; that is, founded on individual rights and personal pursuits. Political identity in France is based on belonging to the nation and participating in the commonweal. In America, citizens are ultimately individuals; in France, individuals are ultimately citizens.

Comparing the Declarations of 1776 and 1789 may be flawed owing to the dissimilar historical circumstances of which they were born. The American proclamation consecrated the struggle for independence by de-legitimizing a former sovereign; the French proclamation sanctified the emergence of a new state that involved the transformation of an absolute into a constitutional monarchy. The American crisis, therefore, would evoke greater resistance to authority and reliance upon individual rights. The French and American contexts, however, were more alike when the Bill of Rights became part of the Constitution. Thirteen years separated the Declaration of Independence and the Declaration of the Rights of Man, but the Bill of Rights and the Declaration of Rights appeared at virtually the same time. More importantly, both nations were then undergoing the transitions of state formation and the creation of new forms of civil authority; thus these documents were more historically congruent. Nevertheless, the first ten amendments to the U.S. Constitution do not mention, let alone avow, the nation, citizens, or the general will. The First Amendment prohibits Congress from "abridging" freedom of religion, speech, the press, and assembly. These and other liberties guaranteed by the amendments derive from "the right of the people" and their referents are "the people" or, more individually, a "person."

In addition to liberty, the Declaration of the Rights of Man and the Bill of Rights also differ over sovereignty. The Declaration of Rights evokes centralizing entities, the citizen, the general will, and the nation. The tenth amendment of the Bill of Rights reserves to the states powers not delegated to the federal government or withheld from the states by the American Constitution. Thus, the Declaration of the Rights of Man expresses a unitary, and the Bill of Rights a pluralistic, type of sovereignty.

Regardless of the difference between the two Declarations and the historical reality that France has tended more toward communal and the United States toward individual rights, the political culture of these countries comprised both types of rights. In Todorov's felicitous formulation, individual rights are associated with freedoms of expression and belief, voluntary association, and protection of property and person; communal or national rights concern the rights of citizenship, that is, equal treatment as a member of national society, as in equality before the law.[29] The French have placed fraternity and equality ahead of liberty, while the Americans have done the reverse, but both countries have honored all these revolutionary-republican commitments.

A universal concept of citizenship, whether emerging in a centralized authoritarian state or a more loosely governed nation, departed from theological and historical precedent and only gradually took hold in the United States and France. In revolutionary and early national America, the route to wider admission was removal of religious disqualification. Later liberalizations, as in France, eliminated property, racial, and gender exclusion. Shedding these restrictions upon full membership in the commonwealth, nationalism achieved its broadest cohesion because the sole prerequisite for citizenship was territorial. Native or naturalized residents belonged to the nation and all others were excluded. In America and elsewhere, however, being inside politically did not confer full social acceptance. A tension thus existed between political and other forms of equality that deterred a fully integrated national identity.

Ardently desiring settlers to foster commercial exploitation, early Anglo and Dutch colonial administrators and adventurers could not fully indulge traditional theological or other ideological proscriptions. Pragmatic opportunism merged with America's peculiar unmitigated individualism to abet the invitation of all white settlers, of any creed, upon the expectation of substantial, if not complete, parity. America early became a land of various enclaves based upon religion, ethnicity, and nationality, all living together in pragmatic accommodation, an association that reified America's inclusive national consciousness.

Inclusiveness also marked the idealistic and mythic phases of American nationalism. Like other nationalisms, it, too, had redemptive and salvational impulses and claimed a special place among the nations and with God. In America's collective sense of itself, however, the pessimism and exclusiveness that curdled German and Russian national consciousness was decidedly less formidable. Unlike other peoples, Americans tended to believe that foreign newcomers could be recreated in the womb of the republic.

Four currents course through the national cultures of Britain, France, and the United States. Individualism, universalism, nationalism, and pluralism sometimes flow confluently and sometimes separately, or even as countercurrents. Of these nations, America more than the others has encouraged ethnic, religious, and governmental variety. Yet this diversity, praised by Tocqueville in its own right and through his celebration of voluntary association, has not, with the intense but impermanent exception of the Civil War, acted as a centrifugal force. By valorizing pluralism, America, in fact, made it a solidifying agent in the national community. France, more structurally centralized and culturally monolithic, proceeded further than America in elevating these inclinations toward uniformity into national ideals. As Tocqueville would affirm, however, uniformity is not unity. Thus the history of France as a national community discloses greater difficulty in achieving solidarity and stronger particularistic impulses toward cultural deconstruction and social and political disintegration.

Civil society is not, Tocqueville to the contrary, an absolute civic virtue. If the state needs pluralism and its embodiment, voluntary association, to resist authoritarian tendencies in the nation-state, civil society requires the nation-state to balance the potential for fragmentation inherent in volitional variety. The national community creates mutual loyalties, values, and aspirations among its members that counteract the centrifugal, particularistic tendencies in pluralism. More directly, state power is necessary to protect and regulate voluntary associations—religions, business corporations, labor unions—from each other, to protect individuals from them, and to provide protection against the state itself. In the latter case, state intervention paradoxically strengthens civil society.[30]

The national consciousness that validates national sovereignty is multidimensional. It is a combination of the objective and concrete (events, land, language, and so forth) and the subjective (historical myth and memory, ethnocultural values, and the like), of the abstract (rational-legal principles) and the emotional (patriotism). It would be an equally false distinction, at least in the cases of France and the United States, to separate national consciousness from civic institutions. The development of national or political cultures in these nations was not an autonomous process; it interacted with nation building and the emergence of the state. Congresses, assemblies, constitutional conventions, and laws mutually nurtured civic culture and state formation. Correspondingly, the emergence of a civic culture gave rise to these instruments of state formation.

Of the many factors in our collective identity, the interplay of nationalism, ethnicity, and religion particularly affected American Jewry. A nation of immigrants, proud of its creedal and ethnic variety, tended to discount common ancestry, faith, history, or ethnicity as criteria for defining the national community. As Michael Walzer observes, Americans do not call their country "fatherland" or "motherland" because their origins are elsewhere.[31]

In the United States, other identities were viewed less as detracting from than irrelevant to, or, conversely, even sometimes supportive of, the national identity. A country that celebrated Judaeo-Christian beliefs in its civic creed signified that Jewish and Christian citizens could feel that their religion and patriotism were mutually reinforcing. Accessibility and accommodation, however, led to assimilation as well as to diversity, to absorption of separate identities into an amorphous Americanism. With membership in the national community acquired as well as inherent, eventually all racial, religious, and ethnic groups were eligible for citizenship. No enclave could use state power, as in other places, to compel its own solidarity. Voluntary association, however, might attenuate group ties. If America was multiethnic, it was also interethnic, or, as some called it, a melting pot in which distinctive cultures merged in a generic Americanism. Pluralism was not the only outcome of accepted diversity.

Although American citizenship is not necessarily ancestral, a nation is nevertheless one big family, as are religious, racial, or ethnic groups. While respecting the integrity of these other families, the national family may weaken or displace them. Even the most tolerant nationalisms cannot avoid giving precedence to national history, language, myths, symbols, heroes, and rituals over those of other reference groups. This quest for national integration may erode the cohesion of other identities and produce conformity. Members of religious and ethnic enclaves might be faced with dual demands, customs, and values, or their special life may be pushed into the private sphere. Of all collectivities by which people define or locate themselves, the nation became the most comprehensive and fundamental, the mediator among, and unifier of, other identities. For most people, national identity transcends gender, class, ethnicity, race, and religion as a determinant of moral legitimacy and, next to the family, commands ultimate allegiance. Even when not contradictory, reference groups could be competitive and, over time, national identity has grown more hegemonic and homogenic.

Ethnicity, religion, and nationalism are collective identities that integrate themselves through inclusive-exclusive boundaries defined by unique historical experience, myth, memory, and heroes, and by their own institutions, values, symbols, rituals, and ceremonies. Judaism, Christianity, and nationalisms are strikingly similar. All have mythic heroes, founding fathers, historical narratives, salvationist impulses, and messianic movements, and each considers itself chosen by God. Ethnic and religious enclaves may further resemble nations in having their own language and territory. No other ethnic or religious group rivaled the Jews in these aspects of separateness and its dialectically related solidarity. The European Jew as a nation within a nation was the oppositional other in a putatively consonant society. In modern times, this alienation was defined by nationalism rather than by religion, as in the past. But in both contexts, Jews could overcome their image of the dangerous outsider by giving up their separate identity—in the Middle Ages by becoming Christian, later by assimilating into the state.

American Jews similarly stood out from other enclaves in their new land. Here, too, they had separate histories, myths, beliefs, and rituals. On both sides of the Atlantic, citizenship raised potential conflicts with the particularistic, communal, and aloof traditions of Judaism, with its essence of Chosenness and its millennial dream of a return to Israel. In the United States, however, Jews were rarely seen as a separate and derided nation and their citizenship was not considered an incentive to overcome, or a reward for rising above, their degenerate way of life.

Given the civic advantages that Christianity retained in America into the nineteenth century, Judaism might have attained denominational equality by sharing in public funding and other privileges with Christian sects. After the Deistic fervor of the Revolution abated in France, that country adopted this path. But America went further in its secularization than did any other country until Soviet Russia. Christian redemption as the end of history was largely replaced by fulfillment in the nation-state. Hence, American nationalism was not rooted in religious identity and the primal, long-standing marginalization and demonization of the Jew was less compelling here than elsewhere. Never shut out from society, the American Jew likewise never developed a strong sense of, or need to defend separateness, as did other Jewish communities. For the same reasons, however, American Jews did not attain the solidarity of other diaspora communities.[32]

Citizenship, which replaced religion as the marker of membership in the territorial community of France, the United States, and other countries, has many meanings: It is a concept, an entitlement, a civic institution, an expression of the nation-state, and a nexus between the individual and the latter. As with so many other facets of national development, in many respects American and French citizenship and naturalization policies were similar. They were foremost among Western industrial countries in freely admitting foreigners and in lenient requirements for citizenship. Both nations conceived of themselves as lands of liberty and opportunity, as refuges for the oppressed (the French Constitution of June 1793 granted asylum to foreigners banished from their homelands in the pursuit of liberty), and were confident of their assimilative vitality. In contrast to German citizenship, which was völkisch, exclusive, and organic, French and American citizenship tended to be inclusive, assimilationist, and state-centered.[33] Nevertheless, these prevalent trends were interspersed with episodes of restrictionist laws, explosive anti-immigrant and anti-ethnic protests and movements, and, for most of American history, racial restrictions on citizenship.

The historical trajectories of citizenship and naturalization in these nations initially converged and, in some respects, subsequently diverged. In ancien régime France, as in the United States, place of birth took precedence over parentage in determining nationality. Revolutionary France also resembled the early American republic in originally welcoming new arrivals. The Constitution of September 1791 created a uniform nationality code and after five continuous years in residence in France granted citizenship to native-born children of a foreign father and to those born abroad of foreign parents. Un-naturalized foreigners were given the same civic rights as Frenchmen. Acceptance of immigrants derived from considerable good will to other countries. France renounced the right of foreign conquest and pledged never to resort to force against the liberty of any people. In the Constitution of June 1793, France continued its generous conferral of citizenship. Newcomers of foreign parentage, however, had to be at least twenty-one years of age, inhabit the country for one year, and make their living there. The threat and reality of war and invasion intensified suspicion of foreigners and raised naturalization requirements. During the year that this Constitution was adopted the government stripped foreigners and nobles of citizenship. Those accused of subverting the Revolution were denied the rights that it made possible. The National Convention, elected in September 1792 after the fall of the monarchy to draft a new constitution, promulgated the Constitutions of 1793 and 1795. By the time of the latter it had turned hostile to foreigners. The Convention excluded foreigners from political activities, forbade them residence in Paris and fortified towns, made them register, and put them under government surveillance. The Constitution of August 1795 increased residence to seven years for eligibility for citizenship and the Constitution of December 1799 added another three years.[34]

Legal terms of citizenship for foreigners were not dictated by radical or conservative politics: The Constitution of 1791 established a constitutional monarchy; Jacobins drafted the Constitution of 1793; the Constitution of 1795 appeared after the Convention was under Thermidorian control; and the Constitution of 1799 legitimized Napoleon's coup against the Republic.

American public policy toward foreigners did reflect political conflicts; naturalization, made more difficult in Federalist administrations, was liberalized after Thomas Jefferson became president. The United

States, like France, at first facilitated naturalization, and then, faced with the prospect of foreign war and invasion, tightened citizenship requirements. In the Naturalization Act of 1790, Congress granted U.S. citizenship to foreign-born residents who had lived in the country for two years or longer. Except for ineligibility for the presidency, naturalized citizens have always possessed the same rights as native citizens. Fears of war and the French revolutionary incubus led Congress in 1795 to lengthen the naturalization requirement to five years of residence in America and, in 1798, to fourteen years. In 1801, however, the probationary period was cut back to five years, where it has since remained.[35]

French and American differences in naturalization laws and immigration generally indicate more expansiveness in the United States. America has had a five-year residence qualification for naturalization and American-born children of aliens automatically received citizenship jus soli. Through a large part of the nineteenth century, aliens in France waited for ten years before qualifying for citizenship; not until 1851 were those two generations removed from their immigrant ancestors automatically given citizenship, and not until 1889 was jus soli extended to those one generation removed. In the French Civil Code, jus sanguinis (citizenship by inheritance) was in an uneasy balance with jus soli (citizenship by territorial birth and residence). Children of French aliens inherited the citizenship of their fathers (jus sanguinis), could not be naturalized until twenty-two years of age, and had to pledge to live in France (jus soli). Moreover, mass migration to the United States began in the late 1830s, about 20 years before a similar influx in France.[36]

National culture created more striking differences between France and America over foreigners than did national variances in legal conditions. America was a newer country than France at the time of their respective revolutions. Indeed, a synonym for the American Revolution was the "War for Independence," which meant that the upheaval of 1776 was perceived as creating a new nation. Citizenship by birthright (jus soli) fitted the needs of the young republic. It reinforced national loyalty, a fragile proposition in a new country with sovereignty divided between state and federal governments. Ascriptive citizenship for the native-born would also encourage immigration because it guaranteed full civil rights to the children of un-naturalized foreigners.[37] These newcomers to the infant republic would help build the new society and it is generally recognized that groups present at the creation of a nation-state tend to be more integrated into the national community than those who come later. Perhaps because Americans are more relaxed about the national identity of their citizens, historically it has been easier to become on American citizen.

Apart from its relatively recent emergence as a national society, America differed from France in that immigration preceded nationhood. In colonial times, the future United States was already a composite of nationalities, ethnicities, and races. During the critical years of nation formation (1775–1815), most of these peoples were still comparative newcomers with individual and collective memories of their ancestral homelands. Even when the huge nineteenth-century influx of immigrants started in the late 1830s, it came to a young nation. If they were not present at its creation, they were nonetheless part of its immediate aftermath. Thus, if citizenship was to be open to substantial portions of the population, jus soli, by minimizing bloodlines as civic determinants, legitimized pluralism and facilitated widespread civic participation, and therefore helped unify these diverse groups. Jus sanguinis, on the other hand, could harden differences of ethnicity and nationality into fragmenting forces.

In France, however, citizenship was determined by bloodline (jus sanguinis), a more rigid and exclusive standard of eligibility. France was an old society in 1789 and its revolution was as much culmination as creation. More fully and rigidly formed than the United States, France was accordingly less open to having immigrants shape its society and more insistent that they conform to the republican image of Frenchness. In contrast to America, mass migration did not begin until at least two generations after 1789 and never reached as high a proportion of the national population.[38]

Related to this distinction is the pluralistic concession to hyphenated groups in America, while such categories do not exist in France. Frequent reference is made to Jewish-Americans, Polish-Americans, German-Americans, Irish-Americans, and now to African-Americans. In France there are no Polish-French, German-French, Jewish-French, and so on because all citizens are supposed to have a single national identity—French. In addition to good character, aliens applying for citizenship are required to "assimilate to the French community" and to the "mores and customs of France." Until recently, ethnicity had no place in French national culture and such ties were supposed to disappear upon the acquisition of citizenship. Apart from "good moral character," America's naturalization requirements are objective and specific: five years of residence and a basic knowledge of the Constitution and the federal government. Unlike France, they mandate no absorption in the national culture. Indicative of America's easier acceptance of newcomers is that during the nineteenth century in many states aliens routinely voted in public elections. Comparative expansiveness continues to the present. Fourteen percent of the American population between 1900–1915 was foreign-born in contrast to 2.8 percent in France in 1911. In 1930, 11 percent of foreigners living in France were naturalized compared to 55 percent in America. Aliens now naturalize at a rate approximately three times higher in the United States than in France.[39]

Gérard Noiriel, an eminent historian of French ethnicity and immigration, concedes that other factors influenced this discrepancy in naturalization patterns, but emphasizes that differences in national culture with respect to ethnicity and immigration significantly account for the higher ratio in the United States. From the outset, the First Republic refused to make ethnicity and nationality part of public life, while America affirmed this diversity. To foster a "unitary myth," French historical research and textbooks largely ignore topics like immigration and ethnicity. But leading American historians, among them Oscar Handlin, John Higham, Eugene Genovese, and C. Vann Woodward, built their careers on these topics and textbooks in America celebrate immigration and ethnic and racial diversity. America made a shrine of Ellis Island, while France razed the selection center in Toul (through which the bulk of Central European immigrants passed). The United States uses ethnic and racial classifications in its census; France does not. In sum, France considers ethnicity inharmonious with citizenship and has thus denied or minimized its impact.[40] A self-proclaimed nation of immigrants, the United States feels that ethnicity and citizenship can coexist and that its vast mosaic of races, ethnicities, and nationalities affirm diversity and pluralism—essential elements of the American creed and society.

The correlative of suppression of diversity is exclusion of those who differ, or are thought to differ, from the national mold. A hint of the convergence of exclusionary nationalism, antirepublicanism, and Jew hatred was the revival of the term "nationalist" in 1892. Originally appearing in 1798 and long discarded, a few years after the advent of modern anti-Semitism in France it was revived by the writer Maurice Barrés, an anti-Semitic avatar who embraced organic and antirepublican nationalism.[41]

Naturalization may have been easier in the United States than in France, but jus soli did not apply to all American inhabitants. Indians and African-Americans were overwhelmingly denied citizenship, even if native-born. In fact, they were deprived of civil rights by a more severe version of jus sanguinis than applied to the children of aliens in France. An even more fundamental violation of liberal consensus by group exclusion inhered in the nature of jus soli. Like jus sanguinis, it was an ascriptive form of citizenship. Citizenship by birthright was automatically conferred as often as was citizenship by bloodline and hence was opposed to citizenship by consent (that is, the classic liberal social contract).[42] Despite the widely proclaimed view that violations of contract and consent were the main causes for the War for Independence and that republican government requires the approval of the governed and should dedicate itself to the preservation of liberty, the American definition of "citizenship" comported neither with the principles enunciated in The Declaration of Independence nor in Tocqueville's concept of voluntary association.

Notwithstanding these reservations, relatively inclusive nationalism, respect for diversity, and commitment to personal liberty precluded America from making demands for political equality and cultural conformity that appeared in France and Soviet Russia. Applied to the subject of this book, citizenship did not entail dejudaization.

PART II

THE ACCOUNT

CHAPTER 3

THE FRENCH EXPERIENCE I:
THE REVOLUTION AND ITS REPUBLIC

In its liberal phase (until August 1792) the Revolution dismantled much of historical France. The country's evaporating past was dynastic and corporative but an idealized future loomed that would be republican and national. The Declaration of the Rights of Man and of the Citizen affirmed individual rights and replaced the political nexus of king and subject with that of state and citizen. Although not always immediately or completely implemented, National Constituent Assembly legislation abolished feudalism; turned peasants into citizens; suppressed the ranks and privileges of nobility; confiscated ecclesiastical property and eliminated church tithes; required the clergy to swear allegiance to the liberal Constitution that body wrote, which transformed an absolute into a limited monarchy and placed the Church under the state; flirted with federalism; and emancipated Protestants and Jews. In the economic sphere, the Assembly banned commercial monopolies, government regulation of trade, and employer and labor associations.[1]

Intervening institutions between state and citizen were removed. "Citoyen"/"citoyenne" became the title of choice, just as "comrade" would be the standard mode of address ushered in by a later revolution. "Citoyen"/"citoyenne" displaced the corporative and stratified designations of Bourbon France and heralded, though briefly, the arrival of republican rule and, more permanently, the emergence of the nation-state. In the Soviet Revolution, "comrade" proclaimed the international brotherhood of workers. Both titles signified the revolutionary elimination of inherited place and privilege and the substitution of the universal for the particularistic. Idealizations of citizen and comrade, however, were rapidly compromised. The events of 1917 did not eventuate in anything resembling global, let alone Russian, comity and compassion and the individualist and federalist inclinations and safeguards of 1789–92 were soon overcome by a centralized authoritarianism that enveloped the infant Republic and the First Empire.

Americans, as reflected in their less passionate and extreme rebellion, preferred the appellation "mister," as in "Mister President" or "Mister Smith." Here was a generic bourgeois designation that signified the middle-class ideology of the United States and verbalized the Tocqueville-

Hartz paradigm of American liberalism. Like "citizen" or "comrade," "mister" applied alike to the foremost and humblest members of the national society. These titles replaced designations that signified now discarded prerevolutionary hierarchies.

Those who would divert or reverse the French Revolution were uncomfortable with "citoyen"/"citoyenne." As Napoleon assumed imperial splendor, he more readily sympathized with royalty and aristocracy and despised and feared the masses. Increasingly hostile to liberty, equality, and fraternity as he distanced himself from the epoch of 1789, the emperor discouraged revolutionary appellations. Although sometimes proclaiming revolutionary credentials, Bonaparte told a royalist leader, "The revolutionary laws will not return to devastate the beautiful soil of France."[2]

Jews and other premodern communities of Bourbon France increasingly came to be regarded as enemies of the Revolution, republican nationalism, and the general will. They whose highest civic aspiration was to be called "citizen," who proclaimed liberty, equality, and fraternity while demanding political uniformity, thought of corporate entities as medieval relics with autonomous statuses, varying rights, and antistate loyalties. Above all such ancien régime enclaves, the Jews of France, and of most of Western Europe as well, were excoriated for subverting the nation. They were historically the most marginalized group in Western civilization.

Before the Revolution, French Jews had no guaranteed rights. They were granted entitlements, frequently circumscribed or withdrawn, due to commercial and financial services and to monarchical and local extortions in the form of taxes, monetary loans, or "gifts." Jews generally could not join guilds, own land, or employ Christians and thus agricultural and artisanal occupations were closed to them. They were severely restricted in commercial activities, prohibited from medicine and other professions, and debts owed them were periodically liquidated. Jews had to swear special oaths in court proceedings and get government permission to marry. In Strasbourg, Paris, and many other cities and towns, they were barred from residence, dwelled without legal status, or could enter for short periods, such as market days, and then only upon payment of special fees, called "*péage corporel*" (body tolls).

French Jewry's impulses toward aloofness were intensified by discrimination, ghettoization, exclusion, demonization, and gratuitous violence. *Lettres Patents* (contracts between Jews and the king or local seigneurs) enabled Jews to live in *kehillot* (self-governing communities) under their own leaders, laws, and courts, collect their own taxes, perform their own rituals, and go to their own schools. Men usually wore beards, distinctively Jewish clothes, and ritual fringes. The primary languages of the French *Sephardim* and *Ashkenazim* were, respectively, Spanish and Ladino and Hebrew and Yiddish. Most Alsatian Jews, the vast majority of Jews in France, spoke Yiddish. Jews had corporate autonomy, which fortified group cohesion. In return they were isolated from gentile communities, marginalized in French society, and subject to private, quasi-public, and official impositions that made life outside their own community uncertain, constrained, and sometimes perilous.[3] Communal autonomy and alienation from the larger society were interconnected; legal enclosure corresponded with legal exclusion. Conversely, emancipation, by enabling Jews to participate as citizens in the nation, threatened the solidarity of their communities.

The Age of Reason and its Jewish counterpart, the *Haskalah*, the incipient weakening of Christianity, and the emergence of republican insurgency and inclusive nationalism began to erode oppression and alienation of the Jews and, less substantially, their allegiance to the Hebraic community and its customs. As revolution approached, the separation, suspicion, and suppression of the Jewish community began to abate slightly.

The pre-1789 situation of French Jewry was replicated in Germany. Here, too, Jews were outcasts having internal communal autonomy and enduring economic and political restrictions and humiliations. During the 1780s, liberation debates with identical contours of controversy commenced in France and the German territories. Actual emancipation, however, differed radically in France and Germany. French Jews received citizenship as a result of a revolution and the emergence of a modern nation. For German Jews, emancipation was a foreign import—the pledge of French victories and conquests. After 1815, these rights were largely withdrawn in the wake of a reaction against Gallic-inspired revolution, rationalism, and republicanism.[4]

In the 1780s, the Bourbon regime undertook several well-intentioned but largely futile initiatives on behalf of the Jews. Nevertheless, these precedents and debates influenced policy and discussion about the Jews during the Revolution, the First Republic, and the First Empire. The péage corporel were abolished and in 1788 the king charged Chrétien Guillaume de Lamoignon de Malesherbes, Tocqueville's great-grandfather, to investigate the situation of the Jews. The "Malesherbes Commission" formulated questions sent to Sephardic and Ashkenazi officials and delegates that were virtually identical with later queries put to Napoleon's Assembly of Jewish Notables. Respondents were asked what could be done to integrate them with Frenchmen, would they accept military service if made citizens, why they practiced usury, would they turn from financial chicanery and parasitism to useful manual labor, and did their laws and rituals prevent them from living like other French people? As would be the case with Napoleon's 1806 meeting of Jews, Malesherbes, an advocate of Jewish regeneration, was concerned with the moral and economic defects of this people. Both inquiries scrutinized whether Judaic beliefs and rituals prevented assimilation and citizenship and thus hindered Jewish regeneration and consequent absorption into the national community. The Revolution terminated the Commission's deliberations. Simultaneous with these ameliorative undertakings, the government also tightened marital and residential restrictions on Alsatian Jews to reduce the Jewish population of that province. In another preview of what was to come, rabbinical and syndical operations of the kehillot were placed under closer government surveillance and, along with other subjects, French Jews had to register births, marriages, and deaths with local authorities.[5]

Most of the historical repressions, however, were not modified, and until well into the nineteenth century Jews and Gentiles remained parted by religious and cultural traditions and historic loyalties, fantasies, and grievances. Even in revolutionary France, the first nation after the United States to emancipate Jews,[6] resisting equality did not stop after conferral of citizenship.

Jews in France, Germany, and the Hapsburg Empire, unlike other corporate groups, had been branded "a nation within a nation." This designation, or more aptly put, this accusation, continued to plague them long after their formal emancipation in Western Europe. It was a label adopted alike by "friends" and foes of emancipation, by those who thought separateness was imposed upon Jews and could be overcome (by their giving up their distinctive religious and cultural identity) and by those who felt that separateness was this people's curse and destiny.[7] They saw Jews as a historically oppositional force, whether they thought that such aloofness necessitated or precluded emancipation. In the Middle Ages, Jews were an alien threat in Christendom; in the modern era, they were the other nation that jeopardized the nation-state. Hence, Jews persisted as the dangerous out-group in a homogeneous society.

Alarm over separatist enclaves in general, and over the Jews in particular, was not a mere flight of imagination fevered by the modern nation's tumultuous emergence. If the overriding impulse of the Revolution was state formation, suspicion of nations within the nation, or, at the very least, antinational forces, would be a concern. Charlotte C. Wells, a historian of early modern French citizenship, notes that as far back as the sixteenth century there emerged a citizen/"bloodsucker" distinction, the latter being a foreigner who betrayed the nation, the antithesis of the upright citizen. The Revolution generated significant antinational and counterrevolutionary challenges. Class and creed contested with citizenship. Large numbers of Catholics confronted the Revolution over its subversion of the Church and many nobles marched with fellow aristocrats from abroad to battle against the new state. Reminiscent of the foreign parasite denigration of the sixteenth century, in 1789 nobles were called "leeches" and "bloodsuckers of the nation."[8]

During the troubled times of the late Bourbon and revolutionary epochs, it would be recalled that the fifteenth- and sixteenth-century *Marranos* who gave rise to the French Sephardic community were granted commercial and residential privileges as members of the "Portuguese nation." Since their arrival, Sephardim and Ashkenazim had largely confined themselves to their own religious communities.[9] Jews were regarded as the most dubious and difficult of groups to become patriotic due to their history and the feeling of gentiles (and, to varying degrees, of Jews themselves) that becoming French would mean surrendering Jewish culture and society. If this allegedly quintessential "nation within a nation" became patriotic, then all other groups could be truly French. Thus, the absorption (or antithetically, but equivalently, the civic exclusion) of the Jews was a test of the nation's capacity to overcome all antinational forces and threats. Throughout their time in Christendom, and here again, the Jews were an entity, a stereotype, and a symbol.

The threat of a religious nation within a nation had a historical urgency in France, which both intensified and contradicted this accusation against the Jews. During the Wars of Religion (1562–98), the Protestant community fought for its life and eventually accepted the Edict of Nantes (1598), which afforded them the protection of state-within-a-state status. Protestants had their own armed forces, fortresses, and governing councils and they regarded autonomy as security against Catholic encroachment, which in its extremity had meant massacre. In the seventeenth century, Protestants were stripped of these rights and their existence as a creed was imperiled. Arrogant and triumphal Catholics faced off against sullen and defeated Protestants, whose smoldering resentment erupted in local rebellion as late as the first decade of the eigteenth century.

Reformation and Counter-Reformation wars contributed in France, as they did in Germany, to fears of a religiously constituted separate nation. Christian sects, no matter how persecuted, however, were perceived by the dominant denomination as an alien creed, not an alien people. Christians were not legally relegated to ghettoes, nor did they speak a foreign tongue and dress strangely. They were considered French or German and by 1789 past conflicts had substantially subsided and French worshippers of Christ, Protestant and Catholic alike, were deemed worthy citizens. For Jews, there was no end to the nation-within-a-nation burden. Even when they entered the culture they were denied the society. Demands to prove themselves loyal French would not cease and proofs offered were never enough.

Citizenship drew the line between those included and excluded from the national community and compelled ultimate civic loyalty. Groups designated as constituting a nation within a nation were, therefore, incapable, by definition, of making the civic commitment necessary for inclusion in the nation. Even in Britain, less monocultural than France, less tribal in its national sentiments than Germany, and harboring less anti-Semitism than either country, the nation within a nation accusation persisted. From the 1820s to the 1860s, opponents of emancipation argued on religious, cultural, or ethnic grounds that English Jews had more in common with coreligionists abroad than with compatriots at home.[10]

Neither in colonial times nor after independence, neither in national consciousness nor reality did America encounter a significant religious entity with the attributes, repute, or self-conception of a nation within a nation. Hence, Jews here never faced demands as rigid, nor made avowals as extraordinary, in order to demonstrate their patriotism. Nor, as events transpired in France and elsewhere in Europe, would they in this respect be as vulnerable or betrayed.

Debate over whether Jews could become French or were destined to remain a separate nation converged with another disputation: Were Jews, by dint of their faith, hopelessly debased or capable of *"régénération"*? Could they become honorable and useful citizens, or were they irremediably parasitic, dishonest, and disloyal? Defenders and withholders of Jewish rights concurred that Jews were debased, just as they did with respect to the imputation of aloofness. They disagreed, again as they did on the issue of Jewish separateness, over whether degradation inhered in religious belief or in persecution.

It was as obvious to contemporary contestants as to later commentators that integration and humanization were indivisible conditions of emancipation. The essay contest of the Royal Academy of Sciences and Arts of Metz in 1785 ("Are there means of making the Jews more useful and happier in France?") was a milestone along the contentious road to citizenship. Abbé Henri Grégoire, a prizewinner in this contest, elaborated upon his response in an influential book, *Essay on the Physical, Moral and Political Regeneration of the Jews* (1789). In 1785, he introduced the term régénération into the discussion. During the Revolution, he vigorously campaigned in the National Assembly for liberation of Jews and blacks.[11]

As the Revolution began, public opinion did not support amalgamation and regeneration. Of the cahiers de doléances with at least one grievance, the percentage that recommended tolerance was 0.0 for the Parish Cahiers, 1.515 for those of the Third Estate, and 1.205 for the Nobility. These documents blamed Christians for Jewish corruption and recommended emancipation and integration. Cahiers recommending persecution had a considerably higher share of those with at least one grievance—respective percentages were .472, 2.525, and 2.410. The main complaints charged Jews with being undertaxed (they were, in point of fact, overtaxed), usurers, and monopolizers of certain items in trade and repeated conventional anti-Semitic charges. These cahiers called for continuing ghettoization, exclusion of Jews from artisanal and commercial vocations, a reduced Jewish presence in Alsace and Lorraine, limits on Jewish communal authority, and backed expulsion or assimilation as alternative solutions to the "Jewish Question."[12]

How do these findings relate to the contention that bourgeois revolutions may harbor an emancipatory impulse that valorizes liberty and universalism?[13] The French Revolution was a middle-class revolution and many of its glorifiers assert that "liberté, égalité, fraternité" was not just its slogan, but its grand narrative. Such uprisings seek to overturn monarchical sovereignty, feudal privilege, and other facets of corporate society in the name of individual rights, equality under law, and universal citizenship. Respecting tolerance, the cahiers affirm this contention. The Third Estate scored highest on the tolerance scale. When it came to Jews, however, the bourgeoisie could also be exceptionalistic and exclusive. Although slightly less tolerant of Jews at the time of the Estates General, the nobility made fewer complaints about them and were less likely to advocate discriminatory measures than did the Third Estate. And this happened not only before and during the French Revolution, but in other countries and at other times, as well.

Distribution of cahier opinion is less clear with regard to another marginalized minority. The percentage of documents with at least one grievance that recommended toleration of Protestants constituted 0.000 of the Parish and Noble cahiers and 0.505 of those of the Third Estate. Thus pro-Protestant cahiers were fewer than pro-Jewish ones. Conversely, the percentage of documents with at lease one grievance that recommended persecution of Protestants was respectively 0.129, 0.000, and 0.505. If more cahiers wanted to help Jews than Protestants, more also wanted to punish Jews than Protestants. But this conclusion may be misleading. Since Jews were more frequently mentioned than were Protestants, it may be that memories of the struggles between Catholics and Protestants, were fast fading and that the latter were more accepted than were Jews. Thus they drew less attention in the documents submitted to the Estates General in 1789.[14]

Concern about usury was absent in consideration of Protestants, but shaped the response to the Jews—although the latter bore no greater guilt than Christians for lending money at exorbitant rates. In frequency of subjects mentioned, usury stood 442nd in the Parish and Third Estate cahiers and 322nd in those of the Nobility.[15] A major source of distress and distaste, it contributed to the discrepancy between Protestants and Jews as they were registered in the cahiers, both with regard to frequency and negativity.

Two features of the Jewish response to the Estates General reflect fundamental and long-term trends in French Jewry: Portuguese and Avignonese Jews of Bordeaux and Saint-Esprit-lès-Bayonne ran in elections to the primary and provincial assemblies, but coreligionists in Alsace and Lorraine were excluded from participation. Sephardim were more accepted and acculturated than were the Ashkenazim, who mostly dwelled in the East, the center of French anti-Semitism. Secondly, at this time and until after the First Empire, gaining political rights was not the priority of most Jews, not even the elite Jewish merchants of Bordeaux. Instead, they wanted equality in taxes and trade, permission to live where they wished, no hindrance to worship (for example, permission to build synagogues as needed), retention of communal autonomy, and, above all, to be left alone.[16]

British Jews had similar priorities two generations later, during the controversy of the 1840s and 1850s over civic rights, as they gradually moved toward definitive political equality granted in the Parliamentary Oaths Act of 1866 and the Promissory Oaths Act of 1871. Across the Channel, Jews also put economic freedom ahead of citizenship.[17]

As the French Revolution proceeded, however, others, including many acculturated and wealthy Jewish leaders, had different agendas. The destiny of the Revolution, human rights, state creation, and citizenship had preoccupied the six-month-old National Constituent Assembly when in three stormy sessions (December 21–24, 1789), which constituted the original public discussion of Jewish citizenship, it considered the emancipation of the Jews. In its new venue, a remodeled indoor riding stable near the Tuilleries Palace (which also had a new, though involuntary, tenant—the royal family) the Assembly deliberated upon a new issue: civic equality for a marginalized and despised people.

Debate opened with motions to decree unhindered "public exercise of all religions" and grant Protestants and Jews citizenship. The most outspoken comments against these proposals came from François Martin Thiébault, deputy and curé for Saint-Croix à Metz: These resolutions violated French tradition and law and the doctrine of the Gallic Church and, accordingly, were "anticonstitutional . . . ; antipatriotic; . . . anticatholic." The curé then proceeded to directly attack the Jews.[18]

Two days later, Stanislas Comte de Clermont-Tonnerre—originally a deputy of the Parisian nobility, who subsequently transferred to the Third Estate and was a major figure in the Assembly—spoke for emancipation. A staunch monarchist who disapproved of the Assembly's abolition of seigniorial rights and had doubts about the Declaration of the Rights of

Man, this grandson of a marshal of France nonetheless espoused Jewish rights. He insisted that citizenship not be linked to religion and that freedom of conscience be immune from government interference. Moving from natural rights to specific refutations, he dismissed conventional reproaches of the Jews: Charges of usury, unsociability, and unwillingness to bear arms to defend the state were dismissed as untrue, irrelevant, correctible by inclusion in the national community, or simply "unjust" and "specious." It was Clermont-Tonnerre who memorably declared, "The Jews should be denied everything as a nation, but granted everything as individuals." He continued:

> They must be citizens . . . they cannot be a nation within another nation. . . . It is intolerable that the Jews should become a separate political formation or class in the country. Every one of them must individually become a citizen; if they do not want this, they must inform us and we shall then be compelled to expel them. The existence of a nation within a nation is unacceptable to our country.

Jews would have to end their separate existence, which meant that the state would terminate their judges, annul their special laws, and dissolve their legal status as a "Jewish corporation." Convinced that Jews would become truly French if given citizenship, he moved that they and Protestants be eligible for public office. This was his most successful revolutionary initiative. Increasingly unpopular as the Revolution became more radical, Clermont-Tonerre was assassinated in 1792.[19]

True nationhood demanded equal rights for all Frenchmen, declared Clermont-Tonnerre, and emancipation equaled rehabilitation. "Usury," "unsociability," and the self-sequestration of the Jews resulted from oppression, not from inexorable Judaic malice. "That usury justly blamed, is the effect of our own laws," he argued. "For men who possess nothing except money, nothing of worth can be done except with money: there is the evil. That they have land and a country and they no longer make loans: there is the remedy." As for their corporate existence, that antinational failing should also not be blamed on the Jews. "[T]ell me [that], the Jews have especial judges and laws" and "I will reply, that is your fault, and you should not suffer it." "Certainly these religious faults will fade away" when "men [become] true citizens".[20]

Phyllis Cohen Albert, an eminent historian of French Jewry, argues that Clermont-Tonnerre asked not that the Jews relinquish their ethnicity, but rather that they surrender their corporate structure ("denied everything as a nation, but granted everything as individuals"). Albert interprets his speech to substantiate her assertion that most Jews did not rapidly assimilate after emancipation and that the French did not demand an exchange of Jewish identity for citizenship.[21]

Albert correctly claims that Clermont-Tonnerre asked the Jews to give up their prerevolutionary status, which made them a nation within a nation. Extensive research also shows that Jews remained a cohesive group long after emancipation. At issue is the contention that Clermont-Tonnerre and other officials or French people did not insist, or at least entreat (albeit unsuccessfully), that Jews forsake their ethnic identity for national affiliation. The difficulty seems to lie in regarding ancien régime Jewish corporate organizations as purely political and legal. In fact, they had comprehensive functions including maintaining the faith and observing custom and ritual. If Clermont-Tonnerre had any familiarity with Jewish communities, he would have realized that culture and structure in this context were inseparable. Furthermore, he promised that citizenship would eventuate in regeneration—an indication that Jewish culture would be significantly altered by integration into the national community.[22]

Another eloquent, and considerably more elaborate, appeal for rejuvenation cum citizenship came from Grégoire, deputy for Nancy, the principal city in Lorraine. The Abbé referred to the Metz competition and his and other works "on the regeneration of this people." As in his *Essay*, he described the "unhappy, proscribed," and prolonged "dispersal of the Jews." Since these remarks were intended for a motion on behalf of Jewish rights (which, incidentally, was not made), Grégoire did not dwell, as he did in his book, on Jewish defects. But he did address the central theme of his writings on this subject:

> I always believed that they were men; a trivial fact, but one that is not yet proven for those who treat them as complete brutes, and who do not speak of them except in a tone of scorn or hatred. I had always thought that one could recreate those people, bring them along to virtue, and leave them in good will.[23]

Adrien-Jean-François Du Port and Maximilien Robespierre similarly spoke for the cause. The former had been chosen as a representative of the nobility from Paris in the Estates General and then defected to the Third Estate. Du Port was a prominent reformer prior to, and then in, the Revolution and advocated citizenship for Protestants and Jews. A leader of the constitutional monarchists, he subsequently presided over the Constituent Assembly. When the Revolution turned to the Left, he was imprisoned for treason; released in 1792, he fled the country. In the December debate, Deputy Du Port asserted: "The law says that the Jews are eligible [for citizenship]; ethics will perhaps object that they be elected, but they [ethics] will be reconciled to the law. Whatever will ensue, you can not refuse to consecrate a grand principle when it is presented to you." Thereupon, Du Port submitted a resolution prohibiting exclusion from citizenship except by an Assembly decree. Clermont-Tonnerre adopted this draft in place of his own resolution.[24]

Democrat and deist, Robespierre was more radical than both Clermont-Tonnerre and Du Port. In 1789, this Jacobin fought for universal male suffrage, free access to public employment and military rank, and against racial and religious (but not gender) discrimination. His defense of Jewish political rights made no concessions to standard anti-Semitic slurs of aloofness (Clermont-Tonnerre) or immorality (Du Port). This relentless predator of Louis XVI and those who would save him, architect and victim of the Terror, allied with two *monarchiens* on behalf of Jewish emancipation. Robespierre agreed with Clermont-Tonnerre that accusations "about the Jews [are] infinitely exaggerated and often contrary to history" and caused by "our very own injustice." The "persecutions of which they have been the victims in the lands of different peoples" are "to the contrary, national crimes that we must expiate, rendering to them the inalienable rights of man of which no human power can deprive them. . . . Return them to happiness, to the *Patrie*, to virtue, by rendering them the dignity of men and citizens." Depriving Jews of political rights would base "the social interest . . . on the violation of the eternal principles of justice and of reason that are the basis of all human society."[25]

Opposing deputies argued that civic equality would not overcome Jewish separatism. "[M]ust one admit into the family [of France] a tribe that is a stranger to oneself," contended Anne-Louis-Henry de La Fare, the Primate of Lorraine, "that constantly turns its eyes toward [another] homeland, that aspires to abandon the land that supports it; a tribe that, to be faithful to its law must forbid to the individuals who constitute it entrance into the armies, the mechanical and the liberal arts, and into the employ of the civil courts and municipalities." Giving Jews citizenship, the Bishop of Nancy predicted, would cause a civic explosion because the people hated them. Several months later, he unsuccessfully moved that the Assembly make Catholicism the state religion.[26]

Abbé (later Cardinal) Jean Siffrein Maury, with still greater denigration and elaboration, resisted emancipation. Intractably opposed to nationalization of church property and the Civil Constitution of the Clergy and by 1791 an adamant counterrevolutionary, the abbé was an outspoken, though conventional, bigot. Deputy Maury presented to the Assembly the usual litany of charges: "The Jews traversed sixteen centuries without assimilating into other nations. They have never done anything except the commerce of money; they have been the scourge of agricultural provinces." In Poland, "the opulence of the Jews" is wrung from the "sweat of Christian slaves." Even in Biblical times the Jews were "solely occupied with commerce, they were what are today like barbaric corsairs." How, then, could this depraved people ever be citizens? They could not become good soldiers or artisans. A nation of mortgage holders in Alsace, they earned the enmity of the French people. Nevertheless, Jews "are our brothers; and anathema to anyone who would speak of intolerance! None may be harassed for their religious beliefs." But Jews "are accordingly protected as individuals, and not as Frenchmen, seeing as they can not be citizens." Maury exempted Protestants from his tirade. Having "the same religion and the same laws as us," Protestants should have "the same rights" as Catholics.[27]

Proponents and opponents of emancipation agreed that Jews were aloof and morally inferior. But the opposing sides disagreed over whether their isolation was a creedal imperative or exaggerated, imposed by Christians and thus reversible; whether "Jewish" vices were the cause or result of their oppressive ghettoization. After the debate, Jewish emancipation barely failed (408 to 403 votes) to pass.[28]

The fundamental laws of the Constituent Assembly arose from the same revolutionary imperative for equal rights that invoked emancipation. In point/counterpoint fashion, the main theme alternated with its variant. Organized on July 9, 1789, that body abolished feudal privileges on August 4th and issued the Declaration of the Rights of Man on August 26th. On the 26th, Parisian Jews demanded citizenship and on the 31st agents of the eastern Jews pressed for civil and political rights as well as to retain communal autonomy. But all was not in harmony. While the Assembly eliminated feudal arrangements and declared for the rights of men and citizens, and Jews and their representatives campaigned for political equality, anti-Jewish riots raged in Alsace. Pulled in contrary directions by those who would create a nation through a rational, philosophical, bourgeois, and novel (though not in the United States) principle of universalizing the rights of citizenship on the one side, and a reactionary and emotional peasantry that still demonized the Jews on the other, the initial bid for emancipation failed the same day (December 24) that the Assembly granted Protestants legal and civil rights. This setback not only temporarily interrupted the advancement of Jewish rights. For the acculturated and wealthy Jews of Bordeaux, the outcome was regressive. The Assembly had voted not to allow Jews to vote in municipal elections, a right already exercised by this enclave.[29]

A disparity existed between the numerous, profound, and agitated discussions in the national chamber and local government bodies of the rights of Jews and the small number and weakness of this enclave. Nor were these debates prompted by a massive outcry from the Jews for political equality. The majority, especially among the Ashkenazim in Alsace and Lorraine, were orthodox in religion and traditional in custom. They preferred to live under their own laws and authorities and were more concerned with lifting restrictions that directly impinged on their lives than with more formal and remote considerations of emancipation and citizenship. For almost two generations, formal civic liberty and equality would have little impact upon the daily lives of most Jews.[30] Consequently, the controversy over emancipation made of the Jews an abstraction or metaphor employed to define the nature of the new state, particularly with regard to equality, citizenship, justice, natural rights, and national culture: What were the liberties of its citizens? Should there be intervening institutions and structures between the state and the citizen? Would all Frenchmen be equal citizens or would there be, as before the Revolution, a France consisting of various corporations with different privileges and responsibilities and a large measure of self-government? Would French nationalism be exclusive or inclusive? Would Jews remain enclosed in a separate institutional body that resembled a nation within a nation or would they be part of *the* nation? Would Jews be defined by creed as a separate people or would they be considered *israélites-française*, French citizens of the Jewish faith?

Disputation about Jewish character centered on whether Jews were hopelessly debased: Did Judaic law, beliefs and rituals, and personal inclination make them incapable of fulfilling the obligations of citizenship, intractably disloyal to the state, venomous to Christians, overconcentrated in finance and commerce, incapable of manual labor, duplicitous and parasitic? Or were these so-called Judaic traits exaggerated and imposed by centuries of persecution and therefore susceptible to régénération through civic equality? Proponents of emancipation sometimes went further in defending Jews: Military service of Jews proved their patriotism and qualified them for citizenship. Mosaic law encouraged tolerance, was compatible with citizenship, and did not promote usury.[31]

Jewish and Christian regenerators alike perceived acculturation and integration as interrelated processes. Except for extreme absorptionists (more likely among Christian than Jewish regenerators), most regenerators envisioned an *israélite-française* enclave. French citizens of Jewish belief would bond to a republic of equal (universal) laws and rights. Groups with special entitlements, that is, corporate autonomy, contradicted the new state's aspirations of equality, universality, and fraternity. Many revolutionaries believed that these goals would be immediately met by edict, example, and insurrectional inspiration, but the transformation of the Jews, as with so many other imperatives of insurgency, proved to be a gradual, partial, and reversible process.[32]

Argument over the outcome of regeneration ramified far beyond the plight or promise of Jewry. If redemption of history's extreme and eternal aliens required only citizenship, the state could assimilate any marginalized group. If the nation could save the Jews, a mission that the Savior and His followers had not accomplished, it was the most powerful and perfect human institution that ever existed.

Defeat of emancipation in 1789 was rapidly reversed, even though equality for Jews was anathema to a majority of the people and many in the Constituent Assembly. On January 28, 1790, what reputedly was the most disorderly dispute in that body up to that time erupted over the issue of citizenship for the Sephardim. Count Charles-Maurice Talleyrand-Perigord, Bishop of Autun, a deputy of the Assembly and subsequent supporter of the Civil Constitution of the Clergy, and wily enough to serve as foreign minister under both Napoleon and Louis XVIII, presented the petition for equal rights of the "Portuguese" Jews of Bordeaux. As in 1789, Abbé Maury opposed emancipation.[33]

The most fervent and extensive speech against citizenship, however, came not from Maury, but from Jean-François Reubell. A member of the bourgeoisie, Reubell was a radical deputy from Alsace, the center of French Ashkenazi Jewry. In 1791 he would successfully propose that the Assembly grant active citizenship to the "free colored" in the colonies. Advocacy of the oppressed, however, did not apply to Jews. Reubell began with a charge he had made in the debate of December 1789: "The Jews joined together in order to exist as a national body separate from the French; they have a distinct role, they have thus never enjoyed possession of the status of active citizen." He then opened a new front in his assault. An Assembly decree of civic rights would "arouse the people" into thinking "that there exists a confederation of Jews and speculators for laying hands on all property." Reubell himself, in 1793, would be charged, not without justification, of stealing the property of the elector of Mainz.[34]

On one side of the Atlantic stood opponents of Jewish emancipation, like Reubell, who favored black freedom. On the other side were slaveholders, Thomas Jefferson among them, who campaigned for religious freedom and against test oaths for federal office holding. This divergence reflected America's greater creedal tolerance and higher regard for Jews and revolutionary France's stronger momentum for black liberty.

Defenders of equal rights for Sephardim made the usual arguments. Rebutting the "nation-within-a-nation" accusation, they asserted that Jews had long been patriots and that no group should be left outside the national body. Some defenders, however, separated the status of Sephardim from that of the Ashkenazim, predominant in Alsace and Lorraine. An argument for the "Portuguese" cause was that, contrary to their coreligionists, the Bordeaux Jews, like those in Avignon and Bayonne, "participate[ed] in the rights of the bourgeoisie" and acted like "citizens" of France. Unlike the Ashkenazim, they were not a nation within a nation. After an hour of interruptions to delay calling the question, by 374 to 224 the "National Assembly decree[d] that all . . . Portuguese, Spanish and Avignonese Jews . . . will continue to enjoy the rights which they enjoyed up to the present, and that had been accorded to them by letters-patent. In consequence they will enjoy the right of active citizens."[35] Along with other events in the Revolution, this resolution combined the conventional with the radical. It emancipated the Sephardim, but their acquisition of citizenship derived from rights granted by ancien régime lettres-patentes. With the incorporation of Avignon and the Comtat into France on September 14, 1791, all Jews in these former Papal States now were citizens.

Sephardim were richer and more assimilated than coreligionists from the Northeast and accordingly encountered less resistance in becoming citizens. No evidence, for example, exists of a recorded Ashkenazi response to questions from the so-called Malesherbes Commission. Bordeaux "Portuguese," however, submitted a lengthy answer, written by their delegates to the Commission, proclaiming allegiance to France and requesting freedom of residence and economic activity. As a prelude to their 1790 emancipation, on February 25, 1789, in Bordeaux, the wealthiest and most adaptable (to French ways) Jewish community, municipal officers allowed Jews to participate in the local electoral assembly. Abraham Furtado, a Jewish leader in that city and at conferences about the Jews from the Malesherbes Commission to Napoleon's Assembly of Jewish Notables, along with several other Jewish leaders in that city served as electors. Such rights were denied the Ashkenazim of Alsace and Lorraine.[36]

Distinctions among Sephardim and Ashkenazim expressed in the National Assembly debate mirrored rifts in the Jewish community. Before the Revolution, Sephardic Jews sought to separate themselves from their Ashkenazic brethren, as did many Christians involved in the controversy over emancipation. The higher regard for Jews of the South and West was reflected within French Jewry. Sephardim looked upon Ashkenazim as less French, less refined, and less virtuous. Conversely, the latter thought themselves more faithful to Jewish law and custom. Not until Napoleon's regime was there any collaboration between these groups. Sephardim felt that they could best advance their rights and interests by remaining aloof, a stance to which they were predisposed. In a memoir sent to Malesherbes, responding to questions he asked of their syndics, *la nation portugaise* sought confirmation of special privileges granted to them between 1550 and 1776 and demanded they not be combined with coreligionists in any prospective laws concerning Jews.[37]

Notwithstanding Sephardic particularistic pleas, since 1789 French Jews and their allies had repeatedly entreated the Assembly for equal rights. Appeals based on imperatives of natural rights, national solidarity, and exemplary service to la patrie—evidence of Jewish régénération—

were conveyed in cadences that mingled pleas, demands, and dispassionate analysis. Sephardic success in 1790 spurred Ashkenazim, at least the wealthier and more assimilated among them, and their supporters to greater efforts to secure citizenship.[38]

Lorraine Jews' "supplication" to the Assembly of February 26, 1790, exemplifies this venue of Jewish-Christian relations. They reassured the tribunal and—through its representation—all of France by "solemnly reiterating the promises of a total devotion to public matters, and of an ardent zeal for the interests of the nation." As proof of such devotion, the petitioners offered "the marks of Patriotism that we gave in this Revolution." Such loyalty merited inclusion in the body politic: "As soon as we serve the country like other Citizens, and with them, then she owes us all that she accords to these." The Lorraine Ashkenazim then moved from national to universal mandates: "The rights [sic] of Man" and "Humanity, Reason, Justice, even the Decrees of the National Assembly on rights for so long ignored men, assure all of us that we will receive . . . the title and rights of *Citizen*." In emancipatory appeals, obsequies often interspersed dignified declarations of patriotism and human rights: "The indulgence that we require is . . . [to] pardon us or to pity us. And, if some interval separates us still from the general Citizens that surround us, they themselves sensed that it was in another order of things that they could require of us all the social virtues." In the end, however, dignity prevailed over diffidence: "How could the National Assembly refuse to give us this Act of justice, that we are soliciting with so much eager willingness, that is so necessary to our welfare, and of which the lengthy suspense caused us such unhappiness; when Nature, Reason, Justice demand it in concert."[39]

In 1790, Ashkenazim made strides in their quest. On January 30th, the General Assembly of the Paris Commune admitted the Jews of the city "to civil status and to all the rights of active citizens." This conferral of rights fused Enlightenment principles, revolutionary zeal, utopian aspirations impelled by state formation, and modern, inclusive nationalism. Emancipation as a reward for Parisian Jews' patriotism expanded into the universal tenet of fraternity: "[A]ll men, living in an empire, should share the same title and the same rights; . . . a difference, in religious beliefs, does not permit any in civil existence; . . . when a people gives itself a constitution, . . . it must hasten to shake off the yoke of prejudices, and to reestablish for equality disregarded rights."[40]

But there were also missteps enroute to emancipation. On January 20, 1791, a deputy requested that the Assembly give all French Jews "the right of active citizen." Prince Charles Louis Victor de Broglie, a liberal noble connected to one of the foremost families of the old regime and fated to perish at the scaffold in 1794, emphatically objected. A deputy from Alsace, he felt that liberating Ashkenazim "hurls alarm in the aforementioned provinces of Lorraine and Alsace, that assuredly have no need at this time of a new germ of heat and fermentation." The prince perceived an "intrigue [that] was concocted by four or five powerful Jews" in the Department of the Lower Rhine. One "acquired an immense fortune at the expense of the State." This cabal enflamed Strasbourg: "never has the public peace been more concerned, no more imperiously called for than by the proposition" for emancipating Ashkenazim. Since anti-Jewish riots erupted in that region in 1789, the argument for order had a powerful impact. Broglie's demand to defer granting all Jews citizenship "passed by a very great majority."[41]

Such mishaps, however, did not divert the process of complete emancipation. In response to a petition of Parisian Jews, on April 26th, 1791, the Directory of the Department of Paris proclaimed religious freedom and vowed to promote citizenship for Jews. On May 7th, the Assembly, prompted by the Directory decision, "declare[d] the principles of religious liberty that it has dictated are the same that it saluted [recognized] and claimed in the declaration [sic] of the Rights of man [sic]."[42]

The Constitution of September 3, 1791, further predisposed the Assembly toward emancipation. Reflecting the liberal phase of the Revolution, it bristled with guarantees of "natural and civil rights" for citizens, including freedom of religious affiliation and expression. It was more generous toward foreigners than any other revolutionary constitution or the subsequent Napoleonic Code. Not only did this Constitution set the lowest requirements for naturalization, it allowed the Assembly to make special grants of citizenship that waved all conditions except residence in France and taking the Civic Oath.[43] Jews were a religious enclave with an alien stigma; therefore, state defense of religious freedom and expansiveness toward foreigners promoted citizenship for French Jewry.

Repeated postponements could not arrest increasing support for equal rights and the issue was conclusively joined on September 27, 1791. Discussion opened with a speech from Du Port, who supported emancipation in the original debate of December 1789. An ardent defender of the Declaration of Rights, the deputy took a robust view of personal liberty:

> I believe that freedom of religion does not permit a single distinction to be made between the political rights of citizens by reason of their beliefs. I believe equally that the Jews can not alone be excepted from the enjoyment of those rights, considering that pagans, Turks, Moslems, Chinese even, men of all sects in a word, are admitted there.

The Assembly adopted, "in the midst of applause," Du Port's measure that "conditions necessary to be a French citizen, and to become an active citizen, are fixed by the Constitution, and that all men who, satisfying the stated conditions, render the civic oath, and engage themselves to satisfy all the responsibilities that the Constitution imposes, have the right to all the advantages that it assures." The second paragraph of his resolution called for annulment of "adjournments, restrictions, and exceptions . . . affecting individuals of the Jewish persuasion, who shall take the civic oath."[44]

Near unanimous passage of the measure supporting citizenship for the Jews did not deter diehards like Broglie and Reubell. The Assembly accepted Broglie's modification of the second paragraph. After the words "who shall take the civic oath," the new decree added: "which shall be considered as a renunciation of all privileges in their favor." If Jews became citizens, Broglie wanted to ensure that their separateness and religious identity would not be legally or institutionally reinforced.[45]

Reubell wrung one further concession. Still preoccupied with "usurious oppression of the Jews," he proposed that the Jews of Alsace give "detailed accounts of their loans"; that provincial officials "determine the known methods of the debtors to acquit these loans" and "pass this information" to "the Directories of the departments of the Upper and Lower Rhine"; and that legislation for "liquidation" or reduction of the loans be considered.[46] This accusation and its suggested solution would continue to vex Jews and be revisited by Napoleon.

In November the emancipation declaration became law—the first formal liberation of Jews. In two years the government had moved rapidly, if in stages, to transform the Jews from a medieval corporation to a modern citizenry. The 1789 Assembly debate over their civic status resulted in a decree that ambiguously placed Alsatian Jews "under the safeguard of the law" and the king. This arrangement blended the old-order principle of monarchical protection of Jews with a degree of civic equality by putting these Jews under the same laws as other French people. The life of this compromise, however, was brief, for shortly thereafter the Assembly made citizens of the Jews.[47]

Actions like emancipation of the Jews moved Tocqueville to rhapsodize about the liberal "heyday of the Revolution; when the love of equality and the urge to freedom went hand in hand; when they wished to set up not merely a truly democratic government but free institutions, not only to do away with privileges but also to make good and stabilize the rights of man, the individual." It was an "age of fervid enthusiasm, of proud and generous aspirations, whose memory despite its extravagances, men will forever cherish; a phase of history that for many years to come will trouble" those "who seek to demoralize the nation and reduce it to a servile state."[48]

Tocqueville's tribute notwithstanding, emancipation was not a pure gift of the fervor for freedom that ennobled the early revolutionary epoch.

The decree of January 28, 1790, emancipating the Sephardim, provoked an anti-Jewish outbreak in the eastern provinces, and fearing worse violence as a result of freeing the Ashkenazim, the Assembly fashioned a quid quo pro for citizenship. It mandated that debts owed Jews be reviewed by district directoires, who determined whether debtors should be excused from their liabilities. Many of these obligations were never met. National Assembly laws of September 28 and November 13, 1791, appeasing peasants in debt to Jewish moneylenders in Alsace and Lorraine, indicated that, while Jews were made citizens, they were still not treated like other Frenchmen. Liberation obviously was not a complete break with the past.[49] More important, the concession unavailingly made to avoid future anti-Semitic uprisings prefigured later revolutionary and Napoleonic policies that compromised civic rights of Jews.

Revolutionary government ostensibly eliminated the historical disabilities of French Jews. But citizenship also terminated their corporate status ("renunciation of all privileges"). Like Protestants, Jews would surrender communal autonomy and a separate identity in order to gain citizenship. Still in its liberal phase, the Revolution granted the Jews civic equality and left them free to voluntarily practice their religion, but, by dislodging legal compulsion to do so, removed their institutional separateness. Subsequent authoritarian revolutionary developments would preserve the exchange of corporative for citizenship status but impede voluntary religious observance and, indeed, outlaw such ritual practice as a retrograde, particularist, corporative attempt to thwart the general will embodied in national citizenship.

In America and England, citizenship fulfilled individual liberty and protected group identity and loyalty to interest or region as well as signifying a commitment to the nation. In France and elsewhere on the Continent, attachments to self, group, interest, or region were not totally abandoned, but citizenship entailed putting the state ahead of them. The nation within a nation would give way to uniform and virtually exclusive affiliation with, and allegiance to, the nation-state. Thus would Jews be transformed, the Revolution completed, and the nation consolidated. "There are no longer in the Republic Jews, nor Protestants, nor Anabaptists, nor Catholics," said the Jacobin leader in Nancy on November 10, 1793, during the Terror, "there are only French republicans."[50]

The Assembly action of September 27, 1791, reflected the most ardent aspirations of the Revolution, epitomized in its battle cry, "liberté, égalité, fraternité." Emancipation verified each facet of this new trinity; thus, in making citizens of the children of Abraham, other Frenchmen pledged the revolutionary creed. Conferral of civic rights enabled the Jews to be rehabilitated, liberated, made equal, and admitted to the national brotherhood. The most alienated and corrupted group in the country, the quintessential nation within a nation, upon receiving liberty, equality, and fraternity, would quit its separate existence.

Momentous modern insurrections—the Puritan Revolution in Britain in the 1640s, the War for Independence in America, the French Revolution, and the Communist takeovers in Russia and China—manifested powerful utopian urges. Their visionary devotions originated in the exhilaration of emancipation, in casting off the constricting past. In 1789, the thrill of freedom initially derived from dismantling feudalism, in 1776 from declaring independence from Britain, and in 1917 from overthrowing capitalism. Liberty was not merely an abstraction, a concept, or even a value. It was much more palpable and intoxicating, a release from accumulated burdens, the prelude to total fulfillment. In the beginning was liberty, but, as the revolutions proceeded, release was tempered with restraint and, varying with the national milieus of the rebellions, gave way to repression, or at least to a quest for regulation. The utopian teleology of these upheavals lay in their messianic aspiration to create national societies—terms of citizenship—that would harmonize the antithetical principles of universalism and particularism, public and private, liberty and order, diversity and unity, individuality and community, the personal, the national and the global, and, finally, idealism and survival. Convinced that they were striving to realize this hope, revolutionaries and sympathetic bystanders alike passionately believed that these were progressive—even transformative—uprisings.

What could be more revolutionary, more transformative, and a fuller realization of the utopian impulses of 1789–91 than to have the moral and civic conversion of the Jews from degenerate outsiders to meritorious citizens proceed from the uprising and from the nation these enthusiasts of a new order were wittingly or unwittingly creating? What could be more revolutionary than regeneration; what could be more regenerative than the Revolution? The Revolution's dismissal of Bourbon feudalism—its emerging political culture of republican universalism—meant that the nation consisted of an autonomous, unified people; a coming together of citizens who determined their own destiny and were equal in rights and under the law. Emancipation of Jews emblematized the Revolution's commitment to these ideals: to bring unity out of turmoil, create a whole nation, and serve as a global beacon.

If the debate over emancipation had brought closure to the controversy over making the Jews equal in rights, it would have been a transformative catharsis that fortified the nation and the republic. An analogous discussion in the American Constitutional Convention produced just such a result. Political conflicts can strengthen the political culture of a nation, but they must be moderate enough so that when the dispute is settled de jure, it is solved de facto. When the legal settlement in the contention over French Jews was not accepted in the country's political culture, the latter was weakened by imperiling republican values of liberty, fraternity, and universalism and intensifying national disunity. From Bonaparte through Vichy, emancipation would be periodically revisited and related to other exclusions that violated the revolutionary legacy, republican values, and French law. Particularization of citizenship reflected a fragmented France, a condition that prevented total realization of nationhood.

Sudhir Hazareesingh, an acute analyst of French political culture, notes that citizenship consists of duties, obligations, guarantees, expectations, and entitlements. These components are refracted through specific and general, individual and collective perspectives. If all of these permutations and combinations are prevalently reinforcing, they foster a cohesive attachment to the civic collectivity and culture. Through these interrelationships, citizenship fortifies the nation by creating a collective identity, a sense of participating in the civic culture and belonging to the civic entity. The state, as the political organization of civic society, legally and institutionally incorporates individuals and different social groups in the same country and implements the national culture, that is, the norms of how the citizens live together in civic space. Political culture and political structure are joined through the nexus of citizenship.[51]

Any disruptions, distractions, or discriminations in these sequences are problematical for individuals and groups so affected and for national solidarity and totality. In France, it would be the fate of Jews and other groups who hovered on the spectrum of inclusion/exclusion never to be certain whether they were inside or outside, French or foreign, citizens or aliens.

Citizenship for Jews and other Frenchmen not only meant liberty, equality, and community; the Revolution stood for other ideals or, put more precisely, imperatives. But the triune conferrals of the Revolution were flexible enough to transpose these interrelated and overlapping imperatives of universalism, participationism, and perfectionism into the rhetorical rubric of liberté, égalité, fraternité.[52] Civic equality for Jews made operable the universalistic values of the Revolution, namely that all citizens had the same rights and were subject to the same laws. Citizenship also enabled the Jews to participate in political society. Finally, emancipation was the perfectionistic instrument by which to redeem the Jews. Once again Jews were cast as witnesses to a messianic transformation. In Christian eschatology their conversion to the One True Faith would usher in the Second Coming, the Kingdom of God. In the eschatology of the French Revolution, the conversion of Jews to the One True Nation would usher in a secular utopia, the attainment of liberté, égalité, fraternité.

As always, the Jews were a metaphor for French society, a circumstance that makes them symbolic of the grand narrative of the Revolution. Like other great revolutions, the upheaval of 1789 contained numerous dichotomies: universalism and particularism, the concrete and the general, the practical and the ideal—indeed, it thematized these antinomies. Contradictions might compromise the revolutionaries, but transcendence inspired them. Hence, as in the uprisings of 1776 and 1917, revolutionary fervor overrode resignation to irreconcilable opposites. As Richard Vernon observes, instantiation, the representation of the abstract in the concrete, was the revolutionary route to overcoming polarization (conceptual or otherwise). Thus, that special entity called the nation became the vehicle to realize universal moral principles—equality, fraternity and liberty.[53] And thus did the really heady stuff of revolution—messianic and utopian aspirations—cohabit with earthly but compelling incitements of national, group, or individual interest and aggrandizement. Instantiation merged the particular and the universal, the political and the moral, might and right.

September 27, 1791, as a sign of the sublime abstractions of liberty, fraternity, equality, and moral redemption, exemplified revolutionary instantiaton. Among other consummate visions and movements that emancipation stood for were republicanism, reformation, and the emergence of the nation-state. Crowning achievements, however, can have crushing consequences. Revolutionaries placed a burden on the Jews that they spared other groups in the nation. This people would have to prove worthy of the Revolution and, especially, the revolutionary gift of belonging to the nation. If Jews succeeded on these terms, the Revolution would be verified. Those who hated it, however, regarded this attainment of civic rights as proof of another kind. For them, it evidenced the sinister core of the Revolution.

Although France was a constitutional monarchy from 1789 to September 1792, the Revolution had already set out to realize universalism, perfectionism, rationality, and liberty by proclaiming the Declaration of the Rights of Man, eliminating feudalism, and placing the Church under civil control, as well as by emancipating Protestants and Jews.

When France became a Republic, these aspirations coalesced into an expectation of the immediate fulfillment of the state as a force for social justice and equality. Politics and morality merged and the nation of virtue legitimatized communal order and individual rights. Its citizens would respect authority and autonomy and thus avoid excessive allegiance to the one, the road to tyranny, or the other, a free-fall into anarchy. Universalism and participationism were instantiated by the role of the sans culottes in the downfall of the monarchy and the Jacobin Constitution of 1793, which declared universal suffrage. The Revolution broke with the past in restructuring power. In the Bourbon regime, power was ascriptive and hierarchical; in the Republic, the general will (of the people) was the source of sovereignty. The Revolution overthrew the king, nobility, and Church, sources of empowerment in the old order, and replaced them with impulses and institutions. This radical and comprehensive departure from the past was justified by pledges of universalism, liberty, republicanism, reason, patriotism, and especially by perfectionism. The essence of perfectionism—that all citizens are capable of equally participating in a rational social order—justified uprooting the ancien régime.[54] And replacement of the old and flawed with a republican utopia of liberty, equality, and fraternity (at least for white male citizens) showed that perfection was not merely possible, but indeed already taking place.

Republican and revolutionary messianism was replete with a salvationist mission (to bring forth a nation based on equality, liberty, and fraternity); transformation (from subject to citizen); redemption (regenerating Jews); and epiphany (storming the Bastille, victory at Valmy, the Goddess of Reason enshrined in the cathedral of Notre Dame) manifesting the emergence of a new divinity, republican France. The revolutionary mission, however, related to older messianisms that it strove to displace. Christian and Jewish messianisms, too, featured salvation, transformation, redemption, and epiphany. Christianity could match its Holy Trinity against the revolutionary trinity of equality, liberty, and fraternity. The mission of the Jewish messiah was to restore the nation of Israel to the Hebrews, just as the mission of the revolutionary redeemers was to recreate for the French the nation of France.

Over a hundred years after 1789, the Revolution still inspired messianic visions among French Jews. "It seemed," to Zadoc Kahn, Grand Rabbi of France at the turn of the century, "as though the era predicted by the prophets of Israel had finally begun." Historian Maurice Bloch also muted the Zionist implications of Jewish messiansism by changing its locus from the restoration of Israel to the Hebrews to the realization of the ideals of the French Revolution. "The new Jerusalem will be everywhere that the Declaration of the Rights of Man will be accepted as truth," he wrote in 1904. "The new Jerusalem will be everywhere the idea of the French Revolution triumphs" and "before this new Jerusalem people will be able to say once again: 'God acts through the French!' " The revolutionary dream and its republican incarnation supplanted Christian and Jewish epiphanies: "The time of the Messiah had come with that new society [the French Revolution], which substituted for the old Trinity of the Church that other trinity whose names can be read on every wall: 'Liberty, Equality, Fraternity.' "[55]

Messianism joined the universalism of the Revolution (liberty and equality for all, perfectionism and utopianism) with the particularism inherent in nationalism (the superiority of French political culture). Nowhere was this union more triumphally projected than in foreign conquest. Although this phase of the Revolution began with the War of the First Coalition on April 20, 1792, it quickened under the Republic. Starting with France defending herself against Louis XVI's protectors and subsequent avengers, the revolutionary wars soon assumed the mission, carried out by republican and Napoleonic armies, of exporting revolutionary principles to such conquered territories as Italy, the Rhineland, and Belgium.[56] As France had ended absolutism at home, so it would terminate it abroad—even while despotism flourished in the First Republic and First Empire.

Like almost everything that went on in the Revolution, these wars were multifaceted, waged as much for particularistic concerns of national defense, interest, and imperial expansion as on behalf of universalistic crusades for liberty and rational order. The same contradictions surfaced at home. Universalism, rational order, participation, and perfectionism turned into coercive centralization. Repression or worse was the fate of many who spurned radical republicanism during the Terror or in the bloody Catholic insurrection against the revolutionary government in the department of the Vendée (1793–95). Only steadfast believers in their own version of the destiny of the Revolution or supreme opportunists could negotiate the contradiction between exaltation and exigency, perfectionism and persecution. For the unshaken faithful, the conviction that episodes of self–, group, and national aggrandizement implemented and fulfilled revolutionary ideals, united the often ugly, or at least worldly and particularistic, course of the Revolution with its lofty aims.

Jews did not oppose the Revolution like Catholics of the Vendée or other diehard monarchists, nobles, and clerics. Despite emancipation, however, French Jewry was not totally comfortable with revolutionary changes that resonated with liberty, equality, fraternity, and rationality. While the Jewish community, at least its acculturated leaders, approved of emancipation, there was concern over dissolution of the kehillot.[57] Before 1789, the Jews were an autonomous, closed, and distinct corporation as defined by French culture and society, law and government. Kehillot administered family life, religious rituals and institutions, and social and economic activity through its charitable, taxing, judicial, and punitive powers.

Emancipation officially ended self-government and limited rabbinical authority to ritual matters. Though weakened, the Jewish community continued to oversee such matters as prayer, marriage, and burial. Habit, belief, anti-Semitism, and the national government's refusal to nationalize kehillot debts perpetuated its existence. In addition to the hostility of Christian France, Jews were isolated by their own aloofness, rites and rituals, which reinforced Judaic uniqueness, and by widespread lack of fluency in the French language and customs. The struggle for, and transformation into, citizenship, therefore intensified identity problems for Jews. Emancipation and le mouvement régénération meant that Jews were now directly subject to the laws of the state and defined in nationalistic terms, particularly by officials, outsiders, and by their more assimilated coreligionists.[58]

Citizenship invited the Jews to move from a closed community of custom and creed to an open, national community of secular rationality and mobility. The shock of this transition generated a discomfort not always relieved by the fact that they were also invited to rise from the repellent designation of "Christ-killers" to the respected status of French compatriots. Later nationalist movements, based on blood and soil rather than reason and rights, sought to return the Jews to their historic reprobation. Once emancipated, and particularly after a much delayed assimilation, Jews found it painful and impossible to revert to their past rejection and exclusion.[59]

Weighing enclosure and autonomy against equality and acceptance was more problematic because citizenship brought to term in Paris did not always thrive in the provinces. Jews could now vote and hold office if they took the Civic Oath and between December 1791 and April 1792 groups of the acculturated elite in Paris, Nancy, and Metz swore their loyalty to the nation in public ceremonies. Some departmental and municipal officials in Alsace and Lorraine, however, hindered Jews from taking the civic oath, taxed them more heavily than they did other French citizens, and prevented Jews from purchasing nationalized property and voting. Moreover, the central government did not nationalize Jewish communal debts as it did the deficits of other dissolved corporations, though it did nationalize Jewish communal property. Historically insecure, uncertain of their real rights, and confronted with continuing hostility, Jews, especially Ashkenazim, remained politically inactive after emancipation. Parisian Sephardim, who joined political clubs in that city and were on lists of eligible electors, were among the most politically vigorous of Jewish enclaves.[60]

Tocqueville was aware of centralizing trends that would erase individual and group freedom: "In the French Revolution there were two impulses in opposite directions, which must never be confounded; the one was favorable to liberty, the other to despotism." Institutions and attachments that intervened between the state and the citizen, that encouraged diversity vital to independence, were undermined by national government. "The Revolution" tended "to republicanize and to centralize." Indeed, "centralized administration" was "one of the great innovations of the Revolution." Nor was the danger of the omnipotent state confined to

France; it inhered particularly in republics. "Despotism," warned Tocqueville in *Democracy in America*, "which is at all times dangerous, is more particularly to be feared in democratic ages."[61]

Although the demand for absorption, especially during the Reign of Terror, led to oppression of Jews, earlier and greater persecutions plagued Protestants (in the 17th and 18th centuries considered more of an enemy of Catholicism than were Jews) and, during the Revolution, the Catholics. By the 1730s, and especially after 1775, the torments of the Protestants lessened. The Edict of Toleration (1787) reaffirmed religious freedom and granted Protestants civil status, thus legitimizing their marriages, births, and last rites. On the eve of the Revolution, however, Protestants could not publicly worship, their pastors could not assume religious functions, they had no political rights, and previously confiscated property was not returned. They became citizens in 1789. A year later, with a Protestant as president of the National Assembly, it awarded heirs of the emigrés of 1685 and those later condemned for religious crimes the property taken from their families and conferred citizenship on returning descendants of religious exiles.[62]

Emancipation did not culminate an overwhelming and irresistible momentum for religious freedom and civic equality for all Christian believers. Unpopular with the Catholic majority, it provoked street demonstrations, particularly among zealots in the West and Southeast. Anti-Protestant agitation continued throughout the Revolution.[63]

The civic gains and continuing persecution of the Protestants immediately before and during the Revolution paralleled the experience of the Jews. Nor were these similarities the only connection between the marginalized enclaves. Malesherbes had been a major factor in the royal edict that gave the Protestants civil status and his probable intent in 1788 was to issue a memorandum on the Jews resembling the one he prepared for the Protestants. His method and motives regarding these two groups coincided. In deliberating on the future of the Jews, Malesherbes solicited opinion from Jewish and Gentile respondents. Reports from the latter, including Protestants, were generally negative about the Jews.[64]

While the prospects of Jews and Protestants improved in the liberal period, Catholicism was severely debilitated by those who professed insurgency in the cause of individual rights. For them, the rights of man and the citizen entailed suppression of the Gallic church. The revolutionaries seized Church property, appropriated its functions, obstructed its rituals, and persecuted its clerics. To everything that the Revolution proclaimed, the Church seemed the most fundamental and dangerous opponent. Enthusiasts for liberty, equality, fraternity, progress, citizenship, the state, nationalism, reason, and secularization regarded Catholicism as the ecclesiastical embodiment of authority, corporatism, hierarchy, and superstition. They regarded the Church as a Bourbon stalwart ever ready to betray the Revolution to a despised past. French Catholicism, a primary opponent of Protestant and Jewish emancipation, thus became the main target of religious persecution by those who liberated worshippers of these other creeds.

Neither the resolve of the majority of the clergy at Versailles in June 1789 to join with the Third Estate—a decision critical to the overthrow of the old order—nor the resounding affirmation of religious freedom in the Declaration of the Rights of Man forestalled the campaign against the Gallic church. Between August 1789 and May 1790 the Assembly nationalized ecclesiastical properties and placed them at the disposal of the government to help pay the state debt; abolished tithes and fees as part of the dissolution of feudalism; cancelled monastic vows and suppressed monastic orders; and rejected a motion to make Catholicism the state creed. The growing cleavage between patriots and priests became a chasm when, in July 1790, approximately between the dates it gave Protestants and Jews full citizenship, the Assembly adopted the Civil Constitution of the Clergy, which organized dioceses in accordance with the new civil departments and made the citizen electorate (including non-Catholics) eligible to elect bishops and curés. In January 1791, the Assembly required the clergy to take an oath of loyalty to the nation, the law, the king, and the Constitution (which included the Civil Constitution of the Clergy), thus detaching the Gallic church from Rome. These decrees eliminated the old-order corporative organization of the Church; state sovereignty displaced apostolic authority and Gallic Catholicism became a branch of the state. In many parishes and dioceses, refractory clerics and their supporters confronted those who pledged loyalty to the state. The Legislative Assembly, elected in September 1791, intensified persecution of clergy who refused to swear the oath, but opposition continued.[65]

Protestantism and Judaism suffered no such official financial confiscation and intervention in ritual and organization. From the perspective of the liberal revolution, Catholicism was the main enemy of the new nation, rational enlightenment, and individual rights; the Church had to be reformed for its integration into the revolutionary state. For devout believers, the Revolution would destroy their freedom of worship and earthly and eternal destiny as members of the body of Christ, and thus became the ultimate foe of the Savior and His flock. The enmity of the faithful was compounded by their belief that the king represented God and defended His Church. The execution of Louis XVI, therefore, was seen as an all-out attack on Catholicism and henceforth defined the struggle between republican and Catholic-monarchist France. Nor did it escape Catholics that the travails inflicted on them and their church transpired in the year of Jewish emancipation. It seemed to the Church's adherents as if the Revolution was elevating one creed while eradicating another and that these contrary trends proceeded from a common source. Then and thereafter they associated revolution, republicanism, and Jewry and intransigently reprehended this unholy trinity.

The liberal era ended when the monarchy fell in August 1792. Jacobin hegemony in 1793 and the Reign of Terror (Fall 1793–July 1794) escalated state authoritarianism and the antireligious furor. During the Terror and its dechristianization campaign, organized Protestantism and Judaism, as well as Catholicism, came under severe and systematic assault. Except in the East, Jews were treated no worse than other groups. Cathedrals, churches, and synagogues were vandalized, closed, or turned into "Temples of Reason"; clubs, stores, and Christian and Jewish communal properties alike were nationalized. Rabbis, priests, and ministers were suspended from their duties and Judaic and Christian rituals were suppressed. Jacobins opposed celebrating the Sabbath either on Saturday or Sunday and Jews were fined for not working on Saturday. Local Jacobin clubs sheared off the beards and side-locks of orthodox Jews. Attacks were made on circumcision and the observance of Jewish holidays. Lighting Sabbath candles and ritual slaughtering were prohibited. Occasionally, intermarriage was coerced and rabbis exiled. Hebrew books were burned, ritual objects confiscated, Yeshivas closed, and Yiddish proscribed (as part of a suppression of foreign and domestic dialects to create a uniform, national language).[66]

Even when discrimination against Jews did not target their religious rituals, as with other faiths, but was inflicted from anti-Semitic motives (for example, exclusion from Jacobin clubs or the National Guard, or denial of certificates de civisme), Jacobins differed in their attitude. Reubell, for example, was unremittingly hostile, but some Jacobin societies still had Jewish members.[67]

But the circumstances of French Jews were not unremittingly miserable. Unlike Catholics, during the Revolution, even at the time of the Terror and the subsequent Thermidorian reaction, few Jews were executed and almost invariably not for their creed, but rather for their faction. "The republic does not know the meaning of the word Jew because this term no longer refers to a people but to a sect," said a Parisian clubbiste on October 27, 1793. "The republic has no interests in sects and deports its votaries only when they disturb the social order."[68]

Many people supported emancipation and Jews were now formally freed of all historical constraints, and de jure, if not de facto, equal to other French people. Exemplary of their new status, they served in the army in the same proportion as other citizens. Religious observances persisted despite persecution, suppression, and destruction. Neither citizenship nor the antireligious and anti-Semitic moods of the Revolution uprooted rabbinical leadership; rabbis swore the civic oath and thus there was no refractory Jewish clergy.[69]

Throughout the Revolution, Protestant and Jewish tribulations paled before anti-Catholic harassment. In September 1792, municipalities took over registration of vital statistics (births, marriages, deaths) from the parishes. Life's passages, traditionally sacramental, became civil matters in yet another attempt to remove any diversions between the individual and the citizen, to make the nation rather than the Church the basic bond, and citizenship rather than Catholicism the primary identity of individuals. Some measures, not decreed by the Assembly, but carried out by officials, local governments, and the army, resembled attacks on other religions fostered by the same individuals and groups: confiscating sacred objects, smashing icons, pillaging and destroying churches, and substituting revolutionary for Catholic ritual. But other onslaughts were unique to Catholicism. In 1792 nonjuring clerics were massacred, especially in September when the Paris Commune killed priests and other suspected counterrevolutionaries to forestall a feared royalist plot and foreign invasion of the city. Many more Catholic clergy were imprisoned, deported, or became exiles.[70]

Depredations coincided with the expanded power of the state. During the Terror, the central government regulated the price, production, and distribution of grain and imposed numerous requisitions and controls on the economy. Suppression of religion, therefore, was one facet of the revolutionary principle that state dominion expressed the general will. Its officials thus believed that the central government was empowered to correct or eliminate all institutions that intervened between state and citizen or that diverted the authority of the former or the loyalty of the latter.[71]

Antireligious and especially anti-Catholic frenzy peaked during the Terror. A republican calendar was adopted that abolished saints' days, holidays, and the Sabbath. Churches were closed and priests ordered to marry. Imprisonment, deportation, and killing of nonjurors continued with renewed vigor. During the Terror, approximately 2,000–3,000 clergy were killed (in addition to Catholic lay people who helped them) and another 32,500 emigrated (five-sixths forcibly). Most priests who pledged to the Constitution, and many Protestant pastors as well, denounced, denied, or deserted their calling.[72]

Repression of traditional creeds, accompanied by robust promotion of a civic creed, in 1793–94 coalesced into a dechristianization campaign. Just as monotheisms can make exclusive demands for spiritual loyalty, so nationalisms can resent other beliefs. The national religion, a deification of reason and the state, would replace Catholicism as the true Gallic spirit. Paris, the national capital, the cockpit of the Revolution, the City of Light or, at this time, at least of enlightenment, would overcome Rome, the center of darkness, the international City of God and the Pope, the citadel of reaction and superstition. Robespierre's Cult of the Supreme Being, festivals and goddesses of Reason, and the transformation of churches and synagogues into Temples of Reason or Liberty created an unlikely union of classical antiquity, the Enlightenment, and the state. The last dominated this trinity. An outburst of passion and pageantry characteristic of the Revolution took place in November 1793, when a Festival of Reason was held at the Cathedral of Notre Dame. An ecclesiastical haven now became a shrine to Reason, where busts of Voltaire, Franklin, and Rousseau looked down on a classically enrobed actress representing the Goddess of Reason or the Deity of Liberty.[73]

Deistic, revolutionary, and republican fetes and pageants heeded the decree of the Constitution of September 3, 1791, the first of France's many national charters (four in the revolutionary era alone). The Constitution of 1791 ordered "the establishment of national festivals to preserve the memory of the French Revolution, strengthen fraternity between citizens and their attachment to the Constitution, the nation, and the laws."[74] Faithful to the Revolution in his own subversive fashion, Napoleon continued to celebrate the republican legacy while betraying it by even more elaborate glorifications of the First Empire.

For the enthusiasts of the 1790s, the civic cult did more than advance the state and defeat believers in Catholicism and other creeds. Revolutionaries proclaimed that their cause—liberty, equality and fraternity—would be unattainable without reason. People could be free only if they formed a nation illuminated by the light of reason. Since universalism was a central constituent of reason, fraternity, like liberty, depended upon rationality. The faculty of understanding was considered innately and commonly human, and, as such, egalitarian, while conventional religions, especially Catholicism, were labeled hierarchical, feudal relics. Judaism, Christianity, and other religions were dark (superstitious) and particularistic, thus nationally divisive. Consequently, reason harmonized with and provided for, and religion offended and endangered, republican equality.

Reason was also associated with another ideal of the Revolution. The civic cult, the Republic of Reason, would fortify secularism, an outlook that most revolutionaries deemed indispensable to liberty, equality, and fraternity because it released the mind from superstitious, slavish obeisance to the clerical hierarchy. Reason and secularism were considered correlative and mutually reinforcing facets of a common temperament. Paradoxically, the Terror imposed this aspect of its agenda with an inquisitional zeal evocative of religious fervor.

The French upheaval and the civic culture it spawned inspired the convergence of revolution, secularism, and nationalism as did no other uprising until 1917. As Ernest Gellner notes, the age of nationalism and revolution ran concurrently, and often interacted, with the age of secularism. The reign of the *philosophes*, the rise of modern capitalism and communism and appearance of their ideological rationales, and development of theories of evolution and psychotherapy coincide with chronological markers of nationalism and revolution: 1775, 1848, and 1917.[75]

The American and French Revolutions radically diverged with respect to reason and religion. Rationalists regularly appeared among the founders of the United States—as revolutionary heroes, formulators of the U.S. Constitution, and early republican leaders—and God was not mentioned in that document. Nevertheless, reason was not enshrined nor religion repudiated during the American Revolution or the creation of the nation state. Hartz correctly asserted that Dissenting ministers became leaders in the War for Independence. Since American religion was revolutionary, he argued, the American rebellion, unlike its French counterpart, neither suppressed religion nor made a religion—a civic, secular cult of reason—of its Revolution.[76] Many American revolutionary and early national statesmen might be personally indifferent, but were not hostile, to religion. In prerevolutionary France, Jews were victimized by the Bourbon-Catholic establishment and excoriated by Enlightenment thinkers. Thereafter, the royal-clerical remnant and rationalists and radicals persecuted Jews. A similar observation pertains to the Russian Revolution. Formulated as a Hartzian dialectic, American Jews were systematically oppressed neither by a reactionary, religious right or a secular, radical left.

Overthrow of the Jacobin dictatorship in July 1794 diminished the antireligious crusade, but Jewish communities remained impoverished and disrupted. Jews persisted in petty trades and as pawnbrokers, defamed occupations that contributed to the persecution that waxed and waned until Napoleon's coup of November 1799. The Concordat of 1801, negotiated between the First Consul and the Pope, set the pattern of Church-state relations for the remainder of the century. Although Napoleon conceded the Pontiff's request that revolutionary cults be abolished and some three-quarters of the Catholic clergy were *refractaires*, the revolutionary disposition prevailed. The clergy was paid by the government, swore loyalty to it, and the Pope had to dismiss intransigent counterrevolutionary bishops, those that refused to accept the agreement. Bonaparte preserved religious pluralism by refusing to make Catholicism the state sect. The government still controlled the Church; hence on another field of conflict the emperor won a victory. When the First Empire displaced the First Republic, sacred buildings no longer were commandeered in the name of the Revolution, reason, the Republic and the state, and people now worshipped openly. Churches, synagogues and religious schools were reclaimed, rebuilt, and reopened.[77]

Since Catholicism was usually officially charged with conspiring to replace the Tricolor with the *fleur de lis*, the Church suffered most. Judaism and Protestantism were not suspected of being Bourbon strongholds, but were still subject to the same abuse, in type if not in magnitude, as the Catholics. Protestants and Jews also endured hostilities of a different, and, in the case of the latter, a more lasting kind. Minorities long loathed by the Catholic majority, these hatreds did not disappear with emancipation and the advent of a new state. Many Catholics looked upon the Civil Constitution of 1791 and its accompanying oath as Protestant plots against Catholicism. Such suspicions aggravated historical turmoil between the two denominations, sometimes to the point of local episodes of mob violence.[78]

Jews, too, found that bigotry and brutality continued despite celebration and acquisition of civic rights. Since medieval times Jews paid special taxes and did so until well into the ninteenth century because when, in 1793, the government nationalized the debts of disbanded corporations, it excluded the Jews. Other refusals to break with the past were more local. As if 1789 had not yet come, cities in Alsace tried to prohibit Jewish residence and commercial activity, levied special taxes on Jews, expelled Jewish inhabitants, and curtailed Jewish visitors. In 1793–94, peasant pogroms again erupted in Alsace. Many of these proscriptions persisted in the First Empire: Restrictions on Jewish moneylending were resurrected, local administrators refused to register marriages of Alsatian Jews to coreligionists in other departments, and Alsatian Jews were denied permission to move to other departments.[79]

Revolutionary rage against Catholicism surpassed animosity against Judaism. As subsequent French history shows, however, intensity is not always depth. Although hostility between the Church and later republics endured, the anti-Catholic paroxysm terminated with the end of the Revolution. Jew hatred was more protracted and eventually more horrible. Long after religion and citizenship ceased to be an issue for Catholics and Protestants, much of France opposed the inclusion of Jews in the nation.

Jewish acquiescence in the attack on Judaism's traditional identity and structure was not invariably coerced or a grudging tradeoff for national acceptance. During the debate over emancipation, an "Address of Alsatian Jews to the People of Alsace" assured Christian compatriots that citizenship would elevate Hebraic character and culture to the national norm and that Jews would abandon certain aspects of their religion and their separate community to become true citizens.[80] Like their gentile allies, Jews seeking civic rights believed in regeneration through political equality.

Immediately after emancipation, another Jewish regenerator, Berr Isaac Berr reviewed for the Jewish congregations of Alsace and Lorraine the flaws of his coreligionists and suggested improvement by adopting the ways of gentile citizens. Son of a rich banker, man of letters, tobacco manufacturer, and prominent among Nancy and national Ashkenazim, Berr was both a delegate of the Jewish community of Alsace and Lorraine during the presentation of its case for civil rights to the National Assembly and an influential member of Napoleon's Assembly of Jewish Notables and Parisian Sanhedrin. A revolutionary nationalist, he attributed emancipation to "the sovereignty of the nation." As a *maskil* (proponent of the Jewish Enlightenment), he thanked "the Supreme Being," not Jehovah, for the Jews' attainment of citizenship. He told his people that self-protection against persecution, which had forced Jews into commerce, also made them "deficient" in "qualification to fulfill the duties of" citizenship. Now that "hardships" of the past no longer prevailed this imbalance would have to be corrected. "[M]oral and intellectual improvement" would "give signal proof" to "our fellow citizens" of the "patriotism so long cherished in our bosoms."[81]

Berr advocated "strict adherence to our religion," through which Jews survived their historic "tribulations." But there were limits to orthodoxy: We must "divest ourselves entirely of that narrow spirit, of *Corporation* and *Congregation* in all civil and political matters, not immediately connected with our spiritual laws" (italics in original). Jews should "appear simply as individuals, as Frenchmen, guided only by a true patriotism and by the general good of the nation; . . . to make ourselves useful to our fellow-citizens, to deserve their esteem and their friendship." Let "us take the civic oath of being faithful to the nation, to the law and to the king." The "oath is nothing but a renunciation of those pretended privileges and immunities which we enjoyed" as a corporate body. What did these privileges consist of? We were "a separate community," excluded from "other corporations," subjected to special and arbitrary taxes, and exempted from military service and public office because "we were deemed unworthy." By pledging the civic oath "we shall enjoy the rights and qualities of active citizens" and "be *constitutionally* acknowledged as French Jews," a status that grants "full liberty to profess our religion" (italics in original). [82]

While congratulating the Jews on becoming politically equal and glorifying the country and Revolution that set them free, Berr advised civic diffidence: "[L]et us avoid grasping at our rights, let us not rush headlong against the opinions of some of our fellow citizens," whose "prejudice . . . will reject the idea of Jews being fellow men." Jews should not attend "assemblies of French citizens" until "we know how to discuss and defend the interests of the country; in short, until our most bitter enemies are convinced, and acknowledge the gross misconceptions they had entertained of us." Ameliorative gradualism would enable Jews to make themselves more useful, ethical, and French. Their fellow citizens would correspondingly become comfortable with the new status of the Jews: "French ought to be the Jews' mother tongue. . . . Why should we continue to bear the name of German and Polish Jews, while we are happily French Jews?" Dropping Yiddish for French involved an educational process that maskilim typically thought would make Jews worthy citizens in their own right and in the eyes of gentile compatriots. Learning the sciences and humanities would remove a Jewish addiction "to that mercantile and trafficking spirit." To accomplish these aims, Jewish children should study in public schools and poorer youngsters be trained in Jewish "houses of industry" as artisans.[83]

Overeager to impress gentile France that Jews could remedy their faults and too willing to accept negative opinion as valid ascriptions of Jewish degradation, Berr approached craven deference. A strong Jewish identity, however, precluded total accommodationism. Hebraic survival, he felt, resulted from steadfast faith in Judaism. His educational proposals, the essence of his Judaic reform program, included fluency in Hebrew, reading the Jewish Bible in that language, and being informed about Judaism generally. These subjects would be taught in Jewish schools. Attending public and Hebrew schools would produce "good Jews and good French citizens." In addition, Berr advocated restoration of Jewish community organizations and election of rabbis to discharge civic and religious functions. Unlike extreme maskilim, who would dissolve the kehillot, Berr favored communal autonomy before 1791, even if it prevented full citizenship, for example, the right to hold office.[84]

Berr deserves examination not only for his eminence in the Ashkenazi community, a standing owed more to elite status and connections with other upper-class Jews and French officials than to influence among the orthodox majority in Alsace and Lorraine. Represented in this letter, however, and more importantly, is evidence of the conflicting impulses harbored by members of both the elite and (increasingly, if belatedly) the larger Jewish community. In it, Berr addressed two communities. To the Gentiles he argued, as did most Jews, that accusations against their community were neither as grave nor irremediable as claimed by opponents of emancipation, imperfections were disappearing, and citizenship would complete regeneration. To the Jews, Berr and his cohorts advocated, at least in secular matters, acculturation over disassociation: French over Yiddish; modern education over teachings in *hederim* and *Yeshivot* (orthodox Jewish schools); manual, agricultural, and professional endeavor over moneylending and other financial activities; and the civil law over the Mosaic Code. Ultimately, if not in the minds of Berr and his contemporaries—who dodged this issue by saying that the nation and the Jewish community were in harmony—the letter's argument was, in sum, the state before the synagogue.

If this regimen was adopted, Berr and other commentators (Jewish and non-Jewish) promised, Jews would fulfill civic obligations and thus deserve civic rights. Recognizing rehabilitation and patriotism, Christians would no longer begrudge political equality. Subsequent generations of Jews struggled with this overly-optimistic prescription as they sought to reconcile allegiance to Judaism with bourgeoning ties to the nation.

While Berr instructed his coreligionists in the virtues of humility and acculturation, the Jews of Avignon in 1794 expressed the same goal of unity with the nation, but in a more aggrieved tone. They petitioned for government assumption of Jewish communal debts and reiterated widespread Jewish resentment against its prerevolutionary status: "The corporation formed a multitude of separate small nations in the midst of the nation itself," argued the petitioners. "All these revolting divisions must disappear. . . . There are no more Catholics, Protestants, Jews [sic] sectarians of any kind, there are only Frenchmen."[85]

Gentile supporters of the Enlightenment and/or the nation-state agreed that Orthodox Judaism was a useless, even dangerous, relic to be discarded in favor of modernism. Maskilim and Jewish patriots in Germany and France—Berr and Moses Mendelssohn are examples—were more hesitant to sever their roots. They, too, however, would radically revise their heritage. Like Berr, Mendelssohn wanted to substitute German for Yiddish and declared his allegiance to the secular state. That icon of the German Haskalah assured hesitant Gentiles that "even in their present debased condition," Jews are "useful to the state" and fit for military service. Wherever Jews are well-treated (given rights), they are loyal and willing to defend the state, which is the duty of all citizens. "Native settlers," he wrote, must become "citizens of the state." And Caesar preceded creed: "The state possesses absolute right, the church limited rights."[86]

Contemporary maskilim were not the original or most celebrated Jewish proponents of civil supremacy. In the previous century, Baruch Spinoza, an early Deist and prototype of the haskalah, with similar intonation anticipated Mendelssohn's formulation of the priority of the state. "All authority in sacred matters rests exclusively with the civil power," theorized Spinoza in 1670, "and religious worship must be in harmony with the institutions of the state if God is to be rightly obeyed."[87]

Conjoined to political issues such as the surrender of communal autonomy for citizenship, was the challenge of modern culture and the modern state to the theology of Zionism. The messianic prospect of ending exile would be displaced by the diasporic reality of living among Gentiles. "The hoped-for return to Palestine," wrote Mendelssohn in 1783, "has no influence on our conduct as citizens." Aside from the very human trait of bonding "wherever Jews are tolerated," without God's intervention "the Talmud forbids *even to think* of a return . . . and a restoration of our nation" (italics in original). A correlative (but not the only Jewish) reaction to national citizenship was assimilative rejection of "next year in Jerusalem." La patrie was the new Palestine.[88]

Disavowing messianic Zionism detracted from the Biblical Hebraic concept of the Jews as a united and chosen People. If Jews belonged to their land of residence rather than remembrance, they no longer were one people. And if they became French, German, English, or American, how were they chosen above other citizens of these countries? Jews now differentiated themselves not only by nationality, but at times intranationally. Jews of Bordeaux saw themselves as a Sephardic patriciate more authentically French than the Ashkenazi in eastern France and, therefore, sought civil rights from themselves alone.[89] A century later, many German-American Jews claimed to be racially different from Jewish immigrants from Eastern Europe. This new Jewish view of Jews and Judaism forged a correspondence between Gentile liberals, nationalists, and dejudaizers and their equivalents among Jews.

Despite the efforts of Berr and other maskilim and patriots to resurrect Jewish community organization, albeit under national auspices, emancipation, particularly the Enlightenment source of civic rights, undercut revival of communal authority. Political equality entailed individual rights and/or citizenship in a secular community and both opposed conventional Jewish authority, which subordinated the individual to the group and maintained a form of corporate autonomy against French nation-state uniformity.[90]

Orthodox culture and community was under a many-sided assault from the eighteenth-century surge of nationalism, secularism, and rationalism among Christians and Jews alike. These trends challenged the Torah and Talmud, Biblical, rabbinic, and messianic Judaism, and Jewish ritual and law. New notions and movements—nationalism, assimilation or acculturation, secularism, individual and natural rights, the law of reason, division of church and state, and tolerance of all faiths—challenged the ideas, customs, and institutions that upheld closed communities and attachment to the myth of exile.[91]

Consider the enormous shock of citizenship to Jewish communities in Western Europe in general and France in particular. Avid seekers of civic equality and those indifferent or resigned to it alike confronted an introduction into modern politics. Living for centuries in their sealed communities, Jews had not, at least extramurally, undertaken political initiatives. Internal autonomy meant political insulation and isolation that fostered external passivity; that is, the Jews were acted upon by outside forces like the king or local lords or municipal councilors. Now Jews were actively involved with, or, at a minimum, the subject of, party and parliamentary maneuvering, public opinion, revolutionary transition, state formation, civic culture, and the surge of nationalism.[92]

Jewish responses to emancipation varied with class and ethnicity and ranged from participation in revolutionary antireligious campaigns, to a desire to assimilate, even to the point of conversion; become true French compatriots and protest against abridgement of their rights as citizens; compromise Judaic ritual and tradition; and in some instances, retain orthodoxy and communal rule. Three models for Jews of the Western world emerged from the Age of Reason and modern state formation. They could embrace Enlightenment universalism as epitomized by Moses Mendelssohn. They could become patriots of their newly formed nation, a lesser-known outgrowth of the Enlightenment. Lastly, they could stay in their traditional communities. In the first case, Jews would forsake nationalism for the cosmopolitanism that soon became an anti-Semitic mantra in the Western world. Taking the second route meant that Jews would become part of civic nationalism, an aspiration of the French and American Revolutions and basic (perhaps *the* basic) trait of the American republic from its beginning and increasingly valued ever since ethnic nationalism culminated in fascism and World War II. Remaining insular would as much be a result of rejection by their hosts as of Jewish "tribalism" and, for both reasons, would leave Jews open to the charge of being an unregenerate nation within a nation. The penultimate Nazi solution to the "Jewish Question" was to return the Jews to this condition and then accuse them of betraying their territorial nation to their spiritual home.

In the era examined in this study, national consolidation and commitment occurred earlier and with greater strength in the United States and France than in Germany; therefore, French and American Jews were likelier to be nationalists and less susceptible to cosmopolitanism than were their German coreligionists. Despite the accommodationism of Berr and other prominent and wealthy figures, French Jewry was on the whole more cohesive and less assimilated than its American counterpart. Consequently, the latter was more attracted to citizenship and integration in national society and, correspondingly, less inclined to preserve or establish self-governing, orthodox religio-ethnic enclaves. Here we contemplate tendencies, not absolutes. However mutually exclusive these three possibilities seem in logic or theory, in real life two, or even all, sometimes joined in varying degrees of harmony and friction.

Assimilation, secularization, and downright repudiation of heritage were driven by the demand that Jews exchange a separate identity for citizenship and by their own national feeling and quest for acceptance. A few abandoned Jehovah to embrace the revolutionary Cult of Reason and, during the worst excesses of the Republic of Virtue, participated in assaults on Jewish institutions and rituals. Intermarriage and conversion, however, only marginally increased through the Revolution and the First Empire. Moderate assimilationists affiliated with Judaism but did not speak Yiddish, read Hebrew or send their children to hederim or Yeshivot. These changes impressed some officials in the First Empire, who argued that since emancipation the Jews had forsaken orthodoxy to become like other citizens and developed a primary loyalty to France. Napoleon's civil servants, like their master, certainly wished this to be the case. As late as the 1820s, a large share of the Jewish population, however, especially the Ashkenazi majority, was literate only in Hebrew.[93]

The Revolution substituted the nation for the body of Christ as the fundamental affiliation of the French people. Citizenship, not Christianity, determined membership in the civic nation. Correspondingly, the Jews moved from odium as Christ-killers and repudiators of Christianity to affirmation as members of the body politic. Accordingly, Jews obtained full civic rights and obligations, including military service. Despite this transformation, assimilationist demands of the gentile public and some of their own leaders, and renunciation or compromise of their heritage by some coreligionists, dejudiazation was not the main response to emancipation.

The greater impact of the Enlightenment on German Jewry by contrast left French Jews less cosmopolitan and more cohesive as a creedal community. According to contemporary reports, as late as the 1820s there were only thirty-six secular Jewish intellectuals in Paris and nineteen in the department of Moselle, which included Metz, the leading Jewish community in northeastern France and center of the French Haskalah in that region.[94]

With longer residence in France, less reinforced by new immigrants, burdened by fewer economic and social restrictions, and more accepted by the national society, Sephardim were quicker to acculturate. They earlier introduced French and other non-Hebraic subjects in their schools and were not as fervent or orthodox in their faith as were the northeastern Ashkenazim. Along with Paris, Bordeaux, a cosmopolitan seaport with many ethnic groups and a Jewish mercantile elite, harbored the most assimilated enclave. Unlike their brethren in Alsace and Lorraine, the Portuguese Jews of Bordeaux, except for civil law, litigated in French law courts. In 1811, however, only seventeen Jewish children in that city enrolled in public schools. Even among the Sephardim conversion and intermarriage were unusual; in Bordeaux, of 390 marriages with at least one Jewish spouse between 1793–1820, only 36 were mixed.[95]

Ashkenazim (approximately 22,500 lived in Alsace in 1789) were more insular. In 1808, Jews in Alsace (26,070) and Lorraine (10,896) constituted 79 percent of the 46,663 in France. Most resided in small towns and villages remote from French society. Strasbourg, the largest city in the region, had just recently admitted Jews. As shown by Paula E.

Hyman and Phyllis Cohen Albert, leading historians of nineteenth-Century French Jewry, attaining fluency in French, the basic element of acculturation, proceeded slowly, and structural assimilation, as defined by intermarriage and other primary group ties, was rare. Resisting pressure from government officials and acculturated leaders in Paris and Strasbourg, most Alsatian Jews remained Orthodox. From 1770 to 1780, 76 percent of Alsatian Jews bore Jewish first names; in 1830, this share (69 percent) had barely diminished. French names began to regularly appear in the 1860s. Until the mid–ninteenth century, Jews in the eastern departments lived in consistories that resembled the corporations of prerevolutionary France, used Yiddish as their primary language, were educated in hederim, worshipped in Orthodox synagogues, revered traditional rabbis, followed old folkways, and had few intermarriages. Unexpectedly, a higher percentage of Ashkenazi children attended French public schools than among Sephardic youngsters in Bordeaux, but the percentages were still small. In Lorraine, the share of Jewish school-aged children who attended public schools reached no more than 20 percent and in two departments of Alsace in 1808 was nearer to 10 percent. Historic loyalty, ties to the global Jewish community, new immigration from Eastern Europe, and anti-Semitism preserved Ashekenazi identity.[96]

Among cosmopolitan French Jews signs of assimilation are surprisingly slight and late; in Paris in the 1860s, only one in three Jewish children attended non-Jewish schools. During the Second Empire, mixed marriages in the Parisian Jewish bourgeois composed only 14 percent of all weddings in that enclave. Approximately 75 percent of an even more assimilated segment (military and government officials), and at a later date (Third Republic), married endogamously.[97]

By all indications, French Jewry was more insular than were coreligionists in Germany and America. Given scant evidence of preliminary inclinations to reject their heritage, comparatively few French Jews took the ultimate step in leaving the Jewish community. Between 1808 and 1840, about 100 families converted to Christianity, and during the Second Empire few defections occurred, even among bourgeois Jews. At the turn of the century, however, apostasy increased.[98]

While Jews generally resisted total integration into national society, they grew more comfortable with life in France. In 1812, Bordeaux Jews started to erect grand synagogues with facades placed on street fronts. Such public displays of Judaism were rare before this date. The less secure and more provincial Jews in the East still sought protection in anonymity. These temples of Judaism did not appear in Alsace until the 1840s.[99]

Jews varied in how much of their heritage they would renounce to feel like, or try to gain acceptance as, citizens. They even differed in how they pursued the quest for civic equality. Not all were as patient, penitent, or thankful as Berr. Some Ashkenazim demanded the equality just granted to American Jews through elimination of the test oath in the U.S. Constitution: "The word *toleration*" is "no longer suitable to a nation that wishes firmly to place its rights upon the eternal foundations of justice," proclaimed a January 28, 1790 petition of French Jews to the Assembly (italics in original). "America, to which politics will owe so many useful lessons, has rejected the word from its code, as a term tending to compromise individual liberty and to sacrifice certain classes of men to other classes. To tolerate is, in fact, to suffer that which you could, if you wished; prevent and prohibit."[100]

Reverend Jean-Paul Rabaut de Saint Etienne, the foremost Protestant leader in the Revolution, future Girondist exile, and supporter of Jewish emancipation, invoked another American constitution: "It is not toleration that I claim," said this deputy in a speech of August 23, 1789, in the Assembly. "That word implies an idea of compassion that degraded man. I demand equal freedom for all." France should "imitate the Pennsylvanians [in their state constitution]. They make exception of nobody. Man, whatever his religious belief, has the right of enjoying all the sacred privileges that belong to mankind."[101]

Aggressive demands for political and religious rights apparently drew on the American experience. At the Virginia Constitutional Convention (1776), James Madison, along with Thomas Jefferson, America's architects of freedom of conscience, suggested an amendment to the Declaration of Rights in the state constitution to "substitute" for the word "toleration" a "phraseology which—declared the freedom of conscience to be a *natural* and absolute right" (italics in original). A member of the committee that prepared a constitution and declaration of rights, Madison prevailed upon his colleagues to broaden religious freedom in another way. The original version guaranteed "the fullest Exercise of Religion." After Madison's revision, the final formulation affirmed "the free exercise of religion."[102]

A decade later, Jefferson told Madison that the Virginia Act for Religious Freedom (1786), America's most uncompromising defense of liberty of conscience, is "in the new Encyclopedie and is appearing in most of the publications respecting America." By 1789, an edition of the U.S. Constitution had gone through four French printings. The federal and state constitutions were widely read by members of the National Assembly and several suggested them and the states' bills of rights as models for The Declaration of the Rights of Man and wanted France to emulate protections of religious liberty in the federal and state charters. The deputies extensively consulted Jefferson, then minister to France, on drafts of the Declaration.[103]

Admiration for America peaked in 1789–90 and remained high until the defeat of the Gironde and the end of amity toward foreigners. *Americanistes* abounded among constitutional monarchists and liberals and Americans were frequent and popular stage characters. Adulation was decidedly less noticeable among unreconstructed Bourbon loyalists, disgruntled aristocrats, and radicals. But even after 1792, emigrés, visitors to America, and the *Idéologues*, a rear guard of philosophes and liberals, praised American republicanism and equality, moderation and freedom from government, and regard for individual rights. Those living abroad bluntly contrasted these conditions with Bonapartism; those who remained at home extolled the same qualities in a silent rebuke of Napoleon.[104]

During the halcyon year of 1789, America inspired many revolutionaries. After the storming of the Bastille, Marquis de Lafayette sent its key to his old commander, George Washington, "because it was American principles that opened its gates." Vicomte de Noailles, Lafayette's brother-in-law and comrade in arms during the War for Independence, and other French officers who served the American cause took the lead on the night of August 4th, when, at a sublime session of the National Assembly, noble supporters of the Revolution relinquished their feudal privileges. In that year, Jean-Marie Roland addressed the Academy of Lyons. His theme was moderation, his model was the American government, and his evaluation of it anticipated the views of Tocqueville and Hartz. "The moderation of the American government creates as zealous patriots as were ever the most famous republicans," said the future Girondist minister and victim of Jacobin radicalism. The example of America was fortified by the mentorship of Jefferson and widely and favorably disseminated in newspapers and pamphlets. America the avatar even appeared on the Paris stage in *La Vallé de Shénandoah en Virginie*, a two-act comedy in which a virtuous Virginian colonist welcomes European immigrants fleeing oppression and undergoing regeneration in their new land.[105]

Franklin and Jefferson, whom the French knew best, were the most revered Americans. Children, shops, and political clubs were named after the former and a play, "*L'Imprimeur ou la Fête de Franklin*," was produced. When he died in 1790, the National Assembly declared a thirteen-day mourning period, accepted a bust of him by Houdon, and the Paris Commune and other revolutionary societies held ceremonies throughout the city and elsewhere. George Washington was less adored, but received honors from Napoleon as well as during the Revolution. Like Franklin, he was sculpted by Houdon, became the hero of a drama, staged in 1791, and was officially mourned. In 1800, shortly after his death, Napoleon ordered Houdon's statue placed in the Tuilleries. Eulogies at a public memorial at the *Invalides* identified the First Consul with America's first president. The Girondist-dominated Legislative Assembly, in August

1792, conferred the title of French citizen upon foreigners who advanced human reason and liberty. Among them were Washington, Madison, and Alexander Hamilton. A few months later, Joseph Barlow, an American poet and active Girondist then living in Paris, received this recognition. The opposition also lauded the United States. Radical as well as moderate Jacobins (Girondists) hung American flags as banners for freedom in their assembly halls. Although enthusiasm for the United States and its revolution waned as France turned left and friction flashed between the two nations, even during the Terror Franklin continued to be celebrated and the American rebellion appeared in the Cult of the Supreme Being and on the revolutionary calendar.[106]

Those less attracted to the republican cause were dubious about America as exemplar. Humbly born Pierre-Paul Royer-Collard was a philosopher and politician in transit from revolutionary enthusiasm to constitutional monarchism. After the Restoration, he would become the intellectual leader of the *Doctrinaires* (a liberal group), president of the Chamber of Deputies, and the friend and mentor of Tocqueville. While in the Council of Five Hundred, Royer-Collard blamed the United States for inspiring imprudent indulgence of religious liberty in the revolutionary constitutions of France. "We have on this head borrowed most of our maxims from American legislation," he told that body in 1797, "without calculating perhaps the prodigious difference that arises when they are applied to a country like ours."[107]

Whatever Royer-Collard thought excessive, the French had certainly not absolutely committed to religious equality. During the Terror, all religions were attacked, but Jacobins tended to single out Jews for commercial and financial persecution. Discrimination persisted through the Thermidor riposte to Jacobin rule. Religious oppression was less intense than economic harassment, but Jews were still punished for observing their holidays and Sabbath. Revolutionary policy and turmoil dissolved or weakened the kehillot, demoralized and deteriorated the rabbinate, disrupted religious services and rituals, repressed traditional customs and culture, and destroyed synagogues and Jewish schools. Jews were hampered in holding public office and the National Guard in many places refused to enroll them. In the 1790s, Alsace defied National Assembly legislation by continuing to impose special taxes upon, and restricting the residence of, Jews. Local administrators and districts in that decade also intervened in Jewish business activities and often used anti-Jewish sentiments to justify fines and taxes levied on Jewish businessmen. The incessantly anti-Semitic French Catholic church, in what would become an ongoing onslaught, identified Jews with the Revolution, thus seeking to discredit that uprising, later republics, and the Jews themselves.[108]

The most egregious violation of citizenship was government refusal to assume prerevolutionary debts of Jewish communities as it did for all other ancien régime corporations. In October 1790, the National Assembly dissolved religious corporate bodies and, in decrees of June and July 1791 and a law passed in 1793, the government assumed the debts of these corporations. Accordingly, in 1792, the Jewish corporative community of Metz tried to disband. Neither the municipal council of the city or the department government permitted this termination because they wanted the Metz kehillah to dun its members to pay off prerevolutionary obligations. Official and fundamental discrimination of this type evoked a similar grievance in another place. "Will the Jews again be treated as before, as citizens only in matters of paying taxes, but as foreigners in matters of rights," protested the Avignon petitioners. "It is not possible to have abolished the corporations and yet to admit the existence of one of them." But the government would not nationalize these debts. To liquidate them, Jews revived their communal organizations as commissions to collect taxes and prosecute delinquents. As late as the 1860s, Jews paid special taxes to discharge these liabilities.[109]

Liberation of the Jews illuminates other contours of the revolutionary landscape and subsequent national topography. While emancipation took place in the liberal era of the Revolution, radicals by no means opposed citizenship for Jews. Jacobin clubs generally supported political equality and some had Jewish members. When asked by their Paris cohorts in January 1790 their opinion on emancipating southern Jews, Strasbourg Jacobins replied that Alsatian Jews should also become citizens.[110]

If granting civic rights drew advocates across the political spectrum, variations of region and religion surfaced during the struggle for emancipation and again in 1793, when anti-Judaism escalated. From the Jacobin triumph to the present, the centralized state has typified France. Yet, as the issue of freedom and equality for Jews shows, centralization was not uniformity. Where Jewish rights were concerned, the Alsace-Lorraine area consistently defied decrees from Paris. And within these former provinces local differences emerged. In 1791, Jacobin clubs in Strasbourg and Colmar disagreed over emancipation and in 1793 over Jewish commercial morality and responsibility for the economic crisis in the region. At both times the Strasbourg club, which had Jewish members, and several other radical societies in Alsace and Lorraine took a position more favorable to the Jews. Alsace-Lorraine and the rest of France continued to diverge after the Revolution. In the late 1850s, years after Jews had been accorded full political equality, as a concession to local anti-Semitism a Jewish lawyer was rejected for an appointment as magistrate in Alsace.[111]

Violation of citizenship rights and therefore the centralized policy of civic equality proceeded from creed as well as place. Opposition from the

Catholic church in 1849 resulted in a Jew being denied a post as teacher of philosophy in a *lycée*.[112]

Ambivalence enveloped France and its Jews. The nation hesitated between inclusion and suspicion of scorned outsiders-turned-countrymen. Jews sought to reconcile Judaic affiliation with modern patriotism. These currents swirled together when French Jews represented themselves to themselves and to gentile citizens by engaging in civic commemorations of the Revolution and Republic. On October 21, 1792, the Jews of Metz, the largest Jewish community in France, participated in a *fête civique*. Jewish and gentile national loyalty converged in this celebration of the victory of Thionville, where a republican army saved the city from a siege. The Thionville troops came to the Metz synagogue, whose rabbi commended their bravery and Jewish allegiance to the Republic. Festivities there included awarding the mayor a civic crown and a Hebrew rendition of "La Marseillaise." This version of the national anthem acclaimed the recent emancipation of the Jews and asserted their loyalty to the Republic and to their French identity.[113] Nevertheless, the Metz affair took place in a private, sectarian site (a synagogue) and largely in the sacred language and was presided over by a rabbi, an official leader of Jewish communities in pre– and postrevolutionary France. At least in the consciousness of these Jews, citizenship and Judaic cohesion were different but blended commitments.

CHAPTER 4

THE FRENCH EXPERIENCE II: NAPOLEON AND THE FIRST EMPIRE

Republicanism, liberty, and the rights of man and the citizen were lega-cies of the Revolution and France recurrently reverted to this inheri-tance. Another legacy of the Revolution, which dominated until the Third Republic, was a kind of state imperium. Power institutionalized in the state was sometimes personified by a Caesar ruling in the name of the people, but not necessarily as their representative. An exemplar of enlight-ened autocracy, Napoleon was the first and foremost of these postrevolu-tionary figures. The bequests of autonomy and authority, more distin-guishable in the abstract than in historical reality, were combined in Bonaparte, who proclaimed himself emperor while considering himself an extension of the Revolution. This chapter explores how imperial urges and revolutionary residues shaped the destiny of the Jews, and through this group, national culture and state formation in the First Empire.

Napoleon, who expanded civic rights for Jews in foreign lands under his influence, nevertheless disliked Jews and his policies toward them in France reflected the regime's and the nation's tenacious prejudice. In the Council of State, the emperor called the Jews "a nation apart" and "a nation within a nation."[1] Corsican-born Bonaparte subordinated his ori-gins to the French nation, which many of his subjects thought he embod-ied. Now Napoleon asked the Jews to do the same, but their reward would be more modest. Citizenship, not supremacy or deification, was the prize for their assimilation.

Bonaparte proceeded as if emancipation had not taken place. Issues ostensibly muted by citizenship were revisited. Jews would have to con-vince their compatriots and the imperial government of their worth in much the same manner they had in the last years of the ancien régime and the liberal era of the Revolution. They would again have to show that they were neither immoral nor unpatriotic. And once more the terms of this proof would be an investigation and alteration of their economic behavior and a demonstrated willingness to put allegiance to France above loyalty to Judaism. Unlike the past, however, the emperor would create institu-tions of Jews—the Assembly of Notables and the Parisian Sanhedrin—to make these changes and sanctify them in a new Mosaic Code. The self-styled inheritor of the Revolution, liberator of Europe, and incarnation of national glory, would now become another Moses to the Jews.[2]

If the emperor reverted to the past while revising it, the Jews endured a severer setback than that implied by a mere recapitulation of what had gone before. The exhilaration of striving for and securing equal rights gave way to the depressing prospect of returning to the struggle after the presumed permanence of the triumph of 1791. Emancipation followed by remarginalization and suppression, however, repeatedly beset European Jews in the nineteenth and twentieth centuries.

In March–April 1805, Napoleon's justice minister reported on Jewish usury to the Council of State. On January 23–24, 1806, Bonaparte heard similar complaints from the prefect and other local notables when he visited Strasbourg. On March 6, Bonaparte asked the Council of State to investigate whether mortgages held by Jews constituted usury and should be voided and such lending discontinued, and whether Jews who had arrived from Poland and Germany in the last ten years should be deprived of citizenship. He even proposed "that from 1 January 1807 the Jews who do not possess property" needed a license to do business and "will not enjoy the right of citizens." To deter Jews from commercial pursuits and vices, Napoleon would revoke emancipation. This self-proclaimed fulfiller and guardian of the Revolution would sacrifice its aspiration—the rights of man and the citizen. The French, particularly Alsatians, feared that Jews would foreclose on peasant debtors and seize a large slice of Alsace. Anti-Semites charged that Jews were usurious leeches whose law and creed authorized them to lend at extortionate rates to non-Jews and, as a result, that Jews were expropriating the land and the toil of Alsatian peasants. Napoleon believed these charges, notwithstanding the facts that Jews held no huge share of mortgages and demanded no higher interest than non-Jews, and further, that high interest rates resulted from lack of stable credit and revolutionary destruction of trading networks. The emperor discounted Jews' claims that they made far fewer loans than anti-Semites claimed, that Christian creditors were also blamed for usury, that Jewish laws did not countenance fraud, theft, or exorbitant interest exactions toward anyone, and that all Jews were being blamed for a few culprits.[3]

Jews of Alsace and Lorraine correctly claimed that the magnitude and malignancy of their lending was extravagantly—even hysterically—exaggerated. Jews held less than one half of the total financial obligations in Alsace and Lorraine around 1800 and this proportion diminished throughout the century. Jews' share of outstanding loans, however, was considerably higher than their share of the population in these provinces. Economic anti-Semitism was exacerbated by the nature, as well as the frequency, of lending. Like their debtors, Jews were mostly poor and their transactions chiefly consisted of extending small amounts of credit to peasants whose own meager resources made default a likely outcome.[4] Regardless of the will or rectitude of the creditors, the flimsy structure of credit inevitably led to defaults, foreclosures, and demonization of moneylenders as usurers. Given the history of folk anti-Semitism among the peasants, creditors would be labeled haters of Christians who sucked the blood out of their Catholic debtors as they had drained the blood of Christ on the Cross and in ritual murders of His innocent surrogates.

Instead of the draconian measures that Napoleon had initially requested of the Council of State, he issued an imperial edict of May 30, 1806, imposing a year-long moratorium on loans by Jewish lenders in Alsace and Lorraine and calling a convention of Jewish leaders. In Council deliberations over suppressing "Jewish usury" and in convening the Assembly of Jewish Notables, Napoleon had been partly motivated by a desire to centralize French credit in the Bank of France and French law in his Civil Code. But the order was chiefly inspired by a conviction that their alleged aloofness and depravity showed that Jews had not assimilated or reformed and, therefore, that emancipation had failed. The government, acting through prominent Jews, would have to ameliorate and integrate the children of Israel. Napoleon ordered a congregation of eminent Jews to advise him on "reestablish[ing] among their brethren the exercise of mechanical arts and useful professions, in order to replace, by an honest industry, the shameful resources to which many of them resorted, from generation to generation, these many centuries."[5]

The imperial decree was another demand for regeneration and the Assembly of Jewish Notables would be the vehicle for reviving Judaic virtue. Bonaparte's convocation of leading Jews understandably evoked little enthusiasm in the Jewish community. Kehillot, especially in Alsace, did not pay delegates' expenses.[6]

If French Jewry was dubious about Napoleon's instrument, it did not summarily reject his program. The Concordat of 1801 and the Organic Articles of 1802 respectively put Catholics and Protestants under official regulation. At this time the Jewish community was still in disarray from revolutionary depredations and from emancipation, which freed Jews from traditional religious, financial, and other communal obligations. Kehillot still existed, but in their weakened condition tenuously maintained communal discipline over such matters as collecting taxes, dispensing charity, providing schooling, and upholding ritual observance. Thus, Jews generally desired Napoleon's offer of an institutional means of ending disorder and rebuilding their community.[7] The Jews, however, did not think they needed everything that Napoleon offered. They wanted official recognition and organization, but did not feel that they were singularly corrupt and required reproof, regeneration, and revalidation of their citizenship and that rejuvenation and rights were interrelated and mutually dependent upon assimilation. Consequently, the Jews and the emperor converged on one part of his program but disagreed on the others. A qualified mutuality of interests between the monarch and his subjects framed the dialogue between him and them that proceeded in the body he soon convened. Ambivalence grasped both sides; they felt threatened by each other but needed to collaborate to accomplish their respective purposes.

The decree of May 30 opened by affirming reports "that in many of the northern departments [Alsace and Lorraine] . . . certain Jews, following no other profession than that of usurers" have "reduced" peasants "to the greatest distress." Napoleon accordingly realized "the urgent necessity, among individuals of the Jewish persuasion" of "reviving sentiments of civil morality, which unfortunately, have been stifled in many of them by the abject state in which they have long languished, and which it is not our intention either to maintain, or to renew." The emperor was ambiguous about whether the "abject state" resulted from oppression or inclination. By straddling the issue of causation, he compromised between the anti-Jewish faction on the Council, led by Count Louis-Matthieu Molé, and the moderates, led by Joseph Marie Portalis and Etienne Denis Pasquin, and emphasized what both sides agreed upon—Jewish degeneracy.[8]

Napoleon disliked Jews but was not a rabid anti-Semite. At a May 7, 1806, Council meeting, the emperor rejected expulsion, the extreme remedy for the Jewish problem. He advocated moral "improvement" and assigned this mission to the Assembly of Notables. "Our goal is to reconcile the beliefs of the Jews with the duties of the French people," Bonaparte wrote in a letter to Minister of the Interior Jean Baptiste Count de Champagny, "and to render them useful citizens, being resolved to bring remedy to the evil that many among them deliver to the great detriment of our subjects." Napoleon then named three commissioners to the prospective assembly and detailed twelve questions to be asked of its deputies. On July 23, 1806, the day after receiving this directive, Count de Champagny sent each member of the Assembly a circular letter communicating the emperor's intentions and expressing his own confidence that the deputies would act in their own and France's interest and fulfill their monarch's objectives.[9]

Mandated by the Decree, members were selected from "rabbis, landholders, and other Jews most distinguished by their integrity and their knowledge." Government prefects appointed the delegates, called deputies. A conclave of notables picked by imperial officials was shrewd policy because a government-vetted elite would be more assimilated and compliant than deputies chosen directly from or by the Jewish rank and file. The 111 men, 95 from France and 16 from Italy, first formally sat on July 26, 1806 in Paris at the Chapel of St. John of the Hotel de Ville. They consisted of Sephardim and Ashkenazim, rabbis and lay leaders, maskilim and the Orthodox, of bankers, manufacturers, merchants, landowners, and included a few municipal officeholders. Two veterans of Jewish rights struggles, Berr and Furtado, emerged respectively as leaders of the Ashkenazi and Sephardic contingents. A virtual freethinker, Furtado was even more acculturated than the maskil Berr. Geographic, ethnic, and ideological diversities ensured vigorous debates.[10]

Orthodox deputies were amazed when some enlightened brethren came in carriages. The emperor ordered a guard of honor placed before the hall of the Assembly and at the disposal of its president, which presented military honors to the delegates when they left the Hotel de Ville. Special headdress and swords were conferred on the deputies and the guards were ordered to salute them on the streets. Such ceremonies for Jews were unprecedented in the diaspora and this ostentation indicated the importance that Napoleon attached to the convention and symbolized the civic dignity, or at least the potential public repute, that Napoleon was prepared to accord French Jewry. Imperial pageantry also showed his recognition of, and perhaps his attempt to magnify, the eminence of the deputies in the Jewish community and displayed Bonaparte's usual mixture of pomp and flattery to make people amenable to his demands.[11] Furtado became president of the Assembly. A landowner, he followed a calling recommended by those (Jew and Gentile alike) who felt that Jews needed moral renewal.

Molé, Portalis, and Pasquin were the imperial commissioners to the Assembly, and their differences over Jewish morality and citizenship carried over from the Council to that body. Appointed chief commissioner, another reflection of Bonaparte's sympathy with the anti-Jewish faction, on July 29th, at its second session, Molé defined the mission of the convention according to the wishes of the emperor. The government had good intentions toward the Jews; their representatives must "prove" that like "all Frenchmen, you do not seclude yourselves from the rest of mankind." Jews must correct their faults or relinquish citizenship: "The wish of His Majesty is, that you should be Frenchmen, it remains with you to accept the proffered title, without forgetting that, to prove unworthy of it, would be renouncing it altogether." The commissioners wished "to report to the Emperor" that Jews were "faithful subjects determined to conform in everything to the laws and to the morality which ought to regulate the conduct of all Frenchmen."[12] In a firm—even condescending—address, the chief commissioner invited the Assembly to make it possible for Jews to join the nation. Fifteen years after they thought emancipation meant integration, they were informed that Jews were suspected of being a nation within a nation and that the responsibility for this crisis, and its solution, lay with them.

After Molé spoke, the commissioners put questions to the deputies, which expressed the Napoleonic imperatives of modification, rehabilitation, and integration. Woodrow Wilson had Fourteen Points; God had Ten Commandments; Napoleon had Twelve Questions. The queries began with seemingly innocuous requests for information and escalated in accusation. Questions Two and Three, for example, respectively asked whether Judaic law allows divorce and forbids intermarriage. But the implications of these queries were ominous. The Second Question proceeded to inquire about a possible clash between French and Judaic law if the latter granted divorces in contradiction of the "French Code" or French courts. Question Three, of course, raised the issue of structural assimilation.[13]

Interpellations Four–Six honed in on alleged Hebraic aloofness. They asked whether Jews considered other French people "as brethren or as strangers?" Question Six summoned the specter of a nation within a nation: "Do the Jews born in France, and treated by law as French citizens, acknowledge France as their country? Are they bound to defend it? Are they bound to obey the laws, and to follow the directions of the Civil Code?"[14]

Questions Two–Six covered relations between the French and the Jews. Questions Seven–Nine pursued an investigation into rabbinic authority and the internal administration of Jewish communal affairs.[15] A major motif weaved through all of the questions: the role of Judaic law in controlling Jewish behavior. Napoleon, through his commissioners' inquiries, seemed obsessed with the *Halakah*. And why not! Was not the emperor a great lawgiver in his own right who had recently given his subjects the French Civil Code? Should he not then concern himself with the Mosaic Code? Legality was not only a virtue per se; law meant order, progress, and civilization, goals that, next to fame, power, and conquest, attracted Napoleon.

Questions Ten–Twelve turned to the reason for calling the meeting of notables. While the last inquiries centered on the commercial corruption of the Jews, Bonaparte's ever-present obsession with the law persisted. As always, the queries became successively more menacing. Question Ten asked whether "their law" excluded Jews from certain professions: Were Jews scroungers attracted to occupations like finance and commerce or could they be industrious tillers of the soil, artisans, or professionals? Question Eleven wondered whether Judaic law forbade Jews "from taking usury from their brethren?" The final interpellation was the sole query addressed directly to the ostensible cause of the conference, extortionate Jewish moneylending. Does the Mosaic Code "allow usury towards strangers?"[16] Question Twelve was set up by Question Eleven and suggested Jewish debasement. If Jews took excessive interest from their own kind, they were universal parasites. If they extorted only from Gentiles, they were leeches on the bodies of all people but their own and could never be French compatriots. In short, were Jews true citizens or did they still think of themselves as a separate, corporate entity? Were they upstanding or reprobates beyond régénération?

The Notables' response ranged from spontaneous to calculated, from eager compliance to subtle or open disagreement. Ultimately, however, the Assembly conformed to the emperor's wishes. The most striking example of unrehearsed fervor for Bonaparte's intentions occurred when Question Six was placed before the body. As the secretary reading the questions reached the section asking whether Jews felt bound to defend France, the delegates "unanimously exclaimed,—*Even to the death*" (italics in original).[17]

At the end of the reading, the president of the Assembly ventured a carefully crafted reply. As with all of the speeches, it fulsomely exalted his most vainglorious majesty. Napoleon's "paternal goodness" created an "opportunity" to "completely reform habits occasioned by a long state of oppression." The emperor's "laws, dynasty, and the return of order, had calmed all the fears we might have entertained of a retrograde motion" and ensured "regeneration of some of our brethren" that is "the result of our new condition." Through "his protecting goodness, we shall enjoy, under his reign, social advantages, which we could expect only from centuries of perseverance." The speech closed with a request that the commissioners "convey our sentiments to His Majesty."[18]

Behind expressed reverence for "the hero of the age," "the common father of all his subjects," and the pledge of regeneration, the president subtly contradicted the emperor's views about Jews. Judaic degradation stemmed from persecution rather than proclivity. "Errors" and "prejudices," not facts or reality, shaped popular opinion about the Jews.[19] Instead of threatening emancipation, Napoleon is the guarantor of civic equality for Jews. And their ethical improvement derives from citizenship; therefore, alleged Jewish deficiencies should not endanger their civic status.

The Assembly's own commission, consisting of twelve members balanced between Sephardic and Ashkenazi enclaves, including Berr and three rabbis, prepared answers to the questions.[20] With little debate, the deputies unanimously and without alteration voted the answer to Question Two. They replied that French Jews accept Western customs and, in matters of divorce, subordination of the rabbinate and the Mosaic Code to the French Code: "In the eyes of every Israelite, without exception, submission to the prince is the first of duties." Next to fealty to Napoleon, the delegates were most eager to demonstrate that in "civil or political interests," Jews recognize that "the law of the state is the supreme law."[21] As happened in Furtado's speech, surface capitulation to the state and

His Majesty masked critical reservations. Jews "rendered unto Caesar what was Caesar's" by putting the state above their creed. But this priority governed the "civic and political" sphere. Would the Assembly be as obliging when it considered spiritual or theological matters?

As indicated by a separate opinion written by the rabbis in the Assembly asserting that Jewish law forbade intermarriage with Christians, Question Three provoked controversy. The commissioners who framed the answer and their supporters argued that the Halakah did not forbid such unions. After vigorous debate of the whole, the commissioners redrafted their answer, a compromise with rabbinical and orthodox opposition, which was approved nearly unanimously. The reply stated that Jewish law prohibited marriages to idolaters. Christianity was monotheistic, and therefore, nonidolatrous, hence the law did not proscribe unions with Christians. The rejoinder, however, mentioned that the rabbis were still against such matrimony. For rabbinical deputies, mixed marriages were valid "civilly but not religiously" and they acknowledged that Jewish men who wedded Christian women were still considered Jews. The response noted that rabbis were no more inclined to bless such unions than were priests. Notwithstanding the reservation of the rabbis and the bold reference to Catholic clergy, Napoleon and his representatives got what they sought. The Notables accepted the principle of intermarriage, the fundamental instrument of structural assimilation.[22]

Question Four also caused contention. Several delegates objected to the length of the original answer and, more significantly, to the distinctions it ostensibly drew between Sephardim and Ashkenazim, a recurrently sensitive issue in the Assembly and the national Jewish community. The president, a Sephardic Jew, observed that when the commission preparing the response alluded to these differences, "it only meant to remark that" Sephardim "made greater progress in civilization, because their hardships were much less" than the Ashkenazim. It is difficult to see how this remark calmed Ashkenazi defensiveness, curbed Sephardic arrogance, or promoted reconciliation in the ethnic conflict that at times divided the convention. Perhaps Furtado himself realized this, because it preluded his decision to drop that part of the response that alluded to differences between these enclaves. The Assembly then unanimously endorsed the answer.[23]

The rejoinders to Questions Four and Five affirmed that Jews regarded Frenchmen as their brothers by emphasizing that the "true spirit of the law of Moses is consonant to this mode of considering Frenchmen." This response not only refuted a specific suspicion, it extolled Judaism. Veneration for their faith permeated the comments of the delegates and contradicted the opinions of Napoleon and his officials and most of gentile France, thus fortifying the integrity of the Notables. The answer to

Question Four concluded with a grandiose reassurance that "now our fate is irrevocably linked with the common fate of all Frenchmen. Yes, France is our country; all Frenchmen are our brethren." France gave the Jews liberty, equality, and an opportunity for rehabilitation; the Jews would give France fraternity. The "glorious title" of Frenchmen, "by raising us in our own esteem, becomes a sure pledge that we shall never cease to be worthy of it."[24] Napoleon and his commissioners told the Jews that they must prove worthy of citizenship; his interlocutors responded that they already belonged to the nation and that this status enabled them to be worthy of it.

Question Five was an extension of Question Four and the answer to it was similar and also adopted unanimously: "At the present time, when the Jews no longer form a separate people," but are "incorporated with the Great [French] Nation" a Jew relates to other Frenchman the way "he would treat one of his Israelitish brethren." The Assembly reassuringly claimed that for Jews the "privilege" of compatriotism meant political "redemption" (once again citizenship prefigured regeneration).[25]

Assurance that Jews were not a nation apart seemed unconditional in the rejoinders to Questions Four and Five. But a close reading of these replies indicates that mutuality between Jew and Frenchman prevails respectively "now" and "at the present time," when they are linked by citizenship. What if in the future Jews again formed "a separate people?" Were the delegates still thinking, "next year in Jerusalem?" And would the existence of a Jewish homeland alter their vow of solidarity with their compatriots? It appears as though the deputies were trying to bridge the gap between allegiance to traditional, messianic Judaism and commitment to the nation where they lived; as Efraim Shmueli puts it "between Holy Land and homeland."[26]

Question Six continued the exploration of queries Four and Five into how the Jews related to France and the French. The answer, therefore, resembles those to the previous two interpellations and was adopted by the Assembly unanimously and without modification. The Notables again placed loyalty to the nation above fidelity to Judaism:

> The love of the country is in the heart of Jews a sentiment so natural, so powerful, and so consonant to their religious opinions, that a French Jew considers himself, in England, as among strangers, although he may be among Jews; and the case is the same with English Jews in France.

Patriotism inspired French Jews to battle "against other Jews, the subjects of countries then at war with France." Jews were no longer one indivisible, chosen people, a nation within all nations. Jews were now devoted nationalists who did not shirk the ultimate sacrifice for their country, whether that sacrifice be forfeiture of life or affiliation with cobelievers. Knowing that Napoleon and many French people doubted this commitment, the answer concluded by reminding Bonaparte and his commissioners of "honorable wounds" and "noble rewards of bravery" earned in the recent war.[27]

Question Eight inquired into rabbinic judicial and police powers and the answer, accepted with little debate and near unanimity, noted that "these tribunals, have, to this day, always depended on the will of governments under which the Jews have lived, and on the degree of tolerance they have enjoyed." Since "the revolution those rabbinical tribunals are totally suppressed" and "Jews, raised to the rank of citizens, have conformed in every thing to the laws of the state." Dissolution of prerevolutionary corporate autonomy "limited" the "functions of Rabbies [sic] . . . to preaching morality in the temples, blessing marriages, and pronouncing divorces."[28] The Notables again "rendered unto Caesar . . ." and left Jehovah a spare residual rule over the spiritual and ritual realm.

In discussing the administration of ancient Israel, the deputies mentioned that the Hebrews "were governed by *Sanhedrim* or tribunals. A supreme tribunal, called *the grand Sanhedrim*, sat in Jerusalem, and was composed of seventy-one Judges" (italics in original).[29] Napoleon kept this in mind when he soon called for a "Great Sanhedrin" to meet in Paris

Questions Ten–Twelve addressed alleged Jewish commercial corruption, an incrimination of Jews and the concrete cause of the convention of Notables. Question Ten suggested that Jews were bound by religious law to exploitative economic activities and correspondingly forbidden to enter useful vocations. If Jews were by creed committed to duplicitous practices, they could never regard others as brothers and thus could not be patriots and did not deserve civic rights. Adopted without debate and unanimously, the deputies' rejoinder was another reminder that Judaism and justice were allied. It stated that the Mosaic Code precluded Jews from no professions and that the Talmud expressly mandated that fathers teach their children a profession.[30] The question implied a severe indictment of the Jews and the response denied that imputation by asserting that it had no validity in Jewish law or theology.

Questions Eleven and Twelve less obliquely addressed Hebraic immorality by asking respectively whether Mosaic Law prevented Jews from usurious exploitation of their "brethren" or only from "strangers" [non-Jews]?[31] To deny that they charged excessive interest on loans made to fellow Jews could inculpate them in the implications of Questions Four–Six. Notwithstanding their answers to these questions, Jews treated Frenchmen as strangers, their law prescribed different (and unethical) conduct toward gentile Frenchmen, and, though born in France and legally citizens, Jews could not truly be confrères and defenders of their country. Thus would be substantiated charges that Jews were an unregenerate nation within a nation.

Given the hazards concealed in Question Eleven, the draft of the answer elicited a dispute among the deputies. One speaker proposed that rabbis should preach "morality" so that "Jews who are ignorant of their duty in money transactions with other Frenchmen, should be made acquainted with them, to be on their guard against the temptation of cupidity." Another delegate agreed with this exhortation and it was seconded. The discussion then shifted to the meaning of "brother" in the answer. A difference of opinion emerged over whether it applied only to fellow Jews or to fellow countrymen. As this dispute waned, a debate erupted over whether Jewish law permitted charging interest on loans. None of these contentions was settled and, after a third reading of the draft of the answer, it passed almost unanimously.[32]

The reply stated that the Mosaic Code bars taking interest. But this interdiction was appropriate for the simple agrarian society of biblical Israel. Now that Jews no longer have a common, independent nation and many live in a complicated commercial society, they distinguish between loans for "charity" and "commerce" and prohibit interest on the former and permit it for the latter. Charity loans are for familial needs and commercial loans for the debtor's speculative and profit-making purposes. Consequently, taking interest for business credit is legitimate. No distinction, however, is allowed on the basis of religion. Charity and commercial loans are handled according to purpose not creed. Curiously, the answer did not specifically forbid usury, the imposition of excessive and/or illegal (according to the nation's laws) interest rates.[33]

The final answer passed without opposition. Unanimity prevailed because it paralleled the rejoinder to the previous inquiry. In both cases the deputies declared that the Mosaic Code forbade treating Jews and non-Jews differently. The Notables conceded that some Jews lent money at draconian rates, but objected to "the general charge made against the Hebrews, that they are naturally inclined to usury." Jews are not prone to this iniquity because offenders are "not so many as is generally supposed" and engage in a "nefarious traffic condemned by their religion." The response closed by boldly asking: "Would it not be deemed an injustice to lay the same imputation on all Christians because some of them are guilty of usury?"[34]

The deputies harmonized religious and national allegiances. Nationality had replaced religion as the forger of the fraternal bond, thus reversing the diaspora and identifying creedal loyalty with territorial loyalty. The delegates insisted that Jews regarded themselves as Frenchmen and treated gentile compatriots as "brethren," defended the country, and obeyed its laws. Mosaic Law and rabbinical authority prohibited usury, in no way contravened the civic code, and operated exclusively in the spiritual realm. The Assembly reconciled Jewish and French law, not by modifying the Mosaic Code to conform with the Napoleonic Code, but by maintaining loyalty to, and the separateness of, both codes while avowing the dominance of French law. Even intermarriage, the most basic act of absorption short of conversion, did not forfeit Judaic membership. Judaism and patriotism, as defined by the Notables, totally coincided and, in any event, the latter took precedence over the former. The Notables might have been certain of all they professed, but long after formal emancipation the Jews of France still had to reassure the state that they were loyal, regenerated citizens.[35]

At ten o'clock in the morning on August 15, 1806, the Notables met to honor Napoleon's thirty-seventh birthday. A bust of His Majesty adorned the Hall; at this sight all of the members cried, "Long live the emperor." President Furtado then presented an ode in Hebrew in glory of the royal hero. At eleven o'clock, they marched in orderly procession to the great synagogue in Paris, which was ornamented with the name of Jehovah and the imperial eagle and other symbols of Napoleon's might and majesty. In Ronald Schecter's insightful account, these emblems also showed that the Jews participated in the glory of the First Empire and thus were full citizens of France. The president and officers of the Assembly sat near the ark, ordinary deputies stood in a circle mingling with Christian spectators; among the latter were distinguished citizens. According to orthodox custom, women had a separate gallery. Schecter notes that, during the ceremony, alms were collected for all religions (no Jewish particularism) and sisters of Jewish soldiers were featured (Jews weren't cowardly or unpatriotic). A popular aria was played, "Where can one better be than in the bosom of his family?" (Jews belonged to the national family). Speeches recalled Jewish suffering and humiliation and praised Bonaparte for ending this oppression. He was the father of the Jews and other faiths (republican fraternity now merged with imperial paternalism). As if to deserve the emperor's patronage, the orators asserted that the Jews had been morally revivified.[36]

Residual Hebraic pride tempered these gestures of assimilation and genuflections to autocracy, thereby preventing total surrender of spiritual independence and integrity. The celebration was held in a holy place whose sacred majesty for Jews equaled, and perhaps neutralized, the usual Napoleonic grandeur. Allusions to the campaign in Egypt underscored the Jews' sense of their Middle-Eastern origin and, consequently, of an identity different from their gentile fellow-citizens. Praise of Judaic history and belief also affirmed Jewish identity and subtly reminded Gentiles that degradation of Judaism was unwarranted. Another recognition of separateness came when birthday songs and odes were chanted in Hebrew and publication of the ceremony contained the Hebrew version alongside the French translation.[37]

Corresponding to Jews' maintenance of their distance from other Frenchmen, the pageant demonstrated Judaic unity on a public occasion. Consequently, the fete did not totally reflect the Assembly. Deliberations there could be contentious and its answers compromises between Sephardic and Ashkenzi, secular and orthodox, factions. Nevertheless, the commemoration culminated the Notables' work, even though they met again, chiefly to prepare the way for their successor, The Great or Parisian, Sanhedrin. The celebration came after the real task—responding to Napoleon's questions—was finished, but was nonetheless the most dramatic reflection of the Assembly's disposition. Like the answers, the ceremony venerated Judaism and the past, revered Bonaparte and France, and looked to the future. It would be extreme to say that the delegates identified Judaism with old times and saw no place for their creed in a national future. It is reasonable, however, to assume that they tended to link Judaism with history and persecution while presently and prospectively associating France with freedom and equality.

After the Assembly submitted its responses, on August 5 and 11 the imperial commissioners filed an unfavorable report of the proceedings. In all likelihood primarily drafted by Molé, it criticized the deputies' truthfulness, patriotism, and morality. Contradicting the commissioners, the Minister of the Interior found the responses sincere professions that Jews regarded themselves as Frenchmen and would fight for their country, that nothing in the Mosaic Code contravened French law, and that their answers on commerce and moneylending were satisfactory.[38]

At the next session of the Assembly (September 18) after the fete, Molé informed the deputies that Napoleon accepted their replies. The emperor embraced Champagny's interpretation.[39] The Assembly "loudly applauded" Molé's speech and President Furtado's response was permeated with the conventional flattery for the emperor. Deferential effusions, however, did not deter Furtado from employing arguments that he doubtlessly knew contradicted the opinions of his monarch and Molé. Furtado recognized that "principles of political right" dictate that "religion must submit to the Sovereign authority" in temporal matters. Accordingly, the Assembly sought "to know in what particulars our religious dogmas coincided or were at variance with the law of the state" and "whether these dogmas, too long considered intolerant and inimical to society at large, were, really, either the one or the other."[40]

Thus far he and Bonaparte agreed, but Napoleon might have disputed Furtado's vindication of the proceedings. Through the Notables' investigation, "the Emperor has acquired the certainty that the religious laws of Moses" contained nothing to "justify the exclusions of its followers from the enjoyment of the civil and political rights of Frenchmen." Furtado conceded that Bonaparte felt that the answers to the Twelve Questions were "satisfactory" but "insufficient," and had called for a Great Sanhedrin "to give to the decisions of this assembly that religious sanction which they ought to have." Nevertheless, the president was gratified that "the ruler of the fate of Europe . . . respects the liberty of religious opinions" and sure that "his reign will be the epoch of the regeneration of our brethren. Europe will be indebted to him for millions of useful citizens."[41] The dialogue between the Assembly and the imperial commissioners and their master had not changed. The emperor and his representatives kept questioning the loyalty and morality of the Jews. Through its leader, the Assembly insisted that Judaic law and custom did not detract from patriotism and citizenship. It would save what it wanted and could of historic Judaism.

After reassuring himself and the delegates of the royal capacity for generosity and about the creation of a "sacred asylum of conscience," Furtado introduced a resolution "to carry to the foot of the throne the expressions of the deep and unshaken loyalty which animates every member" and to form the Sanhedrin according to Napoleon's wishes. It was adopted unanimously and with acclaim.[42]

In the last phase of its deliberations the Assembly turned from considerations of Judaic law and custom and their ramifications for regeneration and citizenship. At the session of December 9th, the deputies ratified a "plan" for governance of French Jewry agreed upon by the imperial commissioners and its own committee. The Revolution wreaked havoc with the rabbinate, synagogues, and Jewish schools and formally (if not actually) dissolved the kehillot. Even Berr, the maskil, long campaigned for restoring community structure and cohesion. Similar appeals by other Jewish leaders were strengthened when, in 1802, as part of the reversal of the revolutionary elimination (*Le Chapelier* law of June 1791) of corporate bodies, the government organized similar institutions for Catholics and Protestants and created a Protestant consistorial system. Jewish leaders requested comparable authorization and assistance. Napoleon restored corporations to foster order and centralization and thus increase his power. He resurrected an old institution, but for a new and contradictory purpose. These organizations would not stand between the state and the individual nor foster autonomy from a central government. Jews wanted these institutions to solidify their community and, contrary to the emperor's aim, at least some hoped that their consistories would intervene between them and the imperium and thus recapture a remnant of the communal authority they exercised in the ancien régime. As later events proved, Jews were divided over whether the organizations should function as instruments of assimilation or to preserve the integrity of the traditional community.

The consistory scheme illustrated the overlapping yet sometimes cross-purposes of the emperor and the Jews. Both agreed on the need for communal organization, but for different reasons and for the attainment of different ends. Nevertheless, they would have to cooperate so that each could realize their own interests, and the necessity for collaboration set limits on the imperium.

The plan called for the establishment of a synagogue and consistory in every department with at least 2,000 Jews. Each synagogue had a grand rabbi and the consistories would be composed of him and three other Jews. Consistory officers from whose ranks usurers were to be excluded, were chosen by the twenty-five largest taxpayers ("Notables") in the district, who were selected by the government. The functions of the consistories were, first and foremost, to make certain that rabbis did not teach or explain Judaic law in a manner contrary to the answers of the Assembly, which were sacredly confirmed by the Sandhedrin. Further, they were to maintain order, manage the synagogues and communal finances, and assess and collect levies for rabbinical salaries and other religious expenses. They would also encourage "Israelites . . . to follow useful professions," and provide the state with the names of Jewish paupers and "the [annual] number of the Israelitish conscripts within the [consistory] district." A Central Consistory, located in Paris, would supervise departmental consistories. It would have the same type of officials, chosen in the same manner, as district consistories.[43]

Rabbis were overseen by the consistory and had to be citizens of France or Italy and, after 1820, would have to understand the respective language of their country. One function of these clergymen was to "inculcate the doctrines contained in the decisions of the Great Sanhedrim." They were instructed to "preach obedience to the laws," especially "to those which relate to the defense of the country." Rabbis would "represent military service to the Israelites as a sacred duty" and "declare" the recruits exempt from "religious practices" incompatible with military service. To inspire patriotism and obedience to imperial authority, rabbis would conduct prayers in synagogues for the emperor and the imperial family. In one of many regulations designed to implement the dominion of civil over religious law, rabbis would celebrate marriages and pronounce divorces after civil authority sanctioned such actions. Finally, rabbis must pledge to uphold the decisions of the Great Sanhedrin, whose members would be preferred for the position of grand rabbi.[44]

Although Jewish leaders wanted to revive a corporate government, the consistory regulations provoked extended debates in the Assembly and did not pass unanimously. Some objections were technical, concerning assessments and expenditures, but others struck at stereotypes held by gentile France and Napoleon. Opposition was voiced to including the word "usurer" on the grounds that it wrongly confirmed the prejudice that extortion was an inherent Jewish vice. Intermittent conflict between Sephardic and Ashkenazi factions surfaced when a speaker objected that although usurers frequented departments in the Northeast (where Ashkenazim were concentrated), this fault was not common to all French Jews (Sephardim were excepted). Criticism also focused on giving consistories police duties over paupers or conscripts. As to the latter, it was asserted that Jews fulfilled their military quotas as much as other Frenchmen; therefore, the provision for conscription implied a false admission that Jews were less patriotic. The opposition, in turn, was reprimanded by a particularly ardent assimilationist who argued that the critics overindulged their coreligionists, considering them not as they were, but as they ought to be. This defender of the plan claimed that some disputed regulations would enhance regeneration.[45]

The plan passed as a resolution on December 18. In addition to the regulations, this resolution included a statement that, coming at the end of the Assembly's tenure, may stand for a summary pronouncement. Reviewing its work, the convention drew "the attention of His Majesty" to what it felt above all "promote[d] the regeneration of the Jews," the "enforce[ment] among the Israelites [of] the obligation of military service, which the country has a right to require from all her children." Consistories were called upon "to remove the remaining objections" that might "prevent the Israelitish youth from following the noble career of arms," and "obedience to the laws of the conscription." The Notables urged their brethren "to shed their blood in battle for the cause of France, with the same zeal and the same bravery which formerly animated their ancestors against the enemies of the Holy City."[46] In the form of a resolution the convention passed on a mandate to French Jews: Regeneration was their new route, Paris their new Jerusalem, France their new Israel.

An imperial decree, the "Organization of the Mosaic Religion" (March 17, 1808), made the plan law. As envisioned by Napoleon, the Consistoire-Israélite, composed of the Consistoire Central in Paris (modeled on an administrative organization for Protestants established when Catholicism was officially rehabilitated) and, under it, the Consistoires Départmentaux would implement the regulations of the Assembly and the Great Sanhedrin and thus coalesce Judaism with patriotism and make Jews worthy citizens. Another imperial decree (December 11, 1808) established consistories—thirteen, each with a synagogue, would administer the 77,162 Jewish residents of France officially recorded in 1808. Consistories were also organized in the Italian, Dutch, and German provinces of the empire.[47]

The state reinvolved itself in the governance of Jews: Synagogues were established by the government, the notables who voted for consistory officers had to be approved by the state, rabbis were appointed by civil authority, and the minister of cults was in charge of executing the decrees. Consistory officials took an oath of "obedience to the Constitution of the Empire and fidelity to the Emperor," and also "to make known anything I might discover which is contrary to the interests of the sovereign or of the state." The Central Consistory did not issue directives to departmental consistories without consulting the ministry of the interior and the latter consistories never made decisions without approval by the local prefect. Thus Napoleon saw the consistory as strengthening his dominion. Centralization would further fortify imperial empowerment. This motive prompted him to impose consistorial organization upon foreign lands occupied by France. The Jews of France—North and South, orthodox and secular, rich and poor, Ashkenazi and Sephardic—belonged to consistories. These institutions supervised basic Jewish community activities, religious practices, schools, synagogues, charity, and discipline. Interrelated goals of order in the community and obedience to the imperium were to be fulfilled by hierarchy, another Napoleonic principle. Authority would flow from the Central Consistory in Paris to departmental consistories and from elite cadres to the people.[48]

As part of Napoleon's order and their communal function, consistories promoted usefulness and uplift. On March 26, 1809, the Central Consistory told the department consistories that the prefects and ministers of cults and the interior were satisfied with these bodies and their members. For the good of the Jews and of the nation they policed the Jews. In the March 26 notification, the Central Consistory emphasized "regeneration" and integration. Moral improvement, education in "sciences and arts," undertaking "useful occupations," and "love of Sovereign, love of homeland," would make compatriots of the once despised "foreigners": "But today we can speak with great pride: We have a homeland, we are Israelites, we are Frenchmen." Rabbis and consistory officials encouraged or compelled industrious labor and military service through education and exhortation and by reporting pauperism, military desertion, and draft dodging to the state. As Scott Glotzer observes, the private (religious) life of the Jews now merged with the public (as an arm of the state and its laws) life of the citizen. Spiritual life was subordinated to secular power through an agency (the consistory) that acted both for the state and for the Jews.[49]

Jews had a more diverse view of the consistories. The prosperous elite came closest to Napoleon's vision. It, too, saw them as instruments of amelioration, acculturation, and deference to the sovereign. On February 27, 1808, the Assembly of Notables of Rhin-et-Moselle "expressed its most profound sentiments of gratitude, recognition, and of admiration felt for the august person of the great hero, regenerator and father of his Israelite subjects who have the pleasure of living under the protecting care of his beloved sceptre." On February 22, 1810, the grand rabbi of Nancy urged the local consistory to curb peddling and vagrancy and promote useful occupations. On March 8, 1810, the Central Consistory ordered synagogues and departmental consistories to enforce the 1808 decree regarding the names of Jews.[50]

Advocates of the Haskalah, however, were not as numerous in the Jewish community as adherents of the Halakah. Poorer, Orthodox Jews composed the vast majority of the Jewish community and for them the consistories were a revivification of the kehillot, designed to maintain community solidarity by perpetuating traditional customs, practices, and interpretations of Judaic law. They ardently resisted Napoleon's attempt at cooptation to facilitate assimilation. The Central Consistory, with the aid of the French government, sought to modernize Jewish customs— circumcision, marriage, and funerals—and arrange the nomination of more progressive rabbis. Other urban consistories made similar attempts to acculturate the clergy and congregations that they oversaw. The Strasbourg Consistory tried to replace traditional Jewish schools (hederim) and orthodox Jewish teachers (melamadim) with schools that would teach an emancipationist curriculum. But, especially in Alsace, clandestine hederim persisted, melamadim still taught, and congregations clung to traditional theology, customs, and rabbis. Despite Napoleon's and the maskilim elite's vision of hierarchical, centralized governance, departmental consistories sometimes ignored or defied the Central Consistory. In turn, local congregations and communities often resisted departmental consistorial authority. Even the reformers utilized the consistories to protest against another imperial decree of March 17, 1808, which constricted Jewish business activity to curb alleged usury, or to urge the state to suppress anti-Semitic riots and publications. In general, however, both acculturalists and traditionalists tried to keep their conflicts intramural and to maintain a low profile in French life.[51]

Consistory acculturalists attempted to make their constituents conform to the nation and to the will of its monarch. Their strategy was to preserve the Jewish community, but modify traditions that they deemed detractive from citizenship. Accommodating Jewish identity to the national identity, however, occasionally moved these bodies to defend Judaism against the French government and populace. In the First Empire, the Central Consistory complained to the government about anti-Semitic propaganda in the press and theater and unsuccessfully opposed the swearing of the *More Judaico* in the law courts of several departments, especially Alsace-Lorraine, Italy, and the German Rhineland cities.[52] But its purpose was the same whether it represented the nation to the Jews or the reverse. Protests against anti-Semitism, official or otherwise, remonstrated against differentiating Jews from other French people.

All sides took something from Napoleon's March 17th "Organization of the Mosaic Religion." Judaism now had a state-recognized, -organized, and -centralized structure just like Protestantism and Catholicism, and, in this respect, these creeds resembled the state government. At this time, however, the state did not pay the salaries of rabbis, as it had for priests and ministers. Another benefit was solidarity. Destabilized by emancipation and revolution, the Jews of France had for the first time a single, centralized institution that, if properly administered, could hold the Jewish community together.

The emperor and his extension, the state, also profited from consistorial organization. Like other Napoleonic institutions, it was hierarchical, bureaucratic, and concentrated power in Paris, thus establishing order and support for the government while aggrandizing Bonaparte and the First Empire. As conceived by Napoleon and his aides, the consistorial system gave Jews organization though not autonomy. It would, in fact, tie them more closely to the imperium and the state. In practice, however, Jews did not forfeit all community authority to Napoleon and France. Consistories faced both ways, policing Jews at the behest of the government while defending the community against official and unofficial persecution and encouraging cohesion. Order strengthened both the state and the Jews, for whom order and unity ensured survival.

Consistories did not fully integrate the Jewish communities, neither with France nor internally. Nor did rifts in the communities necessarily weaken them. Bonaparte's mode of selection of officers for the consistories would establish an enlightened, acculturated, elite governance of the Jewish masses. Departmental consistories, however, did not always obey the Central Consistory and the orthodox majority in the East looked to their own rabbis and congregations for leadership.

Napoleon's approval of the Notables' deliberations and the consistory plan that body had formulated did not conclude his dialogue with the Jews. Molé's September 18 remarks also introduced another imperial summons to French Jewry. Bonaparte would convene a "more dignified and more religious [body]" to convert the Notables' "answers . . . into decisions" that "must find a place near the Talmud, and thus acquire, in the eyes of the Jews of all countries and of all ages, the greatest possible authority." In its present state, the "purity" of the Jewish "law" had no doubt been altered and Jewish confidence in it had been shaken. The proposed body would halt this corrosion by "fix[ing] their [the Jewish community's] belief on those points, which have been submitted to you [the Assembly]." This benefice would be "in return for his [Bonaparte's] gracious protection" (the emperor never gave anything away) and bring for "all of your persuasion, the blessings of a new era."[53]

Napoleon looked to a glorious future in which Jews would be brought into the nation, but his vehicle for absorption was an institution of ancient Israel:

> To find, in the history of Israel, an assembly capable of attaining the object now in view, we must go back to the Great Sanhedrim, and it is the Great Sanhedrim, which His Majesty this day intends to convene.

"This senate . . . will rise again to enlighten the people it formerly governed"; restore "the true meaning of the law" by displacing "the corrupted glosses of commentators"; and "teach them [Jews] to love and to defend the country they inhabit." The Great Sanhedrin will "convince them" that the only nation since the diaspora that freed them deserves the same level of attachment as the Jews held for ancient Israel.[54] Like the rationalists and secular nationalists, Bonaparte, born of the Revolution and nurtured by the Enlightenment, would replace Zion with France, the Mosaic Code with Napoleonic law, and discard biblical, Talmudic, and rabbinic authority as obsolete obstacles to the fulfillment of the modern destiny of Judaism.

Speaking for Napoleon, Molé instructed the Assembly in the composition of the Sanhedrin. It would have seventy-one members, the number of the original body. Appropriate to its sanctifying role, approximately two-thirds would be rabbis—among them the clergy in the Assembly— the other third to be chosen by the Notables from among their ranks. Final approval of candidates was vested in prefects of the empire. Sephardim and Ashkenazim would be equally represented and some deputies would come from outside France. "The duties of the Great Sanhedrim shall be to convert into religious doctrines the answers already given by this assembly," and thus "ratify your answers and give them greater weight."[55] The emperor would do for the Jews what he did for France— give them a new code of law. Ever the self-aggrandizer, Bonaparte would, as Glotzer aptly remarks, rival the great lawgiver of the Hebrews. Another Moses, he would destroy their false rules and beliefs, give them their true law, and sanctify this code. Like his predecessor, the current ruler-prophet would lead them out of their long journey in the wilderness to a new promised land.

Napoleon apparently envisioned a sequential process in matters pertaining to the Jews. The Assembly of Notables rendered opinions and suggested plans. As the foremost prong of his tripartite system, the emperor issued edicts that modified and implemented the deliberations of the Notables, as was the case with the decree "Organizing the Mosaic

Religion." Between the Notables and the imperial government, Napoleon interposed the Great Sanhedrin to sacralize and legalize the responses of the Notables. The Sanhedrin would transform the opinions of the Notables into decisions and the latter, in turn, would be reviewed and implemented by the emperor.

Overlapping with the Assembly in time, personnel, perspective, and purpose, formation of the Great Sanhedrin was decreed by Napoleon on August 23, 1806. The new body contained forty-five rabbis; fifteen of them were also Notables. As conceived by Napoleon, the Sanhedrin would be a "committee" of the Assembly. Hence, the Sanhedrin, like its parent, would be composed of many prerevolutionary leaders of French Jewry or their descendants; of "the principal figures of the Jewish nation;" of "men who fear the loss of their fortune; . . . who do not want to bear the blame for the misfortunes of the Jewish nation." Rabbi David Sintzheim, its president, was an Ashkenazi religious traditionalist and, in July 1808, became the first chief rabbi and president of the Central Consistory. While the Sanhedrin sat (from February to March 1807), the Assembly suspended its meetings and resumed them after the Sanhedrin finished its work. The Assembly of Notables completed its mission on April 16, 1807.

The initial meeting of the Sanhedrin, on February 4, 1807, was as ceremonial as that of the Assembly. Delegates wore a special uniform of black silk and an obligatory sword. Before the meeting began, they went to a synagogue and listened to a canticle composed for the occasion, which compared the emperor and Cyrus, the king of Persia who arranged Israel's first restoration. The king of France would arrange the second restoration, but not in Israel. After the service, the delegates gathered in the chapel of St. John, where the Notables met, from which all Christian ornaments had been removed. Bonaparte, characteristically grandiose, conceived of the Great Sanhedrin as the first universal congress of the Jews.[56]

Sanhedrin sanctification of the responses of the Assembly of Notables into Jewish law, would the emperor felt, encourage "timid" rabbis to support, and discourage orthodox ("fanatic") clergy to resist, the reformation of French Jewry. "[T]he danger of refusal [of the Assembly and Sanhedrin decisions]," Napoleon told his minister of the interior, "would be the expulsion of the Jewish people."[57] Hailed and reviled as the liberator of European Jewry, Napoleon emancipated Jews in territories that he conquered; at home he pursued an antithetical policy based on his real sentiments toward Jews.[58]

A letter dated November 29, 1806, but which did not arrive until February 16 or afterward, contained the emperor's instructions regarding the Sanhedrin to his minister of the interior. Napoleon opened with a declaration of "principles." "It is necessary to remove from the Laws of Moses everything intolerant." The Sanhedrin should "begin by declaring that there are, in the laws of Moses, religious and political provisions; that the religious provisions are immutable but that this does not apply to the political provisions which are susceptible of modification." In biblical times, Mosaic and Israeli law were identical and the Sanhedrin could not distinguish between them. Since the fall of Israel, religious and civic law diverged. Now the Great Sanhedrin, meeting for the first time since the diaspora, could make that distinction. Bonaparte would render the same things to God and to Caesar as did the Assembly of Notables, and he commanded Champagny to ensure that the Sanhedrin affirmed this distribution.[59] The emperor's execution, however, contradicted his intention of separating the spiritual from the political. By convening bodies of Jews who dealt with both types of affiliations and obligations, and subsequently instituting a consistorial system that regulated civic and creedal life, Napoleon merged that which he would distinguish.

The emperor restated his disapproval of the old Mosaic Code: "According to the law [sic] of Moses, the Jews only regard as their brothers those who profess the same religion." The new "Sanhedrin shall establish . . . that one must consider as brothers all men, whatever religion they profess, . . . as long as the Jews enjoy in their midst the same rights as they do." The "application" section of the letter was a series of concrete directives to Champagny that would change Jewish law to integrate Jews with the French people. To accomplish amalgamation via regeneration, he prospectively ordered the Sanhedrin to approve the Assembly's answers to the Twelve Questions.[60]

Bonaparte had accepted the responses of the Notables, as shown by his simultaneous call for a convention of the Great Sanhedrin; however, he was by no means as convinced as the Assembly had hoped that the Jews were ameliorated and patriotic. As Napoleon had said, absorption and expulsion were the alternative solutions to the Jewish problem. Bonaparte's demands as expressed to Champagny were clearly framed in this context. Rabbis must sanction extensive intermarriage. Since "the Jews must consider the Christians as brothers, it follows" that "marriages between Christians and Jews . . . be recommended because they are vital to the nation." "When out of every three marriages, one is between a Jew and a Frenchman, the blood of the Jews will cease to have any unique character."[61]

The emperor also insisted on military service: "When a proportion of the [Jewish] youth is required to enter the army, they will stop having specifically Jewish interests and feelings; they will assume French interests and feelings." Bonaparte also generalized the many constraints he wanted the Assembly to impose and the Sanhedrin to ordain on Jewish economic behavior, for example, partial ban of Jews from commerce and trade and a ten-year moratorium on mortgage loans contracted by Jews who did not own land. One of the "goals" of his proposals was "to rescue several departments [in the Northeast] from the disgrace of finding themselves vassals to . . . a people who, by its morals and laws, forms a unique nation within the French nation." A "secondary object [of the economic measures] is to weaken" the "tendency of the Jewish people toward such a great number of practices which are contrary to civilization and to the good order of society in all the countries of the world."[62]

Rehabilitation might be a daunting task, but not for "that hero whom Providence has sent in his mercy to regenerate the French empire." Napoleon girded himself before the challenge. To "stop the evil" of the Jews entailed "changing the Jews": through intermarriage and military service, such that "when they are submitted to the authority of civil law, all that will remain of them as Jews will be [religious] dogma." Bonaparte elaborated the emphasis on civil law with his own theory of state formation, initiated, according to him, by a people making their religion civil law. He would take the Jews to the next stage: "[T]hey will leave their current state of affairs where religion is the only civil law. This has always been the situation in the infancy of nations." The momentous transition of the Jews from vice to virtue; from a religious nation within a nation to patriotic French citizens; from a people chosen by, and committed to, Jehovah, to a people liberated by, and loyal to, France necessitated "the use at the same time of the Great Sanhedrin, the Jews [sic] Assembly, and the regulations decreed by the Council of State."[63]

The emperor dwelled on differences that he perceived between Jews and other French people and his prescriptions for closing this gap collided with those of many European emancipationists and reversed the original citizenship grant. Yet this course was imperative, for discrimination was not responsible, as many liberals claimed, for degradation. Even in Poland, "where they [Jews] are esteemed and powerful, they are no less vile, dirty, and given to all those customs of the basest dishonesty."[64]

The rejuvenative role of the "Great Sanhedrin" is "to expunge from Mosaic legislation of Moses [sic] all those laws which are atrocious and those which can only refer to the situation of the Jews in Palestine." The rehabilitative power of this sanctifying body significantly derived from its appeal to modern Jews: "The Great Sanhedrin has the best wishes and the respect of all who are enlightened among the Jews of Europe." As with the Assembly of Notables, Bonaparte relied on the reform and acculturated segment to encourage assimilation among their coreligionists. After submission to the French Civil Code, Jews would forsake that part of their religion that functions as civil law. Through the Sanhedrin, the Mosaic Code would be modernized and in particular modified in the direction of the Napoleonic Code. This transformation would end the history of the nation within a nation; Jews would be a religious, but no longer a national, community. Orthodox worshippers were resistant to this grandiose and radical change in Judaic existence as they knew it. In their view, these prescriptions were another in a series of interventions in Jewish life during the Revolution and the First Empire. Even moderate French Jews were not enthusiastic and it was difficult to find enough rabbis willing to serve in that body—a portent that its rulings would not flourish in the Jewish community.[65]

The Sanhedrin accepted Napoleon's charge. Meeting in eight sessions lasting for a month, resolutions were drawn up by Furtado and other Notables and adopted unanimously and without debate. The new body consecrated the Assembly's replies to Bonaparte's queries. In refusing Napoleon's demand that it recommend mixed marriage, the Sanhedrin registered its sole defiance of monarchical will. But this convention of rabbis and laymen accepted their sovereign's demand that exogamous unions not result in excommunication.[66]

After obligatory obsequies to Bonaparte, the Sanhedrin vowed in its April 1807 decisions to "promulgate religious decrees which shall conform to the principles of our sacred laws" and become "a standard to all Israelites." These doctrines "shall teach the nations that our dogmas are in keeping with the civil laws under which we live and that we are in no wise separated from the society of men." Echoing their monarch, the members distinguished, in our "divine law," between "religious dispositions," which were immutable and "absolute," and "political dispositions," which lost their relevancy since "Israel no longer forms a nation."[67] The message was unmistakable; Jewish law was no pretext for accusing Jews of being a nation within a nation. As did the Assembly, the Sanhedrin conceded what their emperor commanded while preserving what they could of their historic faith by assuring him that it harmonized with his policies.

Acquiescence descended to grovelling when the Sandhedrin informed the "prince" who "permitted us to be one with the great family of the State" that "we feel ourselves called upon to contribute to the completion of the moral regeneration of Israel. Thus . . . we hereby religiously enjoin on all obedience to the State in all matters civil and political."[68] As indicated by the Sanhedrin's response to Napoleon's initiative, Bonaparte, ever the supreme manipulator, had created another illusion. The Sanhedrin was ostensibly a decisionary body, as opposed to the Assembly of Notables, which was advisory. By enshrining the responses of the Notables in Jewish law, the Sanhedrin, as the judicial representative of the Jews, was expanding and modifying the Mosaic Code and thus, at least in France, the Jewish people were deciding their own destiny.[69] Reality, however, made a mockery of autonomy.

Great Sanhedrin and grand irony! The body took its name from ancient Israel's supreme council and tribunal, the court that, according to the Gospels, convicted Jesus of violating Hebraic law and turned Him over to the Romans. Seeking assurance that Jews did not constitute a separate and disloyal enclave, Napoleon convened them twice as a distinct group and named the second organization after that body which, in Christian belief, committed history's greatest betrayal.

Despite professions to the contrary, the responses of the Notables, even inscribed as Jewish law by the Sanhedrin, did not appease the emperor. Action alone, not answers and anointments, satisfied him. Two imperial decrees of March 17, 1808, enacted his own policies and prejudices and the plans and codifications of the Assembly and the Sanhedrin. The "Organic Regulation of the Mosaic Religion" concerned the internal governance of the Jewish community and alleged grievances against Jews. The "Decree on the Regulation of Commercial Transactions and Residence of Jews" more bluntly addressed gentile complaints that had generated the formation of the two conventions of prominent Jews and their deliberations and decisions.

The decree on commerce, residence, and military service imposed stringent limitations on Jewish creditors setting interest rates or collecting debts. Jews would have to obtain annual licenses from municipal officials to hold mortgages or conduct business and commerce. Requisite for these licenses was certification by the municipal government that the grantee was not involved in "illicit business" or usury and by the local consistory "attesting to his good conduct and his integrity." Residence was no less restricted than commerce. Jews not permanently living in several departments in Alsace and Lorraine could not move there. In other departments of these provinces, habitation depended on Jews' becoming agriculturalists and not engaging in business and commerce. Bonaparte's edict also set harsh terms for Jewish recruitment in the armed forces. In defiance of French law, which allowed arrangements for substitutes, "every Jewish conscript shall be subject to personal service." The emperor offered consolation in the hope that, "as a result of these various measures made necessary because of the Jews," the provisions would lapse after ten years and "there will no longer be any difference between them and the other citizens of our Empire." The only immediate relief in this relentless anti-Jewish edict, however, was that the Sephardic enclave in Bordeaux and the Southwest was exempted from its mandate.[70]

The decree organizing the consistories was disliked by the orthodox, but that pertaining to commerce, residence, and recruitment was detested by all Jews, who called it the *Décret Infame*. Exemplifying the unification of the Jews under Napoleon, Furtado led the opposition, even though its primary object was not the "Portuguese Nation" in Bordeaux. Until dissolution of the First Empire, he refused all public missions and appointments. The Revolution and Napoleon earlier exported emancipation to the foreign territories under their control, and now this order of restraint was similarly imposed. Within two years, the decree was lifted for the Jews in Paris, southern France, and Italy, but this rescission exempted only one-sixth of the Jews in the empire. Napoleon had again reverted. After creating institutions to merge Sephardim and Ashkenazim, he now, as was the case before 1791, officially favored the former over the latter. Most severely punished were Jews in Alsace and Lorraine, where many debtors stopped paying Jewish creditors and where, particularly in small towns, Jews had difficulty getting trading licenses.[71]

Through their consistories and leaders, French Jews vainly protested and the decree worsened economic conditions for the Ashkenazim. The imperial order treated Jews unlike all other liberated groups in France and, therefore, generated feelings of betrayal and dismay. Jews, at least the Ashkenazim, reverted to their pre-1791 probationary status and, in some respects, to ancien régime practices. Those in the Eastern departments were differentiated from other French people and their unequal treatment was officially legitimized. Once again they had to prove themselves worthy of the citizenship ostensibly granted seventeen years earlier. And, unlike the terms of that emancipation, the acquisition of civic equality, as Glotzer asserts, now depended upon behavior not rights.[72]

The Jews had been found guilty of criminal and sinful acts and were given a ten-year sentence (Simon Schwartzfuchs calls it "probation"). As Napoleon told Champagny, "the mass of [Judaic] corruption can only improve through time."[73] A decade of good behavior would enable Jews to pay their debt to society and thus earn their former freedom. The crucial difference between this and a penal sentence was that they had to enter society in order to be rehabilitated and freed.

A final consequence of the decree was that by exempting Sephardic settlements, it widened the wedge between them and Ashkenazim. This division surfaced early in the Revolution when, on August, 14, 1789, Bordeaux Jews told Abbé Grégoire that the Ashkenazi campaign for citizenship was harming their own chances. In 1790, Gentile and Jewish advocates of Sephardic citizenship distinguished between the latter and Ashkenazim. Internecine conflict continued in the First Empire. Sephardic leader Abraham Furtado attacked alleged Ashkenazi usury at the Sanhedrin meetings. In June 1807, when it became known that the government was preparing a decree about the Jews, the Sephardim petitioned the government to differentiate them from the Ashkenazim.[74]

An incident in the Continental Army and a comment made about the Sanhedrin by a leader of American Jewry dramatically disclose the difference in treatment of Jews in the United States and France. In the

Revolution and subsequent Republic across the Atlantic, armed service was not considered incompatible with Jewish identity. Hart Jacobs, a soldier in George Washington's army, asked for an exemption from duty on Friday nights. His commander granted the request.[75] Suggestive of the different route to religious equality taken by each nation was the comment on the convocation of the Great Sanhedrin made by an eminent American Jew. Gershom Seixas asked his New York congregation to beseech Jehovah that Napoleon "may be a means of accomplishing our reestablishment if not as a nation in our former territory, let it only be as a particular society, with equal rights [and] privileges of all other religious societies."[76] A son of the French Revolution, the emperor sought from the Sanhedrin assurance of the integration of the Jews with the nation. A native-born American, Seixas drew on the American Revolution and the historical experience of Jews in his pluralistic nation in hoping that Bonaparte convened that body to preserve the distinctiveness of the Jews while guaranteeing their equality.

The indefatigable promoter of Jewish assimilation, Napoleon in 1808 made one more effort at absorption. A "Decree Relative to the Names of Jews," issued on July 20th, ordered Jews who had not done so to take family and first names and not to use Old Testament names as last names. Jews were instructed to register their patronymics with the local public records office.[77]

Phyllis Cohen Albert pursues her thesis that the Jews did not assimilate and the French made no serious attempts to stifle Jewish ethnicity by showing that officials and Jews in the First Empire and thereafter used the traditional term *Juif* as a noun and adjective. Thus, the 1808 census referred to *"la population Juive."*[78] Whatever Juif or Juive meant for the Jewish community, it offers no evidence that Napoleonic France was reluctant to challenge the ethnicity of this group. The emperor's, and some of his key underlings', attitudes, correspondence, orders, and conventions of Jews disclose distaste for this people and a persistent desire to change its customs and law to enhance absorption.

If Albert wrongly argues that official France made no sustained attempt to undermine Judaic culture and community, she correctly claims that Jewish identity and cohesion was preserved. Notwithstanding the barrage of integrative ordinances, the real impact of the imperial edicts shows the limits of demands for dejudiazation made by the government and officially designated Jewish leaders. The "infamous decree" was never renewed. Emancipation and the attendant mandate for mergence had little effect on the lives of the vast majority of Jews who lived outside of large cities. Only in these places, especially Paris, was traditional Judaism threatened by French culture. Even secularized leaders wanted acculturation, not absorption. All but the most ardent assimilators disap-

proved of conversion, intermarriage, or even milder forms of secularization, like not learning Hebrew or going to services. Relatively trivial
compromises met with resistance. On March 8, 1810, the Central Consistory demanded that departmental consistories and synagogues enforce
the imperial decree on names and rued that many of these institutions
disregarded the edict.[79] When imperial decrees clashed with religious imperatives, the Jewish community could be obdurate. The intermarriage
order was ignored and mixed betrothals remained rare for several decades
thereafter.

Bonaparte's assimilation policy and Jewish pledges of moral uplift
and total loyalty did not deter the emperor and his Council of State from
undermining integration by reversing emancipation, its fundamental prerequisite. Departmental and local governments, which imposed constraints upon Jews officially repealed during the Revolution, were even
more discriminatory and rejecting.[80] France still erected barriers between
Jews and other citizens. Many Jews pleaded that they were not separate or
irreversibly inferior, but government policy stigmatized and marginalized
French Jewry.

The drawn out engagement between Napoleon and the Jews was
fought over issues supposedly settled in 1791. In this confrontation, Jews
appealed to revolutionary closure and to Bonaparte's claim to be the fulfiller of the Revolution. His treatment of the Jews, on the other hand,
revealed that although the events of 1789 broke with the absolutist past,
ten years later despotism had returned in the guise of the emperor—at
least insofar as he embodied and consolidated the diametric drives of the
Bourbon and revolutionary regimes. This ambivalence and authoritarianism might have edged into Napoleon's awareness. In 1804, he officially
terminated the First Republic, yet he sometimes referred to himself as the
"Republican Emperor."

Napoleon had commanded revolutionary armies, and binding the
First Republic and the First Empire was the confluence of French imperialism and revolutionary messianism that sought to reestablish "the great
French nation" (Belgium and the Rhineland) while exporting revolutionary principles through foreign conquest. Thus continued the 1790s
themes of patriotism (nationalism), universalism (imperialism), and perfectionism (utopianism). Rational order and aggrandizement of civic authority forged another link between Jacobin military ventures and the
victories of the First Empire; put simply, what was good for France was
good for the world. Domestic policy also partly modeled itself on revolutionary universalism—Jacobin style, which meant centralization and amplification of the state through government intervention in what, in
America for example, would be reserved for civil society or the private
sphere. In the Napoleonic, as well as Jacobin, mindset, the state existed

to protect public security and all other public interests. The imperium was further fortified by another revolutionary precedent, secular (state) dominance over spiritual sources of authority,

Napoleon also looked back beyond the Revolution, reverting to the Bourbon past in repairing the ravages inflicted on the Church by the Revolution. But rehabilitation did not mean restoration. State empowerment over religion persisted under a new despot and Catholicism was not reestablished as the state religion. More generally, Bonaparte rejuvenated the hierarchical distribution of authority under the monarchy.[81] The conflation of revolutionary and historical impulses applied to the Jews. Napoleon ended emancipation, but tentatively promised to reinstitute citizenship if Jews merited civic rights. At the same time, he revisited ancient grievances against Jews and reimposed their corporate status and organization. The emperor was less a prodigal son of the Revolution in liberating Jews in the lands he captured than he was in taking away their rights in France.

The Revolution and the old regime were not the only precedents for Bonaparte's treatment of the Jews. An absolutist monarch, he resembled other autocrats, particularly those who believed they ruled in accord with reason. Emancipation, or, in Napoleon's case, the terms for re-emancipation, was not only the result of revolution and republicanism. Enlightened despots, too, undertook such initiatives. Napoleon himself liberated Jews in the parts of Italy and Germany under his control. Even before 1791, or 1789 for that matter, Absolutists of the Age of Reason granted political rights to Jews. Austro-Hungarian Emperor Joseph II issued an Edict of Toleration (January 2, 1782) that lifted some restrictions on Jews in his domain. Even limited freedom came at a price. Reform-minded, Joseph wanted Jews to abandon the use of Hebrew and Yiddish and any document in these languages was invalid for legal and official purposes. His distaste for Yiddish was shared by maskilim who advised coreligionists to drop this dialect in favor of the national language. Two years later, the emperor abolished rabbinical courts and transferred their cases to imperial jurisdiction. An ardent assimilationist, he encouraged Jewish children to attend German schools and directed Jews to take German names.[82] Joseph's removal of some restraints upon Jews harmonized with his despotic desire to exert authority and to eliminate the nation within a nation as an obstacle to imperial empowerment, a purpose and strategy that inspired a subsequent French ruler.

Carried out by reformist liberal nationalists, liberation of Prussia's Jews nonetheless took place under an absolutist monarch and in any case proved temporary. A fuller emancipation than the Edict of Toleration, the Edict Concerning the Civil Conditions of Jews in the Prussian State (March 11, 1812) nevertheless prohibited the keeping of business records in Hebrew and forbade rabbis and Jewish elders to exercise judicial functions. In return for their new civic rights, Jews were required to adopt German surnames and to assume civic duties. King Friedrich Wilhelm, like Emperor Joseph II, would give the Jews rights, but foster national power and unity by curtailing community autonomy. Another enlightened absolutist, Empress Catherine II of Russia, also partly emancipated her Jewish subjects while undermining kehillot authority by making Jews subject to imperial law courts. Not all despots exchanged individual freedom for annihilation of the nation within a nation. Nicholas I drafted Jews into the Russian army, where they were pressured to convert. Less enlightened and reformist than Joseph II or Catherine II, he nevertheless in 1844 abolished the *kahal* (governing body of Jewish communities in Russia).[83]

Despotism—enlightened or unenlightened, liberationist or repressive—commonly sought to dismantle corporate institutions in order to facilitate aggrandizement of the central, monarchical will over all subjects. This approach to the "Jewish Problem," however, was not unique to royal despots. Revolutionary France emancipated the Jews during its liberal phase and demanded the same trade off between rights and autonomy as did Prussian and Austrian autocrats. Despite these similarities, politically active Jews, mostly acculturated members of the educated and economic elites in the Jewish community, on both sides of the Atlantic tended to favor revolutionary, republican, and liberal movements. Yet the despots were not without their supporters. They could be found among "Court Jews," financiers with international connections, and local and national administrators, who helped fund and run the autocratic state. Jews were present in all routes toward nation building. They were active in revolutionary and republican nation-state creation, but were also present in absolutist avenues of modernization and nationalism.[84]

Napoleon blended ancien régime conventions, Enlightenment commitments to reason and rights, revolutionary innovations and aspirations, and, above all, autocratic inclinations in shaping his policies toward French Jewry. To this mix he added, almost inevitably, secularization, and less probably, albeit in formulaic and misused fashion, Jewish customs. The latter was exemplified by the bizarre reconstruction of the Sanhedrin and the analogical resemblance between consistories and the old corporate enclosure of Jewry. In convening the Assembly of Notables and the Sanhedrin, the emperor drafted Jewish leaders to ordain and implement his Jewish program by dissolving their own legal and communitarian traditions. At his behest, the Notables and the Sanhedrin would make state law supreme over the Mosaic Code, except in the spiritual sphere. Repudiation of the old corporate interaction between Jews and the realm would be replaced by benevolent despotic regeneration to enable them to reenter the nation. If incompleteness, need for intensification, random opportunity, or the reluctance of his Jewish designates required direct intervention, the emperor was ever-ready with timely edicts.

Sometimes the course of autocratic empowerment was confused, as in the use of consistories (on the surface a reversion to the decentralized autonomy of the contract between the Jews and the Bourbon regime) to foster absolutistic centralization. But this apparent contradiction was resolved by conceiving the consistorial organization as an agent of state intervention and an institution of centralized control over French Jewry.[85] Yet this paradox was no more opaque than the momentum of Bonaparte's plans for Jews: With their collaboration, he would repeal the rights they had won in 1791 and then guide them along the path of re-emancipation without shadowing his repute as their liberator.

Demeaning discrimination did not end with the First Empire. In 1812, the minister of cults refused a request from the Central Consistory to open a rabbinic seminary; fifteen years would pass before a seminary opened. A generation after Catholic and Protestant clergy were salaried by the state, only after 1831 were rabbis thus remunerated. Not until 1833 did Jewish schools get state funding equal to other religions' educational institutions and many municipal councils disobeyed this law. In 1835, Judaism was finally made a state-supported religion. The more judaico, a special oath that Jews summoned to court had to swear on the Bible, remained in force until 1846. Prerevolutionary Jewish communal debts were reaffirmed throughout the nineteenth century and special taxes for their repayment were approved as late as the 1860s. Qualified Jews were denied entry into the prestigious teacher training school, the École Normale, and into teaching positions in public secondary schools in the 1840s and 1850s and Jewish students were barred from admission to some lycées. On several occasions in the 1850s, Jews were excluded from public ceremonies when other religions were represented, and some towns, as those along the Spanish border and in Alsace, forbade Jewish residents until the 1840s. Anti-Jewish riots recurred in 1819, 1823–24 and in the Revolutions of 1830 and 1848. In the latter upheaval, Jews were suspected of being German agents and in over 20 percent of Alsatian Jewish communities, homes, stores, and synagogues were pillaged. Mob violence against Jews broke out again in the 1850s and subsequent events occurring well into the twentieth century showed that citizenship, the passage of time, and identification with the state and national culture could not halt the war against the Jews.[86]

The narrative of Jews in the Revolution and First Empire illuminates larger discourses about the transformation of Judaism and the emergence of republican government, the nation-state, and nationalism itself. These facets of modernism appeared throughout Western Europe, as well as in France and the United States, and did not proceed in the same way. In Germany and England, for example, formal emancipation was gradual rather than abrupt and not a consequence of a successful revolution, as in the France of 1791.

Citizenship in France and elsewhere in Europe not only intruded upon the old order of separate corporate existence—it also threatened the hegemony of Orthodox Judaism. Changes in ritual, dress, and religious services, introduction of vernacular languages and subjects in Jewish schools and worship, substitution of public schools for hederim and yeshivot and increasing disaffiliation or conversion were not only coerced or opportunistic responses to the nationalist demand that political equality meant integration with the state. Many Jews embraced their new status and eagerly sought to modify their ancestral culture and faith to attain fulfillment as citizens—as French, German, English, or American compatriots.[87]

Wherever the initiative or response lay, or whatever the degree of absorption demanded or exchanged for citizenship, the peculiar structure and culture of each emerging nation-state shaped the destiny of Jews in that country. American and European Jews alike were affected by the rise of capitalism, the advent of the Enlightenment and republicanism, the gradual decline of Christianity, and the age of revolution, but each nation's own history determined how Jews fared in it. As theory these principles are self-evident, but as a problem in comparative history they mandate exhaustive scholarship and intricate delineation.

German nationalism tended to be exclusive, organic, and ethnic or "*völkisch*." French nationalism, at least in its revolutionary, Napoleonic, pre-Romantic, and republican phases was predominantly assimilationist, ideological, and inclusive. Ultimately, Germany distinguished between native-born groups, Jews and Aryans, and stripped the former of citizenship and, finally, of existence.[88] Even Vichy France, however, distinguished between foreign- and native-born Jews; it sacrificed (often eagerly) the former and sought (less zealously) to save the latter. For France, the pivot of exclusion-inclusion turned on citizenship, not ethnicity.

The modern meaning of citizenship emerged from the French Revolution. As defined by that insurgency and later adopted by other countries, it was bounded by the political state. Those inside were, or could become, citizens; those outside were foreigners. Citizenship, however, was not merely territorial. It meant no institutions or loyalties mediating between the nation and its citizens, no errant individual wills frustrating the general will, no nation within a nation, no semi-sovereign communities. As the liberal era of the Revolution closed, in July 1792 the Assembly ordered every commune to have its altar of the Fatherland, with an engraved Declaration of the Rights of Man and the inscription: "The citizen is born, lives and dies for the Fatherland."[89] Citizenship meant uplift as well as solidarity, as in "The Republic of Virtue" (1793–94).

To become citizens, the state demanded, not always effectively, that Jews meet three qualifications: they had to be good, assimilated, and exclusively loyal. This entailed surrendering their traditional communities and beliefs, which most French people regarded as dissonant and degenerate. Thus citizenship and Judaism were antithetical—the nation versus the nation within a nation, virtue versus vice, a corporate past versus a republican future. When modern France defined itself against its image of the Jews, citizenship meant dejudaization—just as revolutionary France, for the same reason, espoused dechristianization.[90]

The Revolution swept away Bourbon hierarchies and privileges of birth, territory, occupation, and faith. Corporate differentiation of immunities and obligations gave way to civic equality and uniformity and, correlatively and ideally, to a direct, unmediated, and seamless relationship between state and citizen. For French Jews, the institution of citizenship meant that emancipation was an invitation, and sometimes an imperative, to assimilation. For avid French anti-Semites, this conception of nationhood meant that Jews could not become compatriots because they could never divest themselves of Jewish ties and traits; they were eternal strangers, always a nation within a nation.

Emancipation did not mean Judaic autonomy. Citizenship supplanted ancien régime incorporation of Jews with incorporation in the nation. Nor was emancipation a Jewish initiative. French Jewry had not the organization, numbers, wealth, power, or political will and experience to move France to give itself equal rights. Furthermore, most Jews felt ambivalent about, or indifferent to, civic and legal parity. Liberation, therefore, was conferred upon the Jews, not won by them. This bestowal was not given in recognition or recompense for previous oppression. Freedom thusly granted would have been considered a particularistic gesture that violated the principles of the Revolution and, correspondingly, insulted the philosophy upon which citizenship was granted to the Jews. Instead, they were liberated according to the abstract, universal values of the Revolution and the state it created. Revolutionary commitment to liberty, rationality, equality, and fraternity, to the rule of law, the rights of man, and the sovereignty of the state negated reconstruction of a particularistic, corporate community. Freedom for Jews, therefore, was freedom to acquire membership in the nation, not freedom to maintain themselves as a separate, religio-ethnic community. If liberation meant the end of the Jews as a separate nation, it also meant the end of traditional messianic Judaism. The destiny of Jews would be diasporic inhabitation rather than return to Israel.

Jews were now admitted into a society, a nation, with a different history and culture than their own. They were allowed to enter on condition that they give up their own past, culture, and nation. Nor were they necessarily welcomed into the new community; they were admitted into a society that harbored strong feelings that Jews and Judaism itself conflicted with its values and customs. Thus, they entered with reservations and misgivings on both sides. For Jews, this created a dilemma that still torments them: What parts of their old identity should they forfeit for acceptance in the national community? To what extent would they be accepted no matter what strategies of assimilation and acculturation they adopted?[91]

The Jews were a microcosm of the Revolution. Perhaps a better formulation is that the Revolution epitomized its interconnected parts and, therefore, the Jewish episode contained themes, transformations, and turmoil that appeared elsewhere and threaded together the whole upheaval. Indeed, the Jewish experience dramatically exemplifies the revolutionary sequence. Like so many other developments, the Revolution broke radically with the past in its treatment of Jews. Rejecting custom, however, did not bring closure. As in other matters and cumulatively, radical departures brought forth an earthquake that tore the social fabric and these fissures did not mend over time. In 1791, France carried out the earliest and most unqualified liberation of the Jews. A century later, it could plausibly be predicted that, at least in the West, France was the likeliest place for an anti-Semitic disaster. The long-resonating clash of inclusion and hostility are commentaries on the Revolution and its echo of recurrent conflict.

The question that agitated France until the near present—indeed was controversial in the Jewish community itself, especially in the first half of the 19th century—was whether the primary attachment of Jews was to the nation or to their religion. Different types of Jews, rich or poor, secularly or religiously educated, acculturated or orthodox, Sephardic or Ashkenazi, tended to give priority to one or the other. Many Gentiles as well as Jews argued, however, that civic and creedal identities were not in conflict. For them, religious affiliation transcended, without contradicting, national loyalty. Nevertheless, the pluralistic resolution of the debate between creed and citizenship was usually a minority and beleaguered view.

The "Jewish Question" had several possible solutions: Jews could be excluded from the nation because they could never amalgamate with non-Jews. Jews could become part of the nation because they could behave like other citizens. Jews could join the nation because religion belonged to the private and citizenship to the public sphere. Jews could enter the nation because denominational affiliation helped the national community cohere. The United States was more amenable to religious diversity and to the principle that voluntarily associated faith could enhance the nation. The disposition that civil society and the civic community could be mutually supportive muted the contention over the issue of creed versus citizenship. In other respects, too, the Jewish experience in the American Revolution and thereafter reflected the nature of that uprising. Contrasted with their French equivalents, the American Revolution and early Republic did not break with history as abruptly or completely; passions were cooler and cleavages not as unbridgeable. Some things settled in the War for Independence and the early national era were not reopened by successive generations. Thus the destiny of American Jewry was settled in the context of comparative compromise and closure upon the formation of the United States.

CHAPTER 5

THE AMERICAN EXPERIENCE

July 4, 1788, was a good day for a parade in Philadelphia. Cloudy but rainless skies and a brisk southern wind brought relief from the clammy summer heat that usually engulfed the city, but the parade would have taken place even if the weather had made marching a sweaty chore. America's largest city was celebrating two defining events of its young history, the twelfth anniversary of the Declaration of Independence and ratification of the U.S. Constitution on June 21st when the last of nine states necessary for approval voted affirmatively. At dawn the peal of church bells sounded a counterpoint to a cannonade from the *Rising Sun*, anchored off Market Street. Later that morning, some five thousand people organized in military companies and "societies" of students, ministers, tradesmen, professionals, artisans, mechanics, and farmers, each with its own officers, flags, and regalia, assembled in a grand procession behind the marshals. Interspersed among these groups were representations of Independence, the French Alliance, the Peace Treaty of 1783, the Constitution, George Washington, and other icons of the Republic. Civic officials and congressmen were present, a band accompanied the marchers, and odes in German and English circulated among the onlookers. The parade ended at Union Green, where an audience of seventeen thousand heard former congressman, member of the Constitutional Convention, and future Supreme Court Justice James Wilson declaim the virtues of the Constitution, enlightened republican government, the Union, and patriotism. After his speech, toasts were drunk to Washington, the Federal Constitutional Convention, the king of France, "the people of the United States," and "the whole family [of] mankind." Festivities ended with the crowd and the participants gathered at tables heaped with food and drink. By all accounts the spectacle was colorful, dignified, joyful, and harmonious.[1]

Benjamin Rush, signer of the Declaration of Independence, delegate to the Pennsylvania ratification convention, and a spectator, was impressed with the diversity of the participants and the sameness of purpose and feeling that united them:

> The clergy formed a very agreeable part of the procession. They manifested the sense of connection between religion and good government. Pains were taken to connect ministers of the most dissimilar religious principles together, thereby to show the influence of a

free government in promoting Christian charity. The Rabbi of the Jews [Jacob Raphael of Congregation *Mikveh* Israel, Philadelphia's only synagogue] locked in arms of two ministers of the gospel was a most delightful sight. There could not have been a more happy emblem contrived of that section of the new Constitution [Article VI, prohibiting religious qualifications for holding office] which opens all its power and offices alike not only to every sect of Christians but to worthy men of *every* religion [italics in original].[2]

Another signer of the Declaration of Independence, Francis Hopkinson, who chaired the committee on arrangements and marched in the procession, also admired this religious display of e pluribus unum. He, too, noticed the "clergy of the different Christian denominations, with the rabbi of the Jews, walking arm in arm." For Hopkinson, the "social idea" of "universal love and harmony was much enforced by a circumstance which, probably, never before occurred in such extent, viz: The clergy of almost every denomination united in charity and brotherly love."[3]

Although the commemoration did not explicitly focus upon religion, the ceremonies honoring the Declaration of Independence and the Constitution were holy acts. As indicated by the symbols and speeches in the parade, these denouements of independence and integration were sacraments in the burgeoning civic creed through which America invented itself as a nation.[4]

Rush's and Hopkinson's observations show that the connection between the parade and religion was more direct than the sacralization of national events and symbols. Emblemized in the marching together of different creeds was the union of the states negotiated in the Constitution.

The conjoining of denominational belief and diversity with liberty, equality, and unity became a point of differentiation between the American and French Revolutions and the consequent creeds of the two countries. Respect for religious variety was manifest at the end of the parade when Jews sat at a separate table. Presided over by Isaac Moses, a Philadelphia cobbler, Jewish patriots ate kosher food.[5] As Rush remarked, the sight of clergy of distinct faiths walking arm in arm and the establishment of a constitutional prohibition against a test oath blended religious belief with republican virtue and political and religious freedom and signified a national unity based on political parity between Judaism and Christianity. Citizenship did not mean, as in revolutionary France, impugning creedal affiliation. Jews and Christians celebrated together as citizens of the republic and then ate separately according to their own rituals and customs. What in France was condemned as a "nation within a nation" was here was praised as an exhibition of "from many, one"—national identity in America was not tied to religion or, for that matter, to disbelief in religion.[6]

Less than a year later, Jews participated in another memorable civic ceremony. David S. Franks, scion of an eminent colonial Jewish family, was one of three marshals at the presidential inauguration in New York City on April 30, 1789. *Hazzan* (cantor) Gershom Mendes Seixas, spiritual leader of New York's Congregation Shearith Israel, walked in the procession beside twelve other clergymen.[7]

Committed to superceding hierarchy, corporatism, and Catholicism with a secular republic whose citizens had equal rights, privileges, and status, most French revolutionaries, especially Jacobins, would not have commemorated July 14th or the anniversary of the Declaration of the Rights of Man and of the Citizen with a prominent role for the clergy. Even less would they have accommodated a display of Judaic separateness. Jewish-American engagement in the Philadelphia fete of 1788 and the presidential inauguration in 1789 differed from French Jewry's participation in the 1792 commemoration of the Thionville victory. The Jews of France celebrated the revolutionary battle and their emperor's birthday in 1806 in their own sacred sites and language, and a rabbi conducted the proceedings. The Jews of America joined in the pageants of 1788 and 1789 with gentile fellow citizens. These variances indicate the presence of a Judaic community in France more solidified and less integrated in the nation than was its American cohort. The festivities also demonstrate America's greater openness to Jews and religious diversity and, at least in this regard, to cultural pluralism.

Although Jews were a tiny enclave in the emerging French nation, the Jewish question addressed many principles, issues and conflicts that shaped the essence and determined the course of modern France: civic versus religious obligation; liberty versus uniformity; the troubled and enduring confrontation between Bourbon France, Catholic France, and the French Republic; and the nature of French nationalism. Jews were even less of a presence in the new United States, but here, too, their experience in the revolutionary and early national eras illuminated many crucial aspects of American history and similarities and divergences between that nation and other Western countries.

The American and French Revolutions were progenitors of nationalism, the modern state, and popular rule, protectors of individual rights and promoters of forces that undermined the historical nexus between church and state.[8] Contemporary and later supporters of these uprisings have also valorized them as spearheads of progress, defined as insurgent republicanism and enlightenment. As with all revolutions, those of 1775 and 1789 were deemed hopeful beginnings. Nor did the impulse for renewal necessarily end with the Revolution. France would periodically start again both constitutionally and politically. America, however, has been the nation par excellence of makeovers. The Massachusetts Bay Colony was founded as a "New Canaan" where the Puritans would at last be unhindered in advancing God's glory on earth and redeem humanity through this beacon in the wilderness. Pennsylvania and Maryland similarly originated as New World oases of freedom for Quakers and Catholics respectively, who had been persecuted in England. In the colonial era, and ever after, immigrants arrived with hopes of commencing a different and better life. The War for Independence was a break with the mother country and was soon to be followed by the emergence of a new nation. "Go West, young man" sloganized the frontier as a symbol of hope through change, a route to a new life. Even the American penchant for divorce at a much higher rate than elsewhere exemplifies the national optimistic attachment to embarkations.

Opponents, then and now, of the French and American Revolutions have, therefore, been labeled reactionary Tories, aristocrats, monarchists, and clerics, as well as recalcitrant peasants. Not the least of the progressive claims about 1775 and 1789 has been that regarding the nationalisms they engendered. Proponents of these insurgencies see these nationalisms as, in the American case, displacing colonial status and imperial and monarchical rule, and for France dismantling a feudal, Catholic, and monarchical relic. These nationalisms have also been lauded for transforming their countries into communities that subordinated and diminished class, sectarian, ethnic, and regional divisions.

If they were better than what they displaced, they were also superior to later nationalisms. Progressive, rational, and republican, they have been regarded as a firewall against subsequent Romantic, organic, reactionary, and authoritarian nationalisms that evoked racialism, genocide, totalitarianism, and war. Despite this common ground, the countries took different paths. At various times, France was a monarchy, a dictatorship, and an occupied country, while America remained a republic with a professed concern for individual rights.

Even within concordant revolutionary experiences, significant variations existed between the nations. France demanded unity through national solidity; America was committed to unity in national diversity. The liberation of French Jews occasioned prolonged and impassioned debate in that country. The equivalent conferral of citizenship in Article VI of the U.S. Constitution. (". . . no religious test shall ever be required as a Qualification to any Office or public Trust under the United States") provoked no such controversy in the Constitutional Convention of 1787, in state ratifying conventions, or in the widespread debate over the Constitution.

Article VI passed after little discussion or dissent with only the North Carolina delegation opposed and Maryland divided.[9] A prominent delegate to the Convention and future governor of, and U.S. senator from,

South Carolina, Charles Pinckney, in his "Plan of Government," advocated "prevention of Religious Tests" as "a provision the world will expect from you, in the establishment of a System founded on Republican Principles, and in an age so liberal and enlightened."[10]

In the ratifying conventions, no state objected to excluding religious tests and only South Carolina, which suggested that the word "other" be inserted between "no" and "religious," wanted any revisions. Indeed, many states, in declarations on the Constitution, announced their attachment to freedom of worship.[11]

Of the few comments made on creedal civic equality, most were favorable. "It puts all sects on the same footing," Governor Edmund Randolph told the Virginia convention. "A man of abilities and character, of any sect whatever, may be admitted to any office or public trust under the United States." A "friend to a variety of sects, because they keep one another in order," Randolph exemplified the harmony-in-diversity sentiment that permeated the infant Republic: "And there are so many now in the United States that they will prevent the establishment of any one sect in prejudice to the rest, and will forever oppose attempts to infringe religious liberties." Delegate James Madison agreed that "freedom [of conscience] arises from the multiplicity of sects which pervades America, and which is the best and only security for religious liberty in any society; for where there is such a variety of sects, there cannot be a majority of any one to oppress or persecute the rest."[12] Pluralism was a cornerstone in the building of the nation, a notion that republican France increasingly found alien and subversive.

James Iredell of North Carolina, soon to be a U.S. Supreme Court justice and the floor leader of the Federalists at the state ratifying convention, comprehensively defended omission of religious tests. Iredell listed all of the objections against such an oath: It would foment intolerance and denominational conflict among believers and hypocrisy among nonbelievers, merge spiritual and civic matters to their mutual detriment, and violate American principles of freedom and reason. He called for an inclusive civic society, where atheists, "pagans" and "Mahometans may be admitted into offices." Like Randolph and Madison, Iredell regarded sectarian variety as necessary for religious freedom: "[N]o sect here is superior to another" and "article [VI of the Constitution] is calculated to secure universal religious liberty, by putting all sects on a level—the only way to prevent persecution."[13]

A few minor figures in the conventions opposed Article VI. While post-1789 French denominational discrimination in granting equality focused on Jews, American advocates of creedal distinctions for citizenship did not single out Jews. Some supporters of religious oaths wanted to apply them against "Papists," "Mahometans," "Pagans," "deists," and "atheists," but omitted Jews from their lists of enemies of the United States.[14]

Even the rare, and always unimportant, delegate who deemed Jews undesirable candidates for citizenship linked them with other alleged foes of the republic. David Caldwell of North Carolina feared that no test oath "was an invitation for Jews and pagans of every kind to come among us." They "might endanger the character of the United States" because "the Christian religion is best calculated of all religions, to make good members of society, on account of its morality."[15] Madison told Jefferson: "One of the objections in New England was that the Constitution by prohibiting religious tests opened a door for Jews [sic] Turks & infidels."[16]

As in the federal and state conventions, few leading pamphleteers in the debate over ratification objected to Article VI and even fewer specified Jews. Luminaries of the early republic, Madison, Tench Coxe, and Oliver Ellsworth lauded the Constitution for guaranteeing religious liberty, identified this principle with political freedom, and praised denominational diversity and freedom of worship in the United States.[17]

Although Article VI enabled Jews to exercise full political rights, religious tests historically had been primarily aimed at Catholics or some Protestant sects. At the time of the Constitution, most states barred nonbelievers from holding public office or voting, some restricted Catholics, a few excluded particular Protestant sects, like the Quakers, and all but two excluded Jews. New York, the first state in the Western world to confer total citizenship upon the Jews (1777), prohibited Catholics from holding government office.[18] American oaths were not specifically targeted at Jews; therefore, their exclusion from the U.S. Constitution was not specifically designed to liberate Jews. The object of the National Assembly action of 1791, on the other hand, was emancipation of French Jewry. American and French dispensations of citizenship, however, commonly eliminated creed as a condition for belonging to the nation. In this universalizing process, liberty, equality, and fraternity had the same meaning on both sides of the Atlantic.

Since test oaths had not singled out Jews, several Anti-Federalist pamphleteers did not specifically mention Jews in criticizing the absence of a religious test for holding office. "Uniformity . . . in religion" was a civic virtue for Boston Brahmin and Harvard Professor James Winthrop.[19] Luther Martin, a Maryland lawyer and delegate to the Federal Constitutional Convention, brooded "that in a Christian country it would be at *least decent* to hold out some distinction between the professors of Christianity and downright infidelity and paganism" (italics in original).[20] Those who would privilege Christianity in the Constitution argued, as in the ratifying conventions, that Christian, or sometimes more narrowly,

Protestant, belief promoted civic order and virtue and prevented infidels from taking power.[21]

As was the custom, pamphleteers seldom singled out Jews among enclaves they sought to exclude. "Cato" and "A Bostonian" grumbled that federal officials could be "Pagans, Mahometans, or Jews," or even blacks or convicts.[22] "Curtiopolis" had a similar litany of undesirables, but departed from the usual Anti-Federalist criticism by specifically stigmatizing Jews. The Constitution "gives the command of the whole militia to the President—should he hereafter be a Jew our dear posterity may be ordered to rebuild Jerusalem."[23]

The few who perceived excessive religious latitude in the Constitution were barely visible compared to the many who feared an insufficient support of freedom. New York, Massachusetts, Virginia, and several other states ratified the Constitution with recommendations for further protection of individual rights, among them liberty of conscience. Accordingly, Congress passed the Bill of Rights in 1789 and the states ratified these amendments in 1791. "Congress shall make no law respecting an establishment of religion, or prohibiting the free exercise thereof," stated the First Amendment. As with remarks on religious issues in the U.S. Constitutional and state ratifying conventions, the congressional discussion was brief and dispassionate.[24]

Jews became full citizens of the United States at the time of its creation; for them political equality was absolute and immediate. This outcome was not replicated in the states. Nor did attainment of civic equality in the states resemble the abruptly uniform emancipation in revolutionary France. In the states political rights were gradually acquired after colonial charters were replaced by state constitutions.

When the colonies became independent, they usually affirmed freedom of worship, yet saw no contradiction between liberty of conscience and public support of religion. The Massachusetts Constitution of 1780 exemplified this discrepancy. Asserted in Article II of the "Declaration of Rights" is that "no subject shall be hurt, molested, or restrained, in his person, liberty, or estate for worshipping GOD in the manner and season most agreeable to the dictates of his own conscience; or his religious professions." In Article III, however, "the happiness of a people, and the good order and preservation of civil government essentially depend upon piety, religion, and morality," which "cannot be generally diffused through a community but by the institution of the public worship of GOD, and of public instruction in piety, religion and morality." The Constitution provided that the "legislature" may "authorize and require" towns and parishes to pay "for the Institution of the public worship of GOD, and for the support and maintenance of public Protestant teachers of piety, religion, and morality."[25]

Rhode Island, New Jersey, Pennsylvania, and Delaware never had an established church in the provincial era and during the Revolution, New York, Virginia, and North Carolina terminated public taxes for sectarian purposes. Although half of the states still provided for public funds for religion, the trend was clear. Those states that continued to support Christianity broadened the scope of their establishments. In colonial days, they officially recognized one or several sects; now they (Maryland, 1776; Georgia, 1777; South Carolina, 1778; Massachusetts, 1780) had multiple establishments that usually included all Protestant faiths and, in Maryland, Catholicism, too. New Hampshire (1784) had a multiple Protestant establishment before and after the Revolution and Vermont (1777), the fourteenth state, also had a general religious establishment. Multiple establishments reflected and promoted the increased diversity in American religion, from which disestablishment ensued. They derived from an indigenous pluralism that resulted in polycentered power structures in many sectors of American life. Before the new nation was formed, its religious structure already differed from that of Europe, where single establishments prevailed.

Disestablishment was completed in South Carolina (1790) and Georgia (1798) after the Northwest Ordinance (1787), the Constitution, and the Bill of Rights affirmed freedom of conscience. Other states (Vermont, 1807; Connecticut, 1818; New Hampshire, 1819; and Massachusetts, 1833) belatedly disestablished religion. No states formed after the United States became a nation provided for funding any creed.[26]

The other state constitutional impingement on equality for Jews was swearing to belief in Christianity in order to hold government posts. Just as many states saw no contradiction in pronouncing freedom of religion while permitting or mandating assessments for sectarian worship, so they saw no inconsistency in declaring liberty of conscience while denying Jews the right to hold office. Either not all civic rights were considered equal or religious equality was not considered a civic right. In the first case, the priority would be to maintain the historical Western tie between the state and Christianity. Membership in the body of Christ was vital to the spiritual and social health of the commonwealth, and therefore a necessary condition of membership in the body politic. While Article VI of the U.S. Constitution prohibited such oaths for federal service, many states required them for their own government. This was true even for those with no religious establishments, as in the Pennsylvania, Delaware, and North Carolina Constitutions of 1776.[27]

The influence of The Virginia Act for Religious Freedom, the Federal Constitution, the Northwest Ordinance, and the Bill of Rights helped ensure that new states did not require Christian oaths and that most of the older states divested themselves of these tests. Within a decade of the

Revolution, Delaware, Pennsylvania, South Carolina, and Vermont rescinded their abjurations, and Georgia did so in 1798. New York and
New Jersey never required religious tests. Connecticut (1818), Massachusetts (1821), Maryland (1825), North Carolina (1868), and New Hampshire (1876) subsequently discarded test oaths.

The "us against them" justification for religious qualification for
holding state posts reiterated the argument of proponents of a federal test
oath. "Deists," "Turks," "Papists," and "Mahometans" were castigated
more often than Jews. The latter were seldom mentioned and then usually
along with other "enemies of Christ."[28] Massachusetts Baptist leader
Isaac Backus hurled a rare shaft aimed at the Jews alone. Long a critic of
Judaism, he applauded the state constitutional provision that kept Jews
from becoming commonwealth officials.[29] A particularized notion of community evoked objection to complete absorption of Jews into the body
politic. For the Massachusetts town of Colrain, even unrestricted admission of Christians was unacceptable: "[W]e move for Amendment [of the
state constitution]," of the oath restricting state office to Christians, "that
the word Protestant be substituted in place of Christian. Reason—we are
a Protestant people."[30]

The Christian commonwealth argument for excluding Jews, of
course, surfaced in debates over civic rights conducted in other countries.
Abbé Maury, it will be recalled, raised this objection in the 1789 National
Assembly discussion of Jewish citizenship. Several generations after this
issue was settled in the American Constitution, during the 1830s–1860s
opponents of emancipating Jews in England employed the Christian state
rationale.[31]

The discrepancy between separation of church and state in the federal
government and favoring Christianity in most early state governments
was partly due to advocates of federal noninterference in matters of
conscience sometimes acclaiming state restraints on religious liberty.
What Backus lauded in the Massachusetts Constitution, he excoriated at
the state convention ratifying the U.S. Constitution. He now argued that
"the imposing of religious tests hath been the great engine of tyranny in
the world."[32]

Supporters of unconditional federal citizenship and religious qualifications for entering state government saw no incompatibility in these
stances. Controls regarded as aggrandizement of national power were
appropriate for state or local governance. This inconsistent attachment
to freedom of conscience did not necessarily entail desertion of religious
liberty. Unlike French centralism, sovereignty divided between state and
federal governments was yet another aspect of an American pluralism
that fostered multiple attachments and tolerance of variant institutions
and beliefs.

Deviation between federal and state emancipations seemingly contradicts the assertion that Jews became full citizens of the United States at its creation. This paradox is resolved by distinguishing between state and national citizenship. As citizens of the nation, Jews were equal to Gentiles even when, as citizens of particular states, they might not yet have received equal rights. Two reasons justify prioritizing the nation over the states. This study focuses on the Jews and the formation of the nation and, therefore, on their capacity as citizens of the United States rather than of a particular state. Secondly, in most states, as well as in the nation, momentum rapidly mobilized on behalf of civic parity for Jews. Indeed, equality of Jews on the national level accelerated a similar trend in the states.

Contrary to the cases of France and the Soviet Union, Jewish emancipation in America took place without a revolution. State constitutions and legislation during the War for Independence did not significantly alter the status of Jews. The gradualism of 1775 compared to the sudden liberations of 1791 and 1917–18 was, of course, not confined to the Jewish issue. The French and Russian upheavals, in contrast to the relatively moderate American rebellion, radically transformed much more than the position of Jews. Thus the history of Jews in the American and French Revolutions verifies the Tocqueville-Hartz minimization of the impact of the earlier uprising and Tocqueville's emphasis on the centrality of the later insurrection.

De jure civic equality for American Jewry was incremental and prolonged.[33] In this, as in many respects, America resembled its parent, Great Britain. Jewish equality in Britain was also gradual, though it started earlier and was completed later than in the United States. Jews in these countries shared historical developments that differentiated them from European Jewry: They lived in nations with greater denominational variety and pluralism. Catholics for long stretches of time were deemed the most dangerous religious enemy. British and American Protestantism was more philosemitic than French Catholicism, German Lutheranism, or the Russian Orthodox church. Neither America nor Great Britain (since the Jews returned in the seventeenth century) had enforced ghettoes and semi-independent, legally recognized communities, trade restrictions, special tolls and taxes on Jews, anti-Semitic movements, or political parties. Finally, American and British Jews entered their respective national cultures earlier than did Jews on the Continent, with the possible exception of the Jews of Holland. Equally, if not more important, was the broader national context. The United States and the United Kingdom historically have weaker *völkisch* urges and political tribulations than the other Western countries. Comparatively free of foreign invasions and conquests, insurrections, constitutional crises, and governmental turnovers, their stability is mutually related to a sturdier national identity.[34]

In France and Russia, de jure emancipation was an abrupt transmutation of Jews from the status of despised and oppressed outsiders, a nation within a nation, to legally undifferentiated citizens. Jews in these countries were liberated before they were acculturated. In the United States, and to a lesser extent in England, however, acculturation, at least of those residing there prior to Jews receiving civic rights, occurred before emancipation. The suddenness of the change in France and Russia compared to the nonrevolutionary Anglo and American cases may account for other national differences in the experience of Jews. Gradual acquisition of civic rights for Jews in the United States is a contributory factor in the failure of emancipatory efforts to evoke mob protests, as they had in France. American governments never singled out Jewish moneylenders as rapacious, cancelled debts owed to Jews, or issued anti-Jewish laws and orders to forestall violent reactions to granting civic rights to Jews. Anglo/American, unlike French/Continental, liberation proved irreversible and did not provoke demands for total absorption in the state.[35] These dissimilarities reaffirm the Tocqueville-Hartz perspective on both the American and French Revolutions and the suitability of the treatment of Jews as an indicator of national culture.

A sequential review clearly differentiates the course of American and European Jewry. European societies had ascriptively stratified along corporate and feudal demarcations. Jews formed one of these particularistic entities. Separateness of birth, rank, and function, in their case, was reinforced by separateness of religious belief. Thus the conviction of the Jews that they were special ("The Chosen People") corresponded to their host communities' assumption that Jews were different, that this difference was degenerate and dangerous, and, therefore, that Jews should be isolated. Avowed by themselves and by Gentiles, the uniqueness of the Jews symbiotically intensified Jewish aloofness. This mutual agreement, however, turned dichotic when the distinctiveness of Jews was evaluated. For them, it was a sign of divine approval; for most Christians it was a mark of Cain.

The French Revolution sought to replace traditional modes of organizing society and alter the perception and reality of the separateness of the Jews by creating a nation founded on liberty, equality, fraternity, rationality, and secularism. This transformation inevitably imposed a radical change in the civil status of Jews. America had a different trajectory. The United States had no medieval past, experienced no religious wars, and realized organically, gradually, and tranquilly many of the objectives that caused fiery eruptions in France and elsewhere in Europe. Consequently, the War for Independence inflicted few of the convulsive disruptions on the Jews or their host society that transpired in the French Revolution. If American Jews escaped the initial trauma of modernism,

however, they did not avoid subsequent anxieties arising from confrontation between their received identity and contemporary intrusions upon
their old culture.[36]

National variations on the nexus of revolution, state formation, and
emancipation are not limited to two models: Anglo/American (evolution-
ary) and French/Russian (revolutionary). The French/Russian model,
however, does not hold together wth respect to another variant of emancipation. While the revolutions of 1775 and 1789 helped usher in their
respective nation states, that of 1917 occurred after Russia had become
a nation. Viewing recent ethnic and nationality clashes in the old Soviet
Union, it might be contended that its revolution inhibited the development of Russian nationalism. In France, revolution and nation formation
formidably contributed to emancipating Jews. In the United States, the
sequence of upheaval and integration was not a crucial factor in liberating
Jews. In Russia, revolution, though not in conjunction with the emergence
of the nation, freed the Jews. Yet another modulation transpired in Germany. Here Jews became citizens in 1871, at the coming together of the
nation, unaccompanied by revolution.

The precedence of adaptation prior to conferral of civic rights may
have facilitated acceptance of Jews in the United States and the United
Kingdom as compared to Russia and France, but this argument does not
apply in Germany. Here, too, many Jews substantially assimilated before
their people became citizens. Nevertheless, the fate of the Jews was even
more horrific than in France and the Soviet Union.

Neither revolution nor the formation of the United States changed
radically the life of American Jews. In colonial times, they often voted
in elections and sometimes held public posts. Taxation for established
Protestant sects did not interfere with their own freedom of worship. Unlike European coreligionists, American Jews were never legally excluded
from commercial and artisanal activity, nor from landholding or military
service, rarely restricted in public worship, and, except in some early settlements, never residentially excluded or confined. Creation of the new
nation did not necessitate the dismantling of official Jewish community
organizations that dated from the Middle Ages. Nor did Jews, as in Europe, have a unifying, distinct foreign language and a coherent, communal
rabbinical authority.[37] Immediately in federal governance and within a
generation of independence in most states, American Jews acquired the
same rights as other citizens.

Although Jews were gratified as the states removed constraints upon their
participation in political affairs and released them from financial obligation to Christian creeds, this final freedom was peripheral compared to
Soviet and French emancipations. In the provincial, as well as in the revo-

lutionary and early national, period, American Jews lived amongst Gentiles, wore no distinctive dress, frequently ignored dietary and other ritual restrictions and attempts at communal control, and intermarried at a rate that alarmed more dedicated followers of Jehovah.[38] Moreover, unlike other countries, Jews were equal citizens at the founding of the nation. Thus it was difficult to look upon them as an alien element against which the United States had to mobilize. Correspondingly, American Jews, as opposed to their European counterparts, did not feel that they had to assume a defensive aloofness for protection against assault from the dominant society.

Assimilationist urges stemmed not only from relatively (to Europe) minimal exclusionist tendencies in a country where Jews had never been traditionally demonized and that, from the start, had been pluralistic in ethnicity, creed, and politics. Jews also sought integration because of their small number and lack of religious organization. Estimates vary, but commonly amount to a fraction of the Jewish populations in England and the major European countries. At the time of the Revolution, between 500 and 3,000 Jews lived in America; during the 1790s, between 1,300–3,000; and during 1800–1812, between 1,600–4,500. The best estimates are that in 1776, 1790, and 1820, under 1,000, 1,500, and 2,750 Jews, respectively, resided in the United States. During these decades Jews composed .03–.04 percent of the total population.[39]

These residents encountered no Jewish communal libraries, no press, and no bookstores for Jewish publications. In fact, colonial Jews, unlike Massachusetts Puritans and Pilgrims, Connecticut Congregationalists, Pennsylvania Quakers, and Maryland Catholics, did not usually come here for religious purposes nor seek to establish a creedal community. Jewish settlers were mostly single young men, and thus the least tied to tradition, age, family, and community, the conventional fortifications of Judaism and most other religions. Institutional weakness combined with demography to deter communal integration. The first native-born hazzan, Gershom Seixas, was appointed to that post in 1768 at Congregation Shearith Israel. Since an ordained rabbi did not serve an American congregation until the 1840s, the hazzan was the spiritual leader. Other elements necessary for creedal and communal coherence also appeared belatedly: Unlike French Jewry, educated mostly in hederim, American Jews almost invariably sent their children to non-Jewish schools. As both cause and consequence, no hederim existed in colonial times, and, before the late nineteenth century, Jewish day schools would be few in number and weak in instruction. Again unlike French Jewry, synagogue attendance was infrequent; after 1800, most American urban Jews did not affiliate with a congregation. (In this respect, America's Jews resembled their Christian compatriots. In 1800, less than 7 percent of the latter belonged to a denomination.) Not until 1814 was a Hebrew Bible printed here and not until 1823 was a Jewish journal published in the United States. Until well into the ninteenth century, American Jews lacked the means to become learned in Jewish law, theology, and the Hebrew language and to employ these resources to strengthen their Jewish communities.[40]

Despite the centrifugal and assimilationist momentum in the New World, American and French Jewry had much in common. Both communities were orthodox in worship and had a similar congregational structure with rich businessmen predominating as leaders. French and American congregations alike assumed responsibility (the latter far less successfully) for educating their young, supporting their poor, and communal discipline, especially with respect to order, observance, and marriage. Those who did not pay dues, keep kosher, observe the Sabbath and other holidays, and wed Jews were, depending on the gravity of the offense, warned, fined, and evicted from the congregation. Emulating its European and West Indian counterparts, Shearith Israel's 1805 bylaws required of every Jew living in the area an annual donation. The apparent orthodoxy and order in American Jewish communities so impressed "a Protestant" (probably a clergyman) that he admonished Christians in Philadelphia to sanctify Good Friday with the same dedication that the city's Jews commemorated Passover.[41]

Resemblance between Jewish communities in France and the United States included the Sephardic-Ashkenazi conflict. With comments that could easily have been voiced in France, this rift drew attention from Protestant clergymen in newly settled Georgia in the 1730s. A Church of England priest reported that "Portuguese" Jews were ritually "lax" while "German" Jews were "strict observers of their law." A Lutheran pastor noted the same discrepancy in obedience to Mosaic Law and claimed that "some Jews in Savannah complained to me the other day that the Spanish and Portuguese Jews persecute the German Jews. . . . They want to build a Synagogue, but the Spanish and German Jews cannot come to terms." Conflict between these groups reopened between the 1780s and the early 1800s, compounded by divisions between native-born American Jews and German-Jewish newcomers.[42]

Notwithstanding certain convergences, French and American Jewry significantly differed, reflecting variances in their respective national cultures. Upon close examination some of the similarities prove partial and shallow. If Sephardim and Ashkenazim in Georgia quarreled like their French equivalents, harmony reigned in the larger and more important Jewish community in New York. In Shearith Israel, both groups worshipped together, jointly administered the congregation, and intermarried.[43]

Following their European origins, American congregations sought to function like old world kehillot. But maintaining communal order and cohesion was more tentative in the United States, where congregations were not corporations vested by civil law and government with disciplinary and other powers. They were another religious voluntary association, whose leverage derived from the desire of members to belong. Since Jews in America moved more comfortably in the larger society and did not live and work in ghettoes officially administered by kehillot, they depended upon the organized Jewish community neither for survival nor as a buffer/intermediary between them and the host society. They could, for example, obtain schooling and charity from their local government, whose services were available via inhabitation not belief.[44] Thus Shearith Israel tithed all Jews in the vicinity, but could only collect from those willing to pay. Refusers and remitters alike had alternative associations and other identities, which they could assume without the grievous consequences these transitions triggered in Europe. This type of autonomy was recognized in the 1789 Constitution of Beth Shalome (Richmond, Virginia), which acknowledged that membership was voluntary. Choice also surfaced within the Jewish community when more than one synagogue opened. Philadelphia started this trend in 1795 when a second congregation appeared.[45]

Structural and cultural factors, less frequent or formidable in France, debilitated American Jewry. Demographic and institutional developments prompted acculturation and structural assimilation in its most extreme form of intermarriage and conversion. These adaptations were further encouraged by pluralism in the host society and an ignorance of Judaic law, language, and ritual in the Jewish community.

Dependence upon West Indian, British, and Dutch congregations for financial support and theological and ritual guidance reflected weaknesses in American Jewry. When the colonies were an outpost of Europe, such need was unexceptional; Catholics and Anglicans looked to Rome and London, respectively. Jewish settlements beseeched larger, richer, and older coreligionist communities for assistance in building synagogues or solving conflicts over observance of law and rite and for candidates for positions of hazzan and *shochet* (ritual slaughter).[46] This reliance persisted into the early republic. When a member of Congregation Mikveh Israel in Philadelphia in 1793 wished to wed a Christian woman who would adopt Judaism, the *parnass* (president) of the congregation consulted the ecclesiastical court of the Spanish-Portuguese synagogue in London. As late as 1818, Shearith Israel received aid from the Curaço congregation to rebuild its synagogue.[47]

Mikveh Israel's appeal in 1785 to Rabbi Saul Lowenstamm of Amsterdam over a marriage—between the daughter of a *Cohain* (the descendant of high priests of ancient Israel) and a Gentile that had been solemnized as Jewish—displays an apprehension of communal endangerment through American individualism and an awareness of the limits of resources that bolstered cohesion in the Old World. The "matter touches the roots of our faith, particularly in this country where each acts according to his own desire," the petitioners told the Dutch rabbi. "Gentile women, some even who are Cohanim" are "completely irreligious people who profane the name of God publicly. . . . The congregation has no power to discipline or punish anyone, except for the minor punishment of excluding them from the privileges of the synagogue." But "these evil people pay no heed and come to the synagogue, since it is impossible to restrain them from so doing because of the usage of the land."[48]

Erosion of old ways was also marked by widespread use of English at a time when Hebrew and Yiddish reigned in the majority of the Jewish communities in France. In 1736 and 1745, respectively, the minutes and accounts of Shearith Israel began to be kept in English. By 1755, the congregational school taught English, as well as Hebrew and Spanish. The first English translation of a Hebrew prayer book was published in 1761 not in London, the publishing center of the empire, but in New York, where lack of fluency in Hebrew made it necessary. Its translator was Isaac Pinto, a learned layman from a prominent New York Sephardic family. Five years later he published another prayer book, in which he explained that insofar as Hebrew was "imperfectly understood by many, by some, not at all; it has been necessary to translate our Prayers in the Language of the Country wherein it hath pleased the divine Providence to appoint our Lot." One of those with an imperfect knowledge of Hebrew, and of Judaic law as well, was Seixas, the next hazzan of the congregation. According to the Constitution of 1805, prayers in Shearith Israel would be in the sacred language, but services would be conducted in English.[49]

Pinto, Seixas, and Shearith Israel would acculturate, but not assimilate; they would change the language, but keep the liturgy. Pinto nevertheless appreciated the "Veneration for . . . our divine service in Hebrew:" The Biblical tongue was "*sacred* by being that in which it pleased Almighty God to reveal himself to our Ancestors," and his fellow worshippers "desire[d] to preserve it, in firm Persuasion that it will be again be re-established in Israel" (italics in original). Pinto adhered to the messianic dream of a regenerated faith and return to the Holy Land. What "induced me to Attempt a Translation in English" was the "hope that it will tend to the Improvement of many of my Brethren in their Devotion. . . ."[50]

In architecture, as in language, Anglo culture made inroads. The initial American synagogue constructed for that purpose was built in 1730 by Shearith Israel in the mode of Sephardic houses of worship in London and Amsterdam. A generation later, in 1763, a gentile architect designed for the Newport, Rhode Island, congregation a synagogue in the neoclassical Palladian style, then fashionable in London and the colonies. Another generation, another place, and yet another type of architecture produced the Charleston, South Carolina, synagogue (1794), which looked from the outside like a Georgian church. The cornerstone dedication in 1792 emulated a Masonic rite.[51]

As synagogue architecture and the tongue of worship began to conform to Anglo-American culture, more fundamental traditions were forsaken and community solidarity dissipated. "The Parnasim & Elders" of Shearith Israel, "having received undoubted Testimony" in 1757 "that severall of our Bretheren, that reside in the Country [areas outside of the city] have and do dayly violate the principles of our holy religion, such as Trading on the Sabath [sic], Eating of forbidden Meats & other Henious [sic] Crimes," declared a graduated series of punishments. Transgressors initially would be cautioned; banishment from the congregation awaited habitual violators. Dismissal meant that they received none of its services, including burial in the synagogue cemetery. Apparently, backsliding was not reversed; the 1790 bylaws contained a similar warning. Nor was this exclusively a New York problem. The 1791 Code of Laws of Congregation Mickva Israel (Savannah, Georgia) included an identical admonishment.[52]

Problems that Shearith Israel had with keeping the old faith started at the top. The leader of the foremost congregation in the largest Jewish settlement in the United States had a sketchy knowledge of the Hebrew language and law and was the original personification of Judaism sanctified in the nation's civic cult a process currently culminating in the nomination of a practicing Jew, Joseph Lieberman, as the vice-presidential candidate of the Democratic Party, the first of his creed to run on a major party ticket for national office. The hazzan marched with other clergymen in the 1789 presidential inauguration procession. He preached sermons on days officially designated for thanksgiving and prayer and consulted with ministers of other faiths to plan such events. Thus he forged ties between Jewish and other religious communities, a role acknowledged by his being called "Reverend" and "minister." He even occasionally preached in St. Paul's Episcopal Chapel and served as a Columbia College regent and trustee (1784–1815). The latter was unprecedented for a Jewish clergyman and the former had not occurred since the medieval disputations.[53]

Civil Judaism in America and France bore a close resemblance. A 1783 resolution of Shearith Israel to New York Governor George Clinton sounded virtually identical to the response of the Assembly of Notables to its emperor. "[N]one has Manifested a more Zealous Attachment to the Sacred Cause of America, in the late War with Great Britain," the congregation assured the governor. "[W]e now look forward with Pleasure and the happy days we expect to enjoy under a [New York] Constitution Wisely framed to preserve the inestimable Blessing of Civilization and Religious Liberty." As the Notables told Napoleon so Shearith Israel said to Clinton: "Taught by our Divine Legislator to Obey our Rulers, and prompted by the Dictates of our own Reason, it will be the Anxious endeavour of the Members of our Congregation to render themselves worthy of these Blessings, by Discharging the Duties of Good Citizens."[54]

Civil Judaism was again on display when, alarmed at the prospect of conflict with Britain and France, President, John Adams on March 28, 1798, proclaimed a day of fasting, prayer and national humiliation. Congregations flocked to their houses of worship to listen to sermons entreating God to rescue America. One such discourse with the Deity took place at Shearith Israel's synagogue on Mill Street. New York's Jews undoubtedly listened intently and probably with some pride as their hazzan preached. Many were successful in business and their professions and among them sat a former parnass who was president and a founder of the Anti-Federalist Democratic Society. If they were pleased with themselves they also esteemed their choice as spiritual leader, a man respected by the genteel and gentile clergy, and the urban elite in general, and the recipient of appropriate honors. Seixas corresponded well to his congregation: He and they shone in their respective callings. He was of Ashkenazi and Sephardic background and his congregation was similarly integrated. Most of all, he epitomized civil Judaism in a congregation that prided itself on being citizens as well as Jews.[55]

The sermon resonated with much of what American Jewry had become. It was delivered in English and Seixas paused to explain the meaning of *tsadaka* (charity) for those in his audience "who are not learned" in "the holy language." As Eli Faber suggests, rumblings of assimilation also echoed in the rhetoric employed by the exemplar of civil Judaism. Christian metaphors of "redemption" and "repentance," of "sin" and "salvation" were incorporated into the sermon.[56] The "Discourse" preached to Shearith Israel early embodied the religious syncretism that combined Protestantism, Catholicism, and Judaism into components of the national civic cult. What began as denominational diversity, as different facets of national culture, blended over time. Reform Judaism, post-Vatican II Catholicism, and mainline Protestantism continue to converge and Tocqueville might have interpreted the growth of mutual tolerance and resemblance as an indication that American pluralism can erode into uniformity.

The leader of Shearith Israel, however, shied away from total assimilation. If the language was syncretic, the purpose was Judaic: "Such are the works necessary to be done to procure redemption and salvation, that we may arrive at that glorious epoch, when we shall be taken from among the nations, and gathered out of all countries, and brought unto our own land." Messianic reservation against absorption in the diaspora surfaced still more revealingly when Seixas contemplated the blessing of American citizenship: "It hath pleased God to have established us in this country where we possess every advantage that other citizens of these states enjoy, and which is as much as we could in reason expect in this captivity."[57]

Notwithstanding the civil Judaism of Seixas and his congregation, a more extreme example of this commitment, and one rarely expressed in France, came not from New York, but from Charleston, home of the nation's most Americanized antebellum Jewish community.[58] On October 15, 1807 Myer Moses, a scion of the Palmetto city's Jewish mercantile elite, addressed the Hebrew Orphan Society. Moses was its vice president; three years later he would become a state legislator and in 1823 commissioner of the city's public schools. The speech epitomizes the emancipatory influence on French and American Jewry. Moses started in the manner of many of his French counterparts by saluting the founding of the nation, "that benign day, when man proclaimed, and Heaven approved, this our country, free and Independent!" He then proceeded to substitute for the diaspora mentalité an American identity. "[F]rom that period must be dated that the Almighty gave to the Jews what had long been promised them, namely, a second Jerusalem!" This epiphany prompted a plea to Jehovah to "collect together thy long scattered people of Israel, and let their gathering place be in this land of milk and honey."[59] "Next year in Jerusalem," at least for Myer Moses, became this and every year in America. Loyalty to a new homeland supplanted hope of return to the Holy Land; the secular, not the sacred, now directed the Jewish mission. Israel was the beginning, but it was also the past; America, however, meant fulfillment and the future. Similar to the French maskilim, but more pervasively in American Jewry, citizenship took priority over creed, modernity over history, and diaspora patriotism over Judaic messianism.[60]

Whether the messianic transpiration took place in America or Israel, eschatological expectations were stirred by the discovery and settlement of the New World.   Starting in the early sixteenth century, European Jewish commentators discerned in that earthly revelation and dispersion a sign of messianic redemption for the Jews. As Jonathan Sarna insightfully notes, many synagogues in the West Indies and the North American mainland bore "messianic names": *Mikveh* (Hope of) Israel; *Shearith* (Remnant of) Israel; *Nidhe* (Dispersed of) Israel; and *Jeshuat* (Salvation of) Israel.   On the basis of religious calculations or natural signs, in 1768, 1769, and 1783 some Jews in North America and Europe believed that the Jewish Messiah was about to come.[61]

The aspirations of civil Judaism seemed on their way to realization. Rebecca Samuel, living in Petersburg, Virginia, in 1791, with less bombast but much the same meaning as Moses, notified her parents that "Jew and

Gentile are as one. There is no *galut* [diasporic exile and rejection] here."
She was perhaps too optimistic or localized, but Jews now had extensive
and cordial business dealings with Christians and served in state legislatures and high municipal offices. Jews enrolled at Yale and in the original
class at West Point (1802) well before they entered English and most European universities or military academies. They were among the founders
of the New York City and Georgia medical societies, masters of high-
status Masonic lodges, and members and officers of prestigious professional organizations, social clubs, and cultural societies in Richmond,
Philadelphia, Charleston, and other cities.[62] Acculturation and assimilation accelerated because of the pull of American acceptance, as well as
the push of a weak Judaic community. In fact, the mutuality of these
developments moots cause and effect analysis.

As the young republic gradually encompassed the Jewish community,
the latter modified or lapsed from ancestral ways. If revolution and nation
building in the United States did not as radically modify its Jewish community as did similar developments in Europe, they nonetheless had an
impact. Americanization of Judaic rituals and a vigorous assertion of civic
rights emerged in this era. Democratization of the synagogue reflected
national valorization of individual liberty, voluntary association, and republicanism, and further distanced American Jewry from the mode of
authority in European Jewish communities. In contrast to French Jewry,
for example, American Jewry had no central organization, grand rabbi,
or government participation in appointment of lay or religious officials
or in Jewish community functions.

During the colonial era, the parnass and other congregation officials
were chosen by an executive board; after independence they were elected
by the congregation. New bylaws and constitutions provided for a small
number of ordinary members (three in the 1790 constitution of Shearith
Israel and the 1791 Code of Laws of Mickva Israel) to call meetings of
the whole to bring up business of their choice.[63]

Representative government in the congregation reflected the republicanism fostered in 1776 and adopted in the federal constitution. "In a
state happily constituted upon the principle of equal liberty, civil and religious," announced the preliminary draft (May 30, 1790) of the Constitution of Shearith Israel. "[T]he several societies, as members of that government," the document continued in a formulation that Hartz would have
surely regarded as validating his thesis, are "free" to enter a "compact"
to preserve and administer "their several communities." This "congregation of yehudim [Jews]," therefore, in the spirit of freedom "enter[s] . . .
into an agreement and covenant" for such "purposes".[64]

Another Lockian Shearith Israel proclamation appeared in the same
year: "Whereas in free states all power originates and is derived from

the people, who always retain every right necessary for their well being individually; and, for the better ascertaining those rights with more precision and explicitly, frequently from [form?] a declaration or bill of those rights," asserted the Jewish Jeffersonians. "In like manner the individuals of every society in such a state are entitled to and retain their several rights, which ought to be preserved inviolate." Therefore, the "congregation of Shearith Israel . . . conceive it our duty to make this declaration of our rights and privileges."[65]

These same forces weakened the power of the synagogue. As in Christian denominations, sectarian pluralism and the divorce of state and church meant that persuasion replaced coercion in securing loyalty to the faith. Before the Revolution, Shearith Israel punished violators of Jewish dietary laws and the Sabbath with ejection from the congregation; after independence, these infractions drew fines or other minor penalties.[66]

Freedom of worship, Enlightenment influence, and the tolerance of the nation eroded orthodoxy as well as authority. Jacob Cohen, who defied the Talmudic ban on Cohainim marrying converted Jews, became a member of Mikveh Israel and in 1810 its president.[67] In colonial times Shearith Israel used the Hebrew calendar to date its records; in the 1770s it used Western and Hebrew dates, and by 1800 the calendar had been dropped.[68]

Although "a Protestant" attested to Judaic piety, other outsiders noticed a falling away from the customs that still solidified Jews in France and elsewhere. The Swede Peter Kalm, son of a clergyman, traveling in the colonies from 1748 to 1751, had "been told by several trustworthy men," including a New York Jew, "that many of them (especially the young Jews) when traveling, did not hesitate the least about this [pork] or any other meat that was put before them, even though they were in company with Christians." At a New York synagogue during services, Kalm noted, "Both men and women were dressed in the European fashion." A generation later, a German mercenary observed that "there are also many Jews now resident in America," who "are not distinguishable from Christians." Unlike those "in Europe," American Jews "are dressed like other citizens, get shaved regularly, and also eat pork, although that is forbidden in their Law." The "women also go about with curled hair and in French finery such as is worn by the ladies of other religions."[69]

Departures from traditional creedal and communal solidarity considerably exceeded those in the orthodoxy that prevailed in Central and Eastern European Jewry and probably even the challenged commitments in England and Western Europe. Both officially and informally, France was more discriminatory and coercive in demanding absorption than was the United States, but French Jewry persevered while many colonial Jews in America lost their Jewish identity.[70]

A revealing symptom of acculturation was anglicization of Jewish first and last names. This transition, already marked in the colonial era, considerably antedated French Jewry's adoption of French names, which did not become frequent until the 1860s.[71] Related to the fact that American Jewry was not primarily literate in Hebrew or Yiddish, while French Ashkenazim were predominantly literate in these languages but not in French, anglicization of names reflected more significant forms of assimilation, as in intermarriage.

British and American Jewry in the period here studied had moderate and high rates of intermarriage, respectively, differing in this respect from the French cohort. According to one systematic survey, of 699 North American marriages uncovered between 1790 and 1840 involving Jews, 201 wedded Gentiles. Since exogamous unions were more likely to remain anonymous, such matches were probably undercounted. The non-Jewish spouse converted to Judaism in only 12 of these 201 unions. A 28.7 percent share of mixed marriages tripled that of the most acculturated segments of French Jewry. Another historian of American Jewry estimates that the first half of the ninteenth-century intermarriage rate approximated 15 percent and that about 8 percent of the gentile spouses converted to Judaism.[72]

In 1805, between 20,000–26,000 Jews lived in England—a number approximately midway between those of France and the United States. A major reason for intermarriage in the United States, extreme scarcity of Jews, would seem to apply neither to Britain nor to France. On closer examination, however, the distribution of Jews in France was dissimilar to that in England. Most Jews in France lived in self-contained and semi-rural or small town settlements in Alsace and Lorraine. About three-quarters (15,000) of the Jews across the Channel dwelled in London, which was, like Paris, the great national metropolis and a center for Jewish assimilation. Similarly, in the Netherlands, 24,000 of Holland's 31,000 Jews in 1805 resided in Amsterdam. In 1789, 500–700 Jews were in Paris; twenty years later, 2,908 Jews dwelled there. Although comparatively few lived in the French capital, moderate-sized groups could be found in smaller cities. In 1789, Metz, in Lorraine, had a Jewish population of 3,025, more than 6 percent of the total inhabitants. By 1806, the Jewish population had shrank to 2,186. In 1808, over 1,330 Jews dwelled in Nancy, another Lorraine city and the home of Berr Isaac Berr. The southern cities of Bordeaux and Saint-Esprit-lès-Bayonne in 1808 and 1809 had, respectively, 2,131 and 1,173 Jewish residents.[73] Unlike those in France, the majority of British Jews located where they had easier access to the host culture and more incentive to assimilate. Thus, rates of intermarriage and conversion, while not as large as in Germany, were higher than in France.[74] In these respects, as well as in others promoting absorption—for example, encountering less hostility—the Anglo and American Jewish communities bore closer resemblance to each other than to France.

The Jewish population in the United States differed from its French equivalent in factors critical to communal cohesion. American Jewry was a microminority, about a fortieth of its French counterpart in 1775. Small numbers and dispersion meant minute concentrations, a circumstance that fostered assimilation. By the 1750s, the few, isolated Jewish families in Connecticut had embraced Christianity. A German mercenary in 1777 reported: "Jews and Christians intermarry without scruple." Rebecca Samuel had ambivalent feelings about these conditions. In 1791, it will be remembered that she extolled individual freedom in the new nation, closeness of Jews with Gentiles, and the absence of diaspora defensiveness and friction between the two religions: "Anyone can do what he wants. There is no rabbi in all of America to excommunicate anyone. This is a blessing here." Samuel subsequently bemoaned the new liberty and amity and the conditions in which it flourished: "Here [Petersburg] they cannot become anything else [but Gentile]. Jewishness is pushed aside here," she told her parents. "We have a shohet [ritual slaughterer] here who goes to market and buys *terefah* [nonkosher meat]. . . . We have no Torah scrolls and no *tallit* [prayer shawls] and no synagogue. We do not know what the Sabbath and the holidays are. On the Sabbath all the Jewish shops are open. . . ." She wanted to move to Charleston, which had a synagogue and was the second largest Jewish community in the United States.[75]

Jews constituted a tiny enclave even in their largest centers of settlement. Estimates of New York City's Jewish inhabitants during the 1770s range from 250–400, in the 1790s from 240–350, and in 1800–15 from 279–500. Jews in Charleston approximated 50–200 (1770s), 53–300 (1790s), and 107–800 (1800–1811). In 1790, Jews composed .73 percent of New Yorkers and 2.5 percent of Charlestonians; three decades later, the respective segments were .40 and 5 percent. Arguably, Jews formed a large enough share in Charleston to at least demographically resist the encroachment of intermarriage. But percentages can be misleading, particularly if the numbers are reduced by those matrimonially unviable due to age, health, or inclination. In 1820, Jews living there amounted to at best 200 families, many fewer than in London, Paris, Bordeaux, Metz, or smaller communities in the Southwest of France or Alsace and Lorraine.[76]

Jews could be found in small enclaves in the South of France and in Alsace and Lorraine. In 1784, the nearly 20,000 Jews in Alsace lived in 179 to 185 locations; 16 had 50 or more Jewish families and 111 had between 1 and 25 families. By 1808, some 26,000 Alsatian Jews dwelled in 203 communities. Before the Revolution, none had as many as 500 Jewish inhabitants—now 5 towns had at least that many. Although scattered in 168 communities in 1808, the nearly 11,000 Lorraine Jews were somewhat more concentrated in urban centers; 3,500 lived in Metz or Nancy.[77] Large or small, urban or rural, the demographic distribution of Jews in France encouraged cohesion. Even tiny communities were usually closer and larger in number than in America and in regions where French Jewry was concentrated. Moreover, kehillot and consistories provided an organized Jewish life for groups of tiny enclaves that individually would have been unable to offer it.

Size and location are critical factors in cohesion. If the number of Jews is tiny, as in the case of the United States in the revolutionary and early national eras, no matter where they live, marrying out will be unavoidable and they may eventually disappear. If the number of Jews is large enough to sustain self-contained communities, as in contemporary England and France, it becomes critical where Jews reside. All things being equal, large cities accelerate assimilation. It may be a historical truism, however, that all things are never equal. Accordingly, in New York City from the 1880s to the 1960s (or for between two and three generations), Jews had few exogamous unions and, relatedly, showed little inclination to other forms of structural assimilation. New York in this period, however, was a much different city than was London or Paris in 1800. From the days of New Amsterdam onward, it was an ethnic city, while the capitals of England and France through the period here under study were representative of their national culture and native stock. More importantly, in the eras we are investigating, Jews composed a minute segment of the people of Paris (581,000 in 1800–1801) and London (959,000 in 1801).[78] When Jews constituted a similarly small proportion of New York's population, many were rapidly absorbed. A century later, however, they made up a large percentage of the residents and, given that city's historic receptivity to multiculturalism, could more easily preserve their ethno-religious customs and solidarity.

The different outcomes of French and American Jewry were due to demographics, background, and national culture. French Jewry was more numerous and deeply rooted, older and more family structured, and had greater institutional and intellectual resources to protect its ethnic and religious identity. National culture was also an important factor in preservation. Intolerance conjoined with insistence on assimilation derived from negative feelings. Most French people and their government felt that Jews should divest themselves of their distasteful traits and be completely French or excluded from the national community. The ambivalence regarding integration was itself a unifying force within the Jewish community. Conversely, the mellowed tolerance of Jews in America undermined Jewish communities and beliefs because there was less to rally against. Acceptance accompanied by indifference inhibited preservationist impulses.

It early became apparent that Jewish communities in the United
States, contrasted with those across the Atlantic—and, for the purposes
of this study particularly, with French Jewry—tended to be adaptable to
the national culture, decentralized, voluntaristic in association and affiliation, and loosely organized.[79] No grand rabbis, congregations, or hierarchy of consistories controlled American Jewry and functioned as agents
of the state. In these respects, the enclave harmonized with its nation of
affiliation. America, too, differed from France and other European countries in being relatively decentralized, individualized, and in preferring
voluntary association to government intervention.

Participation in the struggle for independence and political and religious equality in the Federal Constitution and, albeit gradually, in those
of the states, made Jews feel surer of their place in America. They began to demand rights they felt due them as revolutionaries and contribu-
tors to the newly formed nation and states. In 1776, Newport merchant
Moses M. Hays was outraged that the General Assembly of the Province
of Rhode Island doubted his commitment to the Continental cause and
ordered him to sign a loyalty pledge. While proclaiming support for the
war and love for America, Hays refused the oath: "[I] am an Israelite and
am not allowed the liberty of a vote or voice in common with the rest of
the voters," he told the Assembly. "I ask of your House the rights and
privileges due other free citizens."[80]

Civic assertiveness also moved the Philadelphia Kahal in 1783 to protest to the Pennsylvania Council of Censors (an official committee of the
State charged with safeguarding the rights of the people) against the Constitution of 1776, which prescribed that members of the general assembly
acknowledge the divine inspiration of the New Testament. "[T]his religious test deprives the Jews of the most eminent rights of freemen," asserted the "memorialists." The "stigma on their religion" would discourage immigration to "Pennsylvania from abroad of those who come here
seeking equality and liberty." A test oath caused "displeasure" in the petitioners because "they perceive that for their professed dissent to a doctrine
which is inconsistent with their religious sentiments, they should be excluded from the most important and honourable part of the rights of a
free citizen."[81]

Nearly a generation later, American Jews still vigorously protested
infringements on their citizenship. Although the North Carolina Constitution (1776) required that only Protestants could serve in the state government, Jacob Henry, a Jew, was elected to the House of Commons in 1808.
His service there showed that, as in colonial times, informal arrangements
and an as yet rudimentary bureaucracy enabled Jews to defy legal and
constitutional proscriptions. Henry was reelected in 1809, but this time
his presence in the House was challenged on constitutional grounds, an

indication that although Jews might at times circumvent the law, it could also be used to limit their rights. Henry argued, as had the Philadelphia defenders of Jewish citizenship, that the state constitution guaranteed freedom of conscience in its Declaration of Rights. This "natural and unalienable right to worship Almightly God according to the dictates of their own Conscience," took precedence over the test oath clause.[82]

If not as much was promised to American Jews in 1776 and 1787 as was pledged to their French and Russian counterparts in 1791 and 1917, not as much was demanded of, or forfeited by, them as in the Republic of Virtue, Napoleon's regime, or the Soviet Union. American Jews were not designated a people apart and therefore an obstacle to a united nation, as in France, or to the world dominion of communism. Consequently, their creed was not stringently scrutinized, nor were they coerced into dejudiazation to prove themselves (not always availingly) worthy of citizenship.

America's concept of itself at the time of its founding was relaxed, flexible, and expansive; a confident nationalism open to various religious, ethnic, and nationality groups. "The United States will embosom all religious sects or denominations in Christendom," Yale College president Ezra Stiles told the governor and General Assembly of Connecticut. In this grandiose 1783 election sermon, "The United States Elevated to Glory and Honor," Reverend Stiles noted that America had many sects with none accorded "superiority as to secular powers and civil immunities." Hence, "they will cohabit together in harmony."[83]

In these years, enthusiasm was regularly expressed, agreement on the causes for such hope was widespread. "Our true situation," said Charles Pinckney at the U.S. Constitutional Convention, is "a new extensive Country containing within itself the materials for forming a Government capable of extending to its citizens all the blessing of civil & religious liberty—capable of making them happy at home."[84] "Centinel" (Samuel Bryan), whose arguments widely circulated in contemporary newspapers and as broadsides, opposed the Constitution because it lacked a declaration of religious liberty. Anti-Federalist though he was, Bryan felt that in this country "human nature may be viewed in all its glory. . . . The unfortunate and oppressed of all nations, fly to this grand asylum, where liberty is ever protected, and industry crowned with success."[85]

An assured nationalism, grounded in liberty and diversity, defined contemporary views about immigration, naturalization, and citizenship. The United States was uniquely (among Western nations) relaxed about whom and how many should come here and when and how they should become citizens. Provincial America usually emulated its mother country, but imperatives of military security, labor supply, and population growth to enhance property values and commercial ventures overrode restrictive policies for subjectship and naturalization prevalent in Britain. The colonies generally welcomed newcomers, including Jews. Although some places refused to naturalize Jews, notably Rhode Island, moving to a more liberal colony circumvented such exclusion.[86] Through naturalization, widespread voting, and occasional public service, Jews began to acquire political legitimacy. South Carolina Protestant Dissenters complained to Parliament in 1704 that "Jews, Strangers, Sailors, Servants, Negroes, and almost every Frenchman in Craven and Berkeley Counties" voted in elections.[87]

Protocitizenship gave Jews, and other colonialists, a sense of civic entitlement. During the revolutionary and early republican eras, privileges and liberties were not thankfully received governmental dispensations, but rather individual rights that inhered in the state of nature and the social contract. Economic exigencies and political arrangements resulted in a mingling of ethnic, racial, and religious enclaves to create a national society of pragmatic, pluralistic accommodation.[88] Admitting diverse groups into American society, reflected in widespread freedom of conscience and, after independence, in undemanding naturalization, encouraged assimilation. *E pluribus unum* was inscribed on The Great Seal of the United States. The enduring ideal of variety and unity subsequently appeared in linking race, religion, and original nationality with settlement here. Though frequently disparaged, Jewish-American, Irish-American, African-American, and other hyphenates, became a national type.

America's need for, and attitude toward, recent arrivals changed little after independence. The newly formed states set low barriers for citizenship, requiring, at the strictest, a few years of residence. New citizens were usually permitted to vote or run for office at the time of naturalization or several years afterward. The other conventional requirement was renunciation of foreign allegiance.[89]

Debate over citizenship in the Constitutional Convention joined the issue of whether immigrants would be a bane or boon to the prospective Republic. But the delegates did not seek to define or set general standards for naturalization or admission. They argued, instead, about the length of time the foreign-born must be citizens before serving in the Senate (nine years) and the House of Representatives (seven years). The sole outright exclusion of naturalized citizens was ineligibility for the presidency.[90]

The focus of the debate notwithstanding, opinions foreshadowed later disputes over access to the national society. Pierce Butler, Gouverneur Morris, and Elbridge Gerry, respectively representing South Carolina, Pennsylvania, and Massachusetts, worried that foreign attachments might detract from American allegiance and that foreign customs and ideas would impede adaptation to American ways. Morris even raised the issue of cosmopolitanism, a complaint more frequently heard in the ninteenth and twentieth centuries and from nationalists across the Atlantic. This future minister to France and Federalist senator from New York feared "Citizens of the world . . . in our public Councils." They were untrustworthy "men who can shake off their attachments to their own Country" and therefore "can never love any other."[91]

Spokesmen for an optimistic and inclusive vision in influence and stature overshadowed those wary about excessive embrace of newcomers. "Our Country offers to Strangers . . . a hearty welcome," rejoiced Benjamin Franklin. Immigration "multiplies a nation . . . every Man" here "becomes a Citizen, and by our Constitution" has a "share in the Government of the Country." He wanted no "illiberality inserted in the Constitution." Everywhere "the people are our friends. . . . When foreigners after looking about for some other Country in which they can obtain more happiness, give a preference to ours it is a proof of attachment which ought to excite our confidence & affection."[92]

James Madison, too, "wished to maintain the character of liberality" he found "professed in all the Constitutions & publications of America." The nation "was indebted to emigrants for her settlement & Prosperity. That part of America which had encouraged them most had advanced most rapidly in population, agriculture & the Arts." While Alexander Hamilton saw "possible danger" in the "rule" of recent citizens, he basically agreed with Franklin and Madison. The "advantage of encouraging foreigners was obvious & admitted. Persons in Europe of moderate fortunes will be fond of coming here where they will be on a level with the first Citizens."[93]

Hamilton and Madison also concurred in suggesting that Congress determine naturalization criteria.[94] The Naturalization Act of 1790 granted citizenship to foreign-born residents of two years in the United States and one year in the state from which they applied. In addition, they had to avow support for the Constitution and offer proof of good character. Alarmed at developments in the French Revolution, Congress in 1795 extended the residence requirement to five years, added a few other minor requirements and assumed exclusive control over determining citizenship. Animosity against France and concern that immigrants would likely become Republicans moved the Adams administration to secure passage of the Alien and Sedition Acts (1798), which increased the probationary period to fourteen years. When the Republicans came to power, Congress, in the last major nineteenth-century naturalization law, reinstated the general rules of 1795. After five years' residence, swearing loyalty to the nation and its republican government and demonstrating no character defect, aliens were considered capable of adopting the American way of life and fully participating in the national community, short of being its chief executive.[95]

Jefferson's First Annual Message to Congress (1801) recommended repeal of the Alien Act because of America's historical acceptance of newcomers and the contribution of immigrants to national prosperity. Tradition and practicality, however, were not the only reasons to accelerate naturalization. "Shall oppressed humanity find no asylum on this subject," asked the President? "[M]ight not the general character and capabilities of a citizen be safely communicated to everyone manifesting a bona fide purpose of embarking his life and fortunes?"[96]

Hamilton spoke for the Federalist opposition to Republican repeal of the Alien Act. He seemed on the surface decidedly less welcoming to newcomers than in the debates over ratification of the Constitution. The "safety of a republic" depended on "a common national sentiment; on the exemption of the citizens from foreign bias and prejudice; and on that love of country which will almost invariably be found to be closely connected with birth, education, and family." The "influx of foreigners," therefore, "produce[s] a heterogeneous compound; to change and corrupt the national spirit."[97]

Jefferson and Hamilton, Democratic-Republican and Federalist, respectively, expressed different types of nationalism. For Jefferson, America was a refuge for the beleaguered, a nation eager to accord new settlers equal rights and an open society to which they would readily commit and in which they would be quickly absorbed. Hamilton invoked a European genre of Romantic homogeneous nationalism centered in birth and blood. Since immigrants could not immediately meet these standards, naturalization should culminate a prolonged process of acculturation. Yet even a dedicated Federalist and ascriptive nationalist like Hamilton did not repudiate his previous support of immigration. The country had "a boundless waste to people" and he believed that newcomers could be gradually Americanized through education. While preferring the standard of the Alien Act, he would settle for a "residence of not less than five years."[98]

Welcoming newcomers, evinced by undemanding standards of acquiring citizenship, derived from pluralistic impulses in the young nation and its founding fathers. Franklin "respected" all religions and opposed the test oath in the Pennsylvania Constitution.[99] Jefferson authored the Virginia Bill for Establishing Religious Freedom, an achievement he wanted inscribed on his tombstone, and Madison maneuvered it through the legislature. Less outspoken or consistent a defender of religious freedom, Hamilton nonetheless drafted an act to establish a state university in New York providing that "no president or professor shall be ineligible for or by reason of any religious tenet or tenets that he may or shall profess; or be compelled by any law or others, to take any test oath whatsoever." The charter he wrote for Columbia College when it replaced King's College forbade a religious test or any other creedal exclusion of its president.[100]

Attachment to liberty and diversity evoked an amiability toward Jews virtually nonexistent in European political leaders. "Among the features peculiar to the Political system of the U. States," that most impressed Madison, "is the perfect equality of rights which it secures to every religious Sect. And it is particularly pleasing to observe the good citizenship of such as have been most distrusted and oppressed elsewhere." The "best guarantee of loyalty & love of country; . . . & good will among Citizens of every religious denomination" is "equal laws protecting equal rights." A "mutual respect" among adherents of different faiths is "necessary to social harmony and most favorable to the advancement of truth." Madison specifically brought Jews "fully within the scope of these observations."[101]

Jefferson also emphasized the benefits of religious liberty and comity. The "sufferings" of the Jews "furnished a remarkable proof of the universal spirit of religious intolerance inherent in every sect." American "laws have applied the only antidote to this vice, protecting our religious, as they do our civic rights, by putting all on an equal footing." He regretted the "prejudice still scowling" upon Jews, but prescribed "the moral basis, on which all our religions rest, as the rallying point which unites them in a common interest."[102]

Among America's first four presidents, Federalists and Republicans alike, founding heroes of the Republic, included Jews in avowals of religious freedom and equality. John Adams declared that as the original monotheists, Jews were "the most essential instrument for civilizing the nations." Individually, Jews had "liberal minds, as much honor, probity, generosity and good breeding as any I have known in any sect of religion or philosophy." Collectively, they should "be admitted to all the privileges of citizens in every country of the world. This country has done much. I wish it may do more; and annul every narrow idea in religion, government and commerce."[103]

The substance and timing of his actions and his fame as *the* founding father made George Washington a paladin of creedal pluralism and the legitimacy of American Jewry. Before various sectarian assemblies, he denounced "spiritual tyranny," proclaimed religious liberty and the moral and civic equality of all religious beliefs, and celebrated America for its dedication to freedom of conscience.[104]

Replying to encomiums from synagogues in Philadelphia, New York, Charleston, Richmond, Savannah, and Newport, Washington lauded freedom of worship and expressed respect for Jews. These communications particularly reinforced the principles he pledged because they were publicly voiced while he was president and praised contemporary Jews instead of Old Testament Israelites. "[H]appily the government of the United States, which gives to bigotry no sanction, to persecution no assistance, requires only that they who live under its protection should demean themselves as good citizens," responded Washington to the head of the Newport congregation, who had thanked him for visiting the temple. Americans "possess alike liberty of conscience and immunities of citizenship." Washington conjoined what in France, Russia, and other nations were confrontations between loyalty to Judaism (and sometimes to Christianity) and loyalty to country. In his America, Judaism and patriotism were not contradictory. Believing that creedal communities could harmonize with the national community, the president asserted that "toleration" is no longer "spoken of as if it were the indulgence of one class of people that another enjoyed the exercise of their inherent natural rights." In propounding this higher standard of religious liberty, Washington linked interfaith equality with respect for Jews. "May the stock of Abraham who dwell in this land," he told the Newport congregation, "continue to merit and enjoy the good will of the other inhabitants."[105]

Even more than his rhetoric, Washington's behavior enhanced esteem for Judaism. The president's visit to a synagogue was the latest in a series of gestures that conferred recognition on American Jews, or at least implied good feelings toward Judaic traditions. When the Continental Congress in 1776 considered designs for the nation's seal, Franklin proposed a representation of Moses dividing the Red Sea while the Pharaoh's army drowned in its waters, and Jefferson suggested a portrayal of the Israelites in the wilderness following a cloud by day and a pillar of fire by night.[106] Pentateuch symbolism did not become a civic emblem, but the infant republic, inventing its own past, sought roots in scriptural Israel. More pointed legitimizations occurred at the aforementioned Philadelphia parade and the first presidential inauguration. Instead of seeking to iconize biblical Hebrews, these civic fetes featured rabbis marching with other clergymen and contemporary American Jews in official capacities.

Thus started the admission of Judaism into the civic religion, an interfaith parity symbolized by the obligatory blessing of every national celebration or political convention by a rabbi, a priest, and a minister. Pluralistic and voluntaristic, it is the sacral version of multicultural unity. Private worship might be overwhelmingly Christian and sectarian, but the public God is nondenominational, a division parallel to that of Church and state. A creedless, promiscuous monotheism not militantly anticlerical or anti-Semitic, unlike the secular zealotry of the French and Soviet revolutions, the American faith does not crusade against private religious beliefs and institutions.

The early tendency toward civic parity of Judaism with other religions, in contrast with the more problematic public treatment of Judaism in France, manifested itself in 1811 when New York Mayor DeWitt Clinton drew up and sent to the state legislature a memorial for a charity school run by Congregation Shearith Israel. The legislature granted the

Polonies Talmud Torah the privileges it had conferred upon Catholic and Protestant parochial institutions, and the city council made payments retroactive to the school's beginning.[107] Another twenty-two years passed before France accorded Jewish schools state funding equal to those of other religions and many municipalities ignored this law.

Above all Western countries, the United States advanced Jewry's struggle for freedom. Colonial legacies, which facilitated assumption of full citizenship and differentiated America from France and the rest of Europe, continued after independence. America was the first nation that did not have a medieval past that had demonized, segregated, banished, and massacred Jews. In addition, early modern denominational conflicts that tore Europe apart echoed but faintly here.

If emancipation was most complete in America, the transition—through revolution and formation of the modern state, from alienation and oppression to civic rights and integration—was greater in France. Although America went further in giving its Jews equality, France had further to go to admit its Jews to citizenship. Consider where the Jews of these nations stood in comparative political, legal, social, and economic status in 1775, 1787, 1789, and 1791, and contrast the benign indifference of America and its governments to religion in general, and Judaism and Christianity in particular, and the passionate animosity of much of revolutionary France and its governments in these matters. Such reflections yield the conclusion that the outcome for the Jews was more egalitarian in the United States, but that the magnitude and expedition in acquiring civic rights was more impressive in France.

Revolutionary America and France had different consequences for each country's treatment of its Jews, yet these national upheavals also considerably converged. Neither country in its prerevolutionary or revolutionary ages fixated upon the Jews as its foremost religious foe. Bourbon France recruited Protestantism, and the Revolution of 1789 selected Catholicism, for this role. Another concurrence between the Revolutions was that, in important respects, they were conceived by the Enlightenment and reverenced free expression, individual judgment, and the primacy of reason over faith. Such idealism, unfortunately more de jure than de facto in France, led to formal, if not full, emancipation of Jews. These Republics had the aspiration of new nations to reform and, like early Soviet Russia, sought to implement utopian compulsions by liberating Jews.

As Enlightenment effluvia, the courses of the American and French insurgencies ran together in yet another way. The role of the philosophes in the French and American Revolutions and their republican offspring is well known. Rush, Franklin, Adams, Jefferson, Washington, and other statesmen and religious liberals were in varying degrees rational empiricists, Deists, or religious skeptics.[108] They, again in varying degrees, valorized Enlightenment tenets of individualism and universalism that fostered freedom of conscience. But the limitations of Enlightenment values in securing political equality for American Jews deserves elaboration. Along with French counterparts like Voltaire, Denis Diderot, and Baron d'Holbach, American rationalists and defenders of natural rights sometimes disdained Jews.[109] Rush "anticipated . . . when this once-beloved race of men shall again be restored to divine favor through reunion with Christians" in a "universal savior." Christian triumphalism overpowered deistic inclinations. Contrasting Christ's grace with "Jewish infidelity," Rush "condemned the Jews" for denying "a spiritual kingdom in the Millennium."[110]

Jefferson, America's stellar Deist and fighter for freedom of conscience, sometimes resembled a relentless and pessimistic French regenerator: Judaic theology was "degrading & injurious;" Judaic "ethics" often contradicted "reason & morality" and were "repulsive & anti-social, as respecting other nations." In public a paragon of creedal comity, in private the Sage of Monticello told Lafayette, the "dispersed Jews still form . . . one nation, foreign to the land they live in."[111]

Closely associated with Enlightenment values in promoting sectarian diversity, liberty, and comparative (to Europe) absence of anti-Semitism was widespread religious indifference in the revolutionary and early national periods. Seventeenth-century New England considered salvation essential to preserving the soul and the state, but in late colonial and early republican times, national and individual well-being were perceived as primarily secular matters. Even in New England, by that time, a small minority belonged to a church and doubts about Christianity were often voiced, sometimes in tones of ridicule. Requests for prayers and sermons went unheeded at the U.S. Constitutional Convention and God went unmentioned in the Constitution. Religion was referred to but twice: in Article VI, barring "religious" tests for federal offices; and then again when the Bill of Rights prohibited "an establishment of religion." A congressional chaplain in the Washington and Adams administrations attributed to freethinking the usual absence of two-thirds of the congressmen at prayer meetings. But provincial America, with a few exceptions like seventeenth-century New England, was just as much of a spiritual desert and yet established churches and civic anti-Catholicism and anti-Judaism were routine.[112] As the new century dawned, an evangelical impulse reawakened, people flocked to the churches, and Deism faded.[113] But the religious revival did not halt the momentum for liberty of conscience and equality for Jews.

In establishing themselves here Jews confronted a unique and interrelated promise and challenge. Unprecedentedly incorporated into national society, they experienced unsurpassed (for them) acceptance of their faith as a private belief and constituent in the civic religion. Secularization and individualism helped the Jews gain civic equality, but presented adversity as well. The former undermined Christianity and Judaism alike and the latter fragmented Jewry as it did other traditional communities. National consciousness might not be as ancestral or committed to Christianity as it had been in the Old World, but Anglo-American ethnicity and Protestantism held priority over heritages and creeds of other citizens. Old preferences and bigotries still had the potential to marginalize America's Jews and new liberties might lure them into terminal absorption or disruptive individualism.

PART III

CONCLUSION

CHAPTER 6

THE ARGUMENT

The record of the Jews and the nation from 1775 to 1815 reveals the secure possession of civic rights in the United States, and formal liberation within an uneasy and unequal political situation in France. These dissimilar outcomes bear out the Tocqueville-Hartz theory of American democracy. Validation in one respect, however, is insufficient corroboration; therefore, I now revisit the objections raised in chapter 1 to assess the more universal authenticity of consensus liberalism. The applicability of the Tocqueville-Hartz paradigm will now be subjected to a more rigorous test: Does it provide a coherent and relevant interpretation of the trajectory of groups other than Jews and white males that awaited passage from subjugation to equality? Examined here will be the experience of blacks and women. This exploration will juxtapose their ordeal(s) in France and America to investigate whether a centralized state with authoritarian proclivities (France) can, under certain circumstances and with certain groups, better foster the transition from subordination to liberation than can a decentralized state with pretensions of republican universalism and individual freedom (America). Is the Tocqueville-Hartz thesis a paradigm or a paradox?

History has contradicted some warnings of Tocqueville and Hartz. American freedom has been endangered less by the unchallenged sovereignty of the majority than by a narrow, exclusive, and false conception of democracy. A white male minority has ruled the United States. Women, African-Americans, and Indians have been politically marginalized and, despite recent gains in power, have yet to become full citizens. Partly for this reason, race and gender have become the most formidable challenges to the democratic-liberal consensus and signify its limitations. The Civil War was fought over slavery and resulted in expanding the constitutional (though not for a long period substantive) boundaries of citizenship to include African-Americans. Current fundamental conflicts in the nation concern race and gender, the empowerment of groups that were denied, and now demand, civic equality. America's being a liberal, diverse society in comparison to the statist, homogeneous leanings of France, helps account for the greater freedom of white males, and, to a lesser extent, white females, in the United States in matters of conscience and expression. But in achieving political and economic rights for women, and all liberties for

African-Americans, between 1775 and 1815, vaunted American liberalism and diversity may not have a better record.

Both nations confronted issues of race and gender in the common era of their revolutions and modern state formations. Consequently, an investigation of how blacks and females fared in these countries at this time indicates whether the postulates of American pluralism and individualism, on the one hand, and French authoritarian statism, on the other, comprehensively explain putatively crucial variations in the two national cultures or whether these theories are restricted only to white men and certain rights.

Despite proclamations of liberty, equality, brotherhood (but not sisterhood), and universalism in the revolutionary and early republican epochs of France and the United States, political rights were selectively granted. On the eve of the Revolution of 1848, less than 1 percent of French citizens participated in parliamentary elections. After a brief flirtation with universal (male) suffrage in the Jacobin Constitution of 1793, a temporary restoration in the short-lived Second Republic, and an application diluted and delimited by government interference in the Second Empire, it was not until 1875 that the vote was permanently given to all male citizens. In America, states defined the conditions of political participation. In the 1780s, they started to ease property qualifications for voting, and in the early 1800s began to enfranchise all white male citizens. This process was largely complete by 1845.[1] The trajectory of universal white male suffrage follows the course of American precedence in nonracially mediated citizenship. Except for spasmodic republican episodes during the French Revolution, as well as for racial exclusion, the United States earlier, more comprehensively, and permanently provided enclosure for peripheral groups in the national political community, at least insofar as enfranchisement is concerned.

Revolutionary and republican urges toward universalism only slowly overcame long-standing racialized, gendered, and propertied standards of citizenship. The dominant conception and practice of citizenship from 1775–1815 was white, male, and propertied. Associated with these attributes were the criteria for political participation: Reason (impossible to attain without education); a stake in society (property ownership); and an ability to participate in public life, especially in defense of the nation. Women, blacks, Indians, and those without property were shut out from political participation. They were labeled savages and/or slaves, dismissed as poor, irrational, and uneducated, unfit for public activity and reserved for domestic life. At a time when citizenship was extended to Jews in order to enable them to leave the particular (corporate society) for the universal (citizenship in the nation-state), and to encourage them to think nationally (generally) and not Judaically (separately), these other groups were excluded as allegedly incapable of moving from the private to the public, the particularistic to the general. This exclusion produced a great irony in the political culture of republican nationalism. Citizenship, the putative instrument of universality, became itself particularized.[2]

For Tocqueville, majority rule and centralized government were the critical menaces to freedom in America, but the nation's "black population" and the resentment toward it of Southern whites constituted the gravest perils to "the future of the union." As an active and advanced abolitionist, Tocqueville felt that slavery was degrading and oppressive, deracinating blacks and ensuring permanent hostility between the races. Emancipation, though inevitable, would intensify racial resentments on both sides of the color line to the point of violent conflict. According to Tocqueville, hatred for African-Americans was more malignant in the free North than in the slave South and whites and blacks would never live in harmony. Tocqueville nevertheless considered America the least likely of nations to experience a revolution. Underestimating America's ability to integrate the blacks as fellow nationals, notwithstanding the hesitancy and incompleteness of the process and other ambiguities of black-white relations, Tocqueville located the sole source of insurgency in racial "inequality" and persecution: "If ever America undergoes great revolutions, they will be brought about by the presence of the black race on the soil of the United States." Sectional strife, linked to slavery, also endangered the country's survival. Increasingly anxious about the North's growing prosperity and strength and correspondingly feeling enfeebled and inferior, southern rancor made civil conflict an ever more palpable prospect.[3]

Writing in the 1830s about America did not require uncommon prescience to contemplate race as the exception to the democratic-liberal consensus, the fault line of disunity. Truly remarkable, however, is Hartz's attempt to evade this conclusion nearly a century after the Civil War. The South might proclaim its cavalier image and leave the union, but it could not discard its Lockian liberal essence because it had no feudal origin. Even the bloodiest war in American history did not disrupt Hartz's version of the consensus theory. If internecine carnage did not deter ideological harmony, neither did race. Hartz awkwardly reasoned that the South could not escape the Lockian imprimatur because its whites acknowledged that the Bible, serfdom, and northern wage labor condoned Caucasian-induced bondage and southern slaveholders imputed human traits to their slaves, thus conceding a common humanity with African-Americans. Unlike Tocqueville, who regarded race and slavery as divisive institutions and forces, Hartz considered them to be analytic categories or ideological components of a "reactionary enlightenment"—the South's confused, contradictory, and relatively short-lived self-conception.[4]

Hartz was even more neglectful of Indians, another group that challenged the liberal consensus. They go unmentioned in *The Liberal Tradition in America*. Tocqueville, however, discusses them, along with African-Americans, as dehumanized and atomized by prejudice and oppression. Indians were forcibly dispossessed of their land, economy, and culture: "I believe that the Indian nations of North America are doomed to perish at the hands of the whites." Tocqueville recognized that Indians differ from other racial and ethnic groups in America. They conceived of themselves, and were treated by the American government, as nations with control over the land they occupied, the loyalty of their people, and sovereign functions of treaty making, waging war, and so forth. Only after conquest were they reduced to the status of dependent tribes.[5] Unlike African-Americans or other racial or ethnic enclaves, the Indians were nations within a nation. In this respect, their existence raised problems that Jews presented in European countries: Should and could they become citizens? Did membership in the larger nation mean cultural as well as political absorption into American society?

Tocqueville admitted that race was the exception to the democratic-liberal consensus, while Hartz yielded no ground on ideological harmony. "The Present And Probable Future Condition Of The Three Races That Inhabit The Territory of The United States" (volume I, chapter 18, of *Democracy in America*) is a discussion of relations among Native–, African–, and white Americans and the consequences of their interactions. In the 54 pages devoted to this subject, Tocqueville sympathizes with blacks and Indians and is pessimistic about what white oppression portends for the country.[6]

Hartz ignores the proscription that minority subjugation and exclusion places upon American liberalism and exceptionalism. Since Hartz was no less critical than Tocqueville of the American system, it is difficult to explain his evasion. He, too, rued the compulsive conformity of American culture, but restricted his attack on illiberal Lockian liberalism to political and quasi-Marxian ideological categories of left and right, and thus did not emulate his mentor's confrontation of racial and other negations of the American system. Narrow where Tocqueville was comprehensive, Hartz undermined the legacy of his preceptor. Perhaps this difference was a matter of focus. A historian and social observer, Tocqueville had broader interests than did Hartz, the political theorist. Then again, the divergence may be due to timing. *Democracy in America* came out in the Jacksonian era, when slavery and Indian relations preoccupied the nation. *The Liberal Tradition* appeared when "red" meant Communists, not Indians, and black-white conflicts were in temporary abeyance and seemed solvable.

The topic and time of *The Founding of New Societies* compelled Hartz to address issues he had previously ignored. The book appeared amidst an explosive confrontation over Native– and African-American rights. Moreover, it focused on South Africa, Canada, Australia, and Latin America, as well as the United States—societies with an ugly history regarding blacks and/or Indians. Hartz now indignantly contemplated the treatment of these groups and racism in general. Nonetheless, his analytical framework remained consensus liberalism. He argued that feudal societies, based on status, were less determined enslavers than were liberal societies, with their intense commitment to private property and democracy. Hartz's penchant for the dialectic reappeared in *The Founding of New Societies*. Proceeding from the same premise of human equality, liberal capitalism produced zealous enslavers of blacks or abolitionists, eliminators or protectors of Native-Americans. The distinguishing factor between these polar extremes was whether Indians and blacks were designated "human" or "savage."[7]

Women's lack of political and property rights did not move Tocqueville, as in the case of racial repression, to balefully reflect on America's attachment to democracy. He thought that young women in America were more independent than in France due to the greater individual freedom in democracies. Accordingly, he advocated a worldly education for democracy's daughters. "An American girl scarcely ever displays that virginal softness," Tocqueville deploringly commented on the effects of republican female assertiveness, "or that innocent and ingenuous grace which usually attend the European woman in the transition from girlhood to youth." Self-reliant young American females tended to become "cold and virtuous women instead of affectionate wives and agreeable companions to man. Society may be more tranquil and better regulated, but domestic life has often fewer charms." Once married, however, the republican woman compliantly forsakes her maidenly boldness, if not her hardness, adapts to her husband's ways, and submits to the circumstances of his life. Tocqueville approved this transition from independence to moral guardianship and domestic responsibility. Traditionally inclined in this respect, he nevertheless contemplated women as participants in American democracy and conceded that, at least before marriage, they were more independent and decisive than their counterparts in Europe.[8] Hartz, as usual with social issues, did not mention women in *The Liberal Tradition in America* or *The Founding of New Societies*.

The long exclusion of African-Americans from citizenship is no trivial exemption from the democratic-liberal society postulated by Tocqueville and Hartz. Equally problematic for this theory was the size of the oppressed enclave. The black population in 1790 was 757,808, including

697,681 slaves—African-Americans constituted 19.26 percent of the national population. In 1810, African-Americans numbered 1,377,808, including 1,191,362 slaves—African-Americans composed 19.03 percent of the total population. Large numbers of slaves also lived in the French empire (about 650,000–700,000 in the French Antilles in 1790), but on the eve of the Revolution estimates of blacks and mulattoes living in France range from less than 1,000 to between 4,000–5,000.[9]

Allegedly illiberal France initially gave greater support to civic rights for blacks than did purportedly freedom-loving America. During the French Revolution, blacks served as deputies in the National Assembly and as military officers, occasionally of high rank. Seeking to rally the blacks to the Tricolor against an expected British invasion of St. Domingue, on February 4, 1794, the National Convention decreed emancipation without compensation to the planters. Another of the French Revolution's apparently ardent, but often futile and reversible, quests for freedom, it had no effect where the slaves actually lived. St. Domingue, for example, was already in the midst of a slave rebellion.[10]

The 1794 bill, which also gave citizenship to the freed slaves, nevertheless culminated the revolutionary campaign for racial rights. In March 1790, the Assembly enfranchised the white colonials, but did not mention blacks, still unable to vote, and criminalized incitement to insurgency in the colonies. Seven months later the National Assembly decided not to legislate on "the status of persons" in the colonies. Responding to an abortive slave uprising in Martinique in the West Indies, in May 1791 the Assembly gave full political rights to mulattos and freedmen born of free fathers and mothers, but passed a constitutional decree explicitly safeguarding the slave regime. In September, it withdrew these rights. Seeking assistance against the insurgents in St. Domingue, in March 1792 that body granted civic rights to all freedmen. Fearing future black upheavals, Napoleon reversed the legislative trend toward racial equality. Freed slaves could not come to France without authorization from the minister of Marine and the Colonies, miscegenation was forbidden and, in 1802, Bonaparte, simultaneous inheritor and betrayer of the Revolution, restored slavery and the slave trade.[11]

As with many other issues from 1789 to 1815 government policy was steered by the contrary claims of idealism and interests, freedom and force. Where blacks were concerned, interests and coercion usually prevailed. At the end of that period, with servitude and the slave trade flourishing and blacks all but disallowed from entering France, conditions came full-circle to where they were before the Revolution. Bondage was finally and irrevocably abolished in 1848, with full civil rights for the ex-slaves and no compensation for the former owners.[12]

Liberté, égalité and fraternité clashed with planter pressures, mercantile interests in colonial trade, and considerable ideological racism. Fears of British invasion and slave uprisings in the West Indies impelled the government to conflicting racial policies, depending on whether it thought that placating or repressing blacks was the best defense against these dangers. Strategic and commercial interests prevailed because public opinion was not committed to abolition or racial equality. From the 1760s through the Revolution, antiblack prejudice worsened and protoracist comments regularly surfaced. On the scale of frequency of subjects mentioned in the cahiers, slavery ranked 1088 or last in those of the Parishes, and 419.5 and 533, respectively, in those of the Nobility and the Third Estate. Jews were mentioned considerably more frequently in Parish cahiers and more often in those of the Third Estate, but less so in those of the Nobility. According to Hyslop's study of 522 general cahiers (93 are missing), only 49 called for ending the slave trade or gradual emancipation. The 49 included 17 of the 158 surviving clergy cahiers, 11 of the surviving 154 from the Nobility, 20 of the surviving 190 from the Third Estate, and 1 of the 2 surviving documents that combined the Second and Third Estates. In 1789, the National Assembly refused to seat mulatto delegates from the West Indies. France's first abolitionist organization, the *Société des Amis des Noirs*, was not founded until 1788. Immediately thereafter, *Club Massiac* appeared to oppose Amis des Noirs. The latter was an elite organization that campaigned for gradual emancipation and against the slave trade. Its only successful intervention was on behalf of the passage of the law of April 4, 1792, that gave political rights to free black colonials of mixed blood. Dominated by Girondins, it became virtually defunct by 1793.[13]

Reluctance of revolutionaries to admit blacks to civic society and grant even basic freedoms prevented the state from ending the slave trade—a much more moderate cause than abolition or racial equality. Traffic in slaves peaked between 1783 and 1791. Prohibited in the emancipation decree of 1794, it was reimposed in 1802. Proscribed again in 1815, as resolved by the Congress of Vienna, and revived in 1818, the trade was finally terminated for French slavers in 1831. Throughout these changes in its legal status, the trade vigorously continued until officially halted and sluggishly persisted even after Emancipation. British pressure finally forced France to vacate the trade. As with slavery, the government could not overcome the cacophony of voices and interests and develop a coherent policy.[14]

If calls to do away with slavery, or at least to cease traffic in slaves, did not consistently or prevalently resound at sans cullotte demonstrations, Jacobin club conclaves, national and local assembly meetings, or imperial council sessions, they were even more muted and absent in America. Many southern slaveholders affirmed liberty of conscience and civic equality for all religions. Some champions of this freedom—Washington, Jefferson, Madison, and Edmond Randolph—had moral doubts about slavery. These qualms, however, did not prompt them to publicly agitate for abolition or, except for Washington, to emancipate their own slaves. Charles Pinckney, at the Federal Constitutional Convention, spoke eloquently for religious freedom. In this same forum, he also defended slavery.[15] Further, elimination of religious tests for federal public office passed with little dissent. But twenty-five of the fifty-five delegates were slaveholders and an attempt to generate a petition to outlaw the slave trade, much less to end slavery, was forestalled to avoid disrupting the Convention.[16]

Although revolutionary France was more outspoken against servitude and put free blacks and mulattoes in higher military and civil posts than did revolutionary America, in some respects the countries responded similarly to racial subjugation and a few emancipatory initiatives started in America. The world's first antislavery organization, the Philadelphia Society, appeared thirteen years before the Amis des Noirs and twelve years before The Committee for the Abolition of the Slave trade, Britain's original antislavery association. In 1776, as in 1792, blacks took up arms on behalf of their new republics.[17]

While American congresses did not issue emancipation decrees and France was quicker to abolish slavery, the democratic-liberterian impulses unleashed in the 1770s and the utopian urges of a new nation strengthened religious and political opposition to bondage. It was no coincidence that the Philadelphia Society—officially, the Society for Relief of Free Negroes Illegally Held in Bondage—appeared in 1775. In 1784, it became the Philadelphia Abolition Society, presided over by Franklin, that redoubtable proponent of individual liberty. A year later, the New York Manumission Society was founded, with another revolutionary leader, John Jay, as president. Similar organizations soon appeared in Virginia, Maryland, Delaware, Connecticut, and New Jersey. Many other revolutionary heroes were active in the antislavery movement. Hamilton helped found the New York society; Rush was active in Pennsylvania, and, less visibly, Washington and John Adams opposed slavery.[18]

More important than societies or prominent figures that took up the cause were mainline religious and political forces that embraced manumission. Northern Quakers enthusiastically enlisted in the Christian antislavery crusade. Beginning in the 1760s, several local Yearly Meetings of the Society of Friends disowned members who bought or sold slaves, and, after the Revolution, campaigned to eliminate slavery and the slave trade. Virginia and Maryland Quakers in 1778 and 1784, respectively, required members to free slaves. In the 1780s and 1790s, several state associations of Baptists, Methodists, and Methodist Episcopalians, southern as well as northern, also condemned slavery and the slave trade. These sects advocated gradual abolition with compensation to slaveholders.[19]

Agitation by religious and secular antislavery societies; libertarian sentiments stirred by the Revolution, widely considered a struggle against tyranny; utopian visions evoked by the creation of a new republic; the last rays of Enlightenment egalitarianism—each in its way served to induce the federal and some state governments to move against the slave trade and slavery. Resistance to importation of slaves also derived from less lofty motives—anxiety over the slave revolt in St. Domingue and the calculation that scarcity of slaves would raise their market value.

Shortly before the War for Independence, the Massachusetts and Virginia legislatures passed bills to end importation of slaves, but the royal government disallowed them. The Continental Congresses banned slave importation and American participation in the slave trade. During the Revolution, Delaware and Virginia prohibited slave importation, Vermont constitutionally outlawed slavery, Pennsylvania adopted a gradual emancipation law, and Virginia permitted private manumission. Moreover, about 4,000 African-Americans were in the northern militias of the Continental Army; northern bondsmen who served were freed.[20]

These trends continued after independence. During the late 1780s, slavery lost its legal sanction and disappeared in Massachusetts and New Hampshire and gradual emancipation was enacted in Connecticut and Rhode Island. New York (1799) and New Jersey (1804) subsequently legislated gradual manumission. In the 1780s, Connecticut, New York, Massachusetts, Pennsylvania, and Delaware and Georgia in 1798 forbade participation of their citizens in the slave trade. A majority of states provided for gradual abolition in these years, but they were in the North and had small numbers of slaves. New York's 10,000 slaves constituted the largest group outside of the South. Indeed, more slaves were privately freed in the South than were publicly liberated in the North.[21]

It would take either repudiation of slavery in the South or immense pressure from the federal government to loosen the bonds of the vast majority of American blacks. An emancipationist epiphany never occurred in the South and the national government would not destroy the "peculiar institution" until 1865. Before the Civil War, the federal government moved on only one front, not coincidentally that with the most cooperation from the slaveholders and the least impact upon eventual freedom for blacks. Since the days of the Continental Congresses, public pronouncements and state legislation sought curtailment of the slave trade. Article I, Section 9, of the U.S. Constitution postponed until 1808 federal action against importation of slaves. But, in the 1780s, opposition against such commerce grew, and after the Constitution was ratified, most states outlawed the trade or imposed a prohibitive tariff against importation of slaves. As a result, the national government opposed international traffic in bondage. In 1794, Congress banned Americans from selling slaves in foreign markets and in 1807 Congress prohibited Americans from participating in the trade, the same year that Britain took identical action regarding the English trade and a generation before legal termination in France. Despite public opinion and government policy, the trade peaked between 1780 and 1810 and the U.S. slave population tripled between 1775 and 1820. As with France, formal foreclosure did not immediately stop widespread traffic in African slaves.[22]

Outlawing the slave trade would be the sole consistent initiative taken by the the antebellum federal government against bondage. Southern power in Washington made compromise and retreat the national policy. The politics of accommodation were prefigured in the Revolution. The Second Continental Congress resolved against importation of slaves, but deleted from the Declaration of Independence, that excoriation of tyranny, Jefferson's condemnation of King George III for enslaving Africans. Nine years later, the Confederation Congress rejected his proposal to exclude slaves from all western territories after 1800. The Constitution addressed the issue of racial subjugation, without mentioning slavery, by providing that three-fifths of the slaves should be counted in apportioning taxes and the House of Representatives (Article I, Section 2), by preventing Congress from interfering with the importation of slaves before 1808, and by mandating the return of escaped slaves (Article IV, Section 2). The three-fifths provision legitimized slaveholding insofar as it codified the subhuman status of slaves, made bondage an element in political representation and power, and gave to it a constitutional cachet. In 1790, Congress resolved that it had no authority to interfere with the treatment or emancipation of slaves, but three years later passed a fugitive slave law. Thus Congress claimed that it could not protect slaves, but could preserve investment in them by recovering runaways for their owners. The national legislature also refused to consider abolitionist petitions because of southern protests.[23]

Sectional compromise began in 1787, when the Ordinance of 1787 prohibited slavery in the Northwest Territory. In 1792, Kentucky was admitted into the nation as a slave state, six years later Congress refused to bar bondage from the Mississippi Territory, and, in 1804, it recognized slavery in the Louisiana Territory.[24] Allowing slavery in these territories, the federal government augmented servitude by adding thousands of slaves and millions of acres in slave territory.

The actions of Congress reflected growing southern resistance against manumission. The Methodist Episcopal Church in 1785 suspended a year-old rule requiring members to free slaves. In 1808, the General Conference of this denomination deleted criticism of slavery from copies of its *Discipline* that circulated in the South. Nine years after its adoption, the Virginia Baptist General Committee rescinded its 1785 condemnation of slavery. Virginia in 1782 permitted voluntary emancipation, but in 1806 required freed slaves to leave the state within a year.[25]

What blacks faced can be glimpsed from the relatively enlightened attitude of Jefferson. As a philosophe, the Sage of Monticello felt that the light of reason shone alike on all humankind; as a slaveholder, however, Jefferson stood in contradiction of his own enlightened view. Blacks, he wrote in *Notes in Virginia* (1780–1785), "are in reason much inferior to whites and in imagination they are dull, tasteless, and anomalous." It "has been observed by everyone that mixture with the whites generates the improvement of the blacks in body and mind." Miscegenation "proves that their inferiority is not the effect merely of their condition of life." America's foremost liberal-democrat, however, drew back from unconditional protoracialism: "I advance it as a suspicion only, that the blacks, whether originally a distinct race, or made distinct by time and circumstances, are inferior to the whites in the endowments both of body and mind." Uneasily suspended between nature and nurture, he returned to biological determinism: "It is not against experience to suppose, that different species of the same genus, or varieties of the same species, may possess different qualifications." Unable to settle in his own mind a debate that resonates down to the present, Jefferson was certain that the "unfortunate difference of colour, and perhaps of faculty, is a powerful obstacle to the emancipation of these people. . . . When free, the slave is to be removed beyond the reach of [race] mixture."[26] Great liberal thinkers, Jefferson the slaveholder and Tocqueville the abolitionist, agreed that blacks would be oppressed in, and excluded from, democratic America, an illiberal exception in the land of liberalism.

Comparative assessment of America's liberal Revolution and Republic and the presumptively more coercive Revolution of 1789 and Napoleonic rule indicates that, with regard to racial equality and freedom, any such presumption is misleading. The French were more passionate and expansive—as in so much else concerning their revolution—about black emancipation and citizenship. Again, as in so many matters touched by the upheaval of 1789, these feelings were intermittent and often reversed with the same zeal with which they were previously adopted. In either case, the largest group of freed slaves achieved that status by themselves in the rebellion against France that made St. Domingue independent. Other drawbacks to a rigorous contrast between these nations on the issue of racial servitude are that, beginning in the 1790s, they increasingly retreated from manumission, and the fact that American governments were more steadfast on ending participation in the international slave trade and, at least by law, dismantled it sooner. Nonetheless, slavery ended earlier in France and the debate over it during the Revolution of 1789 was more vigorously pursued and won glorious, if short-lived and mostly rhetorical, triumphs that did not appear in America.

Narrative accuracy does not always amount to analytical acuity. Nothing is amiss in the preceding paragraph save historical interpretation. Let the reassessment commence by juxtaposing two events. The emancipation of 1794 made France the first modern nation to end chattel slavery (score one for France over America in the liberal sweepstakes), but in 1802 France became the only Western country to restore slavery and the slave trade (score one for the United States). From 1799 to 1815, Napoleon, who favored the *colons* and had married one, stifled the French abolitionist movement, but in the "hundred days" of his 1815 return from exile declared an intent (never implemented) to end the slave trade.[27]

From 1789 to 1848, French policy on slavery and the slave trade is contradictory and replete with grand gestures weightier in words than result. Was this the consequence of mighty forces (slavery and antislavery) fighting each other to a prolonged standoff, or was it the effect of national ideological indifference that subjected French policy to changeable exogenous circumstances? Patrice Higonnet, author of a recent study of the Jacobins, hailed the abolition of slavery as "the Jacobins' noblest decision." Their "liberalism and humanism . . . on this issue" made this act, for Higonnet, the Jacobins' finest hour.[28] Some prominent historians of French slavery are less Churchillian in their evaluation. They argue that public tepidity about blacks, the slave trade, or slavery ensured that policy on these issues was mainly determined not by proactive republican principle, but rather by reactive practicality. Liberty, equality, and fraternity had less to do with shaping action than did external factors like slave rebellions and relations with Britain. After revolutionary zeal faded, such factors were increasingly decisive.[29]

The original antislavery society set the tone for the French abolition movement. Amis des Noirs was elitist (its upper-class membership did not seek to rally public support); small (it never exceeded 150 members and never tried to expand its numbers); moderate (its goal was gradual emancipation and, foreseeing a prolonged interval between servitude and freedom, chose to focus on ending the slave trade); temperate (no zealous abolitionists in this group—most members had higher priorities than liberating blacks); and worked through the government, especially the legislature (many of its members were deputies and high officials). The Amis des Noirs pattern would be repeated in subsequent struggles over ending slavery and the slave trade and has been called by Seymour Drescher the "French Way," as opposed to the "British Way," of emancipation.[30]

The Continental/French model of abolition appeared during the Revolution, and not only with respect to the Amis des Noirs. A few months before the 1794 emancipation, one count of treason brought against the antislavery Girondin leaders of the Amis des Noirs was their alleged responsibility for the devastation of St. Domingue incurred during the slave rebellion. The abolition decree itself was glorified as a revolutionary gesture, but in the absence of any popular support for it, the government was mostly motivated by external (as opposed to metropolitan) conditions—an impending British invasion of the West Indies and the slave uprisings in the region. The ninteenth century wrought no significant changes in the abolition movement, which varied from moribund to marginal. The *Société de la moral chrétienne* (1821), in structure and strategy, echoed the defunct Amis des Noirs. Another moderate, gradualist organization of elites integrated with the government, in 1830 it had 388 members. During the last years of the battle against slavery, the abolitionists finally sought popular backing and adopted some tactics of the Anglo/American movement. Their 1847 campaign to mobilize public opinion by besieging the government with antislavery petitions resulted in 12,395 signatures, a tiny fraction of the subscribers that abolitionists in England and America had gathered.[31]

Without massive and enthusiastic endorsement of emancipation, progress in ending the slave trade and black bondage depended upon international and intragovernment negotiations. Slavery ended with the arrival of the Second Republic. Now the liberals controlled the government; the July Monarchy could no longer oppose abolition. Immediate, unconditional, and virtually uncompensated abolition was decreed by the provisional government on April 29, 1848. Despite some progress in mobilizing support and in unifying behind a program of immediate emancipation, slavery ended not by public demand, but by a change of regime. As measured by the press or revolutionary crowds in Paris—prime indicators of public opinion—in the last months before the Revolution no public imperative existed for emancipation. In February and March, newspapers and pamphlets were not concerned with abolition and no record exists of the revolutionary crowd voicing any sentiment whatsoever about slavery.[32]

Abolitionist impulses were more spectacular in the French Revolution than in the American War for Independence, and the first and second (and permanent) French emancipations occurred before America freed its slaves. Nevertheless, at least after their respective Revolutions, America's commitment to liberation was arguably broader, deeper, and more consistent. In fact, that nation's attachment to both abolition (in the North) and slavery (in the South) was more ardent. The liberation movement in the United States resembled that of England. Both countries' abolitionists appealed to the masses through their religious affiliations, widely disseminated publications, political campaigns, petition drives, and the like. Rather than work within the government, the antislavery movement often defied it, organized along middle-class, rather than elitist, lines, and enlisted the support and moral authority of women. In these respects, it so differed from the antislavery movement in France, that abolition historians postulate separate French/Continental and Anglo/American modes of abolition.[33]

French emancipation societies counted their members in the hundreds and their organizations never numbered in double digits. By 1835, there were 200 antislavery societies in the United States; by 1840, some 2,000 auxiliary abolitionist organizations existed and their membership totaled 150,000–200,000. Unlike the situation in France, thousands of antislavery publications in the form of newspapers, pamphlets, tracts, broadsides, and books constantly reminded Americans of the evils of bondage and the imperative to end it. Theodore Weld's pamphlet, *American Slavery As It Is* (1839), sold over 100,000 copies within a year of its publication. French abolitionist popular appeal peaked in 1847, when the emancipation movement collected over 12,000 signatures in 51 petitions. Between December 1838 and March 1839, American crusaders for freedom presented Congress with 1,496 petitions and 163,845 signatures, half from women. In 1848, a coalition of liberationist parties coalesced under the banner of the Free Soil Party and won 291,263 votes in the presidential election. In 1856, the newly founded Republican Party, representing a similar coterie of antislavery adherents, took eleven states in the presidential election.[34] Four years later, the Republicans received a plurality of the vote in the presidential race, setting the stage for a far more spectacular and passionate denouement of slavery than had ever happened in France.

For better or worse, the American encounter with slavery shows a Tocquevillian diversity of divided sovereignty. A national political, or at least legislative, consensus did not, as it did in France, emerge in the United States. The quest for independence and the overthrow of monarchical tyranny celebrated during the American Revolution and in the early republic quickened the antislavery movement in the North and resulted in ending bondage in the states of this region. It had no such effect on the South or on national policy. Pluralism can bring contention and suppression as well as freedom, compromise, and harmony.

American and French confrontations with racial servitude between 1775 and 1815 compromised democratic-liberal principles. Although France evinced more dramatic national emancipatory initiatives, accommodation prevailed in both countries. Thus their national policies on bondage disclose a major flaw in the Tocqueville-Hartz thesis. Race made democratic-liberal values irrelevant for a large segment of the population and contradicted and curtailed the commitment of the white majority to these values.

Despite vivid and important contrasts in the status of Jews and blacks in France and the United States, by the second half of the 19th century some convergence in attitude toward these groups can be discerned. The racialism that engulfed Western thinking after the 1850s initially fixated on putative genetic "Negroid" separateness and inferiority, but soon broadened to differentiate Caucasian peoples. A particularly toxic strain of the latter surfaced as racial anti-Semitism. While not absent in the United States, this facet of racialism was more pronounced in Europe as a component of organic nationalism. African-Americans were distinctive and concentrated in the southern states; Jews were distinctive and concentrated in Alsace in France and, in New York, and other East Coast cities. Both peoples were excluded and persecuted, but Jews fared better in the United States and blacks in France. Since no Dreyfus Affair imperiled the American republic and no equivalent of Édouard Drumont emerged in that country, variations in the treatment of Jews in France and America confirm the contention that the respective national response to Jews validates Tocquevillian distinctions between American liberalism and French authoritarianism.[35] Conversely, lesser antiblack bigotry and repression in metropolitan France reverses these distinctions, thus limiting the scope and power of the thesis of American exceptionalism and its derivation from consensus liberalism.[36]

Taxonomy is description, not explanation, and such is the case with the assignation of different types and intensities of black and Judaic exclusion in different places. Certainly, one explanatory element in the variance of treatment of blacks in France and America was the vastly larger black slave presence in the contiguous United States than in France. This is but one factor, however, and neither relates the black and Jewish experiences in these countries nor connects black emancipation and slavery to other basic topics of explorations in this study—political culture and state formation. An initial excursion into these interactions, and especially into their crossnational comparisons, raises the question of whether a centralized state with intermittent imperiousness can better protect minorities than can a federalized state with incomplete democratic-liberal inclinations.

Evidence from the French Revolution and elsewhere substantiates this notion, but with the tantalizing caveat that so often arises in historical interpretation—not conclusively. The major initiatives for black emancipation came from the radicals, those who believed a homogeneous and powerful state expressed the general will. Blacks belonged to Jacobin societies, Robespierre headed the Paris Society when it excluded a slaveowner and admitted a mulatto, and nearly 300 Jacobin clubs congratulated the

Convention when it ended slavery. The anti-Semitic Jacobin Jean François Reubell on May 15, 1791, proposed in the National Assembly that mulattoes born of free parents be given voting rights. One of the first acts of the Jacobin ministry (formed on March 15, 1792, and under Girondin Jacobin hegemony) was to decree, on April 4, full civic rights for all free adult males in the colonies regardless of color. The Montagnard-Jacobin–dominated National Convention on February 4, 1794, unanimously declared for emancipation without compensation and this act was celebrated in the Temple of Reason, the former Notre Dame Cathedral. Another tableau for racial equality was presented in Peicam de Bressoles's *Fête Américaine*, presented at the Opéra Comique in August. Included in the assortment of symbols in this production were a black and white man, a black and white baby, the Tree of Liberty (a Jacobin icon), and busts of Jacobin leaders. In addition to the Jacobins and the Cult of Reason, immediate, total, and uncompensated emancipation was the cause of the Hébertists, whose leader, Jacques-Rene Hébert, was a member of the Paris Commune, a champion of that city's sans culottes, an intrepid berater of the rich, a fervent dechristianizer, and, ultimately, a victim of the Terror.[37] (By the time of the Terror, not all Jacobins were radicals and not all radicals were Robespierrists.)

Abolition of slavery and citizenship for blacks occurred less than a year after the National Convention on June 24, 1793, ratified the Jacobin Constitution, which replaced traditional deference to property rights with direct universal male suffrage. This constitution and black emancipation had much in common. Both were drafted by the same political faction and ratified by the same legislative body it controlled; both abridged property rights, one with respect to slaves, the other with respect to voting, and neither was implemented. Most importantly, both issued from advocates of a centralized, domineering state. It should not be forgotten, however, that while Jacobins were conferring civil rights on black slaves, they were persecuting Christians and Jews.

A bizarre relic of the radical tolerance for blacks surfaced in what otherwise might be considered a reactionary, fascist, and racist regime. Vichy France was corporatist, antirepublican and anti–French Revolution, as well as antiforeign, antirefugee, anti-Gypsy, and anti-Jewish, but not antiblack. No restrictions against blacks were implemented in the Unoccupied Zone, a French West Indian native was a member of Henri Pétain's cabinet, and the National Council and several blacks served as deputies. France had a history of accepting assimilated blacks as part of the nation, and while Vichy denied this same national tradition to Jews, the regime honored it for blacks.[38]

Other revolutions and overbearing, monolithic regimes at first glance confirm the contention that such dominion can be selectively solicitous of minorities. For example, the Soviet Union, or at any rate its government, was sympathetic to black civil rights; in fact more sympathetic to racial equality than to religious freedom. Like most radical Jacobins, Russian Communists tended more toward anti-Judaism. The proposition that such states protect minorities, at any rate blacks, better than do ostensibly liberal and pluralistic states is flawed, however. Nazi Germany was totalitarian *and* intensely racist. Perhaps the Third Reich, as in so many other ways, was a grotesque anomaly. A regime closer to revolutionary France, however, re-enslaved blacks. The First Empire made Bonapartism a synonym for autocracy, yet Bonaparte on May 20, 1802, restored ancien régime racial practices in colonies still controlled by France. In Guadeloupe and Martinique, this regression meant discrimination against freed slaves, refusal of their entry into France, and proscriptions against miscegenation. Napoleon sought to revivify the economy of the Caribbean territories and repress rebellion there, but racism also shaped his policy. Like Hitler, though less demonically, he disliked blacks and regarded them as savages.[39]

Viewed from an angle more acutely congruent with France, the putative cohabitation of centralized authoritarianism and racial emancipation becomes more suspect. If the push for abolition during the Revolution came largely from radicals besotted with power, the emancipation they delivered to blacks proved more dramatic than climactic. The emancipation decree of 1794 basically ratified the result of the slave uprising in St. Domingue; it resulted in no permanent, or even long-term, cessation of French chattel slavery. Revolutionary emancipation of the Blacks was not a turning point for that race in the manner that the revolutionary emancipation of the Jews was for that people. Moreover, the French model of abolition ultimately derived from the Amis des Noirs, an organization that had been destroyed and whose leaders had been imprisoned or sent to the scaffold by radical Jacobins. It could be argued, however, that the Amis des Noirs focused on ending the slave trade rather than slavery itself and envisioned liberation as a gradual and prolonged process. In other words, the radicals were behaving like radicals; militant foes of slavery, they wanted its immediate and total termination. For them, the Amis des Noirs was a group of temporizing hypocrites. Another counterclaim is that its members were persecuted and the society suppressed not for anti-slavery activity, but because it was a Girondin stronghold. Nevertheless, an accusation leveled by the Montagnards was that the Amis des Noirs was responsible for the St. Domingue uprising.

Not all radicals acted the part where black freedom was concerned. Reubell, who denied the Jews, but defended the blacks, personifies a paradigm that can be found in the French and other revolutions and authoritarian regimes—but his was not the only road taken. A Jacobin clubbiste from Strasbourg was more symmetrical in his oppositions. In March 1791, he regarded as premature a call from the Society of Angiers to support a plea to the National Assembly on behalf of colonial blacks because the demand would cause trouble in slave-trading maritime towns and because the matter of Jewish rights had been tabled.[40] Many Jacobin clubs admitted blacks, but some excluded them—the same mixed reception that Jews and women encountered. With regard to the emancipation of mulattoes, in February and March 1791, clubs located in port cities tended to be neutral, while the other Jacobin societies favored liberation. Between 1789–92, radical Jacobins withheld their participation in the antislavery movement. No Jacobin club, for example, corresponded with the Amis des Noirs until 1791. Radicals were revolutionaries, but also property owners and businessmen; hence their ambivalence about manumission.[41]

The postrevolutionary impetus for emancipation came largely from liberals. Starting in the 1820s, opposition to the slave trade and advocacy of gradual abolition emanated primarily from moderate liberals and liberal monarchists—among them was Tocqueville. When the Revolution of 1848 brought liberals to power, the Second Republic issued an edict of immediate emancipation and conferred citizenship upon the ex-slaves.[42]

Whatever happened thereafter, during their Revolutions, the French manifested a greater inclination to emancipate blacks than did the Americans, and the radicals in the French Revolution were the most racially egalitarian; certainly moreso than constitutional monarchists or Girondins. Under radical rule, colonial planters fell into disfavor. For the revolutionary Left, at least for those who backed the decree of 1794 as a matter of principle, among other motives, the Montagnard Constitution of 1793 and the suppression of slavery were realizations of the Declaration of the Rights of Man and of universal citizenship, of liberty, fraternity, and equality. If the radical vision of the state was centralized and authoritarian, embedded in it was an egalitarian negation of the individual will, a fraternal incarnation of liberty in the general will.

It is often overlooked, by critics and advocates of American liberalism alike, that property is an essential component of that ideology and often conflicts with its nonhierarchical, inclusive, and humanitarian values. Property as a constitutive element of liberalism is certainly neglected by Hartz and subsequent liberal theorizers Rogers Smith and Desmond King. This subject is absent from the indexes of *The Liberal Tradition in America* and King's *In the Name of Liberalism*, and the only entries for it in *Civic Ideals* are scattered and concern property tests for determining voting eligibility.[43] Tocqueville, a more acute observer, recognized the centrality of property in America. As quoted in chapter 1, he asserted that "in no country in the world is love of property more active and more anxious than in the United States."[44]

Comparison between radical factions in the French Revolution—who opposed, albeit incompletely, the privileging of property either with respect to slavery or suffrage—with America's entrepreneurial liberals, who fought against England, bears out Tocqueville's contention. Emancipatory impulses in France, at least during the radical reign, were less constrained by commitments to property. The War for Independence, however, was fought to secure private ownership and other individual rights from despoilment by an allegedly tyrannical king and parliament. These aims ruled out freedom for slaves. Those owning no property and belonging to others were not independent and were, in fact, exemplary of the holdings that the revolutionaries were trying to protect. Unlike St. Domingue's blacks, American slaves had not liberated themselves. For these reasons, freedom and citizenship for blacks would not follow from a successful revolution. American slaves found that support in Enlightenment liberalism for dissolving an oppressive social contract had been grievously diluted because they neither consented to that arrangement before entering into it nor rebelled against it and reverted to a state of nature. Liberal ideology was impaled on its central contradiction—the rights of private ownership versus the rights of individual freedom.[45]

As a type of ownership, human bondage occupied a much more central place in America, whose slaves resided in the home country, than in France, where they lived mostly in the colonies. Many American revolutionary leaders were slaveholders, while French planters were largely colonials more remote geographically and politically from the power elites involved in the French Revolution. From the U.S. Constitutional Convention through the Civil War, slavery was a recurrently central concern and this preoccupation simultaneously made emancipation more difficult and the abolition movement more intense and widespread.

Having analyzed attitudes toward rights for blacks among various factions in the French Revolution and between France and the United States, one more change must be rung on this subject. This final analysis explains variances in the treatment of blacks and Jews. Here, too, we begin with the Revolution of 1789. After the demise of feudalism, nobody in France or its colonies owned Jews. Consequently, the more conservative and property-conscious revolutionaries would not be offended, because of their attachment to the rights of ownership, by Jewish emancipation. These conservatives also envisioned a nation with a decentralized and pluralistic political structure and a loyalty to individual freedom, and thus would be less anxious about alleged separatist proclivities of Jews. Conversely, the revolutionary Left, less attached to property rights, would be more eager to emancipate the slaves. On the other hand, radicals, believing in a centralized state governed by the general will and whose authority should not be challenged by individual liberty, would be less eager to give civic rights to Jews on grounds of religious freedom and more reluctant to liberate them because of their reputation as a nation within a nation. Blacks, however, were not regarded as a menace to national solidarity due to historical aloofness and self-containedness. The treatment of these two minorities in the First Empire is less complicated. Napoleon deprived Jews and blacks of previously won political rights: he disliked both groups and had little regard for democracy, freedom, the poor, or the oppressed.

It is easier to show that racial attitudes and policies in the United States undermine the Tocqueville-Hartz interpretation of American political culture and civil society than to argue the related proposition—the American Revolution and early republic was no more liberal than the French Revolution and the First Empire. Even conceding that on racial matters, especially black slavery and civil rights, during their revolutions, France was freer than America does not mean that France was intrinsically more liberal. Consider this comparison between blacks and Jews: America was more tolerant of Jews, but France made greater progress in overcoming anti-Semitism. The demography of blacks and slaves in the two countries makes for an analogous argument about slavery—in this case recognizing the more intractable problem of race and bondage in the United States. Nearly all French slaves and blacks lived in territorial possessions distant from the homeland, while virtually all American slaves and blacks resided in the home country. Consequently, it was considerably easier for France to advocate emancipation and other liberal racial policies. In both nations, abolition sentiment concentrated in areas with few slaves; for France at home rather than in the colonies, and for the United States in the North rather than the South. Thus circumstances, not ideology, may have ultimately determined American and French attitudes toward blacks and slavery. For women's rights, it may be noted no such demographic problems exist. In both nations, half of the population was female and that half lived in the mother country.

Race and gender are often linked together, as in the currently historically correct triumvirate of race, class, and gender. Marxian and other critics have used perceived injustices in these categories to unveil inconsistencies, limitations, hypocrisies, and other offenses of liberalism. The mildest of these reservations is to relegate liberalism to the realm of an innocent idealism constantly violated by the powerful realities of racial oppression, class exploitation, and sexism. (Liberals and other anti-Marxists, of course, conversely use the reality of the Soviet Union against the prescriptions of socialism.) Numerous past and current episodes, however, attest to the fact that getting one category "right" does not necessarily entail a "correct," or even similar, stance on the others. One such case was the French Revolution.

A more complicated problem regarding race and gender is that they constitute distinct entities and thus are in some key respects incomparable. It is clear, for example, that slavery is not a voluntary association. It is less certain that marriage, even in the eighteenth and ninteenth centuries, was a similarly coercive institution for women. Equation of race and gender could consequently result in the distortion of reality by imposing present values and conditions upon the past. In this case, historical reality may be violated by contemporary reformism. In fact, this argument is presented as an alternative contention to the hypothesis that suppression of human rights is an abstract and operational breach of liberty, even if those subdued are unaware or even collaborate in their own subjugation. Hence, I consider the treatment of women in France and America as a limitation upon, and contradiction of, the liberal consensus. Consensus may be achieved with the consent of the oppressed, but liberal ideas and a liberal society cannot be realized under such conditions.

Race and gender conjunction or disjunction additionally relates to national culture and the liberal consensus. In the United States, struggles for black and women's rights have been interconnected; in France, for the most part, they have been separate concerns. Antebellum American female abolitionists were sometimes impelled to feminism because males, whether for or against emancipation, condemned their antislavery campaigning as unladylike. Women's service during the Civil War further inspired momentum for equal rights. Granting civil rights to former slaves accelerated, in emulation and indignation, agitation for emancipation of women.[46] A century later, the black liberation movement became a model for its women's and gay/lesbian equivalents.

No such sequences emerged in France. Perhaps this was because racism, at least of the black versus white variety, had a stronger presence in the United States. A more intriguing, if less obvious, possibility is that the American overlap between race and gender rights indicates the greater power of democratic liberalism in the United States than in France. The conjunction of race and gender equalities thus affirms the Tocqueville-Hartz thesis about America.

Contention over the role and rights of women, as in nearly everything connected with their revolutions and the creation of their nation-states, was more volatile in France than in the United States. In the public sphere the women of France acted more freely and vigorously, but suffered greater reversal of progress than did their transatlantic sisters. Uprisings and state formation, however, had a similarly slight impact on the expansion of economic and political rights for women in both countries. Since women played a secondary role in the public events of these years, until relatively recently, they, and blacks, drew meager scholarly attention. Standard references on the French Revolution, a *Historical Dictionary of the French Revolution, 1789–1799* (1985) and *A Critical Dictionary of the French Revolution* (1988), have no separate articles on slavery, race, gender, feminism, or women.[47]

The clarion calls of the American and French Revolutions, the Declaration of Independence and the Declaration of the Rights of Man confirm that these struggles for freedom excluded women. Among the "truths [found] to be self-evident" in The Declaration of Independence were that "all men are created equal." To "secure" the "unalienable Rights" of "Life, Liberty, and the pursuit of happiness. . . . Governments are instituted among Men, deriving their just power from the consent of the governed."

Similar in intent, the full title of the French manifesto is The Declaration of the Rights of Man and the Citizen. Its preamble proclaims the "rights of man." Article I asserts: "Men are born and remain free and equal in rights." Article II lists "liberty, property, security, and resistance to oppression" as the "imprescriptable rights of man," whose "preservation" is the "aim of every political association." Article IV mentions "each man's exercise of his natural rights." In Article IX, "Every Man is presumed innocent until he has been found guilty. . . ." Article X states, "No one must be disturbed because of his opinions." This phallocentric construction of liberty moved constitutional monarchist Olympe De Gouges to draft a "Declaration of Rights for Women and Female Citizens." A protest against the patriarchic proclamation of rights, it would eliminate genderized property, social, and political privileges. Gouges sent the document to the National Assembly in September 1791 as a foundation for the prospective constitution, which subsequently rejected the feminist declaration.[48]

Additional evidence of revolutionary indifference to women's rights comes from the cahiers. References to women's rights—or even women—are extremely rare in these documents. Hyslop's survey of the general cahiers disclosed that 33 (16 from the Clergy, 9 from the Nobility, and 8 from the Third Estate) recommended education for "girls." But the nature of this education was not specified, and the fact that Clergy cahiers were the most numerous indicates that the schooling would be traditional and submissive. Gilbert Shapiro's and John Markoff's more exhaustive investigation of the cahiers ranked enfranchising women at the bottom of the table of subject frequencies: 1088 for the Parish cahiers, 1121 and 1125, respectively, for those from the Third Estate and the Nobility. But this sole tabulated reference to women has a standing similar to adult, non-Catholic, and general enfranchisement. Consequently, it is impossible to conclude whether the low ranking for women's franchise is due to unconcern for women, voting rights, or both.

Regardless of their contributions to, or the consequences that befell them due to, civic developments from 1775 to 1815, French and American women were part of the revolutionary crowd. Reflecting the more highly charged atmosphere of the French Revolution, French women were more militant than their American counterparts. They were at the forefront of Parisian bread riots in 1789, parading into the National Assembly to demand that the deputies discuss subsistence problems. In addition, 6,000 women marched on October 5 of that year to bring Louis XVI and the royal family back from Versailles to the capital. Radical in substance, traditional in form, this procession, by bringing back "the baker," "the baker's wife," and "the baker's little boy," continued an ancien régime ritual of urban, working-class females demonstrating at Versailles over food prices. In 1790, political clubs began to admit women and the *Société Fraternelle des deux Sexes* was formed, a Jacobin organization advocating marriage and divorce reform and better education for women. At this time, women's newspapers and clubs appeared that also supported these causes. In the summer of 1791, revolutionary women participated in radical republican clubs and democratic societies, sat in the galleries of sectional assemblies and the national legislature, contributed commentary to newspapers and political journals, petitioned for the vote, and urged Frenchmen to defend the Revolution. In 1792–93, women joined the *enragés* and the Paris Commune to bring down Girondins and the king. When foreign war broke out in 1792, women rolled bandages, made uniforms, accompanied troops to the front, and petitioned the National Convention to form women's legions. The Convention refused to form such units, but some local authorities issued arms and uniforms to women. In addition, about one hundred women crossdressed to serve in uniform at the front. Shortly before the Reign of Terror, in May 1793 militant Jacobin women founded the *Club des citoyennes républicaines révolutionnaires*. Some fifty women's Jacobin Clubs were organized, the majority between 1791–93 and mostly in the cities. Of the 4,800 primary assemblies formed in July 1793 to ratify the Montagnard constitution, at least two dozen had women members. Allies of the sans-culottes, these Republican Revolutionary Women spurred the radical insurgency of 1792–94.[49]

All female political agitation was not on behalf of the Revolution. If widely known, it is seldom mentioned that as a counterrevolutionary force women had their greatest impact on the Revolution and the First Empire. These women, many peasants, demonstrated against revolutionary deities, state cults, and civic religion festivals. They boycotted the constitutional clergy, rebuilt churches, celebrated the Christian Sabbath instead of the *decadi*, and protected clandestine refractory priests. By winter

1795, their efforts helped defeat dechristianization and constitutional Catholicism and restore the traditional Church.[50]

The apex of black civil rights was reached in 1794, during the Terror. The high point of women's rights came between September 1792, and March 1793. In the fall of 1792, Girondin Jacobins were ascendant; by spring 1793, Montagnard Jacobins contested control of the government. On the earlier date, the National Assembly mandated divorce on an equal basis for both spouses. Completing a legislative process begun in 1791, the National Convention in March 1793 equalized inheritance of property between the sexes. Females could now contract debts and consequently had some control over their property.[51]

Marital and property reforms were limited by an inability to leverage them for full citizenship and by their rapid reversal. While women made advances during the ascendancy of the Gironde, they were, according to the Constitution of 1791, "passive" rather than "active" citizens because they could not vote, bear arms for the country, and had limited ownership and control of property. Although property requirements for suffrage and military service were eliminated for white males in August 1792, the Convention refused to organize female military units. A year later, the Convention called for a *levée en masse*. Its decree stated: "Young men will go to battle; . . . women will make tents, uniforms, and serve in the hospitals." Four years of revolution had not altered the customary gender division of labor—men were ordered to fight, women to sew and nurse. Thus women were denied essential functions of citizenship.[52]

Momentum for women's rights, like Jewish rights, accelerated in the liberal era. A law of August 16, 1790, instituted a *tribunal de famille* (family court) to democratize the family by giving women and children more influence, thus diminishing patriarchal power. The liberal Constitution of 1791, drafted in September by the National Assembly, established marriage as a civil contract. Another advance for liberty and secularization occurred in that month when Jews were emancipated. In 1791, the Assembly also legislated partial succession rights (inheritance of property) for females. But not all went well for women in 1791. The Constitution that made marriage a civil contract also made women passive citizens.[53]

Unlike Jewish emancipation, however, progress on women's rights at first continued when the Revolution moved to the Left as a result of the fall of the monarchy on August 10, 1792, the election of the National Convention, and proclamation of the Republic in September. On the day (September 20) that the Legislative Assembly gave way to the Convention, under Girondin (moderate Jacobin) dominance marriage ceased to be a sacrament and the most liberal divorce law in the world was passed. With Girondins in the process of losing control of the government to Montagnards (radical Jacobins), the Convention further liberalized divorce and enhanced women's property rights. Moreover, under Girondin leadership the Convention refused to form female military units.[54] Advocacy of, or opposition to, women's rights was not associated with any era or faction of the Revolution. As the Revolution became radicalized, however, women became more active and militant for or against the Revolution, on behalf of Girondins or Montagnards, defending or attacking different factions of radical Jacobins, and in support of the Jacobin or the White Terrors.

Many Jacobin males supported divorce reform and, according to the revolutionary principle that women were citizens of the Republic, property rights for women. The Montnagard-controlled Convention on June 10, 1793, gave women equal rights and an equal say in the distribution of common lands. Numerous male Jacobin clubs supported the founding of sister societies, albeit with more than a whiff of paternalism. Several Jacobins lauded women soldiers and a few advocated that women form National Guard battalions. The impulse to liberate women stemmed from the revolutionary ideals of universality and equality, a vision that spurred emancipation of Jews and blacks.[55]

Radical women rallied to the Jacobin cause; despite some support from male allies, however, they did not fare well during the Terror. Along with Jews and believing Christians, they were oppressed and, unlike these other enclaves, never recovered from civic persecution. The trial of Louis XVI (December 1792–January 1793) marked the end of Gironde salience in the Convention. On April 30, a month before the Convention ratified the Montagnard Constitution (never applied) that provided for universal white male (but not female) suffrage, that body expelled women who accompanied the army but performed no vital services and those who actively served.[56]

Although this decree was not strictly enforced, it heralded an assault on women's rights. On May 31–June 2, Girondins were purged from the Convention and a Montagnard regime emerged. On October 28, the Convention banned women's clubs and popular societies. Government repression was explicitly rationalized as reinstating a natural order that returned females from the public sphere to domesticity. Less than four months later, the Convention emancipated slaves and gave blacks citizenship. This same legislature in effect outlawed women's right of public assembly, which removed them from the street, and, by 1794, curtailed all attempts at legal and social reform for women. Thermidorian triumph curbed or ended Montagnard political and religious persecution for many groups, but not for women. In May 1795, females were barred from the Convention galleries and in the anti-Jacobin backlash, divorce for women became more difficult to obtain. The passing of Thermidorian hegemony did not halt the decline of women's freedom. In May 1796, the Council of Five

Hundred excluded women from senior teaching posts. Although the Napoleonic Civil Code of 1804 preserved revolutionary legislation requiring that estates be divided among all sons and daughters and giving women rights to guardianship of their children, the Code reinforced the authority of the paterfamilias, resurrected unequal standards of divorce, and restored constraints on women's property rights. Wives could not own property without a husband's consent, be civil witnesses, or plead in court in their own name. In legal terms, married women were effectively minors.[57]

Aside from these reverses, Bonaparte, who shared the Jacobin outlook on women—namely that domesticity was female destiny—allowed education for girls to wither. Napoleon did not permit Josephine to talk politics with him. Waving his hand in dismissal of this possibility, he once said: "Let her weave, let her knit." Refusal to engage his wife in political discussion reflected the emperor's misogyny. From his St. Helena exile, the former scourge of Europe admitted, "I don't like women very much," a late and perhaps final comment on that subject. At least he was consistent in conventional disparagement of Jews, blacks, and women. Prospects for the latter, however, did not improve with the removal of the emperor—after the Bourbon Restoration of 1815, they completely lost the right of divorce.[58]

Apart from increased political involvement, the Revolution was a disappointment to the few who hoped it would engender women's rights. Gender equality was, at best, a marginal issue and feminist advances were rare, superficial, and temporary. Indeed, formulations like feminism, gender, or women's equality arguably are impositions of current concepts and values upon the past. Revolution, republicanism, and modern state formation left women's rights in no better, and in some respects worse, shape than under Bourbon reign. During the last decades of the old order, women could sometimes vote and act as regents, and a few nobles and women in religious orders participated in early meetings of the Estates General.[59] Even at the height of revolutionary feminism, these political and representational privileges were not preserved.

Women did not mobilize for civic equality. They reflected national divisions into radical, moderate, and reactionary factions. Those who joined the clubs and mobs that ushered in Jacobin rule did not speak for the leading feminist ideologue of the Revolution. Gouges, a Girondin and moderate royalist, castigated Robespierre. Her ideas and invective led to her arrest and execution. A broader fission opened between the *poissards* (market women) who had rallied around the Revolution in 1789 and the Republican Revolutionary Women who were the female legions of the Terror. The poissards opposed the Jacobins because the Law of the Maximum (September 29, 1793) regulated commodity prices and would hinder their profits. Their conflict with the radical women was enflamed when the Convention, on September 31, decreed that all women must wear the national cockade. Some female enragés were wearing not only the national cockade, but also the red cap of liberty and trousers worn by male sans-culottes. Poissards feared that Montagnards would impose male dress on them and beat up Jacobin women who appeared on the street wearing the red caps. This conflict led to the suppression of women's clubs, in no small part because the radicals often belonged to the *Club des citoyennes républicaines révolutionnaires*, an organization detested by the Robespierrists. Aside from strife between moderates and montagnards, women who differed over the liberal and radical versions of the Revolution were commonly hostile to women defending traditional Catholicism.[60]

Another reason women did not mobilize for full citizenship was that, like the nineteenth-century abolitionist movement and the civil rights and anti-Vietnam campaigns of the 1960s, women focused on issues other than feminism, or at least feminism as presently defined. Female enragés, members of the Club des citoyennes or other Jacobin societies, or simply those who showed up for demonstrations, did not usually emphasize feminist issues in their revolutionary agenda. Instead, they agitated for militant republicanism, staged bread riots, petitioned for female legions (the exception), or joined husbands, sons, and lovers at the front. But food riots and accompanying the army were customary in Bourbon times, as traditional as defending the Church against revolutionary encroachment.

Revolutionary men envisioned the role of revolutionary women, including female Jacobin political societies, as regenerative, benevolent, didactic, and decorative. As republican mothers, women were to teach revolutionary and republican principles, preferably to their children, engage in charitable and hospital work, serve as exemplars of purity, and beautify revolutionary-republican fetes. These functions would harmonize with the natural feminine domains of education, esthetics, empathy, self-sacrifice, and maternal feeling. Women's club members often shared this outlook and founded their organizations to instruct themselves and their families in revolutionary ideology, aid the war effort, and promote and participate in revolutionary festivals. In pursuit of their uniquely feminine incarnation of family and morality, several women's club members took oaths not to marry aristocrats and to give their hands and hearts solely to soldiers or patriotic citizens. The radical women of the *Société Citoyennes* subscribed to the conventional gender division of labor when they believed that women should stay in the home front and catch traitors while men marched away to the battlefront.[61]

Feminist issues like the rights to vote, bear arms, and obtain political representation did not dominate the program of the women's clubs.

Enough societies, however, discussed or agitated for these matters to alarm male Jacobins. The political consciousness of these organizations is reflected in name changes in the course of the Revolution. In 1791, the societies frequently called themselves *Amies de la Constitution*. Following the fall of the constitutional monarchy in the autumn of 1792, many redesignated themselves *Amies de la liberté et égalité*. By 1793, some took yet a new name, *Amies de la République*. A hint of the disjoined expectations of men and a minority of politically conscious women came in the response from a citoyenne clubbiste to the male chauvinism of Louis-Marie Prudhomme, a radical journalist: "We do not limit ourselves at all, Citizen Prudhomme, to singing the hymn of liberty, as you advised us; we want also to engage in civic acts."[62]

Widespread, if not unanimous, agreement on female roles and the alleged natural traits that genderized them disqualified women from political affairs. Hence, the major reason why women's rights were neglected was that the revolutionary commitment to civic rights did not include women. Under Jacobin hegemony slaves were formally freed and given citizenship, but elementary political rights—namely, that of assembly—were stripped from women. The repeated explanation for depriving women of the vote, military service, and full control over their property was that the public sphere was an unnatural place for women. Gouges was executed as much for feminism as for subversion. While not as uncompromisingly feminist as Gouges, other Girondin female leaders and reformers were nevertheless cut down by the radicals. Théroigne de Méricourt, a former *demimondaine* turned speaker for women's rights, was flogged by female enragés, a public humiliation that made her renounce political activity. Etta Palm d'Aelders, who lobbied the National Assembly for legal and educational reform for women and tried to organize a network of women's clubs, was arrested on the charge of being a royalist agent of Holland. Madame Jeanne Philipson ("Manon") Roland, the politically ambitious and influential wife of the Girondin Minister of the Interior, was arrested and executed.[63]

These figures may have been eliminated for their Girondin affiliation as well as their gender and prominence in women's reform activities. But in April 1794, with Robespierre still in power, Anne-Pauline Léon, a founder of the Société Citoyennes and an intrepid anti-Girondin street fighter, was arrested. Claire Lacombe, another militant radical opponent of the Girondins and successor of Léon as the leader of the Society, was arrested in March. Although Lacombe and Léon were radical Jacobins, factional conflict contributed to their deposition. They and their club allied with the enragés, the champions of direct democracy and the Parisian poor. Jacques Roux, the enragé leader, early in 1793 supported the food riots and his speeches militantly divided the world into the poor and the rich. Robespierre opposed the demonstrations and as an opponent of direct democracy, along with many other bourgeois Montagnards, grew alarmed at Roux's call for class warfare. Fearing public disorder, always an apprehension for radicals when in power, Roux was arrested in the fall of 1793.[64]

Revolutionary male leaders of every faction, especially radicals, disliked politically active women. In November 1793, a deputation headed by Jacobines appeared before the General Council of the Paris Commune. The Commune president, Pierre-Gaspard Chaumette, a National Assembly Deputy and Cult of Reason fanatic guillotined by Robespierre for dechristianization zealotry, was outraged by their presence. "[I]t is dreadful, it is contrary to all the laws of nature that a woman wants to make herself a man," he told the delegation. "Since when is it permitted to foreswear one's sex? Since when is it decent to see women abandon the pious attention of their household, the cradle of their children, in order to come to public places, to harangue the tribunes there. . . . Is it to men that nature confided domestic cares? Did she give us breasts to suckle our children? No, she" reserved for men "the hunt, labors, political matters." Nature commanded woman "to be the goddess of the domestic sanctuary" and "reign" there "by the invincible spell of grace and of virtue." Proceeding from the general to the particular, Chaumette reviewed for the delegation the fate of "impudent women, who want to become men":

> Recall that arrogant woman of a boneheaded and perfidious
> spouse, *la Roland*, who considered it proper to govern the Repub-
> lic, and who ran to her downfall; recall the impudent Olympe de
> Gouges, who, the first, instituted the societies of women, who aban-
> doned the cares of her family to embroil herself in the Republic,
> and whose head fell under the iron vengeance of the law. Is it for
> women to make motions? Is it for women to put themselves at the
> head of our armies? [italics in original]

After this diatribe, often interrupted by vigorous applause, Chaumette asked that the deputation be dismissed and the council no longer receive delegations of women. His request was unanimously adopted.[65]

An apostle of the Terror and member of the Committee of General Security, Jean Baptiste André Amar, speaking for the Committee, in October, 1793, blamed "women associated with democratic societies" for brawls between enragés and market women. The Committee asked, "Should women exercise political rights, and interfere in the affairs of the government?" As for citizenship, it concluded: "Universal opinion repudiates this idea" that "women have the moral and physical force to exercise" civic "duties."[66]

The Committee then queried, "Should women assemble in political associations?" It answered: "No, because they would be obligated to sacrifice more important cares to which nature calls them." Like Chaumette, Amar believed "that social order results from the difference that there is between man and woman." Natural endowments of "great energy, audacity and courage" and a profound "intelligence" qualify males for public life. "[W]omen are little capable of high conceptions and serious meditations." The "charm of their sex" and "their natural timidity and decency" confine women "to the care of the household" and "to prepare the minds and heart of children for public virtues." Amar and the Committee "believe[d] accordingly that a woman may not go out from her family to immerse herself in the affairs of the government" or "exercise political rights." The Committee proposed to the National Convention prohibition of women's political clubs and societies, a recommendation decreed by that body.[67]

Robespierre looked upon women in politics as unnatural, "sterile as vice," and wanted them to be wives and mothers. Prosecutors and judges in the radical Republic similarly degraded women who opted for demonstrations instead of domesticity. These officials charged women under their jurisdiction with lesbianism or promiscuity; male defendants were not denigrated in this manner. Another sign of contempt for women who left the hearth for the barricades surfaced in the May 1794 Convention debate over the imposition of civil dress for citizens. The proposed uniform was restricted to males.[68]

Men of the Revolution generally believed that biology and culture made the domestic sphere the proper place for women. "*Aux Republicaines*," a November 17, 1793, editorial in the *Feuille de salut public*, a government sponsored newspaper, conveys Jacobin rage over women who challenged the feminine stereotype. Addressed to the women of the Republic, it is a savage obituary of Marie-Antoinette, Gouges, and Mme. Roland, arguably the foremost female figures in the Revolution. The government had recently beheaded the Queen, and Gouges and Roland soon followed her to the guillotine. "Aux Republicaines" opens with a harsh warning: "In a short while the revolutionary tribunal is going to give women a great example which without doubt will not be lost on them; because justice, always impartial, places without cease the lessons on a level with the severity."[69]

As for the females subjected to retributive punishment, Marie-Antoinette was "ambitious" and betrayed France to monarchical Austria. But the *Feuille de Salut Public* discharged its most toxic venom on the personal, not the political. "She was a bad mother, a debauched spouse, and she died charged with the imprecations of those whose ruin she had wanted to consummate. Her name will forever be a horror to posterity."

Gouges, too, was indicted as much for her gender as alleged sedition. She deliriously aspired "to divide France" and "to be a statesman, and it seems that the law will punish this conspirator for having forgotten the virtues that befit her sex." The last of the unholy trinity, "The woman Roland," a "monster by all reports," she "distributed favors, positions and money," and scorned "the people and the judges chosen by them." Along with the others, violations of public trust were less vilified than violations of feminine virtue: "Although she was a mother, she had sacrificed nature, by choosing to elevate her sex, and that negligence, always dangerous, finished by causing her to perish on the scaffold."[70]

The editorial-obituary began with a clarion of caution, proceeded to describe the evils and calamities of those who transgress political and gender norms, and concluded with patronizing patriarchic counsel to cleave to the canons of true womanhood: "Women! Do you want to be republicans? Love, follow and teach the laws that call your husbands and your children to the exercise of their rights; . . . stay pure in your place, labor in your household; never attend the popular assemblies with the desire to speak there."[71]

The revolutionary rank and file echoed the sentiments of their leaders, spokesmen, and government officials. When the Convention dissolved women's political clubs, it mandated that male societies admit women. A few male Jacobin clubs refused, but even the majority, which allowed women to join, followed the policy of their predecessors with mixed memberships. Women regularly had to sit in a segregated area of the hall and as a rule they could not vote or make motions. The Jacobin Club of Toul resolved that women who sat on benches reserved for men be arrested. Chateauroux clubbistes declared that women should sweep the hall and men be exempted from this chore; women who participated in Jacobin fetes similarly cleaned up or served food. Grenade Jacobins asserted that the first duty of women was to teach their children revolutionary principles; Republican motherhood would also become the prime mission of contemporary American women. Women who did not behave in a conventional manner were subject to ridicule from the revolutionary crowd as well as from prominent Republicans. Parisian sans-culottes referred to the republican society *des deux sexes* as the *société hermaphrodite*; hermaphrodite was a term applied to men who defended women's rights.[72]

If men of the Revolution, with rare exceptions, reprehended politically inclined women and suppressed any initiatives that resembled the present-day feminist agenda, women of the Revolution, again with few exceptions, did not agitate for equal rights. In fact, they agitated for virtually everything else. Women campaigned against the monarchy and the Gironde, for the radicals, and for supply of, and price controls on, food, and in support of the traditional Gallic church. Yet, it may be argued that much of this activity, even when engaged on behalf of the Revolution and the emerging nation, derived from women's conventional defense of the family rather than from aspirations for full political rights. Those women who championed civic equality did not reflect the sentiments of the vast majority, who simply did not think in modern terms about their womanhood. Thus, it is anachronistic to define in current gender discourse conflicts over women's place in the revolutionary Republic and the First Empire.

Despite the proviso of anachronism, it is clear that during the Revolution divorce and property-holding reforms and occasional advocacy of women's rights did not prevent women from being excluded from the liberal discourse, at least as applied to full citizenship. Their position did not improve under the radicals. Unlike liberal monarchists and Girondins, Montagnards executed and imprisoned women leaders and closed women's political societies. Radical Jacobins also unleashed a tirade against women who forsook traditional domesticity for the public sphere.

The barrage of denunciation and repression was a male attack (many men would say counterattack) in the revolutionary war of the sexes. In modern parlance, it was a weapon of choice in the genderized struggle over the contested terrain of the public sphere. Men were willing to concede that women could be republican mothers and patriotic wives, inculcating revolutionary and republican virtue in their families. As women of the revolution, they should also dispense charity, uphold morality, and appropriately (according to their feminine nature) assist the war effort and other public causes. These were considered activities properly conducted in the private sphere, that is, chiefly at home. Political and military functions (taking part in civic debates, holding office, voting, bearing arms), however, were reserved for men because they were in the public sphere. Montagnards might be radical revolutionaries, but in gender matters they were conservatives. Hence they were frightened and outraged by the minority of women who staked a claim in the public realm and even by the majority of women clubbistes who worked for the Revolution without crossing conventional borders.

The anger and anxiety of male Robespierrists was misogynistic, but not misconceived. Women organizing, deliberating, and demonstrating, even within the professed confines of a woman's true place, threatened to erase distinctions between public and private and thus between masculine and feminine. As shown by Suzanne Desan, revolutionary men warned women not to be frivolous, a trait regarded as both feminine and aristocratic. Members of women's societies responded by claiming that their revolutionary activities had made them serious-minded. Gravity and rationality, however, were considered masculine qualities, virtues in men, but dangerous, unfeminine traits that eroded gender boundaries. In the course of their revolutionary and republican activities, some women not only discovered that they were patriotic, courageous, and rational, characteristics appropriate for the public realm, but they also came to realize that many men they encountered there were irresolute and emotional, qualities attributed to women and deemed tolerable only in domestic life.[73]

The assault on women, therefore, was, as Desan asserts, an attempt to revert to conventional gender boundaries. Male radicals argued that the Revolution had not changed women; they were still flighty, fickle, gullible, hysterical, and incapable of political action. Those women who aspired to public visibility or evinced talents and traits that won them this notoriety were impugned as unnatural amazons. Both condemnations aimed to fortify male supremacy, which, in turn, was believed by the majority of men, and probably by most women, to be the indispensable route to restoring public order. Accordingly, much vilification of civically active women was sexually charged. They were besmirched as seductresses, "hussies," and "prostitutes," and sympathetic men were belittled as "hermaphrodites."[74]

Historians of French and American women of that era agree that the birth pangs of the modern nation did not gestate dramatic transformation in the status of women. Those that make comparisons between the two countries also concur that France tended toward more vigorous rhetoric and reforms than did America.[75] The radical climate of the French Revolution activated women and the Church, and women's guilds or guild-like associations facilitated their recruitment and coordination. Paris was another mobilizing factor. The commercial, civic, cultural, and revolutionary cockpit of France, locus of bread riots and other demonstrations that shook and toppled governments, home of the enragés, sans-culottes and the Commune, Paris radicalized and galvanized its inhabitants, male and female alike. These conditions and institutions were peripheral or absent in America. It should be noted, however, that France also experienced greater regression, and that the persistence of the Napoleonic Code and the pervasiveness of traditional Catholicism made the reaction more permanent than the improvements made before 1793.

Despite comparative moderation, American "daughters of liberty," marched, signed petitions, demonstrated, sang, cheered and jeered, took part in street theater, attended meetings, and joined riots. The street became an ungendered public forum, which before the War for Independence amplified resistance by enforcing homespun campaigns and boycotts of British goods. Females even met by themselves to raise money or spin cloth to further the Continental cause. They accompanied the troops to sew, cook, launder, and haul water for the soldiers. After the daughters of liberty had become "republican mothers," women made limited ad-

vances in acquiring divorces and control over their property. Divorce became more widespread and women received alimony and regained control
of their property when they were innocent parties to the break-up of the
marriage. Termination of primogeniture also enhanced women's ownership rights by making daughters more likely to share in family inheritance.
Changes appeared as well in female education. To school future republican wives and mothers, postrevolutionary women's academies included
civic knowledge in their curricula. Political rights for women also mod-
estly expanded during the Revolution and immediately thereafter. The
New Jersey Constitution (1776) did not explicitly deny women suffrage
and in the 1780s and 1790s; as in colonial times, women occasionally
voted in local elections.[76]

If gender equality inspired few women in the French Revolution, it
had even less transatlantic appeal. American women did not join or form
clubs, petition their governments, seek to organize combat units, or make
passionate speeches to stir revolutionary fervor. Pre-1793 reforms were
reversed in France, but even less was accomplished in the War for Independence and the early Republic. As in France, much of women's activity,
spinning cloth and accompanying troops, was traditional. Divorce increased, but never on the basis of the gender parity that briefly existed in
France. In the young United States, it was still difficult for women to dissolve their marriages, but not as impossible as in France after 1815. Not
until the late 1830s was the English Common Law doctrine of coverture
breached. Thus the early national period ended without wives having significant control over their property. They could not make contracts or a
will and their capital remained in the hands of their husbands. In some
respects, pertaining to dower rights, women's standing worsened.[77]

American and French women faced the same prejudice. Expressing
an attitude voiced as well by Napoleon and Robespierre, John Adams
answered the question he put to himself about women voting and undertaking government service: "[T]heir delicacy renders them unfit for practice and experience in the great businesses of life, and the hardy enterprises of war, as well as the arduous cares of state." Fragility and other
facets of femininity ensure that women's "attention is so much engaged
with the necessary nurture of their children, that nature has made them
fittest for domestic cares."[78]

In this private letter, Adams approvingly mentioned another exclusion from the liberal polity—the revolutionary leader also opposed enfranchising those without property. Thomas Jefferson, the great democrat, had no reservations about the propertyless voting; he agreed,
however, with Adams's assessment of women. "But our good ladies, I
trust, have been too wise to wrinkle their foreheads with politics," he
wrote one woman. "They are contented to soothe and calm the minds of

their husbands returning ruffled from political debate. They have the good sense to value domestic happiness above all other, and the art to cultivate it beyond all others." Jefferson addressed this subject to another female friend with what in those days was conventional wisdom, but would currently be considered insufferable condescension: "The tender breasts of ladies were not formed for political convulsion; and the French ladies miscalculate much their own happiness when they wander from the true field of their influence [the home] into that of politicks [*sic*]"[79]

Since founding fathers in France and the United States did not support gender equality, apart from minor variances women had the same low civic status in both countries. Unlike the French convent girls' schools, women's academies taught their students civic responsibility but, as did the French nuns, educated potential republican spouses and parents to focus on the family and home. Women became citizens of the new United States—they could be naturalized, subject to laws, and taxed as single adults. But female citizens could not vote, hold office, or perform military service, and as wives had little control over their property. Lacking these qualifications for full civic participation, citizenship mainly obligated the republican wife and mother to maintain and instill moral values in her husband and children. Citizenship thus defined and developed was not a bastion of rights for women, and New Jersey in 1807 further weakened women's civic status by specifically disenfranchising females. No state extended suffrage to females. Revolution and nation building in France and America were patriarchic processes.[80]

The republican wife and mother resembled in her conformity to conventional womanhood another contemporary female icon—the woman captive of the Indians. Nurturer and paragon of domesticity and victim, martyr to savagery, represented the paramount heroines of true womanhood, the loftiest idealizations of feminine virtue. These figures as well represented the most extreme and complete antithesis and negation of the icon of modern feminism, that paragon of gender equality, the liberated woman.[81]

In the early epochs of the modern French and American nations, Jews, blacks, and women faced distinct difficulties in acquiring equal rights. Either full citizenship was never granted (women), granted, but not implemented and subsequently withdrawn (blacks), granted, but never fully attained and ultimately compromised (French Jews), or granted in the civic realm, but often withheld in civil society (American Jews). As demonstrated in the discussion of blacks and Jews, the degree and explanations of liberation differed within and between the nations. The experience of women is now included in this comparison of emancipation and subjection. Obviously, neither race nor religion figured in the civic and social standing of white gentile women in the United States or France.

Men and women of this type were considered equally French or American, while blacks (almost always) and Jews (frequently), even when citizens, were deemed lesser members of the national community.

If men and women of the right creed and ancestry belonged alike to the nation, they were dissimilar in their civic role and status. In France, they were passive instead of active citizens; in America, they were daughters of the Revolution or republican mothers, and this association of women's national and biological-familial roles was not coincidental. While these images did not signify the malignance conveyed by many stereotypes of blacks and Jews, they did delimit the civic rights and functions of women. When blacks and Jews were emancipated, they were given full legal rights of citizenship. When women were made citizens, they did not receive equal civic rights. Upon emancipation, black and Jewish men in both countries could legally vote, control property, and serve in the armed forces. These rights were conferred upon women long after they became citizens and this prolonged delay constricted them politically; for example, until the twentieth century they were citizens who could not vote. Citizenship for Jewish and black males was a declaration of their independence; citizenship for women was circumscribed by (and thus inscribed) their continued legal dependence.

French and American revolutionaries and nation builders and most males in these countries could not transcend—as they could, at least intermittently, in the case of alleged civic deficiencies of Jews and blacks—their belief that women were essentially mothers, wives, or daughters. According to this view, women were unable to manage their property or take up arms in national defense. Military service to preserve the country is a basic function of the citizen in all forms of nationalism. It is widely recognized as a particularly desirable form of bonding. Citizens acting together out of loyalty to, and sacrifice for, their nation are generally looked upon as exemplifying the quintessence of civic fraternity, the pinnacle of patriotism. Property has a dimmer halo, but is considered a fundamental component of American liberalism. Excluded until relatively recently by received opinion from property management and military service, women were relegated to the domestic sphere by imputations of nature and virtue. Men, however, even if black and Jewish, were eligible for the public sphere. Whatever differences existed between French and American political culture and national identity, both nations held a common view of women and hence accorded them similar civic status. Women were differentiated from other citizens and thus became a particularistic deviation from the universal values of consensus liberalism. When fraternity was equated with masculinity, liberty and equality were genderized.

At the deepest level, gender posed a different problem than did race or creed. Blacks and Jews were either going to be incorporated into or separated from the national community—emancipated or excluded. Women, like Jews and blacks, could be subordinated, but not segregated, as could Jews from Gentiles or blacks from whites. They were, after all, part of the family and unless family and country were to be isolated from each other, they belonged, as well, to national society. During the French Revolution, therefore, white men and women were similarly addressed as "citoyen" and "citoyenne" at a time when most blacks were slaves. In America, white males and females bore the equivalent titles of "Mr." or "Mrs." and "Miss", while most blacks were in bondage, and even the few who were free were rarely so called.

Nevertheless, imputed to women were traits that differentiated them from men and disqualified them from fundamental civic activities. Accordingly, their citizenship derived from alleged gender differences and these distinctions led to the creation of a private sphere, the domain of women, and a public sphere where men ruled. A pretense of parity in these spheres thinly disguised a reality of subservience and dominance. The gender hierarchy politically manifesting itself as sexual bifurcation dictated social specialization, which, in turn, defined different types of citizenship for men and women. Women were citizens of France and America at the same time or before Jews and blacks, but belatedly, or have not yet, acquired full civic rights and obligations.

No argument can reconcile American racism from 1775 to 1815 or thereafter with the claim that a liberal consensus is a comprehensive feature of the national culture. Historical oppression of Native-Americans and Asian-Americans, as well as African-Americans, contradicted national attachments to freedom and democracy. In this respect, France more justly validates the Tocqueville-Hartz thesis. Women's rights, however, is a more complicated issue. Although in 1800 women in America and France experienced an approximately equal deprivation of rights, in the long run America's Tocquevillian predilections may have inclined more to gender than race and thus contributed to an earlier and more extensive achievement of civic equality for women in the United States.

Affirming a more favorable outcome for women's rights in America than in France can feasibly begin with an argument of omission. Unlike France under the regressive Napoleonic Code, America, with one important exception, never reversed federal legal gains on gender equity. Despite irrevocable erosion of coverture and momentum for female suffrage, the Expatriation Act (1907) contradicted the gradual trend toward equality. Congress now mandated that American women who married un-naturalized foreigners lost their citizenship. For women, matrimonially derived civic status replaced equally gendered nationality rights. In 1934, the historic situation of equal nationality rights was restored. But the regression of 1907–34, on balance, left America more egalitarian than

France in this critical aspect of women's rights. Although France anticipated America by seven years in substituting female equal nationality
rights for spousal-derived civic status, this phase of gender equality was
new to that nation. From the promulgation of the Napoleonic Code until
1927, a wife forfeited French citizenship if she married an alien, that is,
nationality effectively derived from the husband.[82]

More positive evidence of greater progress in women's rights in the
United States is the precedence of American women in the quest for full
citizenship. French women were not enfranchised until 1944, twenty-five
years after the passage of the Nineteenth Amendment to the U.S. Constitution. Moreover, for some time before 1919, women could vote in some
local and state elections or on some matters—for members of school
boards or on tax and bond issues—especially in the West, and were
elected to government office, even to Congress. Women in America voted
before they did in France and, as a consequence, held elected governmental and party posts well in advance of French women. In the 1930s, for
example, one woman was in Franklin Roosevelt's cabinet, two became
foreign ministers, one a federal circuit court judge, and, in 1936 the gender ratio on the Democratic Party Platform Committee was equal.[83]

American women have maintained an edge in political participation
even after French women have been enfranchised. In the 1990s, President
William Clinton appointed women to head the State and Justice Departments, which along with Treasury and Defense, are the most important
cabinet posts. Women currently compose 8.7 percent of French national
legislators. The equivalent share of the 107th Congress is 13.5 percent
(13.6 percent of the House of Representatives, 59 of 435 members, and
13 percent of the Senate, 13 of 100 members). While the female contingent among American legislators is nearly one-third as large, the percentage difference is a less impressive 4.8. Neither of these cradles of national
republicanism, however, has much to boast about. France is last in the
fifteen-member European Union in percentage of women legislators, behind Germany (29.6 percent) and the United Kingdom (17.1 percent).
The United States, that allegedly nonpareil liberal society, would rank
ahead of only Greece, Italy, and France.[84]

American women also preceded French women in attaining higher
levels of education. Since inferior, or, at least, less schooling had been a
justification for suffrage restrictions, the proliferation of American
women in colleges undermined gender distinctions regarding equal citizenship. From the start, unlike France, American public primary and secondary schools were coeducational and, for primary schools, coequal in
gender attendance. In 1848, 40 percent of French girls had no formal
education; two years later, the government mandated primary schools for
girls, but in 1860 less than one-quarter of them were for girls. When the

first French female undergraduate enrolled in the 1860s, women had been going to several American colleges for two decades. In 1870 over one-fifth, in 1890 more than one-third, and by 1920 over two-fifths, of American college students were women. Correspondingly, in France in 1900 there were 624 native French women students in that nation's higher educational system and 2,547 in 1914; not until the 1960s did French women equal the share of American women in 1920 among college students in their respective countries. In addition, women were awarded one-third of graduate degrees granted by American universities in the 1920s. Equally crucial in facilitating civic entry, American women were more likely than their French sisters to receive a secular education.[85]

Women's lack of control over property was another powerful argument made for male civic bias. Accordingly, it is not surprising that American women were economically empowered, as they attained political rights, sooner than were French women. During the early years of the Third Republic, women were still under the constraints of the Napoleonic Code. Wives had to obey their husbands, live where their spouses chose to live and get their permission to seek employment, husbands administered their wives' property, and fathers had full control over their children. These repressive regulations were relieved by husbandly "tacit consent," which, when granted, enabled women to act concerning their property and in other related economic matters.[86]

Starting in the 1880s, female autonomy in France was placed on firmer legal ground. But American women were there first. In 1839, Mississippi, the first state to legislate women's control over their own property, contrary to English common law, started the trend. New York's legislature passed The Married Women's Property Act of 1848, which gave women in that state control over property acquired by inheritance, bequest, or gift. Twelve years later, a New York law gave women control over their wages, allowed them to make contracts or bring suits, and have joint custody of their children. The Empire State was no exception. Between the 1840s and the 1880s, a series of married women's property and community property enactments in most states recognized the right of women to total control over property that they inherited, brought into the marriage, or were given by a third person. Between 1869 and 1887, thirty-three states and the District of Columbia granted married women the sole right to dispose of their own earnings and wages, thirty specifically provided for a separate estate for women, and five adopted community property laws, that is, family property was held in equal shares by each spouse. By 1900, women had significant property autonomy. Three-quarters of the states allowed wives to own and control property, two-thirds permitted similar rights over their earnings. In most states, women could make contracts and bring suits. Women achieved extensive ownership as well as control. By 1880, in no jurisdiction in the United States were less than one-third of probated decedents or testators female. Twenty years later, one-third of all estates belonged to women and they held one-quarter of all probated property.[87]

French women belatedly attained such economic parity. Before 1886, they could not open bank accounts. Until 1897, they were ineligible to be witnesses in civil action. Only in 1907 did wives acquire the legal capacity to freely dispose of their own earnings.[88] It may be alleged that the discrepancy between American and French women was de jure rather than de facto ("tacit consent"). Until the 1880s, patriarchal judges in the United States blunted some of the married women's property legislation. It is also true, however, that, as late as World War I, some French banks turned women away when they tried to open accounts.[89]

Social, as well as political and economic, activities were more liberally engendered in America. In 1884, France reintroduced the right of divorce. By banning dissolution by mutual consent, which had been in the 1792 divorce law, the renewal was narrower in scope than the original. Divorce laws were less restrictive in many American states and the national divorce rate has always been considerably higher. No necessitous connection exists between divorce and women's freedom. In fact, some patriarchal societies allow divorce, usually when desired by husbands. But in America wives petitioned most legal dissolutions. Two-thirds of the divorces in the 1860s were granted to women; a century later this share had risen to three-quarters.[90]

Bearing arms on behalf of the state has been as vital as property ownership and education as a historical indicator of civic rights. Those who cannot fight for the state are ipso facto not full citizens. This prescription for citizenship is underscored by the centrality of war and the nation's armed forces in state formation and the development of nationalism. The right of women to military service is of recent recognition in France and the United States, and after their respective Revolutions both nations followed the same trajectory. In World War I, women served in conventionally female roles as nurses and ambulance drivers. During World War II, they enlisted in the armed forces as uniformed, noncombat auxiliary personnel. Subsequently, the armed forces of these nations made these corps part of their regular services and promoted women to flag rank at approximately the same time. Nonetheless, in the postwar era, women in the American military have been considerably more prominent than their French counterparts. Between 1973 and 1980, the percentage of women in the U.S. military climbed from 2.7 to 8.1. In the latter year, women composed 2.75 percent of the French armed forces. In 1986–87, comparative shares of American and French servicewomen were, respectively, 10.1 and 3.7 percent of the total in uniform. At this time, 10.3

percent of U.S. military officers were women; females constituted 2.6 percent of French officers.[91]

Greater gender parity in the United States than in France continues to the present. In 2001, the United Nations issued a "Gender-related Development Index" ranking of 151 nations according to "a long and healthy life, knowledge and a decent standard of living—adjusted to account for inequalities between men and women." America ranked fourth and France tenth.[92]

Some aspects of female empowerment and equity favored France over America. During the twentieth century, a higher percentage of French women have been in the work force and the gender wage gap has been narrower in France than in the United States[93] In precedence and magnitude, however, American women surpassed their French sisters in political participation, defense of the state, control over property, extent of education, individual autonomy, and familial equality. A key clue to this national gender differential lies in the trajectories of French and American feminism. An Anglo/American and a French/Continental mode may be distinguished and these different modes correspond to the contrasting abolitionist campaigns in these countries. Anglo/American agitation for women's rights was a mass movement that engaged religious affiliations and alliances with other reform crusades, exploited women's organizational experience in these activities, and employed such tactics as lectures, fairs, pamphlets, newspapers, massive petitions, meetings, marches, demonstrations, and extensive advertising to generate popular support for the cause.[94]

Although French and American feminism emerged in the late 1840s, their courses soon diverged. Lacking the education and organizing skills of their transatlantic sisters and following a different antislavery reform model, French feminists formed small groups and preferred to encourage government legislation rather than mobilize popular support. *Association pour le Droit des Femmes* (1870), founded to emulate feminist organizations in the United States and England, had 100 members. *Ligue Française pour le Droit des Femmes* (1882), a moderate legal reform oriented society, started with 200 members, half of them male, and shortly thereafter dwindled to 100 and was run by men. Other women's rights organizations had similar numbers. Many legislative advances in women's education and divorce that started in 1880s were due more to anticlericalism than to a commitment to women rights. "During the nineteenth century, no feminist group attempted to organize women into a mass political movement," wrote a historian of French feminism. "[F]eminists . . . functioned either as propagandists and/or organized small local groups whose purpose was to pressure the Paris-based government to decree or legislate reform. In this respect, they functioned like other nineteenth-century French political groups."[95] Similar variances between French and American feminism and abolitionism substantiate Tocqueville's observation that voluntary association or, as it is now called, civil society, was further developed in the United States than in France.

Differences in size and strategy of women's rights movements in France and the United States appear in a comparison between the numbers who signed an 1854 petition organized by Susan B. Anthony for the right of wives to their wages and equal guardianship of their children, on the one hand, and subscribers to nineteen French petitions between 1881–85 for women's suffrage, on the other. The American solicitation had 6,000 signatures, the largest of the French petitions 2000.[96] It may be argued that the French appeal, addressed to the franchise, demanded a higher level of feminism; then again, it came a generation later. A more illuminating contrast is between the principal suffrage societies in France and America, the *Union française pour le Suffrage des Femmes* (1908) and the National American Woman Suffrage Association (1890), respectively. In 1914, the UFSF had 12,000 members and in 1915 the NAWSF had 200,000. The French organization restricted its campaign to the municipal franchise. French suffragette leaders explicitly ruled out demands of English and American suffragettes for full voting rights and opposed the street demonstration tactics of Anglo/American feminists.[97]

Inconclusive endings are inherently unsatisfying, but research on past and present racism and sexism in the United States precludes the absolute resurrection of the liberal consensus hegemony of the previous generation. Its burial and the ensuing fragmentation of American historical scholarship may nevertheless be premature.[98] The study of marginalized and repressed groups dilutes, but does not obliterate, the validity of the paradigm. Consensus liberalism essentially denies the history of America's African– and Native-Americans and largely distorts the experience of Asian-Americans and American women. Trends toward gender equality, however, appeared earlier and proceeded more effectively in America, partially due to the national commitment to individual liberty and equality.

The Tocqueville-Hartz thesis offers truer explanations for America's allegiance to liberty of conscience and to the acquisition of full citizenship by male European immigrants from diverse national and ethnic extraction. Inclusive nationalism, republican pluralism, and individual freedom may be selective and conditioned, but are nonetheless powerful impulses in American culture and society. They are also dynamic. Since the 1950s, these bedrock beliefs have been a fulcrum for those historically excluded but now advancing toward civic equality. The battle to redress previous imbalances still persists for these groups, but the gains have been basic and dramatic. What can be dynamic, however, can contract as well as expand. And lapses in equal rights have happened in American history, as was the case after Reconstruction and with the tightened restrictions on immigration. Over the past generation, however, racial and gender marginalization has been significantly and unprecedentedly reduced and this outcome would be unimaginable without the national belief, flawed though it still is, in liberty, individualism, and pluralism.

A second major issue here addressed is how the liberal consensus differentiates the United States and France. America has demonstrated inclinations toward authoritarian statism, and for designated racial groups, outright tyranny, and France has shown a persistent, if often not prevalent, propensity for individual freedom. These nations are kaleidoscopic; each presented different facets of itself depending upon era, event, and enclave. France and America have nevertheless in important respects considerably diverged and these differences involve cleavage to statism and some variance of unrepresentative rule versus individualism and republicanism. The United States has been a republic since its Revolution, while France until 1870 was, outside of two brief periods, under monarchical or despotic government. Even the relatively long life of the Third Republic was threatened and finally ended by an antirepublican coterie of anti-Semites, clerics, Bourbons, and fascists. And the Fourth and early Fifth Republics' "man-on-the-horse" charisma of Charles De Gaulle had no equivalent in George Washington or any other American leader.

A final reservation awaits disposition. What if structural and cultural analyses of France and America that dichotomize centralism and pluralism, authority and freedom, and the state and the individual are irrelevant? What if the real differences between these countries derive not from internal and ideological factors, but from external developments? Would France have been more liberal and stable if, from the Revolution of 1789 until the end of Vichy, the nation had been spared wars on its own soil and civic upheaval? In 1792–93, 1813–15, 1870–71, 1914–18, and 1940–44, France was invaded and partly occupied; in 1814 and 1815, 1871, and 1940, it suffered humiliating defeats. Regimes were overturned in 1789, 1792, 1794, 1799, 1815, 1830, 1848, 1852, 1870, 1940, 1945, and 1958.

Much of the domestic turmoil, however, did not prevent a liberal consensus, but rather derived from the absence of such agreement. Conversely, widespread belief in individual freedom and republican government unified American civic society. Foreign wars, invasions, and occupations undoubtedly disturb domestic tranquility, but America was also invaded and partly occupied in 1776 and 1812 and, in the interval between these wars, was often threatened by, and sometimes in actual strife with, France and England, yet these conflicts did not inhibit the emergence of the liberal consensus or throttle the young Republic.

The Civil War, which combined war, rebellion, and, for the South, invasion and occupation, does challenge the contention of a national accord over representative government and personal rights. The ready reunion of the North and South and the lack of any subsequent fundamental domestic division, however, indicate the strength and stability of America's commitment to Lockian liberalism. But this outcome, particularly in contrast to the virtually serial civil strife in France from 1789–1945, comes with the usual exception; the renewed commitment to civic peace and liberty was contracted over the deprivation of these conditions for African-Americans.

At this juncture of causal analysis, we face alternative explanations of the emancipation and other experiences of French and American Jewry and the genesis of national culture, particularly as the cultures of these countries touch on the conceptions of liberalism expounded by Tocqueville and Hartz. I have examined these matters by exploring the Anglo-American/Continental European dichotomy as represented by the United States and France from 1775 to 1815. My contention is that the late-eighteenth-century revolutionary experiences and heritages of France and America were shaped by long-developing pluralistic and tolerant milieus in the Anglo-American Atlantic that began in the seventeenth century, as well as by a comparative absence of these milieus in the ancien régime. These differences in French and American civic cultures were accentuated by dramatic and significant variances in the French and American Revolutions and these variances, in turn, reflected preexisting historical developments in these nations.

I have now introduced the possibility that contrasts between France and America in their treatments of Jews, their national cultures, and their encounter with patterns of liberalism may be also accounted for by "exogenous" factors like wars, invasions, occupations, and civil conflicts. Accordingly, the primacy of genetic or "exogenous" factors must be resolved. My initial contention is that in the period 1775–1815 and in the American Civil War, both nations underwent similar exogenous experiences and that, therefore, the different consequences of these experiences in France and America implies that exogenous elements had a secondary impact. Their subordinate role is further substantiated by the history of a new nation. Since acquiring independence in 1948, Israel has been surrounded by countries that have conspired and fought against its independence, survived four wars and two invasions, and a hostile Palestinian population that has mounted two uprisings. Yet Israel's political culture and national values, as in America, have sustained—freedom of thought, political stability, and, at least for its citizens (the majority of the inhabitants), democratic rule.

A more profound stipulation, however, undermines the exogenous explanation. Wars and civil conflicts, as I attempt to show throughout this study, were not external intrusions into, but outgrowths of, the revolutionary heritages and their historical contexts in France and America. The rebellion of the South, for example, grew out of issues of slavery and the locus of ultimate sovereignty unresolved in the War for Independence, the formulation of the U.S. Constitution, and the early national era. In sum, the exogenous is, in reality, the inherent.

In the operative sphere, as in the operatic, things are not always what they seem. Put more ponderously, there are unintended consequences, unanticipated developments, and unanalyzed sentiments. Religious liberty, diversity, and tolerance was stronger, and formal demands for total assimilation were weaker, in America than in France, but, until the second half of the nineteenth century, the Jewish community in the United States was less cohesive and enduring than its cohort across the Atlantic. America celebrates itself as the land of the free, the home of the voluntary association, and the pinnacle of individualistic, unregulated capitalism. France emblazons the general will and the interventionist state and has intermittently embraced kings, emperors, and surrendered to charismatic authoritarians. Yet when perspectives are changed from those of republican constancy, creedal tolerance, and ethnic pluralism to that of race, it is France that may be a more resolute defender of diversity and freedom. America's heritage of liberty and equality, however, facilitated advances in women's rights before and further than in France, but this heritage has been belatedly, and as yet incompletely, applied to gender matters. Thus we end where the argument started. The Tocqueville-Hartz thesis illuminates important dimensions of American life and history and distinctions between France and the United States, but obscures the contradiction between racism and sexism, on the one hand, and individual liberty, universal republican values, and national consensus, on the other.

CHAPTER 7

THE OUTCOME

In 1989, Anne Sinclair, a television journalist, was chosen to represent Marianne, the female figure of republican France; there is nothing noteworthy in this selection except that Sinclair was Jewish. Five years before, a French public opinion survey reported that 94 percent of the respondents felt that Jews were "French people like all the rest." Concurrent approval was recorded in America: Ninety-two percent of the respondents in a 1981 public opinion poll would let Jews into their neighborhoods, 73 percent would vote for a Jewish presidential candidate, and 66 percent would not object to their child marrying a Jew. Further evidence that Americans were disinclined to distinguish Jews from other people came from a 1981 poll that tested public support for admission of various ethnic groups. Russian Jews, Northern Europeans, and Italians ranked highest with respective affirmative percentages of 39.0, 40.9, and 41.7. The former achieved the same approval rating as Northern Europeans, a stunning reversal of the racialist thinking that prevailed from the 1880s until after World War II.[1] In the 1990s, two Jews sat on the U.S. Supreme Court, another headed the Federal Reserve System, arguably the second most important post in the national government, and Jews or ex-Jews occupied two of the three most powerful cabinet posts (State and the Treasury). A Jew ran as vice president to enhance the electability of the 2000 Democratic presidential candidate and the Albert Gore-Joseph Lieberman ticket won the popular vote. Jews now have apparently fulfilled their own aspirations and those of the many who supported their liberation. They have indeed become useful, moral, and full citizens of France and the United States. If their attainment in these countries is virtually identical in type and degree, however, the route to this destination has sometimes diverged.

As the Age of Napoleon passed, the Jews of France were organized in cohesive creedal communities and most worshipped in the manner of their ancestors. Formally emancipated, they faced an enduring struggle for political equality and affirmation by the gentile community. At this time, the Jews of America, not as solid a religious enclave, were more confident of their civic status and national acceptance. I now summarize the subsequent history of the Jews of these countries. As in the preceding narrative and analysis, I examine Jewish identity per se and the way in which it connects to national identity and relate that interaction to the Tocqueville-Hartz theory of liberalism.

Considerable convergence occurred in the American and French Jewish communities. In 1815, they were minor demographic outposts of world Jewry. Presently, France, next to Russia, has the largest Jewish population in Europe and more Jews live in the United States than anywhere else. In addition, America is the cultural, financial and political center of diaspora Judaism. Jews of both countries congregated in cities and especially in Paris and New York. Ethnic composition is another parallel between the groups. Sephardic Jews came first, assimilated earlier and were the dominant enclave in the ancien régime and the colonial period. In the nineteenth century, Ashkenazim of German extraction predominated in both countries. At mid-century, Reform Judaism made inroads, especially among German Jews in America and France. Later in the century, however, an infusion from Eastern Europe rejuvenated orthodoxy. Similar tensions developed in the United States and France between Sephardic and German Jews and between German and Russian Jews.

French and American Jews had the same occupational trajectory, starting out as artisans and petty tradesmen and ascending in wealth and status as professionals and businessmen. Many American and French Jews were committed to the labor movement and, more than other ethnic and religious groups, to intellectual activity. The Jews of France and America, whether from Sephardic, German, or Eastern European origins, have culturally and to a lesser but still considerable, degree, structurally assimilated. Starting during the Civil War and the 1880s, respectively, Jews in America and France encountered (in France, reencountered) a rising tide of anti-Semitism, which crested during World War II. Nevertheless, they have been patriotic citizens who deem their diasporic residence the true Promised Land.

Despite extensive resemblance, these national Jewish communities diverged in important respects. The demographic increase of American Jews was continuous until the 1960s. Cessation of Alsace and Lorraine in 1871 reduced the number of Jews in France. But immigration from Eastern Europe and since the mid-1950s from North Africa more than compensated for the loss of 1871. Newcomers from Tunisia, Morocco, and Algeria were Sephardic, giving French Jewry an ethnic profile unlike the overwhelming Ashenazi composition of the American community. In contrast to French Jewry, Jews in America had an uninterrupted presence since early settlement and were never banished. Another dissimilarity was that until the Civil War, Jews in the United States seldom surfaced in the consciousness of their gentile compatriots.

While French Jewry was originally more cohesive, in the 1840s American Jewry began to acquire the numbers, resources, and institutions that fostered solidarity. Communal integrity was achieved in different ways in France and America. Until the late nineteenth-century arrival of Eastern European coreligionists, the Jews of France were organized in a consistorial establishment. Jewish-American communities were organized in congregations. One system reflected French centrality, the other American pluralism.[2]

Regardless of the tighter organization and earlier cohesion of French Jewry, by the twentieth century American Jewry was just as consolidated, or, perhaps more realistically put, at a no more advanced stage of disintegration: While American Jews earlier initiated modification of their Hebrew and Jewish names, 85 percent of the name changes among French Jews from 1803 to 1957 took place between 1945 and 1957. Intermarriage, a more important indicator of disintegration, also showed that the French had caught up with the Americans. A larger share of early American Jews married out. Contrary to this situation in France, however, after 1840, intermarriage in America declined. Greater numbers, as well as the revival of orthodoxy as a result of the greater influx of Eastern European Jews to America, accounted for the rise in endogamous unions. Between 1908–12 in New York City, which then contained approximately half of America's Jews, 1.7 percent of the Jewish population entered into mixed marriages, the lowest rate of intermarriage of any group except for black-white marriages. Among New York Jews, the French-born had the highest endogamous marriage rate (6.5 percent), perhaps due to a vastly smaller enclave of French-born Jews than those of other national origins. A 1957 U.S. Census Sample Survey reported that 7.2 percent of America's Jews married out, but this may be an undercount, and, according to one estimate, 10–15 percent of Jews by birth had wedded Gentiles. Between 1965–74, the rate was 26 percent, compared to about 40 percent for French Jews between 1966–75. Between 1985–90, 53 percent of American Jews chose a non-Jewish spouse.[3]

Over the *longue durée* from liberation to equality and acceptance, the clear trend in both French and American Jewry was to integrate with the nation. This process was cyclical as each subsequent wave of immigrants transited (most often intergenerationally) from newcomer to acculturated American or French. Spanish-Portuguese Marranos, German and Eastern European Jews, each in its time, gradually assimilated and all became indistinguishable from their compatriots save, for those who kept the faith, in denominational affiliation. Given, relative to France, the centrifugal tendency of pre-1840 American Jewry and the openness and diversity of American society, it would be expected that American Jews would earlier join the national community. More frequent name-changes and intermarriages among early American Jews evince this integration.

Name changing is a unilateral effort at adopting aspects of the national culture, but intermarriage, since it depends upon collaboration with Gentiles, is a bilateral process of assimilation. The appearance of Jews in public office, prestigious educational institutions, and as icons in the national culture is similarly mutual. If the initiative might come from Jews, its success depends upon a positive reaction from fellow citizens of other religions. At first glance, the commonsense supposition seems true that America antedated France in these aspects of integration. In the late eighteenth century, Jews regularly attended what later became the University of Pennsylvania and Gershom Seixas was a trustee of Columbia College. During the first decade of the next century, Jews enrolled at Yale and West Point. At this time and throughout the antebellum era, Jews were among the founders of state and city medical societies, as well as members and officers of highly reputed professional organizations, elite social clubs, and cultural societies. By the 1840s, Jews served in Congress, and, in 1860, Commodore Uriah P. Levy became a naval flag officer.[4]

If intuitive assumptions are invariably correct, historians' work might verge on the trifling and redundant. Fortunately for historians, counterintuitive conclusions are often valid. This aspect of the comparison between American and French Jewry is one such case: the U.S. government never legally discriminated against Jews, while the last vestige of de jure civic inequality in France, the more judaico, was not abolished until 1846. Nevertheless, the first Jew in the Chamber of Deputies was elected in 1834, seven years before his counterpart appeared in the U.S. Congress. Jews regularly served as deputies starting in the 1840s and the first Jewish cabinet ministers were in the provisional government (February 2, 1848) of the Second Republic. By contrast, the original Jewish-American cabinet member sat in the Confederate government of 1861 and his initial Jewish equivalent in the Federal government appeared in 1906. In every aspect of national life, French Jews participated more prominently (and usually earlier) than their American coreligionists. The Rothschilds established a presence in French banking in the 1790s, and, by the First Empire, James Rothschild was the leading French financier. During the 1830s, he and the Periere brothers were key factors in launching the French railroad industry. By the late nineteenth century, Jews were among the foremost figures in art, music, theater, philosophy, and the social sciences. They attended and were on the faculties of the country's foremost Écoles and universities. Even in the army, a citadel of anti-Semitism and antirepublicanism, Jews made their mark. Between 1867 and 1907, they constituted 3 percent of the regular army officers. In 1866, Jews composed .23 percent of the population and in 1872, after the loss of Alsace and Lorraine, .14 percent.[5]

Since American Jews outnumbered their French coreligionists by the 1850s, the greater national eminence of the latter was not due to its larger population. Nor was the comparative notability of French Jews due to less anti-Semitism in that country. One important demographic difference between the French and American Jewish communities accounts for the relative national anonymity of the latter: French Jewry was largely a long-settled community while American Jewry was overwhelmingly composed, especially after 1830, of newcomers.

More important than the numbers of Jews in eminent positions was their commitment to Judaism. American Jews in the highest antebellum political posts (U.S. Senators David Yulee and Judah P. Benjamin, and August Belmont, Minister to The Netherlands and Chairman of the Democratic National Committee) married out and disaffiliated with Judaism. Not until the 1850s would Jews who did not discard their heritage be elected to the House of Representatives; not until 1879 would they serve in the Senate.[6]

Belmont was a luminary of New York high society, in part because of marriage to a patrician family, and the nation's ranking banker of Jewish birth. His financial position came from being the American representative of the Rothschilds. A comparison between his own commitment to Judaism and that of his patrons reflects the greater solidarity of French Jewry. The Rothschilds wedded Jews, funded Jewish causes and charities, and served as presidents of the Central and Paris Consistories. While Jews in American politics severed their religious roots, Adolph Crémieux, a deputy and Minister of Justice in the Second Republic, was the leading Jew in France. He was president of the Central Consistory and the *Alliance Iraélite Universelle*. Loyalty to Judaism was characteristic of civic and military officers of that faith. In the Third Republic, 95 percent of the Jewish prefects, 83 percent of the twenty-five Jewish generals, and 78 percent of the Jewish deputies and senators married Jews.[7]

Increasing renown and visibility of Jews in France and the United States regrettably did not reflect declining anti-Semitism. Until 1945, hostility ascended along with Jewish participation and accomplishment; after World War II, the curves of animosity and achievement disjoined. Bigotry diminished at the same time and for the same reasons in France and the United States, but its course did not always proceed identically in these countries. This meditation on the Jews and the nation fittingly concludes by contemplating the rise and fall of anti-Semitism, a phenomenon that illuminates the condition of the Jewish communities in France and the United States as these groups interact with nationalism and civic culture. Liberal and republican values in fundamental ways shape the political culture of these countries, and thus, although they did not write about

Jews, the experience of that people in these nations extensively engages the concepts of Tocqueville and Hartz.

Anti-Semitism in America symbiotically coalesced with the advent of racialism and organic and restrictive nationalism. In the late nineteenth century, Jews began to be barred from resorts, clubs, and certain occupations; in the twentieth century, they were excluded from residential neighborhoods and quotas were imposed on Jews attending institutions of higher education. These developments proceeded simultaneously with the late nineteenth-century founding of ancestral and immigration restriction societies, official barriers against foreign entry, and the eugenics movement. The mergence of xenophobia in general with Jew hatred in particular led to some notable victories for integral nationalism, especially the Immigration Restriction Acts of 1921 and 1924, which effectively ended the arrival of Jewish and other ethnic groups from Southern and Eastern Europe.[8]

Contrary to uninterrupted escalation in America, anti-Semitism in France waxed and waned. Prejudice against Jews was profound from the ancien régime through the First Empire. Bigotry did not vanish with the exile of Napoleon. Revolutions and other crises triggered mob attacks on Jews in 1819, 1823–24, 1830, 1832, and 1848. Thereafter, hostility diminished until the 1880s.[9]

Anti-Semitism in the modern era in the United States starts during the Civil War, in Germany in the 1870s, and in France a decade later. The outbreak in America in the 1860s, however, differed from the German and French varieties because it was largely based on traditional grievances against alleged Jewish business chicanery and exploitation and hatred of Christianity. By the 1880s, however, anti-Semitism, without discarding its commercial and christological dimensions, had taken on modern traits of scientific racialsm. The new outlook mainly consisted of assumptions, about Darwinian hypotheses, unalterable genetic predispositions, and eugenic panaceas, combined with a zealous attachment to xenophobia. Translated into the perspectives of this study, the negation of Jews involved integral or organic nationalism featuring particularistic and exclusionary values. American animosity, however, differed from the French variety in being less intense and not singling out Jews.

Ideology and organization joined in the late nineteenth century to invigorate an imperative for rejection of Jews. In the 1880s, ancestral, patriotic, and immigration restriction societies emerged to confront alleged Judaic and other racial threats to the United States. The American Legion (1919) and the 1920s resurgence of the second Ku Klux Klan (1915) indicated that strident and xenophobic patriotism escalated in the twentieth century. Defensive and exclusionary nationalism became public policy. Restriction started with the Exclusion Law of 1882, initiating the barring of Chinese immigrants, and culminated in the National Origins Act of 1924, which imposed quotas that favored emigrants from "Nordic" countries and cut annual immigration from Southern and Eastern Europe to less than 15,000.

At the same time, scientific racialism established its gloomy reign over genetics, biology, eugenics, and the social sciences. These disciplines legitimated the doctrines of unalterable inherent racial traits: a hierarchy of races topped by the Nordic peoples and the threat of an inferior racial influx and race mixing polluting the national stock and bringing about an American defeat in the inevitable struggle for existence among the races of the world and the nations they inhabit. The titles of the formative works of racialism convey their creators' pessimistic, predatory worldview in which the operative code is the law of the jungle and the overriding commandment is survival of the fittest: Madison Grant's *The Passing of the Great Race: Or the Racial Basis of European History* (1916), was largely ignored until the 1920s, but by 1923 had sales of 16,000; Grant and Charles Stewart Davison, *The Alien In Our Midst or "Selling our Birthright for a Mess of Pottage"* (1930); Lothrop Stoddard, *The Rising Tide of Color Against White World-Supremacy* (1920), and *The Revolt Against Civilization: The Menace of the Under MAN* (1922); Henry Pratt Fairchild, *The Melting Pot Mistake* (1926).[10]

As in America, the resurgence of French anti-Semitism coincided with the advent of scientific racialism, xenophobia, organic nationalism, and immigration from Eastern Europe. But Jew hatred in France also differed in trajectory, intensity, and etiology. It was more volatile and frenzied than in America, dramatically surging in the 1880s, peaking during the Dreyfus Affair (1894–1906), plummeting with the defeat and discrediting of the anti-Dreyfusards, rising sharply in the 1930s, and attaining its greatest virulence in the Vichy period.

Despite some common causation, the revival of anti-Semitism in France was not always inspired by the same factors as in the United States: France had suffered a recent defeat in war and an accompanying loss of territory; underwent a severe and prolonged economic crisis in the 1880s; Jews figured in a sensational case of corporate fraud (the Panama scandal 1888–1893), which ruined thousands of small savers; and the republican government mounted an anticlerical campaign to divide Church and state. To the extent that anti-Jewish feelings are aggravated by assimilation and the attainment of civic—ten Jewish generals served during the Dreyfus Affair—and social prominence by Jews, this source of bigotry had greater force in France, and also in Germany, than in America, where Jews were more marginal. A product of envy and fear of displacement, this source of hostility exacerbated an abhorrence that festered into the Dreyfus outrage and Vichy and Nazi malevolence.

The key antipathetic difference in these countries was that in France Jews were regarded as the most dangerous and degenerate alien threat. An extensive and important clerical element and many lay Catholics adamantly opposed Jews. In America, a Protestant nation, the Church was feared more than the synagogue, and Catholics in that nation did not, until the 1930s, turn against another persecuted group. In fact, during the Dreyfus Affair, conservative French Catholics criticized their American fellow believers as too democratic and tolerant of the equality of other creeds. Finally American, unlike French, anti-Semitism, was never conflated with recurrent conflicts over the legitimacy of its Revolution or Republic, over whether the nation should be secular or Catholic, monarchist or republican.[11]

Comparison of French and American anti-Semitism reveals greater historical revulsion in France and a more intense conflation of feelings toward Jews with those regarding the state. Consequently, American bigotry resulted in no sensational incident, no reviled (or revitalized) figure, and no mob violence—factors that imbued the accusation, trial, and restoration of Alfred Dreyfus with a passion and significance absent from American prejudice against Jews.

These national variances in antagonism are reflected in the fact that America had no contemporary equivalent of Édouard Drumont, France's original anti-Semitic demagogue. A xenophobic nationalist, Drumont was the first Frenchman to stipulate a racial conflict between Christians and Jews; that is, a war between Aryans and Semites. He penetrated France in the 1880s like a flaming meteor and soon won fame by writing *La France juive*. Published on April 14, 1886, this diatribe of hatred within two months sold over 70,000 copies. At the end of the year, over 100,000 copies of the book had been bought and it became the best seller in France. By 1887, *La France juive* was in its 145th printing; ultimately, it became, after the *Protocols of the Elders of Zion*, the most influential anti-Semitic tract. Not until the New Deal would a Jew hater with equivalent celebrity and popularity emerge in America, and the mass appeal of Charles E. Coughlin had a much shorter life than that of Drumont and was not revived in a later period. *La France juive* was among a number of French anti-Semitic books and journals that began to appear in the 1880s. Anti-Semitic leagues and clubs were formed in that decade and, in the 1890s, overtly anti-Jewish candidates ran for the Chamber of Deputies. In January 1898, a wave of mob violence against Jews and their property and places of worship erupted in nearly every city in France.[12]

Organized French Jewry reacted passively to the first outbreak of modern French anti-Semitism. No direct Jewish institutional confrontation occurred because French Jews sought to prove (yet again) their national loyalty, were convinced of the Third Republic's capacity to survive and commitment to universalistic citizenship, and defensively desired not to draw attention to themselves.[13]

The outcome of the Dreyfus case seemed to verify the sentiments of the Jewish establishment. Dreyfus was exonerated and promoted, the Republic prevailed over its opponents, and the Jewish presence increased in high civic and cultural circles during and after the Dreyfus trials. Anti-Dreyfusards were morally, but as later events proved, not mortally, defeated. Elected to the Chamber of Deputies in 1898, Drumont was defeated in 1902. Subsidence of hostility owed much to the combat record of Jews in World War I (no such pleasant fate awaited the German and American Jews who also distinguished themselves in the trenches) and to the image of victory as a triumph of the élan of a united la patrie. Jewish war sacrifice and the *union sacrée* of the war prompted anti-Dreyfusard Maurice Barrés, an organic nationalist and anti-Semite, to recognize Jews as one of the "spiritual families" of France. *La Parole*, Drumount's anti-Semitic newspaper, which had a daily circulation of 300,000 in 1889, died for lack of readership in 1924. Rancor against Jews was also reduced by France's need for immigrant workers due to economic growth and wartime casualties. During the 1920s, naturalization requirements were eased and in 1929 France had a greater percentage of newcomers than the United States or any other country.[14]

The American-Jewish community did not endure the ordeal inflicted on their French brethren between 1880 and 1906. On the other hand, it did not experience a subsequent reduction of antagonism. Without the usual stimuli of defeat in war or economic depression, aversion for Jews in America climbed steadily until the end of World War II. In 1915, a unique event happened—the lynching of Leo Frank. An anti-Semitic crusade in Georgia ended with the only recorded Jew in America being killed largely because of his religion. As Frank's anti-Semitic nemesis, Tom Watson rehabilitated his political career and in 1920 was elected to the U.S. Senate. The 1920s witnessed the first American elected to high federal office in part because he hated Jews and the first national hero to publicly champion anti-Semitism. Henry Ford financed an anti-Semitic journal and the publication and dissemination of the *Protocols of the Elders of Zion*. More important than individuals, however, were structural developments reflecting increasing aversion to Jews. Colleges and professional schools, many vocations and neighborhoods, and clubs and recreational resorts excluded or imposed severe quotas on Jews. Public policy and voluntary organizations mounted attacks that, in typical American fashion, included other despised minorities. The Johnson Acts of 1921 and 1924 suppressed immigration of Jews along with other groups from Southern and Eastern Europe. After 1920, a revitalized Klan dedicated itself to the xenophobic mission of tormenting Catholics, Jews, African-

Americans, foreigners, and anyone else it deemed a foe of its brand of WASP patriotism.[15]

Until the early 1900s, organized Jewish resistance to anti-Semitism was low-keyed, as in France. Even in the 1890s, however, Jews seemed more vigorously resistant. By then, American Jews were considerably more numerous than their coreligionists in France and they lived in a country more consistently liberal, pluralistic, and republican. When Jew-hater Hermann Ahlwardt came to America from Germany in 1895 to organize an anti-Semitic movement, he was heckled by Jews and others at public meetings (New York City Police Commissioner Theodore Roosevelt organized a bodyguard to protect Ahlwardt). In 1906, just as French hostility toward Jews was on the wane, the American Jewish Committee was formed. It fought biased ads for public resorts, college quotas, and immigration restriction. 1927 culminated American Jewry's most effective counterattack on anti-Semitism and the leading American Jew-hater. Fearing grievous business losses in the face of a Jewish boycott of Model T automobiles, Henry Ford apologized for his previous animus, disavowed the "International Jew" pieces in his Dearborn *Independent*, and professed mortification over the circulation of the "Protocols," which he now declared a fiction and a forgery.[16]

Ford's recantation did not make America safe for its Jews. Quotas and exclusions did not abate and popular anti-Semitism intensified. Assimilation and assumption of higher positions in business, the professions, and government heightened fears of Jewish competition and mastery. In many ways, the circumstances of America's Jews worsened as the country plunged into the Great Depression and then entered World War II. Until the 1930s, Catholicism was the most detested creed in the Protestant-dominated national culture. In this decade, however, Christian America affixed this designation upon Judaism. Henry Ford's 1920s onslaught heralded this switch in antagonists; now others shifted. Evangelical preacher Gerald Winrod, founder and leader of the Defenders of the Christian Faith, had a large following in the Midwest. A Catholic-baiter in the 1920s, he muted this sentiment after 1935, and, by 1939, called for a united Christian patriotic front to thwart a Jewish thrust toward global rule. William Pelley, the most rabid hatemonger of the era, was founder and commander of the Christian American Patriots (Silver Shirts). Most members of this fascistic association were Protestants, but focusing, as did Winrod and Coughlin, on a Jewish-Soviet conspiracy to destroy Christian civilization and rule the world, that group neither openly opposed the Church nor banned Catholics from its ranks.[17]

As a popular and charismatic anti-Semite, Coughlin, a Catholic priest, became the American Drumont. Where the latter's weapon of choice was the printed word, the former wielded the microphone. By

1938, Coughlin rode the airwaves as America's most widely admired Jew-hater. In December 1938, 45 radio stations carried his weekly vilification, 3.5 million Americans listened regularly, and two-thirds of the faithful agreed with his views. Another 15 million heard him at least once. Public opinion polls, which began in the 1930s, confirmed the appeal of Cough-lin's message. In a 1938 survey, approximately 60 percent of the respon-dents held a low opinion of Jews, labeling them "greedy," "dishonest," and "pushy."[18]

The time of depression and war, however, was far from an unmiti-gated downward spiral for American Jewry. While excoriation mounted, three Jews sat on the U.S. Supreme Court in the 1930s, another became the first Jewish member of the inner cabinet as secretary of the Treasury and several Jews were among Franklin Roosevelt's close advisers. The New Deal was a political coming-of-age not only for Jews, but also for Italians, and was the first administration since Reconstruction to make overtures to African-Americans. It could be claimed that Roosevelt's poli-cies toward those of Southern– and Eastern European origins and Afri-can– and Native-Americans inaugurated the gradual reversal of the ero-sion of American liberalism that Rogers Smith explores.

Long influential in American popular culture, Jewish visibility rose in intellectual and academic circles. More important than personal repute were cultural changes that undermined the basis of discrimination against Jews and other minorities. Nazi propaganda bestirred dislike of Jews, but as Germany increasingly loomed as the enemy, the ideology of the Third Reich discredited racialism, the scientific rationale for anti-Semitism and other forms of xenophobia and particularistic nationalism. By the 1930s, racialism and eugenics were routed by scientific research, social science scholarship, and academia.[19]

Countertrends notwithstanding, as measured by public opinion polls, excoriation and exclusion of Jews escalated throughout World War II and peaked in 1946.[20] A wartime climate of xenophobia and zealous patrio-tism also produced the incarceration of Japanese-American citizens on the West Coast. Again, however, countercurrents emerged. Inspired by an American version of union sacrée and the discrediting of scientific racism, and especially since the country was now at war with fascist powers, the standing of African-Americans improved symbolically (The Fair Employ-ment Commission of 1941 and the first black general) and substantively (*Smith v. Allwright*, the 1944 Supreme Court decision outlawing the all-white Democratic Party Primary in Texas). In some respects, the situation of Jews also improved. If Coughlin was an American Drumont, his reign did not last nearly as long. He launched his crusade in 1935 and, by 1942, largely as a result of government pressure, was silenced by the Church. Other hate hucksters of the 1930s and their publications, Winrod and

Pelley among them, were similarly suppressed by government action in that year.[21]

The plight of American Jewry during the 1930s and 1940s was bliss relative to what happened in France. Nevertheless, hostility toward Jews in these countries had common features. Economic crisis and Nazi propaganda contributed significantly to the upsurge of antipathy in both nations. The 1930s outbreak of anti-Semitism in France also had much in common with its previous resurgence in the 1880s, including some of the same figures. In both eras, France was plagued with economic depression and high unemployment, and, in the 1930s, reminiscent of a half century ago, there was a financial scandal (the Stavisky Affair of 1933–34) that involved Jews. As in the 1880s, the bigotry of this decade coincided with a rise in Jewish immigration.

France's first Jewish premier, Léon Blum, headed the Popular Front government in 1936–37. Antirepublican, xenophobic, and anti-Semitic fervor mounted. Naturalization and anti-immigration laws eased in the previous decade were now tightened, mob demonstrations and anti-Semitic rallies unleashed a tornado of abuse against Blum's regime, the readership of anti-Jewish publications spectacularly increased, and anti-Semitic associations remobilized their frenzy practiced during the Dreyfus Affair—the spirit of Drumont once again seduced *la belle France*. Beleaguered and bemused, the consistorial establishment, as in the Dreyfus crisis, rode out the storm with a moderate and dignified response. A minority enclave, leftists and recent immigrants from the East, pursued a more vigorous riposte. Establishment Jews and their adherents relied on a record of patriotic service and sacrifice, long-standing citizenship, and the routinized revolutionary-liberal values of the Third Republic, that perennial protector of French Jews.[22]

This time, however, the outcome was different and disastrous. Military defeat, forfeiture of territory, occupation, and the fall of the Third Republic completed the array of incendiary anti-Jewish forces. Nazi conquest and Vichy collaboration ignited a conflagration that threatened to consume French Jewry. Vichy statutes defined Jews by race (namely, inheritance), barred or severely restricted them from many vocations and from military command, "aryanized" Jewish property, facilitated their internment, and forced them to wear the Yellow Star of David. These laws moreover were passed and strictly enforced without German pressure. France was unique among occupied countries of Western Europe in voluntarily adopting anti-Semitic policies.

Jews bore the brunt of Vichy's Catholic, corporative, authoritarian, and xenophobic mission to create a homogeneous (of 15,174 revoked naturalizations, 6,307 were Jews) and morally rehabilitated nation by suppressing the anti-Semite's most feared degenerative force. Vichy also

enthusiastically cooperated in the deportation of over 75,000 Jews, nearly
one-third French citizens. Henri Philippe Pétain's government nevertheless retained faint residues of the Revolution: It attempted to distinguish
between native– and foreign-born Jews by working (not always successfully or earnestly) to protect the former and eagerly sending the latter to
the death camps. Apart from this half-hearted attempt to shield Jewish
citizens, all of the other outrages fell alike on un– or de-naturalized newcomers and those with intergenerational ties to the country.[23]

Self-righteous, exclusionary nationalism ironically was the passionately held conviction of those who surrendered, and then collaborated,
with France's conqueror and, since 1870, great enemy, and who in the
past frequently denounced Jews for allying with Germans to destroy
France. By execrating Jews for conspiring with Germany, pre-Vichy anti-
Semites united their primary internal and external foes.[24]

Two leagues founded during the Dreyfus Affair are emblematic of the
ramifications of anti-Semitism for liberalism and national culture. The
League for the Rights of Man came into existence in February 1898; in
January 1899, the League for the French Fatherland was formed in opposition to the earlier association. Obviously, "the Rights of Man" was
taken from the Declaration of 1789, but it could easily have been a slogan
from the American Revolution because the phrase valorizes human freedom and brotherhood. "French Fatherland" connotes an organic, particularistic nationalism (French) comprising authority, family, blood (father), and territory (land). The League for the Rights of Man supported
Dreyfus and its opponent was an anti-Dreyfusard organization. Dreyfusards defended Dreyfus as a citizen of France, anti-Dreyfusards attacked
him as a Jew, and therefore an adversary of France.[25]

As indicated by the names of the leagues, Dreyfusards defended the
republican principle that the nation was a civic community. Membership
in that community was defined by citizenship rather than religion, race,
or ethnicity. The French Republic's primal scene, its moment of creation,
was the Revolution and the redemptive message of that upheaval was
liberty, equality, and fraternity. As in another drama of salvation, the Revolution had its own trinity and mission. They were secular, but their
epiphany also issued from their empowerment of universal redemption.
Another eruption of anti-Semitic forces contradicted these principles, be-
sieged the Third Republic in the 1930s, and ended its existence in 1940.

Tocqueville pointed out that in the United States the state is weak
and civil society is strong while in France the opposite prevails. American
empowerment of voluntary associations affirmed the national society's
commitment to diversity, and that commitment worked in favor of Jews.
A dominant central state, however, does not necessarily harm Jews. Nor

does its form of government seem a determinative factor in the civic circumstances of Jews. They were emancipated under a constitutional monarchy and oppressed by the revolutionary Republic. Napoleon's strictures against the Jews lapsed during the Bourbon Restoration. The last vestiges of official discrimination were removed under the July Monarchy. French Jewry made gains in the Second Republic, but lost no ground in the Second Empire. Nevertheless, no regime defended Jewish citizens as consistently as did the Third Republic, even during the Dreyfus incident. In this Republic, the state and republicanism finally fused and secularism was basic to this conjunction. This association—republicanism, secularism, and defense of Jews—therefore fostered a convergence of anti-Semitism and anti-republicanism from monarchists, integral nationalists, and Catholics.

Anti-Semites identified the Republic with the Jewish menace (a conflation encouraged by Jews being citizens and government officials) and attacked both by accusing the republican state (universalistic) of subverting the nation (particularistic). This dimension of the Jew as antagonist could not develop with the same fury in more decentralized America. A prime consequence of converging opposition to Jews and the Republic was that the severest persecution of Jews in modern French history coincided with the overthrow of the Republic. Vichy reversed the integration of Jews and the state, which they felt had culminated in a Jewish dominion with Blum and the Popular Front. Now the assault was not against Jews as outsiders (a nation within a nation), but as insiders (masters of the state under the Republic). Once again Jews became a metaphor for national conflicts unresolved from the time of the Revolution. Vichy substituted emotion for reason, hierarchy for equality, authority for liberty, exclusion and particularism for fraternity and universalism, and tradition (as conceived by Vichy) for modernity.[26]

The Dreyfus Affair, anti-Blum demonstrations, and Vichy showed that failure to resolve "the Jewish Question" was a recurrent national disaster per se and a symptom of other exclusions that violated revolutionary and republican values as well as French law. At various times between 1789 and the present, civic rights of Catholics, black and white colonials, immigrants, socialists, communists, and women, as well as Jews, were threatened, withdrawn, or not wholly granted.[27] These transgressions of citizenship fragmented France, thus preventing the full realization of nationhood.

From the end of the war until the 1980s, anti-Semitism steadily declined in France and the United States; correspondingly, a growing majority saw Jews as no different from other citizens.[28] Formal and informal, public and private disabilities inflicted upon Jews virtually disappeared.[29] In the United States, subsidence of hostility was accompanied by dramatic gains in acceptance and parity for other historically persecuted groups, women, African-Americans, Native-Americans, and Asian-Americans, as well as Jews. Affirmative action, agency, empowerment, and so forth moved the once-marginalized closer to total acceptance and integration.

France and America corresponded in the gradual but cumulatively sharp diminution of anti-Jewish sentiment, but past episodes of that prejudice had been more intense and devastating in France and postwar aftershocks reverberated with greater force. In the 1940s, Gerald L. K. Smith inherited the role of the American hatemongers of the 1930s. Smith labored diligently to spread anti-Semitism, but with less effect than his predecessors. In France, however, in the parliamentary elections of January 1956, candidates of the Poujadist movement, tinged with populist anti-Semitism, won 2.5 million votes (11.5 percent of the total) and elected fifty deputies. Jean-Marie Le Pen was one of them; he now heads the xenophobic National Front. In the European parliamentary elections of 1984, Le Pen's party received 11 percent of the French vote and in the 1986 elections won thirty-five seats. In the French presidential election of 1988, he received 14 percent of the vote, and in the regional elections of 1992, the National Front got 13.9 percent of the vote. Like Anti-Dreyfusards and Vichyites, he campaigns against republican values and flirts with anti-Semitism; for example, intermittent denial of the Holocaust.[30]

Le Pen's American equivalent is Pat Buchanan. They are populists with an antiforeign, anti-immigrant platform and a penchant for anti-Semitic innuendo. Buchanan, too, had some success in the 1990s, especially in Republican Party presidential primaries. Running as an independent for president in 2000, however, Buchanan received only 1 percent for the vote.

As with Jews, trends toward acceptance of other minorities had a similar trajectory in France and the United States Public opinion, always more affirmative toward blacks in France than in the United States, nevertheless advanced in the same positive direction in both countries. Nor did the nations appreciably vary on opinion about immigration. Surveys in the 1980s in France and America, and Italy, Germany, and Britain as well, showed no significant differences in anti-immigration sentiment.[31] Le Pen's popularity, however, partly based on a general xenophobia and particular distaste for Arabs and North African immigrants, may belie the similar poll data from America and France.

Growing acceptance of Jews in France and America is remarkable in view of developments that historically would have challenged feelings of fraternity and equality. Since the Six-Day War in Israel (1967), Jews in these and other countries have become more militantly Zionist. Jews in France and America have formed political pressure groups (American-

Israel Public Affairs Committee [1954] and *Comité Juif d'Action* [1973; in 1980, renamed *Renouveau Juif*]) and held mass rallies to influence public elections, opinion, and policy on behalf of the Jewish state. Formerly, such activity would have stigmatized French and American Jewry with the allegation of dual loyalty (a nation within a nation). These initiatives presently have not increased doubts about the civic rights or commitment of Jews in France and the United States.[32]

The improved reputation of the Jews did not solely depend on public opinion. Structural changes in France promoted integration of the Jews and the nation. Catholicism, both Gallic and ultramontane, had long created problems for Jews. After World War II, however, the power of the Church in France weakened and, by the 1960s, Rome had begun to revise its views of Judaism and its role in the war. As of 1958, 92 percent of the French population was baptized, but by 1983 only 65 percent underwent this rite; in 1955, 24 percent attended religious services, but in 1988, 12 percent.[33]

Another important development ameliorated the condition of Jews. France has recently encouraged decentralization and regional and ethnic diversity. Since 1980, authority has devolved from Paris to local and regional institutions, promoting multiculturalism and civil society; official policy no longer employs the educational system to uproot the native cultures of children of immigrant workers. "The time has come," said ex-President Valéry Giscard d'Estaing in 1977, "to state there is no contradiction between being fully French and continuing to live according to local or regional traditions, customs, and cultures." François Mitterand successfully campaigned for the presidency in 1981 with a program that endorsed "the right to be different." After election, Mitterand appointed a presidential committee to advise the government to recognize the cultural autonomy of minority groups. In response to the report, Minister of Culture Jack Lang created a National Council of Regional Languages and Cultures.[34]

Government endorsement of heterogeneity and decentralization was of benefit to Jews. Immediately after the war, French people were still dubious about Jews. A public opinion survey of 1947 revealed that only 37 percent of the respondents felt that Jews were "French like all the rest" of the citizens. For a long time, the French ignored Vichy's responsibility for anti-Semitic persecutions and French historians regarded the Dreyfus Affair and Pétain's regime as isolated and anomalous episodes. And a clerical network protected Vichy criminals who organized murders of Jews during the war.[35]

In recent years, these attitudes have been drastically modified. French bishops issued a "Declaration of Repentance" on September 30, 1997, for the collaboration of the Church with Vichy. This mea culpa was read during a memorial ceremony at the Drancy internment camp. On the 53rd anniversary of the Vel d'Hiv round-up (July 16–17, 1942) of 12,884 Jews for transportation to concentration camps, President Jacques Chirac acknowledged "the responsibility of the French state" and the nation's "collective blame" for the 76,000 Jews killed during the Vichy era. A public opinion survey recorded 72 percent of the respondents in agreement with this assessment. On July 20, 1997, Prime Minister Lionel Jospin announced that the government would support a commission charged with inventorying Jewish property and financial holdings plundered during the Occupation and would aid in the building of a Holocaust museum in Paris.[36]

Israel's reaction to the Second Intifada, however, has dramatically escalated anti-Semitism in Europe and particularly in France, where one synagogue was destroyed and several others damaged. These cases of vandalism appear to be chiefly the acts of young, alienated, second-generation North African immigrants. Ethnic diversity does not always result in national harmony. From the opposite side, the resurgence of the intermittent anti-Semite Le Pen, master of the politics of xenophobia, has concerned Jews in France and elsewhere. When the Left fragmented in the first round of the presidential election (April 21), Le Pen displaced incumbent Prime Minister Lionel Jospin. His second place finish put him up against Jacques Chirac in the final round (May 5). Chirac was overwhelmingly reelected, but Le Pen received 5.8 million votes (nearly 18 percent) his highest level ever.[37] In America, where public opinion is more sympathetic to Israel, the recent turmoil in the Middle East has aroused no insurgence of hostility toward Jews and has produced congressional declarations of support for Ariel Sharon's policies.

The present has been a halcyon era for America's Jews. Buchanan was defanged in the last presidential election and transgressions of individual Jews have not dispersed the atmosphere of approval. In the 1980s and 1990s, a Jewish-American civilian employee of the Navy was sent to jail for giving vital defense information to Israel; Jewish-American capitalists and Wall Street barons were found guilty of financial fraud and tax evasion; and a Jewish-American woman was involved in a sex scandal with President Clinton. Betrayal of diasporic citizenship to benefit Israel and fellow Jews, commercial duplicity for monetary gain, and sexual degeneracy, conventional anti-Semitic fears and stereotypes, even when exemplified in these incidents did nothing to disturb the favorable opinion and position of American Jews.

When liberal republicanism, for the first time since the early 1870s, seems to be fulfilling its promise, Rogers Smith and others stress its shortcomings. Such was also the case a half century ago when Hollywood (*Gentle-*

man's Agreement) and serious scholarship (*The Authoriarian Personality*) delved into anti-Semitism just as it began to wane. As marginalized groups—Jews, women, gays and lesbians, Indians, Latinos, and Asian- and African-Americans—gain acceptance, they increasingly attract national attention. Their previous afflictions are more compassionately contemplated and their subsequent struggle for recognition is celebrated. Laws are passed on their behalf, and officials rue their former oppression and extol their more recent progress; their travails and triumphs are heralded in civic ceremonies, studied in schools, explored in scholarship, and depicted in the public media.

Yet, for all their advancements, these once-alienated (and not yet fully integrated) groups are still haunted by the long duration of their ordeal. Jews have moved further than many marginalized peoples from the periphery to the center, from aversion to affirmation. But the Holocaust casts a shadow over this transformation due to the intense trauma of genocide and to the feeling among Jews in France, the United States, and elsewhere that their post–World War II rehabilitation is in significant part the result of that cataclysm. As long as previous victimization shapes responses toward Jews, they can never be normal citizens—at any rate not in the nations that participated in their mass liquidation. And they will always wonder what their civic standing will be in those places when their former tribulations no longer influence their treatment.

Chapter 1
The Prospect

1. Gilbert Shapiro and John Markoff, *Revolutionary Demands: A Content Analysis of the* Cahiers de doléances *of 1789* (Stanford: Stanford University Press, 1998), p. 438; Esther Benbassa, *The Jews of France: A History from Antiquity to the Present* (Princeton: Princeton University Press, 1999), pp. 79–80.

2. Ronald Schecter, "The Jewish Question in Eighteenth-Century France," *Eighteenth-Century Studies* 32 (Fall 1998): 84, 86; idem, "Impression Management, Cultural Performance and Jewish Self-Preservation in Napoleonic France," *Proceedings of the Annual Meeting of the Western Society for French History: Selected Papers from the Annual Meeting* 25 (1998): 219–21; idem, "Competing Proposals for the Regeneration of the Jews, 1787–1789," ibid., 24 (1997): 283–93; idem, "Rationalizing the Enlightenment: Postmodernism and Theories of Anti-Semitism," *Historical Reflections/Réflexions Historique* 25 (Summer 1999): 287–301; see also Gary Kates, "Jews into Frenchmen: Nationality and Representation in Revolutionary France," in *The French Revolution and the Birth of Modernity*, ed. Ferenc Fehér (Berkeley: University of California Press, 1990), pp. 103–16.

3. For an interesting discussion of different aspects of emancipation, see Pierre Birnbaum and Ira Katznelson, "Emancipation and the Liberal Offer," in *Paths of Emancipation: Jews, States, and Citizenship*, ed. Pierre Birnbaum and Ira Katznelson (Princeton: Princeton University Press, 1995), pp. 5, 11–12, 30–34.

4. Daniel T. Rodgers, "Republicanism: The Career of a Concept," *The Journal of American History* 79 (June 1992): 11–38; and idem, "Exceptionalism," in *Imagined Histories: American Historians Interpret the Past*, ed. Anthony Molho and Gordon S. Wood (Princeton: Princeton University Press, 1998), pp. 21–40.

5. Keith Windschuttle, *The Killing of History: How Literary Critics and Social Theorists are Murdering Our Past* (New York and London: The Free Press, 1997).

6. Some of the salient contributions in this debate are: Laurence Vesey, "The Autonomy of American History Reconsidered," *American Quarterly* 31 (Fall 1979): 455–77; Michael Kammen, "The Problem of American Exceptionalism," ibid. 45 (March 1993): 1–43; Thomas Bender, "Wholes and Parts: The Need for Synthesis in American History," *The Journal of American History* 73 (June 1986): 120–36; Nell Irvin Painter, "Bias and Synthesis in History," ibid. 74 (June 1987): 109–12; Richard Wightman Fox, "Public Culture and the Problem of Synthesis," ibid.: 113–16; Roy Rosenzweig, "What Is the Matter with History?," ibid.: 117–22; Thomas Bender, "Wholes and Parts: Continuing the Conversation," ibid.: 123–30; John Higham, "The Future of American History," ibid. 80 (March 1994): 1289–1309; Ian Tyrrell, "American Exceptionalism in an Age of International History," *The American Historical Review* 96 (October 1991): 1031–55;

Michael McGerr, "The Price of the 'New Transnational History,' " ibid.: 1056–67, and Ian Tyrrell's response, 1067–68; Dorothy Ross, "Grand Narrative in American Historical Writing: From Romance to Uncertainty," ibid. 100 (June 1995): 651–77; *Is America Different? A New Look at American Exceptionalism*, ed. Byron E. Shafer (Oxford: Clarendon Press, 1991).

7. "The Discourses of Michel Foucault," chapter 4 in *The Killing of History*, is Windschuttle's lengthy and vituperative denunciation.

8. Hayden White, *Metahistory: The Historical Imagination in Nineteenth-Century Europe* (Baltimore and London: The Johns Hopkins University Press, 1975), pp. ix–xii, 1–42, 426–34, quotes on pp. ix–x, 426; for Windschuttle on White, see Windschuttle, *The Killing of History*, pp. 232–41, 245, 250, quote on p. 233.

9. Maurice Aynard, "The Annales and French Historiography (1929–1972)," *The Journal of European Economic History* 1 (1972): 496–97, Robert Forster, "Achievements of the Annales School," *The Journal of Economic History* 38 (March 1978): 74–75; Peter Burke, *The French Historical Revolution: The Annales School, 1929–89* (Stanford: Stanford University Press, 1990), pp. 1–5, 14, 43–45, 49–50, 54, 65–69, 97, 106–7; Joyce Appleby, Lynn Hunt, Margaret Jacob, *Telling the Truth About History* (New York and London: W. W. Norton, 1994), pp. 82–84, 208, 232–33; Colin Lucas, "Introduction" to the 1985 English edition of *Constructing the Past: Essays in Historical Methodology*, ed. Jacques Le Goff and Pierre Nora (Cambridge, London, and New York: Cambridge University Press), pp. 1–11. See also the following articles all in *Histories: French Reconstructions of the Past*, ed. Jacques Revel and Lynn Hunt (New York: The Free Press, 1995): François Furet, "French Intellectuals: From Marxism to Structuralism" (1967), pp. 227–30; Roger Chartier, "Intellectual History or Sociocultural History? The French Trajectories," (1982), pp. 287–88; Le Goff and Nora, preface to their *Constructing the Past* (1974), pp. 319–20, 323–27; Immanuel Wallerstein, "*Annales* as Resistance" (1978), pp. 366, 369; François Dosse, "History In Pieces" (1987), pp. 469–70; Jacques Revel, "The Paradigms of the *Annales*" (1979), pp. 472, 474; The Editors of *Annales*, "History and Social Science: A Critical Turning Point" (1988), p. 480; and "Let's Try the Experiment" (1989), p. 490.

10. John Demos, *The Unredeemed Captive: A Family Story from Early America* (New York: Vintage Books, 1995).

11. Alexis de Tocqueville to Eugène Stoeffels, 16 February 1839, *Memoirs, Letters and Remains of Alexis de Tocqueville*, ed. Gustave de Beaumont (Boston: Ticknor and Fields, 1862), 2 vols., 1: 375–76; Tocqueville to Louis de Kergorlay, Oct. 18, 1847, *Alexis de Tocqueville: Selected Letters on Politics and Society*, ed. Roger Boesche (Berkeley, Los Angeles, and London: University of California Press, 1985), p. 191; Robert Nisbet, "Many Tocquevilles," *The American Scholar* 46 (Winter 1976–77): 59–60; André Jardin, *Tocqueville: A Biography* (New York: Farrar Straus Giroux, 1988), pp. 224, 228; J. P. Mayer, *Alexis de Tocqueville: A Biographical Essay in Political Science* (New York: The Viking Press, 1940), p. 36.

12. See footnote 6, especially Higham, "Future": 1297–1300 for references to similar historiographical interpretations. For a specific critique of the limits of the liberal school and of Tocqueville and Hartz, see Rogers Smith, "The 'American

Creed' and American Identity: The Limits of Liberal Citizenship in the United States," *The Western Political Quarterly* 41 (June 1988): 225–51; idem, "Beyond Tocqueville, Myrdal, and Hartz: The Multiple Traditions in America," *The American Political Science Review* 87 (September 1993): 549–66; and idem, *Civic Ideals: Conflicting Visions of Citizenship in U.S. History* (New Haven and London: Yale University Press, 1997). Another interesting critique of Hartz is James T. Kloppenberg, "In Retrospect: Louis Hartz's *The Liberal Tradition in America*," *Reviews in American History* 29 (2001): 460–78.

13. See index to Appleby, Hunt, and Jacob, *Telling*, pp. 310–22; Seymour Drescher, "Foreword," in Francoise Mélonio, *Tocqueville and the French* (Charlottesville: University Press of Virginia, 1998), pp. vi–ix; and idem, *Dilemmas of Democracy* (Pittsburgh: University of Pittsburgh Press, 1968), pp. 3–7; Lynn L. Marshall and Seymour Drescher, "American Historians and Tocqueville's Democracy," *The Journal of American History* 55 (December 1968): 512–32; Claude Lefort, *Democracy and Political Theory* (Minneapolis: The University of Minnesota Press, 1986), pp. 14–15; Daniel T. Rodgers, "Exceptionalism," pp. 21–40; Louis Hartz, *The Founding of New Societies: Studies in the History of the United States, Latin America, South Africa, Canada, and Australia* (New York: Harcourt, Brace & World, 1964).

14. Alexis De Tocqueville, *Democracy in America* (1834, 1840; New York: Vintage Books, 1945), 2 vols., 2: 38; Seymour Martin Lipset, "American Exceptionalism Reaffirmed," in *Is America Different?*, ed. Shafer, p. 1.

15. Louis Hartz, *The Liberal Tradition in America: An Interpretation of American Political Thought Since the Revolution* (New York: Harcourt, Brace & World, 1955), pp. 3–6, quotes on p. 4.

16. Tocqueville, *Democracy*, 1: Index, viii; Joshua Mitchell, *The Fragility of Freedom: Tocqueville on Religion, Democracy, and the American Future* (Chicago and London: University of Chicago Press, 1995), p. 36.

17. Tocqueville, *Democracy*, 1: 58–59, 73.

18. Tocqueville to Kergorlay, 18 October 1847, *Alexis de Tocqueville: Selected Letters*, ed. Boesche, p. 191.

19. Tocqueville, *Democracy*, 2: 108.

20. Hartz, *Liberal*, pp. 35–86 quotes on pp. 35, 66. Hartz reiterated this view of the American Revolution in *Founding*, pp. 73–85.

21. Hartz, *Liberal*, pp. i, 5, 66, 146.

22. For Tocqueville's disagreement with Gobineau over racism, see Tocqueville, *"The European Revolution" & Correspondence with Gobineau*, ed. John Lukacs (Gloucester, MA: Peter Smith, 1968); Tocqueville to Arthur de Gobineau, 15 May 1852, p. 222; cf. same to same, 11 November 1853, p. 224; 17 November 1853, pp. 226–30; 20 December 1853, pp. 231–32; 8 January, 1856, p. 270; 30 July, 1856, pp. 291–95; 14 January, 1857, pp. 304–6.

23. Tocqueville, *Democracy*, 1: 28.

24. Ibid., 2: 314–15.

25. Ibid., 1: 315. These two paragraphs developed out of a discussion with Seymour Drescher.

26. Hartz, *Liberal*, pp. 68–69, 71.

27. Ibid., pp. 50–51, 47.

28. For a similar formulation in another context, see Oscar and Lilian Handlin, *Liberty and Equality: 1920–1994*, vol. 4 of their *Liberty in America: 1600 to the Present* (New York: HarperCollins, 1986–1994), p. xii.

29. Hartz, *Liberal*, pp. 40–41.

30. Tocqueville, *Democracy*, 1: 13.

31. Tocqueville to Eugène Stoeffels, 21 July 1848, *Alexis de Tocqueville: Selected Letters*, ed. Boesche, p. 215; cf. to Kergorlay, 15 December 1850, p. 254; to Gustave de Beaumont, 6 March 1855, p. 316.

32. Alexis de Tocqueville, *Recollections* (New York: Anchor Books, 1971), p. 83.

33. Alexis de Tocqueville, "On the Middle Class and the People" (1847), *Tocqueville and Beaumont on Social Reform*, ed. Seymour Drescher (New York, Evanston, and London: Harper Torchbooks, 1968), p. 175; and idem, *Recollections*, p. 5, cf. p. 130; cf. *"European"*, ed. Lukacs, pp. 72–73, 79.

34. Tocqueville, *"European "*, ed. Lukacs, p. 160; Hartz, *Liberal*, pp. 3–5, 8–9, 20–21, 35, 43–44, 68–71, quote on pp. 43–44.

35. A similar view of Tocqueville is put forth in White, *Metahistory*, pp. 193, 195, 210–11, 224–25. White, however, does not sufficiently differentiate Tocqueville's less tragic view of America. He omits, for example, Tocqueville's claim that voluntary associations in America resist centralized government and thus preserve liberty.

36. Tocqueville, *Democracy*, 2: 268, 270.

37. Hartz, *Liberal*, pp. 51, 74.

38. Tocqueville, *Democracy*, 1: 6–7; 2: 28–29; 1: 312.

39. Ibid., 1: 310–26.

40. Ibid., 1: 322–23; Alexis de Tocqueville, *The Old Régime and the French Revolution* (1856; New York: Anchor Books, 1955), p. 5, and *"European"*, ed. Lukacs, p. 108; cf. idem, *Democracy*, 1: 325.

41. Tocqueville to Claude-François de Corcelle, 17 September 1853, *Alexis de Tocqueville: Selected Letters*, ed. Boesche, p. 294.

42. Tocqueville, *"European"*, ed. Lukacs, pp. 108, 126, 162 and *Old Régime*, pp. 207–8.

43. Tocqueville, *"European"* ed. Lukacs, p. 111; cf. p. 172, and idem, *Old Régime*, pp. 12–13.

44. Tocqueville, *Democracy*, 2: 19.

45. Hartz, *Liberal*, p. 10.

46. Tocqueville, *Democracy*, 2: 19.

47. Hartz, *Liberal*, p. 59.

48. Tocqueville, *Old Régime*, pp. 20–35, 192.

49. Tocqueville to Pierre Freslon, 16 March 1858, *Alexis de Tocqueville: Selected Letters*, ed. Boesche, p. 371.

50. Tocqueville, *Democracy*, 2: 7.

51. Ibid., 1: 117–18.

52. Hartz, *Liberal*, pp. 73, 43, 85–86. Hartz repeated this assessment in *Founding*, pp. 73–85.

53. Tocqueville to Kergorlay, 29 June 1831, *Alexis de Tocqueville: Selected Letters*, ed. Boesche, p. 48.

54. Tocqueville, *Democracy*, 1: 310–26; 2: 21–33, quotes in 1: 314, 323.

55. Tocqueville, *Old Régime*, pp. xii, 8–9, 19–20, 207–10, quote on pp. 274–75, and *Democracy*, 1: 3–8, 56, 90, 93–100, 192–93, 202–3, 270–71, 273, 341–42; 2: 98–104, 115–17, 213, 304–52.

56. Ibid., 1: 273, 106.

57. Hartz, *Liberal*, pp. 11, 288, 302; cf. 11–23, 50–51, 55–59, 157, 177, 228–83, 285, 305–7. Tocqueville and Hartz were not alone in accentuating democratic conformity as an American attribute. "This the land of the free! Why, if I say anything that displeases them, the free mob will lynch me, and that's my freedom," wrote D. H. Lawrence in *Studies in Classic American Literature*. He continued, "Free? Why, I have never been in any country where the individual has such an abject fear of his fellow countrymen. Because, as I say, they are free to lynch him the moment he shows he is not one of them." D. H. Lawrence, *Studies in Classic American Literature* (London: Mercury Books, 1965). p. 3.

58. Tocqueville to W. R. Gregg, 27 July 1853, *Memoirs*, ed. Beaumont, 2: 219.

59. Tocqueville, *Democracy*, 1: 117–18, 169–77, 192–93, and idem, *Journey to America*, ed. J. P. Mayer (New Haven: Yale University Press, 1960), pp. 60, 216.

60. Tocqueville, *Democracy*, 2: 123, 342, and *Journey*, ed. Mayer, p. 212.

61. The conceptualization in this paragraph derives from Richard Vernon, *Citizenship and Order: Studies in French Political Thought* (Toronto, Buffalo, and London: University of Toronto Press, 1986), pp. 119–22.

62. Tocqueville, *Journey*, ed. Mayer, p. 263, and *Democracy*, 1:. 451–52.

63. Tocqueville, *Journey*, ed., Mayer, p. 211.

64. Tocqueville, *Democracy*, 1: 56, 58; cf., 14, 300–301, 311.

65. Tocqueville to Gustave de Beaumont, 6 August 1854, *Memoirs*, ed. Beaumont, 2: 265.

66. Tocqueville, *Journey*, pp. 168–69.

67. Tocqueville, *Old Régime*, p. 210, and "*European*," ed. Lukacs, p. 172; cf. pp. 100, 130, 136, and *Old Régime*, p. 211.

68. Tocqueville, *Democracy*, 1: 273, 14, 45.

69. Hartz, *Liberal*, pp. 5, 285.

70. I discuss the distribution of power in Frederic Cople Jaher, *The Urban Establishment: Upper Strata in Boston, New York, Charleston, Chicago, and Los Angeles* (Urbana, Chicago, and London: University of Illinois Press, 1982), pp. 726–30. Robert A. Dahl, "A Critique of the Ruling Elite Model." *American Political Science Review* 52 (June 1958): 463–69, is still a powerful analysis on behalf of a democratic distribution of power.

71. Rogers M. Smith, *Civic Ideals*, p. 707. Another example of the revival of Tocqueville among political scientists is political theorist Sheldon Wolin's exploration of Tocqueville's concept and practice of political theory, idea of democracy as a political and theoretical project, and place in the politics of modernity, in Sheldon S. Wolin, *Tocqueville between Two Worlds: The Making of a Political and Theoretical Life* (Princeton and Oxford: Princeton University Press 2001).

72. Robert D. Putnam, *Bowling Alone: The Collapse and Revival of American Community* (New York and London: Simon & Schuster, 2000), pp. 292, 25.

73. Desmond King, *In the Name of Liberalism: Illiberal Social Policy in the USA and Britain* (Oxford and New York: Oxford University Press, 1999).

74. For another discussion of these issues see Smith, " 'American Creed' ": 225–51; idem, "Beyond Tocqueville": 549–66, and idem, *Civic Ideals*; Linda K. Kerber, "A Constitutional Right to be Treated Like American Ladies: Women and the Obligations of Citizenship," in *U.S. History as Women's History: New Feminist Essays*, ed. Linda K. Kerber, Alice Kessler-Harris, and Kathryn Kish Sklar (Chapel Hill: University of North Carolina Press, 1995), pp. 17–35, applies the principles of King and Smith to American women.

75. For Smith's view of Tocqueville and Hartz as central figures in the misleading orthodoxy, see Smith, *Civic Ideals*, pp. 1–30. Political scientists far outnumber historians currently perpetuating the Tocqueville-Hartz thesis; see ibid., pp. 27–30.

76. Ibid., "Epilogue," pp. 470–506, esp. pp. 504–506, quotes on pp. 471–72.

77. Tocqueville, *Democracy*, 2: 11, 241–43, 324.

Chapter 2
The Nation

1. Beatrice Fry Hyslop, *French Nationalism in 1789 According to the General Cahiers* (New York: Columbia University Press, 1934), pp. 284–86.

2. Gilbert Shapiro and John Markoff, *Revolutionary Demands*, pp. 476–82, especially p. 476.

3. E. J. Hobsbawm, *Nations and Nationalism Since 1780: Programme, Myth, Reality* (Cambridge and New York: Cambridge University Press, 1992), p. 12.

4. Lynn Hunt, *Politics, Culture, and Class in the French Revolution* (Berkeley and Los Angeles: University of California Press, 1984), pp. 149–79.

5. Henry Lachouque, *Aux Armes, Citoyens! Les Soldats de la Révolution* (Paris: Libraire Académique Perrin, 1969), plates facing p. 142; *French Caricature and the French Revolution, 1789–1799* (Los Angeles: Greenwald Center for the Graphic Arts, Wight Art Gallery, University of California at Los Angeles, 1988; distributed by the University of Chicago Press), p. 215. I am indebted to Prof. John Lynn for bringing this material to my attention. The decrees of August 27 and September 15, 1797, are in Raphael Mahler, *Jewish Emancipation: A Selection of Documents*. Pamphlet Series Jews and the Post-War World, no. 1 (New York: The American Jewish Committee, 1941), pp. 28–29.

6. Hobsbawm, *Nations and Nationalism*, pp. 18–21, 41–42, 87–88.

7. Georges Le Febvre, *The French Revolution From Its Origins to 1793* (New York: Columbia University Press, 1962), p. 124; Milo M. Quaife, Melvin J. Weig, and Roy E. Appleman, *The History of the United States Flag from the Revolution to the Present* (New York: Harper & Row, 1961), pp. 26–53; Whitney Smith, *The Flag Book of the United States* (New York: William Morrow, 1970), pp. 53–56, 58–68; *Concise Dictionary of the United States*, ed. Wayne

Andrews (New York: Charles Scribner's Sons, 1962), p. 358–59; Continental Congress Resolution is on p. 358.

8. Quaife. Weig, and Appleman, *The History of United States Flag*, pp. 26–53; Smith, *The Flag Book*, pp. 53–56, 58–68.

9. For references, see fn. 8.

10. For the Pledge of Allegiance, see *Encyclopedia Britannica*, 29 vols. (Chicago: Encyclopedia Britannica, 1997), 9: 515.

11. *Historical Dictionary of the French Revolution, 1789–1799* (Westport, CT: Greenwood Press, 1985), ed. Samuel F. Scott and Barry Rothaus, 2 vols., 2: 637–38.

12. *Encyclopedia Americana* 30 vols. (Danbury, CT: Grolier, 1999), 25: 609–10; *Concise Dictionary*, ed. Andrews, p. 896.

13. .*Concise Dictionary*, ed. Andrews, p. 1042; *Encyclopedia Americana*, 29: 648.

14. *The Oxford English Dictionary* (Oxford: Clarendon Press, 1989), prepared by J. A. Simpson and E. S. C. Weiner 2d ed., 22 vols., 10: 235; *Dictionairre De La Langue Française* (Paris: Libraire Hachette Et Cie, 1873), ed. É. Littré, 2 vols., 2: 692. The *Dictionairre* did not contain entries for the words "nationalist" or "nationalism."

15. *Historical Dictionary*, ed. Scott and Rothaus, 1: 82–83; Michel Winock, *Nationalism, Anti-Semitism, and Fascism in France* (Stanford: Stanford University Press, 1998), p. 6.

16. Another discussion of these matters is in Tzvetan Todorov, *On Human Diversity: Nationalism, Racism, and Exoticism in French Thought* (Cambridge and London: Harvard University Press, 1993), pp. 175–76, 187–89.

17. Ibid., pp. 387–89.

18. Ibid.

19. David Carroll, *French Literary Fascism: Nationalism, Anti-Semitism, and the Ideology of Culture* (Princeton: Princeton University Press, 1995), p. 95.

20. For a comparison between French and German citizenship, see William Rogers Brubaker, *Citizenship and Nationhood in France and Germany* (Cambridge and London: Harvard University Press, 1992); Yasemin Nuhoglu Soysal, "Changing Citizenship in Europe: Remarks on Post National Membership and the National State," in *Citizenship, Nationality and Migration*, ed. David Cesarini and Mary Fulbrook (London and New York: Routledge, 1996), pp. 17–18; Patrick Weil, "Nationalities and Citizenships: The Lessons of the French Experience for Germany and Europe," in ibid., pp. 76–77. For discussions of civic and ethnic nationalism, see Bernard Yack, "The Myth of the Civic Nation," in *Theorizing Nationalism*, ed. Ronald Beiner (Albany: State University of New York Press, 1999), pp. 103–88; Kai Nielsen, "Cultural Nationalism, Neither Ethnic nor Civic," in ibid., pp. 119–30.

21. Gérard Noiriel, *The French Melting Pot: Immigration, Citizenship, and National Identity* (Minneapolis and London: University of Minnesota Press, 1996), p. xviii.

22. Todorov, *Human Diversity*, pp. 386–87.

23. A discussion of this point may be found in Richard Vernon, *Citizenship and Order*, pp. 1–11, 222–26.

24. Michael Walzer, "The Civil Society Argument," in *Theorizing Citizenship*, ed. Beiner (Albany: State University of New York Press, 1995), pp. 167–68; Jurgen Habermas, "Citizenship and National Identity," in ibid., pp. 180–83.

25. Iris Marion Young, "Polity and Group Difference: A Critique of Universal Citizenship." in ibid., p. 175.

26. *Historical Dictionary*, ed. Scott and Rothaus, 1: 317–22; 2: 942–46, 961–65; François Furet, *Revolutionary France 1770–1880* (Oxford, UK and Cambridge, MA: Blackwell, 1992), pp. 70–72, 88–89, 133–36, 152–53; J. F. Bosher, *The French Revolution* (New York and London: W. W. Norton, 1988), pp. 133–57; Patrice Higonnet, *Sister Republics: The Origins of French and American Republicanism* (Cambridge: Harvard University Press, 1988), pp. 2–3, 5–7, 89–91, 230–33; Jean-Pierre Hirsch, "Revolutionary France, Cradle of Free Enterprise," *The American Historical Review* 94 (December 1989): 1281–89; Thomas E. Kaiser, "Property, Sovereignty, the Declaration of the Rights of Man, and the Tradition of French Jurisprudence," in *The French Idea of Freedom: The Old Regime and the Declaration of the Rights of 1789*, ed. Dale Van Kley (Stanford: Stanford University Press, 1994), pp. 300–39; "The Declaration of the Rights of Man and of the Citizen (1789)," in ibid., pp. 1–3; Isser Woloch, *The New Regime: Transformations of the French Civic Order, 1789–1820s* (New York and London: W. W. Norton, 1994), pp. 51–59.

27. *Historical Dictionary*, ed. Scott and Rothaus, 2: 589–90; Alan Forrest, "Army," in *Critical Dictionary*, ed. Furet and Ozouf, pp. 419–20; Woloch, *New Regime*, pp. 385–87; Simon Schama, *Citizens: A Chronicle of the French Revolution* (New York: Alfred A. Knopf, 1989), pp. 760, 762–63.

28. For a discussion of the movement from universal to national rights in the Declaration of the Rights of Man, see Julia Kristeva, *Strangers to Ourselves* (New York: Columbia University Press, 1991), pp. 148–51.

29. Todorov, *Human Diversity*, p. 200.

30. Walzer, "Civil Society," pp. 168–71.

31. Michael Walzer, *What it Means to be an American* (New York: Marsilio, 1992), pp. 24–25.

32. The discussion of nationalism, citizenship, ethnicity, religion, and the Jews draws on the following: ibid., and *Obligations: Essays on Disobedience, War, and Citizenship* (Cambridge: Harvard University Press, 1970); Noiriel, *The French Melting Pot*; Brubaker, *Citizenship and Nationhood*; Higonnet, *Sister Republics*; Todorov, *Human Diversity*; Oscar and Mary Handlin, *The Dimensions of Liberty* (Cambridge: Harvard University Press, 1961); Ernest Gellner, *Nations and Nationalism* (Ithaca and London: Cornell University Press, 1983), and idem, *Culture, Identity, and Politics* (London and New York: Cambridge University Press, 1987); Peter H. Schuck and Roger M. Smith, *Citizenship Without Consent: Illegal Aliens in the American Polity* (New Haven and London: Yale University Press, 1985); Jurgen Habermas, *The Structural Transformation of the Public Sphere: An Inquiry into a Category of Bourgeois* (Cambridge: MIT Press, 1989), and "Citizenship and National Identity," in *Theorizing Citizenship*, ed. Beiner, pp. 261–64; Benedict Anderson, *Imagined Communities: Reflections on the Origin and Spread of Nationalism* (London and New York: Verso, 1993); Thomas Hylland Erikson, *Ethnicity and Nationalism: Anthropological Perspectives* (Lon-

don and Boulder, CO: Pluto Press, 1993); *Multiculturalism: Examining the Politics of Recognition*, ed. Amy Gutmann (Princeton: Princeton University Press, 1994); Liah Greenfeld, *Nationalism: Five Roads to Modernity* (Cambridge: Harvard University Press, 1992); Paul R. Brass, *Ethnicity and Nationalism: Theory and Composition* (New Dehli and London: Sage Publications, 1991); Steven M. Cohen, *American Modernity and Jewish Identity* (New York: Tavistock Publications, 1983); Benjamin Azkin, *State and Nation* (New York: Hutchinson, 1964); *The Moral Foundations of the American Republic*, ed. Robert H. Horwitz (Charlottesville: University of Virginia Press, 1986); Alasdair Macintyre, *Is Patriotism a Virtue?* (Lawrence: University of Kansas Press, 1988); *Ethnicity and Nationalism*, ed. Anthony D. Smith (Leiden, New York, and Cologne: E. J. Brill, 1992); Anthony D. Smith, *Theories of Nationalism* (New York: Holmes & Meier, 1983); idem, *The Ethnic Origins of Nations* (Oxford: Basil Blackwell, 1986); idem, *National Identity* (Reno, Las Vegas, and London: University of Nevada Press, 1991); Julia Kristeva, *Strangers to Ourselves*, and *Nations Without Nationalism* (New York: Columbia University Press, 1993); Hobsbawm, *Nations and Nationalism*; *Theorizing Nationalism*, ed. Beiner, especially Yack, "Myth" pp. 103–18 and Kai Nielsen, "Cultural Nationalism," pp. 119–30; Sudhir Hazareesingh, *From Subject to Citizen: The Second Empire and the Emergence of Modern French Democracy* (Princeton: Princeton University Press, 1998), and idem, *Political Traditions in Modern France* (Oxford and New York: 1998); Vernon, *Citizenship and Order*.

33. *Acte Constitutionnel Du 24 Juin 1793*, in *les Constitutions de la France*, ed. Charles Debbasch and Jean-Marie Pontier (Paris: Dalloz, 1983), Article 120, p. 47; Brubaker, *Citizenship and Nationhood*, p. 445, and "Introduction," *Immigration and the Politics of Citizenship in Europe and North America*, ed. William Rogers Brubaker (Lanham, MD, New York, and London: University Press of America, 1989), pp. 7–9, 11–13; Donald L. Horowitz, "Immigration and Group Relations in France and America," in *Immigrants in Two Democracies: French and American Experience*, ed. Donald L. Horowitz and Gérard Noiriel (New York and London: New York University Press, 1992), pp. 4–7.

34. *"Constitution du 3 Septembre 1791,"* in *Constitutions*, ed. Debbasch and Pontier, Section 2, Articles 2–4, pp. 11–12, Section 6, p. 37; *"Acte Constitutionnel Du 24 Juin 1793,"* Articles 4–6, p. 147; *"Constitution Du 5 Fructidor An III* (22 August 1795)," Section 2, Articles 8–10, p. 63; *"Constitution Du 22 Frimaire An VIII* (13 December 1799), Articles 2–3; p. 100; *The Code Napoleon or the French Civil Code* (New York: Halsted and Voorhies, 1841), pp. 3–4; *Code Civil* (Paris: L. Larose & Forcel, 1885–1898), pp. 74–81. Brubaker, *Citizenship and Nationhood*, pp. 44–45; Wells, *Law and Citizenship*, pp. 140, 143–44; Patrick Weil, "Nationalities and Citizenships: The Lessons of the French Experience for Germany and Europe," in *Citizenship, Nationality*, ed. Cesarini and Fulbrook, p. 76.

35. A more detailed discussion of American citizenship laws, with references, is in Chapter 6.

36. *Code Napoleon*, p. 3; *Civil Laws*, pp. 22–23; *Code Civil*, Book 1, Section 1, Article 13, p. 79; Stephan Thernstrom, "American Ethnic Statistics," in *Immigrants in Two Democracies*, ed. Horowitz and Noiriel, p. 81; Gérard Noiriel, "Difficulties in French Historical Research on Immigration,"in ibid., p. 69; Rox-

ana Silberman, "French Immigration Statistics," in ibid., p. 112; Brubaker, *Citizenship and Nationhood*, p. 85; Wells, *Law and Citizenship*, pp. 145–46; Weil, "Lessons," p. 77.

37. Schuck and Smith, *Citizenship Without Consent*, pp. 52–53.

38. For other discussions of these matters: Andrei-Clément Deconflé, "Historic Elements of the Politics of Nationality in France (1889–1989)," in *Immigrants in Two Democracies*, ed. Horowitz and Noiriel, pp. 362–63; Horowitz, "Immigration," in ibid, pp. 7, 9; Schuck and Smith, *Citizenship Without Consent*, pp. 49–63, 70–71; Gérard Noiriel, *The French Melting Pot*, pp. xxii, 6–7, 258–66; Catharine Collomp, "Immigrants, Labor Markets, and the State; a Comparative Approach: France and the United States, 1880–1930," *The Journal of American History* 86 (June 1999): 41–66.

39. Peter H. Schuck, "Immigration, Refugee, and Citizenship Law in the United States," in *Immigrants in Two Democracies*, ed. Horowitz and Noiriel, p. 335, and "Membership in the Liberal Polity: The Development of American Citizenship," in *Immigration and Politics*, ed. Brubaker, pp. 52, 55; Brubaker, *Citizenship and Nationhood*, p. 33; idem, "Citizenship and Naturalization: Policies and Politics," in *Immigration and Politics*; ed. Brubaker, pp. 118–20, quotes on French naturalization requirements are on p. 111; Noiriel, *The French Melting Pot*, p. 259, and *Workers in French Society in the 19th and 20th Centuries* (New York: Berg, 1990), pp. 119–23; U.S. Bureau of the Census, *Historical Statistics of the United States: Colonial Times to 1970* (Washington D.C.: GPO, 1970), 2 parts, 1: 105–9; Collomp, "Immigrants, Labor Markets": 45.

40. Noiriel, *The French Melting Pot*, pp. 3–5, 8–10, 259, and *Workers in French Society*, pp. 122–23. For a similar view, see Collomp, "Immigrants, Labor Markets": 41–66.

41. Winock, *Nationalism, Anti-Semitism*, p. 6.

42. Schuck and Smith, *Citizenship Without Consent*, pp. 49–71.

Chapter 3
The French Experience I

1. François Furet, *Revolutionary France 1770–1880* (Oxford: Blackwell, 1992), pp. 70–71, 82–85, 88–92; Mona Ozouf, "De-Christianization," in *A Critical Dictionary of the French Revolution*, François Furet and Mona Ozouf eds, (Cambridge and London: Harvard University Press, 1989), pp. 25–26; Ozouf, "Federalism," in ibid., pp. 54–63; Furet, "Civil Constitution of the Clergy," in ibid., pp. 449–56; J. F. Bosher, *The French Revolution*, pp. 133–57, 168; Patrice Higonnet, *Sister Republics*, pp. 230–33; George Armstrong, "The Jacobin and Liberal Contributions to the Founding of the Second and Third French Republics," in *Liberty/ Liberté: The American and French Experiences*, ed. Joseph Klaits and Michael H. Haltzel (Baltimore and London: Johns Hopkins University Press, 1991), pp. 131–32; François Bourricaud, "The Rights of the Individual and the General Will in Revolutionary Thought," in ibid., pp. 10, 23–26; Jean Rivero, "The Jacobin and Liberal Traditions," in ibid., pp. 121–22; Jean-Pierre Hirsch,

"Revolutionary France, Cradle of Free Enterprise," *The American Historical Review* 94 (December 1989): 1286–89; Thomas E. Kaiser, "Property, Sovereignty, the Declaration of the Rights of Man, and the Tradition of French Jurisprudence," in *The French Idea of Freedom*, ed. Dale Van Kley, pp. 300–1, 324–25, 337–39; "The Declaration of the Rights of Man and of the Citizen," in ibid., pp. 1–4.

2. Alan Schom, *Napoleon Bonaparte* (New York: HarperCollins, 1997), p. 296.

3. The findings in this and the previous paragraph are based on the following works: Zosa Szajkowski, *Jews and the French Revolutions of 1789, 1830 and 1848* (New York: KTAV, 1970), pp. xii–xvi, xviii, xliv, 28–29, 45–46, 221–24, 241–45, 282–83, 299, 303–4, 314–20, 331–32, 374, 576–77, 599–620; Reinhard Rurup, "Jewish Emancipation and Bourgeois Society," *Year Book* (New York: Leo Baeck Institute), 14 (1969), pp. 69–72; Frances Malino, *The Sephardic Jews of Bordeaux: Assimilation and Emancipation in Revolutionary France* (Birmingham: University of Alabama Press, 1978), p. 48; idem, *A Jew in the French Revolution: The Life of Zalkind Hourwitz* (Oxford and Cambridge, MA: Blackwell, 1996), pp. 15, 21; and idem, "Attitudes toward Jewish Communal Autonomy in Prerevolutionary France," in *Essays in Modern Jewish History*, eds. Frances Malino and Phyllis Cohen Albert (Rutherford, NJ: Fairleigh Dickinson University Press; London and Toronto: Associated University Presses, 1982), pp. 96–97; Arthur Hertzberg, *The French Enlightenment and the Jews* (New York: Columbia University Press, 1969), pp. 52–59, 83, 107–9, 118, 122–24, 138–40, 165–75, 188–247, 318–22; S. Posener, "The Immediate Economic and Social Effects of the Emancipation of the Jews in France," *Jewish Social Studies*, 1 (1939): 271–81; Gary Kates, "Jews into Frenchmen: Nationality and Representation in Revolutionary France," in *The French Revolution and the Birth of Modernity*, ed. Ferenc Féher (Berkeley and Los Angeles: The University of California Press, 1990), pp. 109–10; Paula Hyman, *The Emancipation of the Jews of Alsace: Acculturation and Tradition in the Nineteenth Century* (New Haven: Yale University Press, 1991), pp. 13–14, 16, and idem, *The Jews of Modern France* (Berkeley, Los Angeles, London: University of California Press, 1998), pp. 1–15; Simon Schwarzfuchs, *Napoleon, the Jews and the Sanhedrin* (London and Boston: Routledge & Kegan Paul, 1979), p. 3; Scott Glotzer, *Napoleon, the Jews, and the Construction of Modern Citizenship in Early Nineteenth Century France* (Ann Arbor: UMI, 1997), pp. 15–33, 57–65, 119–21; Esther Benbassa, *The Jews of France: A History from Antiquity to the Present* (Princeton University Press, 1999), pp. 61–71; Jonathan I. Israel, *European Jewry in the Age of Mercantilism* (London and Portland, OR: Littman Library of Jewish Civilization, 1998), pp. 43, 55–56, 95–96.

4. Werner E. Mosse, "From 'Schutzjuden' to 'Deutsche Staatburger Judischen Glaubens': The Long and Bumpy Road of Jewish Emancipation in Germany," in *Paths of Emancipation*, ed. Pierre Birnbaum and Ira Katznelson, pp. 60–74; Raphael Mahler, *A History of Modern Jewry 1780–1815*, pp. 129–76, 201–6.

5. The "Commission," in fact, never met or actually existed. Benbassa, *Jews of France*, pp. 67–68, 78; Hertzberg, *French Enlightenment*, pp. 110–21, 135–

36, 190–92, 316, 318–20, 323; Rurup, "Jewish Emancipation," pp. 69–70; Szajkowski, *Jews and French Revolutions*, pp. xlv, 76–77, 311–21, 358–59, 371–77; *French Revolution*, ed. Ferenc Féher, pp. 109, 316, 319; Hyman, *Jews of Modern France*, pp. 1–24, and *Emancipation*, p. 14; Malino, *Sephardic*, pp. 28, 31–37; Paul Meyer, "The Attitude of the Enlightenment Toward the Jews," *Studies on Voltaire and the Eighteenth Century* 26 (1963): 1203–5; Léon Poliakov, *The History of Anti-Semitism* (New York: Vanguard Press, 1965–1974), 3 vols., 3: 149; Glotzer, *Napoleon, the Jews*, pp. 119–29, the questions are reprinted on pp. 128–29.

6. The United States was arguably the first nation to emancipate Jews because Article VI of the Constitution prohibited religious tests for office, thus removing the widespread colonial obstruction against Jews holding office, effective because such oaths required Jews to affirm the divinity of Jesus and the New Testament.

7. *Abbé* Henri Gregoire, *Essai sur la Régéneration physique, morale et politque des Juifs* (Paris: Stock, 1988), p. 108, and "Take Oath of Civil Constitution of Clergy On Behalf of the Jews," (1789), in Ray L. Carol, *Two Rebel Priests of the French Revolution* (San Francisco: R & E Research Associates, 1975), pp. 18–33; *The Jew in the Modern World: a Documentary History*, ed. Paul Mendes-Flohr and Jehuda Reinharz (New York and Oxford: Oxford University Press, 1995), pp. 42–44, 49–50; Shanti Marie Singham, "Betwixt Cattle and Men: Jews, Blacks, and Women, and the Declaration of the Rights of Man," in *The French Idea of Freedom*, ed. Dale Van Kley, pp. 125–26. For accounts of the "nation within a nation," see Hertzberg, *French Enlightenment*, pp. 328, 334, 350–68; Malino, "Attitudes toward Jewish Communal Authority," pp. 95–117; Szajkowski, *Jews and French Revolutions*, pp. 576–82, 606–20; Rurup, "Jewish Emancipation," pp. 69–72; Jacob Katz, *Emancipation and Assimilation: Studies in Modern Jewish History* (Westmead, UK: Gregg International Publishers, 1972), pp. 3–4, 31–36, 56–65; Hyman, *Jews of Modern France*, pp. 20–25; Glotzer, *Napoleon, the Jews*, pp. 55–56, 65–71, 74–92.

8. Charlotte C. Wells, *Law and Citizenship in Early Modern France* (Baltimore and London: The Johns Hopkins University Press, 1995), pp. 139–40.

9. Hyman, *Jews of Modern France*, pp. 3–22; Benbassa, *Jews of France*, pp. 40–72.

10. Israel Finestein, "Jewish Emancipationists in Victorian England: Self-imposed Limits to Emancipation," in *Assimilation and Community: The Jews in Nineteenth-Century Europe*, ed. Jonathan Frankel and Steven Zipperstein (Cambridge and New York: Cambridge University Press, 1992), pp. 43–47; David Cesarini, "The Changing Character of Citizenship and Nationality in Britain," in *Citizenship, Nationality and Migration in Europe*, ed. Cesarini and Mary Fulbrook, pp. 60–61.

11. Gregoire, *Essai*. The best discussion of "renegeration" is in the articles of Ronald Schecter: "Competing Proposals for the Regeneration of the Jews, 1787–1789," *Proceedings of the Annual Meeting of the Western Society for French History* 24 (1997): 483–93; idem, "The Jewish Question in Eighteenth-Century France," *Eighteenth Century Studies* 32 (Fall 1998): 84–91; and idem, "Rationalizing the Enlightenment: Postmodernism and Theories of Anti-Semitism," *Histori-*

cal Reflections/Réflexions 25 (Summer 1999): 287–301; see also Hyman, *Jews of Modern France*, pp. 15–25; Glotzer, *Napoleon, the Jews*, pp. 55–56, 78–92, 128–29, 141–49; Jay R. Berkovitz, *The Shaping of Jewish Identity in Nineteenth-Century France* (Detroit: Wayne State University Press, 1989), pp. 14–15, 41–42, 128–49; Benbassa, *Jews of France*, p. 77.

12. Gilbert Shapiro and John Markoff, *Revolutionary Demands*, pp. 123, 476; David Feuerwerker, *L'Émancipation Des Juifs En France De L'Ancien Régime A La Fin Du Second Empire* (Paris: Éditions Albin Michel, 1976), pp. 262–85; Glotzer, *Napoleon, the Jews*, pp. 135–37; Berkovitz, *Shaping*, pp. 41–42; Benbassa, *Jews of France*, pp. 79–80.

13. See, for example, Iris Marion Young, "Polity and Group Difference: A Critique of Universal Citizenship," in *Theorizing Citizenship*, ed. Ronald Beiner, p. 175.

14. Shapiro and Markoff, *Revolutionary Demands*, p. 476.

15. Ibid., p. 449. The total number of frequencies of subjects mentioned is on p. 1.

16. Benbassa, *Jews of France*, p. 80; Michael Graetz, *The Jews in Nineteenth-Century France: From the French Revolution to the Alliance Israélite Universelle* (Stanford: Stanford University Press, 1996), pp. 20–25.

17. Geoffrey Alderman, "English Jews or Jews of English Persuasion: Reflections on the Emancipation of Anglo-Jewry," in *Paths of Emancipation*, ed. Birnbaum and Katznelson, pp. 128–29, 133–36.

18. *Archives Parlementaires de 1787 à 1860, Premier Série (1789 à 1799)* [hereafter *AP*] (Paris: Librairie Administratif de Paul Dupont, 1878), 10, du 12 Novembre 1789 au 24 Decembre 1789, pp. 693–95; speech of François Martin Thiébault is on pp. 705–12.

19. Speech of Count Stanislas de Clermont-Tonnerre to the National Assembly, 23 June 1789, in *Jew in the Modern World*, ed. Mendes-Flohr and Reinharz, pp. 114–15, and in *AP*, 10, pp. 754–56. For information on Clermont-Tonnerre and the emancipation debate, see Hertzberg, *French Enlightenment*, pp. 355–68; Gary Kates, "Jews into Frenchmen," in *The French Revolution and the Birth of Modernity*, ed. Ferenc Féher, pp. 111–14; *Historical Dictionary of the French Revolution*, ed. Samuel F. Scott and Barry Rothaus, 1: 194–95.

20. Clermont-Tonnere, *AP*, 10 23 Decemeber 1789, p. 756.

21. Phyllis Cohen Albert, "Israelite and Jew: How did Nineteenth-Century French Jews Understand Assimilation?" in *Assimilation and Community*, ed. Frankel and Zipperstein, pp. 88–109. The Clermont-Tonnerre interpretation is on p. 91.

22. In chapter 4, I will consider Albert's opinion that the French did not generally demand assimilation.

23. Grégoire, *AP*, 10, p. 764.

24. *AP*, 10: 758. Biographical information on Du Port is in *Historical Dictionary*, ed. Scott and Rothaus, 1: 338–40.

25. *AP*, 10: 757.

26. Speech of Anne-Louis-Henry de la Fare, Bishop of Nancy and Primate of Lorraine, in ibid., pp. 757–58, and in *Jew in the Modern World*, ed. Mendes-Flohr and Reinharz, pp. 115–16; François Furet, "Civil Constitution of the

Clergy," in *A Critical Dictionary of the French Revolution*, ed. Furet and Mona Ozouf, p. 450.

27. The Abbé Maury's remarks are in *AP*, 10: 756–57. Biographical information on Maury is in *Historical Dictionary*, ed. Scott and Rothaus, 2: 645–46.

28. *AP*, 10: 758; Malino, *Sephardic*, p. 48; Hertzberg, *French Enlightenment*, pp. 339–40.

29. Ibid., pp. 80–81; Pierre Birnbaum, *Jewish Destinies: Citizenship, State and Community in Modern France* (New York: Hill and Wang, 2000), p. 21; *AP*, 10 (24 December 1789), p. 783; Burdette C. Poland, *French Protestantism and the French Revolution: A Study in Church and State, Thought and Religion, 1685–1815*, (Princeton: Princeton University Press, 1957), p. 105.

30. Berkovitz, *Shaping*, pp. 111–26.

31. A summary of the arguments for and against emancipation may be found in Glotzer, *Napoleon, the Jews*, pp. 142–49.

32. A good discussion of these points is in Benbassa, *Jews of France*, p. 84.

33. The remarks of Talleyrand and Maury are in *AP*, 11 (28 January 1790), p. 364.

34. Statement of Reubell is in ibid., p. 364; his 1789 remark is in ibid., 10, p. 695; Biographical data is in *Historical Dictionary*, ed. Scott and Rothaus, 2: 818–20.

35. *AP*, 11, pp. 364–65. For the historical account of this debate, see ibid., pp. 363–65; Malino, *Sephardic*, pp. 51–53; Hertzberg, *French Enlightenment*, pp. 339–40; Kates, "Jews into Frenchmen," p. 111.

36. Malino, *Sephardic*, pp. 31–42; Glotzer, *Napoleon, the Jews*, pp. 129–31, 133–35; Paula Hyman, "The Social Contexts of Assimilation: Village Jews and City Jews in Alsace," in *Assimilation and Community*, ed. Frankel and Zipperstein, p. 111; Graetz, *Jews in Nineteenth-Century France*, p. 25.

37. Malino, *Sephardic*, pp. 24, 46–50; Benbassa, *Jews of France*, pp. 71–72, 78; Birnbaum, *Jewish Destinies*, pp. 21, 36–38. 42–43; Hyman, "Social Contexts," pp. 110–29; Graetz, *Jews in Nineteenth-Century France*, pp. 20–25.

38. See, for example reports, deputations and petitions to the National Assembly in *AP*, 10 (14 October 1789), pp. 755–65; 10 (28–30 January 1790), pp. 758–63; 11 (28 January 1790), pp. 363–65; and 3 September 1789, 25 January 1790, and 26 February 1790 reprinted in *Les Juifs de France: De l'émancipation à l'intégration (1787–1812)*, ed. Richard Ayoun (Paris and Montreal: L'Harmattan, 1997), pp. 103, 119–21.

39. "Nouveau Mémoire pour les Juifs de Lunéville et de Sarguemines, presented to the Assembly, Feb. 26, 1790, *Juifs de France*, ed. Ayoun, pp. 119–21.

40. *AP*, 10 (28–30 January 1790), pp. 758–63, quote is on p. 763.

41. National Assembly, 18 January 1791, reprinted in *Juifs de France*, ed. Ayoun, p. 123; biographical information is in *Historical Dictionary*, ed. Scott and Rothaus, 1: 127–28.

42. National Assembly, 7 May 1791, reprinted in *Juifs de France*, ed. Ayoun, pp. 124–25.

43. "Constitution du 3 Septembre 1791," in *les Constitutions de la France*, ed. Charles Debbash and Jean-Marie Pontier, Titre Premier, pp. 10–11; Titre II, arts. 1–4, pp. 11–12.

44. National Assembly, 27 September 1791, *AP*, 31, pp. 372–73; biographical information is in *Historical Dictionary*, ed. Scott and Rothaus, 1, pp. 338–40.

45. National Assembly, 27 September 1791, *AP*, p. 441; the Resolution is also in *Jews in the Modern World*, ed. Mendes-Flohr and Reinharz, p. 118.

46. *AP*, pp. 441–42.

47. Hertzberg, *French Enlightenment*, pp. 339–40, 350–68; Malino, *Sephardic*, pp. 51–55; Schwarzfuchs, *Napoleon*, pp. 11–14; Kates, "Jews into Frenchmen," pp. 110–11; Hyman, *Jews of Modern France*, pp. 26–31.

48. Alexis De Tocqueville, *The Old Régime*, pp. x–xi.

49. Benbassa, *Jews of France*, pp. 82–83; Graetz, *Jews in Nineteenth-Century France*, p. 28.

50. Kates, "Jews into Frenchmen," pp. 112–15; quote in Zosa Szajkowski, "The Attitude of French Jacobins to the Jewish Religion," *Historia Judaica* 18 (October 1956): 110.

51. This discussion derives from Sudhir, Hazareesingh, *Political Traditions in Modern France*, pp. 4–5.

52. For a discussion of these issues, see ibid., pp. 68–72.

53. Richard Vernon, *Citizenship and Order*, p. 217.

54. Ibid., pp. 68–72.

55. This point is made by Dominique Schnapper, *Jewish Identities in France: An Analysis of Contemporary French Jewry* (Chicago and London: The University of Chicago Press, 1983), p. 104, Kahn quote is on p. 104; Maurice Bloch, "La Société Juive En France Depuis La Révolution," *Revue des Études Juives*, 48 (1904): xli, xx.

56. Vernon, *Citizenship*, pp. 132, 157; Hazareesingh, *Political Traditions*, pp. 130–31.

57. On the division between more assimilated Jewish leaders and the mass of eastern Jews, who were orthodox in belief and practice, uninterested in civil rights and, above all, wanted to be left alone, see, Benbassa, *Jews of France*, p. 83.

58. Berr Issac Berr, "Letter to His Brethren on the Occasion of the Right of Citizenship Decreed on 28 September 1791," reprinted in M. Diogene Tama, *Transactions of the Parisian Sahedrin or Acts of the Assembly of Israelitish Deputies of France and Italy, Convoked at Paris by an Imperial and Royal Decree Dated May 30, 1806*, trans. F. D. Kirwan, printed in *Historical Views of Judaism* (New York: Arno Press, 1973), pp. 11–29; Glotzer, *Napoleon, the Jews*, pp. 155–56; Poliakov, *History of Anti-Semitism*, 3: 255–57; Berkovitz, *Shaping*, pp. 14–15, 86–80, 111–26, 247.

59. These matters are discussed in Ernest Gellner, *Culture, Identity, and Politics* (Cambridge, London, and New York: Cambridge University Press, 1987), pp. 74–79.

60. Szajkowski, *Jews and French Revolutions*, pp. 494–95, 525–37, 627–46; Kates, "Jews into Frenchmen," pp. 214–15; Glotzer, *Napoleon, the Jews*, pp. 156–58; Birnbaum, *Jewish Destinies*, p. 21.

61. Alexis de Tocqueville, *Democracy in America*, 1: 100; 2: 109.

62. Victor L. Tapié, *France in the Age of Louis XIII and Richelieu* (Cambridge and London: Cambridge University Press, 1984), pp. 199–202; John A.

Lynn, *The Wars of Louis XIV: 1667–1714* (London: Longman, 1999), pp. 174–81; Poland, *French Protestantism*, pp. 20–25, 77, 79–81, 105, 116, 151, 158–59; Bosher, *French Revolution*, p. 141; Timothy Tackett, *Religion, Revolution, and Regional Culture in Eighteenth-Century France: The Ecclesiastical Oath of 1791* (Princeton: Princeton University Press, 1986), pp. 208–10; Szajkowski, *Jews and French Revolutions*, pp. 378–80.

63. Schama, *Citizens*, pp. 259, 501.

64. Benbassa, *Jews of France*, pp. 78–79.

65. Bosher, *French Revolution*, pp. 145–46, 271; Féher, "The Cult of the Supreme Being and the Limits of the Secularization of the Political," in *French Revolution*, ed. Féher, pp. 180–82; Tackett, *Religion, Revolution*, pp. 3–11, 20–55, 159–204; Ozouf, "De-Christianization," pp. 25–27, and "Revolutionary Religion," in *Critical Dictionary*, ed. Furet and Ozouf, pp. 552–66; Furet, "Civil Constitution," in ibid., pp. 449–56; Adrien Dansette, *Religious History of Modern France* (New York: Herder & Herder, 1961), 2 vols., 1: 41–54, 57–58, 67–73; Ralph Gibson, *A Social History of French Catholicism, 1789–1914* (London and New York: Routledge, 1989), pp. 34–40; Furet, *Revolutionary France*, pp. 82–85, 89–92; Olwen Hufton, "The Reconstruction of a Church, 1796–1801," in *Beyond the Terror*, ed. Gwynne Lewis and Colin Lucas (Cambridge: Cambridge University Press, 1983), pp. 21–52; Schama, *Citizens*, pp. 483–84, 487–91.

66. Schwarzfuchs, *Napoleon*, pp. 16–17; Szajkowski, *Jews and French Revolutions*, pp. 785–816, and "Attitude": 113–20; Calvin Goldscheider and Alan S. Zuckerman, *The Transformation of the Jews* (Chicago and London: The University of Chicago Press, 1984), p. 37; Hyman, *Emancipation*, p. 15; idem, *Jews of Modern France*, pp. 32–34; Poland, *French Protestantism*, pp. 141–60; 181–92; Singham, "Betwixt Cattle," p. 123; Schama, *Citizens*, pp. 774–79, 855; Glotzer, *Napoleon, the Jews*, pp. 158–61, 163–64; Benbassa, *Jews of France*, p. 85; Kennedy, *Jacobin Clubs in the French Revolution, 1793–1795*, pp. 182–88; Patrice Higonnet, *Goodness Beyond Virtue: Jacobins during the French Revolution* (Cambridge and London: Harvard University Press, 1998), pp. 236–37.

67. Higonnet, *Goodness*, pp. 236–37.

68. Richard Cobb, *The French and their Revolution: Selected Writings edited and Introduced by David Gilmour* (London: John Murray, 1998), p. 192; Higonnet, *Goodness*, p. 237, quote on p. 237.

69. Glotzer, *Napoleon, the Jews*, pp. 156–57; Szajowski, *Jews in French Revolutions*, pp. 554–75. 785–98, 800–8, 810–23; Salo Wittmayer Baron, "Newer Approaches to Jewish Emancipation," *Diogenes* 29 (Spring 1960): 70–71; S. Posener, "Immediate Economic and Social Effects": 307–8, 315–18.

70. Poland, *French Protestantism*, pp. 196–97; Dansette, *Religious History*, 1: 32–33, 82–83; Ozouf, "De-Christianization," p. 27; Philippe Raymond, "Democracy," in *Critical Dictionary*, ed. Furet and Ozouf, p. 653; *Historical Dictionary*, ed. Scott and Rothaus, 2: 891–96; Gibson, *Social History*, p. 42 ; Emmet Kennedy, *A Cultural History of the French Revolution* (New Haven and London: Yale University Press, 1989), p. 155; Schama, *Citizens*, pp. 774–79, 855.

71. Furet, *Revolutionary France*, pp. 133–36; Ozouf, "Federalism," in *Critical Dicionary*, ed. Furet and Ozouf, pp. 54–63; Rivero, "Jacobin and Liberal," pp. 131–36: Kaiser, "Property," pp. 329–30; Robert Gildea, *The Past in French*

History (New Haven and London: Yale University Press, 1994), pp. 172–73; Gibson, *Social Forces*, pp. 43–46, 52; Schama, *Citizens*, pp. 774–79, 855.

72. Gibson, *Social History*, pp. 43–46, 52; Dansette, *Religious History*, 1: 72–90; Kennedy, *Cultural History*, pp. 358–61; Poland, *French Protestantism*, pp. 198–222, 252, 255, 265; Ozouf, "De-Christianization," pp. 20–32; Schama, *Citizens*, pp. 774–79, 855.

73. Poland, *French Protestantism*, pp. 198–206; Féher, "Cult," pp. 174–97; Kennedy, *Cultural History*, pp. 338–65; Dansette, *Religious History*, 1: 84–91, 94–98; Ozouf, "De-Christianization," p. 26, and "Revolutionary Religion," pp. 562–67; Gibson, *Social History*. pp. 44–46; Schama, *Citizens*, pp. 774–79, 855.

74. "Constitution Du 1 Septembre 1791," Debbasch and Pontier, *Constitutions de la France*, Titre Premier, p. 13.

75. Gellner, *Culture, Identity, and Politics*, p. vii.

76. Louis Hartz, *The Liberal Tradition in America*, pp. 40–41. For the role of the ministers, see *The Pulpit of the American Revolution: or The Political Sermons of the Period of 1776*, ed. John Wingate Thornton (Boston: Gould and Lincoln, 1860).

77. For references for this and the preceding paragraph, see Gibson, *Social History*, pp. 48–51, 54; Poland, *French Protestantism*, pp. 254–60, 263–69, 276–77; Dansette, *Religious History*, 1: 97–102, 110–11, 121–37; Martyn Lyons, *Napoleon Bonaparte and the Legacy of the French Revolution* (New York: St. Martin's Press, 1994), pp. 82–86; Hufton, "Reconstruction," pp. 35–37; Benbassa, *Jews of France*, p. 85.

78. Poland, *French Protestantism*, pp. 124–40; Tackett, *Religion, Revolution*, pp. 207–28; Schama, *Citizens*, p. 501.

79. Hyman, *Emancipation*, pp. 15–16; idem, *Jews of Modern France*, pp. 33–34; Szajkowski, *Jews and French Revolutions*, pp. 51–53, 97, 336–72, 381–82, 796–97; idem, *Agricultural Credit and Napoleon's Anti-Jewish Decrees* (New York: Editions Historiques France-Juives, 1953), pp. 17, 21–22, 24, 26, 37–39, 62–65, 87; Singham, "Betwixt," pp. 123–27; Schwarzfuchs, *Napoleon*, pp. 123–81; Glotzer, *Napoleon, the Jews*, pp. 158–60, 194–95, 201–20, 239–40, 263–65, 269, 301–3, 367–73; Berkovitz, *Shaping*, pp. 36–38, 41–45, 82, 151–52, Franz Kobler, *Napoleon and the Jews* (New York: Shocken Books, 1976), pp. 134–46. Tama, *Transactions*, pp. 93–94, 105 (Imperial Decree of 30 May 1806), 131–32 (Louis-Matthieu Molé, Address to the Assembly of Notables, 29 July 1806), 244–45 (Molé, Statement to the Assembly, 18 September 1806).

80. Hertzberg, *French Enlightenment*, pp. 348–49.

81. Berr, "Letter," in Tama, *Transactions*, pp. 11–12.

82. Ibid., pp. 16–17.

83. Ibid., pp. 18–25, quotes on pp. 18, 21–22.

84. Ibid., pp. 15, 18–23, 27–28, quote on p. 23; Berkovitz, *Shaping*, pp. 70–71.

85. Petition of Avignon Jews quoted in Szajkowski, *Jews and French Revolutions*, pp. 584–85.

86. Efraim Shumeli, *Seven Jewish Cultures: A Reinterpretation of Jewish History and Thought* (Cambridge and New York: Cambridge University Press, 1990), Mendelssohn quote on native settlers is on p. 168; Moses Mendelssohn to

Ernst Ferdinand Klein, 29 August 1782, in *Moses Mendelssohn: Selections from His Writings*, ed. Eva Jospe (New York: Viking Press, 1975), p. 106, and *Jerusalem and Other Jewish Writings* (New York; Schocken Books, 1969), p. 23; idem, "Preface to Menasseh ben Israel's *Vindiciae Judaeorum*" (1782) in *Jew in the Modern World*, ed. Mendes-Flohr and Reinharz, pp. 39–40; idem, "Remarks Concerning Michaelis' Response to Dohm" (1782), in ibid., p. 43; Mahler, *History of Modern Jewry*, pp. 169–202.

87. Benedict [sic] Spinoza, *Tractatus Theologico-Politicus* (London: Trubner, 1862), pp. 284–86, 317–18, 321–23, 327–41, quote on p. 327.

88. This discussion follows Efraim Shmueli's brilliant exploration of these matters in *Seven Jewish*, pp. 168–77; Mendelssohn, "Remarks," p. 43.

89. Shmueli, *Seven Jewish*, pp. 168–69.

90. Ibid., pp. 172–73.

91. Ibid., pp. 172–74, 176–77.

92. Michael Graetz, "Jewry in the Modern Period: The Role of the 'Rising class' in the Politicization of Jews in Europe," in *Assimilation and Community*, ed. Frankel and Zipperstein, pp. 167–68; David Vital, *The Future of the Jews* (Cambridge: Harvard University Press, 1990), pp. 66–71.

93. Szajowski, "Attitude": 119–20, and "Secular Versus Religious Jewish Life in France," in *The Role of Religion in Modern Jewish History*, ed. Jacob Katz, (Cambridge, MA: Association for Jewish Studies, 1975), pp. 109–13; and idem, "Jewish Education," p. 3; Schwarzfuchs, *Napoleon*, p. 17; Posener, "Immediate": 308–10, 319–23; Hyman, *Jews of Modern France*, pp. 31–35; Berkovitz, *Shaping*, pp. 90, 94–97.

94. Zosa Szjakowski, *Jewish Education in France: 1789–1939* (New York: New York Conference on Jewish Social Studies, 1980), pp. 2–3; Berkovitz, *Shaping*, p. 60.

95. Malino, *Sephardic*, pp. 25–26, 29–39, 49–50, 56; Szajkowski, "Jewish Education," p. 2, and "The Demographic Aspects of Jewish Emancipation in France During the French Revolution," *Historia Judaica* 21 (April 1959): 16–17; Berkovitz, *Shaping*, pp. 59–60, 90, 98–99; Benbassa, *Jews of France*, p. 97; Graetz, *Jews in Nineteenth-Century France*, pp. 22–23.

96. Szajkowski, *Jews and French Revolutions*, pp. 579–82, "Attitude": 119–20, and idem, "Secular," pp. 109–13; Schwarzfuchs, *Napoleon*, p. 17; Posener, "Immediate": 308–10, 319–23; Hyman, *Emancipation*, pp. 12, 53, 64–68. 75–82, 94–95, 98–103, 112–13, 120–21, 138–39; idem, *Jews of Modern France*, pp. 33–35, 48–76, and idem, "Social Contexts," pp. 110–29; Phyllis Cohen Albert, "Ethnicity and Jewish Solidarity in Nineteenth-Century France," in *Mystics, Philosophers, and Politicians: Essays in Jewish History in Honor of Alexander Altermann*, ed. Jehuda Reinharz and Dan Swetschinski (Durham, NC: Duke University Press, 1982), pp. 249–74; Berkovitz, *Shaping*, pp. 59, 90, 94–97, 151; Benbassa, *Jews of France*, pp. 99, 102, 114, 127; Birnbaum, *Jewish Destinies*, pp. 28–29, 33, 38–40, 43.

97. Benbassa, *Jews of France*, pp. 115, 127.

98. Ibid., pp. 124–25.

99. Ibid., p. 94.

100. "Petition des juifs établis en France peur parvenir à l'entière juissance des droits de citoyens," January 28, 1790, *AP*, 13 April 1790, 12 (1790): 722.

101. Speech of Saint Etienne, *Gazette Nationale, ou Le Moniteur Universel Du 23 Au 26 Aout 1789*, no. 46: 189. See also Lewis Rosenthal, *America and France: The Influence of the United States on France in the XVIIIth Century* (New York: Henry Holt, 1882), pp. 207–8; and Max J. Kohler, "Phases in the History of Religious Liberty in America, with Special References to the Jews," *Publications of the American Jewish Historical Society*, 11 (1903): 58; Hertzberg, *French Enlightenment*, pp. 346–47.

102. James Madison to George Mason, 19 December 1827, in *Letters and other Writings of James Madison* (Philadelphia: J. B. Lippincott, 1865), 4 vols., 3: 606; 4: 678; *James Madison on Religious Liberty*, ed. Robert S. Alley (Buffalo: Prometheus Books, 1985), pp. 147–48; *The Papers of James Madison*, ed. William T. Hutchinson and William M. E. Rachal (Chicago: The University of Chicago Press, 1962), 11 vols., 1: 170–79; *James Madison: A Biography in His Own Words*, ed. Merrill D. Peterson (New York: Newsweek, 1974), pp. 40–41.

103. Thomas Jefferson to James Madison, 16 December 1786, in *Madison on Religious Liberty*, ed. Alley, p. 69; Raymond Birn, "Religious Toleration and Freedom of Expression," in *French Idea*, ed. Van Kley, p. 267;, Marcel Gauchet, "Rights of Man," in *Critical Dictionary*, ed. Furet and Ozouf, pp. 819–21; Durand Echeverria, *Mirage in the West: A History of the French Image of American Society to 1815* (New York: Octagon Books, 1966), pp. 163–68; Bernard Fäy, *The Revolutionary Spirit in France and America: A Study of the Moral and Intellectual Relations between France and the United States at the End of the Eighteenth Century* (New York: Harcourt, Brace, 1927), pp. 252–60; R. R. Palmer, *The Age of Democratic Revolution: A History of Europe and America, 1760–1800* (Princeton: Princeton University Press, 1959, 1964), 2 vols., 1: 487, 518–21.

104. Echeverria, *Mirage*, pp. 143–44, 216–24, 245–46, 260–80; Fäy, *Revolutionary Spirit*, pp. 252–335; Joyce Appleby, "America as a Model for the Radical French Reformers of 1789," *William and Mary Quarterly*, ser. 3, 28 (February 1971): 274–86.

105. André Maurois, *The Miracle of America* (New York and London: Harper & Bros., 1954), pp. 131, 158–59, Bastille quote on p. 159; Fäy, *Revolutionary Spirit*, pp. 134, 176, 254–59, 269–70, 307, Roland quote on p. 258.

106. Echeverria, *Mirage*, pp. 119, 165, 170–71; Fäy, *Revolutionary Spirit*, pp. 287–93, 315, 319, 335–36, 432–36; Palmer, *Age of Democratic Revolution*, 2: 51; *AP*, 39, p. 10.

107. Royer-Collard, speech to the Council of Five Hundred, in Amable G.P.B. De Barante, *La Vie Politique de Royer-Collard: Ses Discours et ses Écrits* (Paris: Didier, 1861), 2 vols., 1: 30. For biographical information, see George A. Kelly, *The Humane Comedy: Constant, Tocqueville, and French Liberalism* (Cambridge and New York: Cambridge University Press, 1992), pp. 17–37.

108. Hertzberg, *French Enlightenment*, pp. 350, 354, 356, 359, 366–67; Szajkowski, *Jews and French Revolutions*, pp. 388–98, 425–29, 508–10, 525–37, 555–57, 785–91, 796–97, and "Jewish Autonomy Debated and Attacked," *Historia Judaica* 17 (1957): 23–28; Hyman, *Jews of Modern France*, pp. 32–34; Glotzer, *Napoleon, the Jews*, pp. 160–61; Berkovitz, *Shaping*, pp. 88–90, 151–

52. For later French anti-Semitism see Michel Winock, *Nationalism, Anti-Semitism*, pp. 84–102, 114–30, 219–24; Hyman, *Jews of Modern France*, pp. 56, 64, 93, 95–117, 135, 138, 145–52, 187, 189, 209–12.

109. Hertzberg, *French Enlightenment*, pp. 364–65; Szajkowski, *Jews and French Revolutions*, pp. 584–91, 627–46, Avignon Jews quote on p. 584; Schwarzfuchs, *Napoleon*, pp. 14–15, 19–21; Phyllis Cohen Albert, *The Modernization of French Jewry: Consistory and Community in the Nineteenth Century* (Waltham: Brandeis University Press, 1977), pp. 155–56.

110. Michael L. Kennedy, *The Jacobin Clubs in the French Revolution: The First Years* (Princeton: Princeton University Press, 1982), pp. 13, 154, and idem, *The Jacobin Clubs in the French Revolution: 1793–1795* (New York and London: Berghahn Books, 2000), p. 183; Higonnet, *Goodness*, p. 236.

111. Kennedy, *Jacobin Clubs in the French Revolution: 1793–1795*, pp. 183–86, 188; Higonnet, *Goodness*, pp. 236–37; Hyman, *Jews of Modern France*, p. 95.

112. Hyman, *Jews of Modern France*, p. 64.

113. Ronald Schecter, "Translating the 'Marseillaise': Biblical Republicanism and the Emancipation of the Jews in Revolutionary France," *Past and Present* 143 (May 1994): 108–35.

Chapter 4
The French Experience II

1. Napoleon quoted in Simon Schwarzfuchs, *Napoleon*, pp. 21, 28.

2. Jay R. Berkovitz, *Shaping*, pp. 77–78; Scott Glotzer, *Napoleon, The Jews*, pp. 194–95; Franz Kobler, *Napoleon and the Jews*, pp. 134–39.

3. Napoleon, "Note for the Grand Judge," *Correspondance de Napoléon Ier* (Paris: Imprimerie Impériale, 1858–1869), 32 vols., 12: 190; Schwarzfuchs, *Napoleon*, pp. 45–67; Szajkowski, *Agricultural Credit*, pp. 17, 21–22, 24, 37–39, 62–65, 87; Glotzer, *Napoleon, the Jews*, pp., 201, 203–20; Kobler, *Napoleon and the Jews*, pp. 134–38; Benbassa, *Jews of France*, p. 86.

4. Eugen Weber, "Reflections on the Jews in France," *The Jews in Modern France*, ed. Frances Malino and Bernard Wasserstein (Hanover, NH and London: The University Press of New England for Brandeis University Press, 1985), pp. 13–14.

5. Benbassa, *Jews of France*, pp. 86–87; Schwarzfuchs, *Napoleon*, pp. 45–67; Glotzer, *Napoleon, The Jews*, pp. 194–95, 202–3. Kobler, *Napoleon and the Jews*, pp. 137–39; Berkovitz, *Shaping*, p. 82; Imperial Decree of 30 May 1806, in M. Diogene Tama, *Transactions*, pp. 105–6, quote on p. 105.

6. Raphael Mahler, *A History of Modern Jewry 1780–1815* (New York: Schocken Books, 1971), p. 62.

7. Benbassa, *Jews of France*, p. 86; Michael Graetz, *Jews in Nineteenth-Century France*, pp. 29–32.

8. Imperial Decree of 30 May 1806, in Tama, *Transactions*, p. 105; Glotzer, *Napoleon, the Jews*, pp. 202–3, 219–20; Kobler, *Napoleon and the Jews*, pp. 141–42.

9. Glotzer, *Napoleon, the Jews*, pp. 220, 239–40; Napoleon to Jean Baptiste Count de Champagny, 22 July 1806, *Correspondance de Napoléon Ier*, 12: 700–2, quote is on 700–1.

10. Imperial Decree of 30 May 1806, in Tama, *Transactions*, p. 105; ibid., pp. 108–18; Glotzer, *Napoleon, the Jews*, p. 239; Berkovitz, *Shaping*, pp. 78–79; Kobler, *Napoleon and the Jews*, pp. 139–41; Benbassa, *Jews of France*, p. 87; Graetz, *Jews in Nineteenth-Century France*, pp. 35–36.

11. Kobler, *Napoleon and the Jews*, p. 141.

12. Molé, Address to the Assembly of Jewish Notables, in Tama, *Transactions*, pp. 131–33.

13. The commissioners' questions are in Tama, *Transactions*, p. 133. They were originally framed in the Council of State and transmitted by Napoleon to Champagny: see Napoleon to Champagny, 22 July 1806, in *Correspondance de Napoléon Ier*, 12: 701–2.

14. Tama, *Transactions*, pp. 133–34.

15. Ibid., p. 134.

16. Ibid., p. 134.

17. Ibid., p. 135.

18. Fortado's speech, ibid., pp. 135–38, quotes on pp. 136–38.

19. Quotes in ibid., p. 137.

20. Ibid., p. 139.

21. Ibid., pp. 140–42, 151–54.

22. Ibid., pp. 142–48, 154–55.

23. Ibid., pp. 171–73, quote on p. 172.

24. Ibid., pp. 176–80, quotes on pp, 176–77, 179–80.

25. Ibid., pp. 173–74, 180–81, quotes on pp. 180–81.

26. Efraim Shmueli, *Seven Jewish Cultures*, p. 168.

27. Tama, *Transactions*, pp. 174, 181–82, quotes on p. 182.

28. Ibid., pp. 184, 194–96, quotes on p. 195.

29. Ibid., p. 194.

30. Ibid., pp. 184, 196–97.

31. Ibid., pp. 197, 201.

32. Ibid., pp. 185–89, quote on p. 185.

33. Ibid., pp. 197–201.

34. Ibid., pp. 185, 201–7, quotes on p. 207.

35. Excellent evaluations of the responses of the Assembly are in Glotzer, *Napoleon, the Jews*, pp. 240–61, and Berkovitz, *Shaping*, pp. 78–82.

36. Ibid., pp. 212–42; Ronald Schecter, "Impressions, Management, Cultural Performance and Jewish Self-Preservation in Napoleonic France," *Proceedings of the Annual Meeting of the Western Society for French History* 25 (1998): 221–25. This and the next paragraph are a summary of Schecter's essay.

37. Tama, *Transactions*, pp. 212–42; Schecter, "Impressions": 221–25.

38. Glotzer, *Napoleon, the Jews*, pp. 263–68; Schwarzfuchs, *Napoleon*, pp. 68–69, 71–73, 75–80, 101–2, 202 (note 20), 203 (note 28).

39. Molé, address to the Assembly, 18 September 1806, in Tama, *Transactions*, pp. 242–47.

40. Furtado's speech, 18 September 1806, in ibid., pp. 247–53.

41. Ibid., pp. 251–52.

42. Resolution of 18 September 1806, in ibid., pp. 254–56; quote from Furtado on p. 252, quote from the Resolution on p. 254.

43. "Plan" in ibid., pp. 285–89.

44. Ibid., pp. 289–92.

45. Ibid., pp. 294–311.

46. Resolution of 9 December 1806, in ibid., pp. 292–94.

47. Napoleon, "Organic Regulation of the Mosaic Religion," 17 March 1808, in *A Documentary Survey of Napoleonic France*, ed. Eric A. Arnold, Jr. (Lanham, MD: University Press of America, 1994), pp. 281–86; and "Decree Establishing Jewish Consistories," 11 December 1808, in *An Analysis and Translation of Selected Documents of Napoleonic Jewry*, ed. Simeon J. Maslin (Cincinnati: Hebrew Union College-Jewish Institute of Religion, 1957), pp. 44–45, the census is on p. 45; "Consistorial Installation Decree," 19 October 1808, in ibid., pp. 64–65, quote on p. 65. For imposition of the consistorial system in French-conquered Holland, see Hans Dalder, "Dutch Jews in a Segmented Society," in *Paths of Emancipation*, ed. Pierre Birnbaum and Ira Katznelson, pp. 45–51; Mahler, *History of Modern Jewry*, pp. 97, 100–1.

48. Napoleon, "Decree Establishing Jewish Consistories," 11 December 1808, in *Analysis and Translation*, ed. Maslin, pp. 44–45, and "Consistorial Installation Decree," 19 October 1808, in ibid., pp 64–65, quote on p. 65; Glotzer, *Napoleon, the Jews*, pp. 186, 328–31, 349–50; Frances Malino, *The Sephardic Jews of Bordeaux*, pp. 94–95, 110–13, Schwarzfuchs, *Napoleon*, pp. 115–16, 179–94; Phyllis Cohen Albert, *The Modernization of French Jewry*, chaps. 1–2, 9–10; Benbassa, *Jews of France*, pp. 90–91; Mahler, *History of Modern Jewry*, p. 76.

49. The Central Consistory to Departmental Consistories, 26 March 1809, in *Analysis and Translation*, ed. Maslin, pp. 84–88, quotes on pp. 85, 88; Glotzer, *Napoleon, the Jews*, pp. 330–31. References in fn. 48 also apply in this paragraph.

50. Excerpts from a meeting of the Assembly of Notables of Rhin-et-Moselle, 27 February 1808, in *Analysis and Translation*, ed. Maslin, pp. 96–98; quote on pp. 97–98; The Grand Rabbi of Nancy to the Consistory of Nancy, 22 February 1810, in ibid., pp. 110–12; Extract of the Central Committee Proceedings at a Meeting of 8 March 1810, in ibid., pp. 89–90.

51. Frances Malino, "From Patriot to Israelite: Abraham Furtado in Revolutionary France," in *Mystics, Philosophers, and Politicians*, ed. Jehuda Reinharz and Dan Swetschinski, pp. 244–45; Phyllis Cohen Albert, "Ethnicity and Jewish Solidarity in Nineteenth-Century France," in ibid., pp. 253–54, and *Modernization*, pp. 45–311; Paula Hyman, *The Emancipation of the Jews of Alsace*, pp. 53, 138–54, and *Jews of Modern France*, pp. 44–46, 48, 52, 54, 57, 64–67, 71–72, 74; Berkovitz, *Shaping*, pp. 90–126, 151–52; Berr, "Letter," in Tama, *Transactions*, pp. 18–23; Glotzer, *Napoleon, the Jews*, pp. 186, 394–96.

52. Mahler, *History of Modern Jewry*, p. 76.

53. Molé, address to the Assembly, 18 September 1806, in Tama, *Transactions*, p. 245.

54. Ibid., pp. 245–46.

55. Molé's speech, 18 September 1806, in ibid., pp. 246–47; quotes on p. 246; Napoleon to Count Jean Baptiste de Champagny (his minister of the interior), 29 November 1806, in *Analysis and Translation*, ed. Maslin, p. 19. A good account of the Sanhedrin is in Mahler, *History of Modern Jewry*, pp. 68–72.

56. For references to this and the preceding paragraph, see Napoleon to Champagny, 3 September 1806, *Correspondance de Napoléon Ier*, 13: 158–60; Same to Same, 29 November 1806 in *Analysis and Translantion* ed. Maslin, p. 19; Kobler, *Napoleon and the Jews*, pp. 156–59; Glotzer, *Napoleon, the Jews*, pp. 291–92; Malino, *Sephardic Jews*, pp. 90–111; Schwarzfuchs, *Napoleon*, pp. 88–114; Mahler, *History of Modern Jewry*, pp. 68–72; Graetz, *Jews in Nineteenth-Century France*, p. 36.

57. Napoleon to Champagny, 3 September 1806, *Correspondance de Napoléon Ier*, 13: 158.

58. For Napoleon's imperial, as opposed to domestic, policies regarding Jews, see Schwarzfuchs, *Napoleon*, pp. 149–63.

59. Napoleon to Champagny, 29 November 1806, in *Analysis and Translation*, ed. Maslin, p. 16.

60. Ibid., pp. 17–22. Lengthy excerpts from this letter are reprinted in Schwarzfuchs, *Napoleon*, pp. 99–100, and in Glotzer, *Napoleon, the Jews*, p. 300–3. Glotzer's translation is felicitous and his commentary on the letter and the Sanhedrin in general (pp. 299–319) is insightful.

61. Napoleon to Champagny, 29 November 1806, in *Analysis and Translation*, ed. Maslin, pp. 16–22, quotes on pp. 17, 19, 21.

62. Ibid., pp. 21–22.

63. Description of Napoleon in a speech by Deputy Baruch Cerf-Berr to the Assembly of Notables, July 1806, in Tama *Transactions*, p. 157; Napoleon to Champagny, 29 November 1806, in *Analysis and Translation*, ed. Maslin, p. 22.

64. Napoleon to Champagny, 29 November 1806, in *Analysis and Translation*, ed. Maslin, p. 22.

65. Ibid., p. 23; Schwarzfuchs, *Napoleon*, pp. 89–90, 99–100, 165–78; Glotzer, *Napoleon, the Jews*, p. 308; Kobler, *Napoleon and the Jews*, pp. 150–57.

66. Mahler, *History of Modern Jewry*, pp. 70–71.

67. Doctrinal decisions of the Sanhedrin, April 1807, in *The Jew in the Modern World*, ed. Paul Mendes-Flohr and Jehuda Reinharz, p. 135.

68. Ibid., p. 136. For accounts of the Sanhedrin, see Schwarzfuchs, *Napoleon*, pp. 92–112, 165–78; Malino, "Patriot," pp. 240–44; Hyman, *Jews of Modern France*, pp. 43–45, 47, 51–52, 66, 69, 72, 81; Glotzer, *Napoleon, the Jews*, pp. 308–19; Kobler, *Napoleon and the Jews*, pp. 150–57; Berkovitz, *Shaping*, pp. 57–58, 82.

69. Benbassa, *Jews of France*, p. 89.

70. Napoleon, "Decree on the Regulation of Commercial Transactions and Residence of Jews," 17 March 1808, in *Jew in the Modern World*, ed. Mendes-Flohr and Reinharz, pp. 139–40. Another imperial decree on Jewish recruits having to find substitutes from among other Jews was issued on 9 July 1812. This law was reprinted in *Journal de l'Empire*, 13 August 1812, p. 2a, in *Analysis and Translation*, ed Maslin, p. 83.

71. Werner E. Mosse, "From 'Schutzjeiden', to 'Deutsche Staatburger Judischen Glaubens': The Long and Bumpy Road of Jewish Emancipation in Germany," in *Paths of Emancipation*, ed. Birnbaum and Katznelson, pp. 68–71; Mahler, *History of Modern Jewry*, pp. 74–75; Graetz, *Jews in Nineteenth-Century France*, pp. 37–38.

72. Schwarzfuchs, *Napoleon*, pp. 123–29; Glotzer, *Napoleon, the Jews*, pp. 186, 368–70; Szajkowski, *Agricultural*, pp. 26, 87; Benbassa, *Jews of France*, p. 90.

73. Napoleon to Champagny, 29 November 1806, in *Analysis and Translation*, ed. Maslin, p. 22.

74. Szajkowski, *Agricultural*, pp. 96–97; Pierre Birnbaum, *Jewish Destinies*, pp. 25, 36–38, 42–43.

75. Certificate of exemption for Hart Jacobs, 22 January 1776, in David and Tamar De Sola Pool, *An Old Faith in the New World: Portrait of Shearith Israel, 1654–1954* (New York: Columbia University Press, 1955), p. 35.

76. Gershom M. Seixas sermon to Congregation Shearith Israel, 11 January 1807, in *Publications of the American Jewish Historical Society*, 27 (1920): 141.

77. Napoleon, "Decree Relative to the Names of Jews," 20 July 1808, in *Analysis and Translation*, ed. Maslin, pp. 59–60; Benbassa, *Jews of France*, p. 90.

78. Albert, "Israelite and Jew," p. 94.

79. Extract of the Proceedings of a Central Consistory Meeting, 8 March 1810, in *Analysis and Translation*, ed. Maslin, pp. 89–90.

80. Szajkowski, *Jews and French Revolutions*, pp. 52–53, 97, and *Agricultural*, p. 26; Hyman, *Emancipation*, pp. 16–17; Berkovitz, *Shaping*, pp. 45–56, 142.

81. For a discussion of Napoleon and his relation to the Revolution and the ancien régime, see Sudhir Hazareesingh, *Political Traditions in Modern France*, pp. 29, 75, 152–53, 157, 159.

82. Joseph II, "Edict of Toleration," 2 January 1782, in Raphael Mahler, *Jewish Emancipation*, pp. 18–20; David Biale, *Power and Powerlessness in Jewish History* (New York: Schocken Books, 1986), pp. 93–94; Mahler, *History of Modern Jewry*, pp. 229–31.

83. Friedrich Wilhelm, "Edict Concerning the Civil Conditions of Jews in the Prussian State," 11 March 1812, in Mahler, *Jewish Emancipation*, pp. 32–35, and *History of Modern Jewry*, pp. 198–214, 373–77; Biale, *Power and Powerlessness*, pp. 92–95.

84. Benjamin Ginsberg, *The Fatal Embrace: Jews and the State* (Chicago, University of Chicago Press, 1993), pp. 13–18.

85. The ideas in this and the preceding paragraph are discussed in Biale, *Power and Powerlessness*, pp. 95, 104.

86. Schwarzfuchs, *Napoleon*, p. 137; Szajkowski, *Jews and French Revolutions*, pp. 53, 1028–32; Albert, *Modernization*, pp. 50, 152, 155–56; and idem, "Ethnicity," pp. 263–65; Hyman, *Emancipation*, pp. 18–27, 103; idem, *Jews of Modern France*, pp. 56, 64; Michel Winock, *Nationalism, Anti-Semitism*, pp. 84–102, 114–30, 219–24; Benbassa, *Jews of France*, pp. 96, 134–45, 162–63, 167–78; Birnbaum, *Jewish Destinies*, pp. 101–77.

87. The advent of Reform Judaism was most prominent in Germany: Heinz Groupe, *The Rise of Modern Judaism: An Intellectual History of German Jewry, 1650–1942* (Huntington, NY: R. E. Krieger, 1979), pp. 103–4, 165–69, 197–99; Michael A. Meyer, *The Origins of the Modern Jew: Jewish Identity and European Culture in Germany, 1749–1824* (Detroit: Wayne State University Press, 1967); David Sorkin, "The Impact of Emancipation on German Jewry: A Reconsideration," in *Assimilation and Community*, ed. Jonathan Frankel and Steven Zipperstein, pp. 175–98; Mosse, "From 'Schutzjuden'," pp. 77–83. Moses Mendelsohn's dilemma of Judaism and modernism is discussed in his *Jerusalem: or on Religious Power and Judaism* (Hanover, N.H.: University Press of New England, 1983).

88. Rogers Brubaker, *Citizenship and Nationhood*.

89. Adrien Dansette, *Religious History of Modern France*, 1: 92.

90. Shmuel Trigano, "From Individual to Collectivity: The Rebirth of the 'Jewish Nation' in France," *Jews in Modern France*, ed. Malino and Wasserstein, pp. 249–52.

91. The formulations in the last two paragraphs partly derive from David Vital, *The Future of the Jews*, pp. 19–20, 128–29.

Chapter 5
The American Experience

1. Francis Hopkinson, "Account of the Grand Federal Procession Performed at Philadelphia on Friday the 4th of July, 1788," in *The Miscellaneous Essays and Occasional Writings of Francis Hopkinson, Esq.* (Philadelphia: T. Dobson, 1792), 3 vols., 2: 349–401; Benjamin Rush to Elias Budinot, 9 July 1788, in *The Letters of Benjamin Rush*, ed. Lyman H. Butterfield (Princeton: Princeton University Press, 1951), 2 vols., 1: 471–77; Naphtali Phillips to John McAllister, Jr., 24 October 1868, in *Jews and the American Revolution: A Bicentennial Documentary*, ed. Jacob Rader Marcus (Cincinnati: American Jewish Archives, 1975), pp. 247–49.

2. Rush to Budinot, 9 July 1788, in *Letters of Benjamin Rush*, ed. Butterfield, 1: 474.

3. Hopkinson, "Account of the Grand Federal Procession," 2: 399, 420.

4. Catherine L. Albanese, *Sons of the Fathers: The Civil Religion of the American Revolution* (Philadelphia: Temple University Press, 1976), pp. 214–15.

5. Phillips to McAllister, Jr., in *Jews and American Revolution*, ed. Marcus, p. 249.

6. Jonathan D. Sarna, "The Impact of the American Revolution on American Jews," *Modern Judaism* 1 (May 1981): 154.

7. N. Taylor Phillips, "Unwritten History: Reminiscences of N. Taylor Phillips," *American Jewish Archives* 6 (June 1954): 99; Samuel Rezeneck: *Unrecognized Patriots: The Jews in the American Revolution* (Westport, CT: Greenwood Press, 1975), p. 163.

8. Patrice Higonnet, *Sister Republics*.

9. *The Records of the Federal Convention of 1787*, ed. Max Farrand (New Haven: Yale University Press, 1966), 4 vols., 2: 468.

10. Charles Pinckney, "Observations on the Plan of Government Submitted to the Federal Convention in Philadelphia on the 28th of May 1787," in ibid., 3: 106.

11. *Documents Illustrative of the Formation of the Union of the American States*, ed. Charles C. Tansill (Washington, D.C.: GPO, 1927), pp. 1009–50, 1052–53, 1064; *Debates in the Several State Conventions on the Adoption of the Federal Constitution*, ed. Jonathan E. Elliott (Washington, D.C.: Taylor & Maury, 1854), 4 vols., 1: 277, 326–27, 331, 344.

12. Edmund Randolph speech to the Virginia Constitutional Convention, 2 June 1788, in *Debates*, ed. Elliott, 2: 204; James Madison remarks to the Convention, 12 June 1788, in ibid., 2: 330; cf. Governor Samuel Johnson, speech at the North Carolina Ratifying Convention, in ibid., 4: 199.

13. James Iredell, speech at the North Carolina Ratifying Convention, in ibid., 4: 192–93. For other defenses of Article VI, see ibid., 2: 118–20, 148–49, 202; 4: 199–200.

14. Ibid., 2: 44, 118–19, 148; 4: 212, 215.

15. Ibid., 4: 199.

16. Madison to Jefferson, 17 October 1788, in *James Madison on Religious Liberty*, p. 72.

17. Tench Coxe, "An American Citizen," 1 (1787), in *The Debate on the Constitution: Federalist and Antifederalist Speeches, Articles and Letters During the Struggle over Ratification*, ed. Bernard Bailyn (New York: The Library of America, 1993), 2 Parts, 1: 20; Oliver Ellsworth, "A Landholder," 7 (1787), in ibid., 1: 521–24; James Madison, "The Federalist," 51 (1788), in ibid., 2: 166.

18. On this point, see Robert A Goldwin, "Why Blacks, Women & Jews Are Not Mentioned in the Constitution," *Commentary* 83 (May 1987): 33.

19. James Winthrop, "Agrippa," 18 (1788), in Bailyn, *Debate*, 2: 161.

20. Luther Martin, "The Genuine Information" (1788), in ibid., 1: p. 655.

21. *The Complete Anti-Federalist*, ed. Herbert Storing (Chicago and London: University of Chicago Press, 1981), 7 vols., 4: 193, 195–96, 242–48; 5: 126–27.

22. "Letters from the Federal Farmer," 12 (1788), in ibid., 2: 295; "A Bostonian" (1788), 4: 232.

23. "Curtiopolis," *New-York Daily Advertiser*, 14 January 1788, in *The Hartford Courant*, 28 January 1788, p. 3.

24. House of Representatives Debate, 15 August 1791, in Leonard Levy, *The Establishment Clause: Religion and the First Amendment* (New York: Macmillan, London: Collier Macmillan, 1986), pp. 76–81. The Senate debate was not recorded.

25. Massachusetts Constitution: Articles II and III, in *The Federal and State Constitutions, Colonial Charters, and Other Organic Laws of States, Territories, and Colonies Now and Heretofore Forming the United States of America*, ed. Francis Newton Thorpe, (Washington, D.C.: GPO, 1909), 7 Vols., 3: 1889–90.

26. The best general analysis of established religion in America is Levy, *Establishment Clause*, pp. 1–63. Colonial charters and state constitutions are in *Federal*, ed. Thorpe.

27. *Federal*, ed. Thorpe, 1: 566, 568; 5: 2793, 3100.

28. *Pennsylvania Evening Post*, 24 September 1776, p. 476; 26 September 1776, p. 479; Henry Melchoir Muhlenberg to unknown recipient, 2 October 1776, in *Pennsylvania Magazine of History and Biography* 22 (1898): 129–30; Amherst County, Virginia petition to the Virginia Assembly, 10 November 1779, quoted in Thomas E. Buckeley, *Church and State in Revolutionary Virginia, 1776–1787* (Charlottesville: University Press of Virginia, 1977), p. 51.

29. Isaac Backus, "A Door Opened to Liberty," (1783), in *Isaac Backus on Church, State and Calvinism: Pamphlets, 1754–1789*, ed. William G. McLoughlin (Cambridge: Harvard University Press, 1968), p. 436.

30. *The Popular Sources of Political Authority: Documents on the Massachusetts Constitution of 1780*, ed. Oscar and Mary Handlin (Cambridge: Harvard University Press, 1966), Return of Colrain, 26 May 1780, p. 551.

31. David Cesarini, "The Changing Character of Citizenship and Nationality in Britain," in *Citizenship, Nationality and Migration in Europe*, ed. David Cesarini and Mary Fulbrook, pp. 60–61.

32. *Debates*, ed. Elliott, 2: 148–49.

33. Frederic Cople Jaher, *A Scapegoat in the New Wilderness: The Origins and Rise of Anti-Semitism in America* (Cambridge: Harvard University Press, 1994), pp. 86–96, 99–105, 112–13, 119–28.

34. *Toward Modernity: The European Jewish Model*, ed. Jacob Katz (New Brunswick, NJ and Oxford: Transaction Books, 1987), pp. 226–42; Todd M. Endelman, *The Jews of Georgian England 1714–1830: Tradition and Change in a Liberal Society* (Philadelphia: The Jewish Publication Society of America, 1979) and idem, *Radical Assimilation in English-Jewish History 1656–1945* (Bloomington and Indianapolis: Indiana University Press, 1990), pp. 21–22; Israel Finestein, "Jewish Emancipation in Victorian England," pp. 43–47; Geoffrey Alderman, "English Jews or Jews of English Persuasion? Reflections on the Emancipation of Anglo-Jewry," in *Paths of Emancipation*, ed. Pierre Birnbaum and Ira Katznelson, pp. 128–37; M. C. N. Salbstein, *The Emancipation of the Jew in Britain: The Question of the Admission of the Jews to Parliament, 1828–1869* (Rutherford, NJ: Fairleigh Dickinson University Press; London and Toronto: Associated Universities Presses, 1982); Cesarini, "Changing Character," in *Citizenship, Nationality and Migration*, ed. Cesarini and Fulbrook, pp. 57, 60–61.

35. Salo W. Baron, *The Russian Jew Under Tsars and Soviets* (New York: Macmillan, London: Collier Macmillan, 1976), pp. 173–76, 199–200, 226–27, 231–34, 245–47; *The Jews in Soviet Russia Since 1917*, ed. Lionel Kochan (London, New York, and Toronto: Oxford University Press, 1972), pp. 88–89, 102–24, 162–69, 172–83, 293; Michael Stansilawski, "Russian Jewry, the Russian State, and the Dynamics of Jewish Emancipation," in *Paths of Emancipation*, ed. Birnbaum and Katznelson, pp. 266–81; Eli Lederhendler, "Modernity Without Emancipation or Assimilation? The Case of Russian Jewry," in *Assimilation and Community*, ed. Frankel and Zipperstein, pp. 324–43.

36. Another discussion of the matters in this and the previous paragraph is in Steven M. Cohen, *American Modernity and Jewish Identity* (New York and London: Tavistock, 1987), pp. 13–14, 16–25.

37. Jaher, *Scapegoat*, pp. 103–5, 121–22.

38. Peter Kalm, *Travels in North America*, ed. Adolph Benson (New York: Dover Publications, 1964), pp. 130, 630–31; Rebecca Alexander Samuel to Mr. and Mrs. Aaron Alexander (her parents), 12 January 1791; and a second letter from 1791 (date unknown), both in *In Love, Marriage, Children—and Death, Too: Intimate Glimpses into the Lives of American Jews in a Bygone Age as Told in their Own Words*, ed. Jacob Rader Marcus (New York: Society of Jewish Bibliophiles, 1965), pp. 43–44; Rudolf Glanz, *Studies in Judaica Americana* (New York: KTAV, 1970), p. 220; Jacob Rader Marcus, *The Colonial American Jew: 1492–1776* (Detroit: Wayne State University Press, 1970), 3 vols., 2: 959–60, 1025–26, 1085–86; 3: 1174, 1187–88; idem, and *Early American Jewry*, (Philadelphia: The Jewish Publication Society of America, 1951, 1953), 2 vols., 1: 92, 107–8, 175–78; 2: 184–88, 495–513; idem, *United States Jewry: 1776–1985* (Detroit: Wayne State University Press, 1989–93), 4 vols., 1: 266–67, 373–79, 381, 387–88, 396–401, 597–602; Naomi W. Cohen, *Jews in Christian America: The Pursuit of Religious Equality* (New York and Oxford: Oxford University Press, 1992), p. 34; Leon A. Jick, *The Americanization of the Synagogue, 1820–1870* (Hanover, NH: Brandeis University Press and the University Press of New England, 1976), p. 6; Hyman Grinstein, *The Rise of the Jewish Community of New York: 1654–1860* (Philadelphia: The Jewish Publication Society of America, 1945), pp. 211, 334–35.

39. Arthur Goren, "Jews," in *Harvard Encyclopedia of American Ethnic Groups*, ed. Stephan Thernstrom (Cambridge: Harvard University Press, 1981). p. 571; Marcus, *Early American*, 1: 3; 2: 393; Dov Weinryb, "A Hundred Years of Jewish Immigration to America," *American Jewish Year Book*, 5, ed. Menachem Ribalow (New York: Histradruth Ivrit, 1940), pp. 327–28; Jacob Lestschinsky, "The Economic Development of American Jews," ibid., 7 (1942), p. 503; Ira Rosenwaike, "An Estimate and Analysis of the Jewish Population of the United States in 1790," *Publications of the American Jewish Historical Society*, 50 (September 1960): 23, 20; idem, "The Jewish Population of the United States as Estimated in the Census of 1820," *American Jewish Historical Quarterly* (formerly PAJHS), 53 (December 1963): 132, 148; and idem, *On the Edge of Greatness: A Portrait of American Jewry in the Early National Period* (Cincinnati: American Jewish Archives, 1985), pp. 2–3, 17; Jacob Rader Marcus, *To Count a People: American Jewish Population Data, 1585–1984* (Lanham, MD, New York, and London: University Press of America, 1990), p. 237.

40. Marcus, *Colonial*, 2: 927–28, 1085–86, and *United States Jewry*, 1: 42–43, 265, 373–79, 381, 387–88, 396–401, 597–602; Jick, *Americanization*, pp. 3–4, 6, 8–9; Grinstein, *Rise*, pp. 84, 211–12, 229, 362n.

41. "The Earliest Extant Minute Book of the Spanish and Portuguese Congregation: Shearith Israel in New York 1728–1760," ed. Jacques J. Lyons, *Publications of the American Jewish Historical Society* 21 (1913): 1–82; "Minute Book of the Spanish and Portuguese Congregation Shearith Israel in New York, 1760–1786," ed. Lyons, ibid.: 83–171; "Items Relating to Congregation Shearith Israel, New York," ed. Lyons, ibid. 27 (1920): 2–34; Jacob Rader Marcus, *American Jewry: Documents Eighteenth Century* (Cincinnati: Hebrew Union College, 1959), pp. 95–96, 129, 157, 161, 166, 179, 188; David and Tamar De Sola Pool, *An Old Faith in the New World: Portrait of Shearith Israel 1654–1954* (New York: Columbia University Press, 1955), pp. 235–36, 264. For the 1805 tax on

Jews, Constitution of Shearith Israel (1805), Article X, in *A Double Bond: The Constitutional Documents of American Jewry*, ed. Daniel J. Elazar, Jonathan D. Sarna, and Rela G. Monson (Lanham, MD, New York and London: University Press of New England, 1992), p. 110; "A Protestant" (probably Rev. Charles Crawford), *Pennsylvania Packet and Daily Advertiser*, 23 December 1784, in Marcus, *American Jewry: Documents*, pp. 136–37. Jonathan D. Sarna, "The Jews in British America," in *The Jews and the Expansion of Europe to the West, 1450 to 1800*, ed. Paolo Bernardini and Norman Fiering (New York and Oxford: Berghahn Books, 2001), pp. 519–31, stresses the synagogue-congregation as the key factor in organizing and maintaining cohesion in Jewish-American colonial communities. Our interpretations generally agree but differ in emphasis. My evaluation places more emphasis on the limits of the synagogue in this regard.

42. Rev. S. Quincy quoted in Malcolm H. Stern, "New Light on the Jewish Settlement of Savannah," *American Jewish Quarterly* 52 (March 1963): 184; Rev. Belzius to Johann Heinrich Callenberg, 21 February 1738, in ibid.; 185; Eli Faber, *A Time for Planting: The First Migration 1654–1820* (Baltimore and London: The Johns Hopkins University Press, 1992), pp. 124–25.

43. "Earliest Extant": 5, 8–11, 172; Pool and Pool, *Old Faith*, p. 463.

44. A good discussion of these issues is in Faber, *Time for Planting*, pp. 76–83; see Sarna, "Jews in British America," pp. 519–31, for a greater emphasis on cohesion.

45. Constitution of Beth Shalome (1789), in *Double Bond*, ed. Sarna, Elazar, and Monson, p. 112; Jacob R. Marcus, "The American Colonial Jew: A Study in Acculturation," *The American Jewish Experience*, ed. Jonathan Sarna (New York and London: Holmes & Meier, 1986), pp. 26–27.

46. "Earliest Extant," ed. Lyons: 37, 73; "Items, " ed. Lyons: 2–9; Pool and Pool, *Old Faith*, pp. 85, 164–67, 411, 413, 415–19; Marcus, *American Jewry: Documents*, pp. 86–88.

47. Benjamin Nones to the *Beth Din* of Congregation Shagnar a Shamaim, 7 August 1793, in Marcus, *American Jewry, Documents*, p. 188. In 1794, the couple were married in the Philadelphia synagogue; Pool and Pool, *Old Faith*, p. 414.

48. Congregation Mikveh Israel to Rabbi Saul [Lowenstamm] of Amsterdam, March 1785, in *The Jewish Experience in America: Selected Studies from the Publications of the American Jewish Historical Society*, ed. Albert J. Karp (Waltham, MA: The American Jewish Historical Society, New York: KTAV, 1969), p. 139.

49. Pool and Pool, *Old Faith*, pp. 460, 213; [Isaac Pinto], *Evening Service of Roshashana, and Kippur. Or The Beginning of the Years, and the Day of Atonement* (1761), facsimile in *Beginnings, Early American Judaica: a Collection of Ten Publications in Facsimile*, ed. Abraham J. Karp (Philadelphia: The Jewish Publication Society of America, 1975); [Isaac Pinto], *Prayers for Shabbath, Rosh-Hashana, And Kippur, or The Sabbath, the Beginning of the year, And The Day of Atonements; With Tha Amidah and Musaph of the Moadim, or Solemn Seasons* (New York: John Holt, 1766), p. iii; Faber, *Time for Planting*, p. 92; Constitution of Shearith Israel (1805), Article III, in *Constitutional Documents*, ed. Elazar, Sarna, and Monson, p. 105.

50. Pinto, *Prayers for Shabbath*, p. iii.

51. Marcus, *American Jewry: Documents*, pp. 87–88; Faber, *Time for Planting*, pp. 87–88, 116.

52. "Earliest Extant," 14 September 1757, ed. Lyons: 74; "Laws" of Shearith Israel, 22 August 1790, in Marcus, *American Jewry: Documents*, p. 166; "Code of Laws, Congregation Mickva Israel, 25 July 1757, in ibid., p. 179.

53. Jaher, *Scapegoat*, pp. 122, 125; Faber, *Time for Planting*, pp. 118–20; Rev. G. Seixas, "Discourse Delivered In the Synagogue In New-York. On The Ninth of May, 1798, Observed As A Day Of Humiliation, &c. &c, Conformably to a Recommendation Of The President Of The United States of America," facsimile in *Beginnings*, ed., Karp.

54. Resolution of Congregation Shearith Israel to Gov. George Clinton, 9 December 1783, in "Items," ed. Lyons: 33–34.

55. Details on Seixas, the sermon and Shearith Israel are in *Beginnings*, ed. Karp, pp. 18–22.

56. Seixas, *Discourse*, pp. 8–9, 11, 18–19, 27; Faber, *Time for Planting*, pp. 118–20.

57. Seixas, *Discourse*, pp. 18, 23, cf. 26.

58. Jaher, *Scapegoat*, pp. 125–26, 186–87.

59. Myer Moses, "An Oration Delivered Before the Hebrew Orphan Society, On the 15th day of October, 1807," facsimile in *Beginnings*, ed. Karp, pp., 18, 32. Biographical information on Moses is in Karp, *Beginnings*, p. 23.

60. This formulation is based on Efraim Shmueli, *Seven Jewish Cultures*, pp. 168, 172–77; see also Naomi W. Cohen, *Encounter with Emancipation: The German Jews in the United States 1830–1914* (Philadelphia: The Jewish Publication Society of America, 1984), p. 170. An acute discussion of messianism in the colonial American Jewish community may be found in Sarna, "Jew in British America," p. 520.

61. Noah J. Efron, "Knowledge of Newly Discovered Lands Among Jewish Communities of Europe (from 1492 to the Thirty Years' War)," in *Jews and Expansion*, ed. Bernardini and Fiering, pp. 49–58, 66; Benjamin Schmidt, "The Hope of the Netherlands: Menasseh ben Israel and the Dutch Idea of America," in ibid., pp. 91, 97–99; Sarna, "Jew in British America," p. 520.

62. Rebecca Samuel to Mrs. And Mrs. Aaron Alexander, 12 January 1791, in Marcus, *American Jewry: Documents*, p. 52; ibid., pp. 311–475; Jaher, *Scapegoat*, p. 122; Pool and Pool, *Old Faith*, pp. 471, 473, 480–83.

63. Compare the Constitutions of Mikveh Israel, Philadelphia, in 1770 and 1782, in *American Jewry: Documents*, ed. Marcus, pp. 95, 118. See also the Constitutions of the Congregation of Shearith Israel (New York, probably 1790), the Code of Laws of Congregation Israel Mickva (Savannah 1791), and the "Parliamentary Rule" (24 March 1782), and 1798 Constitution of Mikveh Israel (Philadelphia), in ibid., pp. 121, 128, 150, 153, 157–58, 177–78. Compare the former with the Shearith Israel Constitutions of 1728 and 1761, in Pool and Pool, *Old Faith*, pp. 499–500, and the prerevolutionary Constitution of Mikveh Israel in Marcus, *American Jewry: Documents*, p. 95. See also the 1789 Constitution of Beth Shalome (Richmond), in *Double Bond*, ed. Elazar, Sarna, and Monson, p. 112.

64. Preliminary draft of the constitution of Shearith Israel, 30 May 1790, in Marcus, *American Jewry: Documents*, p. 150.

65. Declaration of rights of Shearith Israel, 1790, in ibid., p. 154.

66. Grinstein, *Rise*, pp. 334–35.

67. Marcus, *Early*, 2: 184–87.

68. Grinstein, *Rise*, pp. 211–12; Jick, *Americanization*, p. 10.

69. Kalm, *Travels*, pp. 130, 631, cf. pp. 630–31; Abraham Vossen Goodman, "A German Mercenary Observes American Jews During the Revolution," *American Jewish Quarterly* 59 (December 1969), Diary of Johann Conrad Dohla, 3 June 1777: 227.

70. Marcus, *Colonial*, 3: 1157–72; Daniel J. Elazar, *Community and Polity: The Organizational Dynamics of American Jewry* (Philadelphia and Jerusalem: The Jewish Publication Society, 1995), pp. 53–54, 57, 60–61.

71. Marcus, *United States Jewry*, 1: 42, 590.

72. Malcolm H. Stern, "Jewish Marriage and Intermarriage in the Federal Period (1776–1840)," *The American Jewish Archives* 19 (November 1967): 142; Faber, *Time*, p. 93; Max I. Dimont, *The Jews in America: The Roots, History, and Destiny of American Jews* (New York: Simon & Schuster, 1978), pp. 58, 89. On conversion, intermarriage, and other forms of assimilation, see Benbassa, *The Jews of France*, pp. 66, 70, 86, 92–93; Endelman, *Radical Assimilation*, pp. 5–6, 10, 12, 15–33, 37–38, 41–57; and *Jews of Georgian England*, pp. 248–71.

73. The population statistics are in W. D. Rubinstein, *A History of the Jews in the English-Speaking World: Great Britain* (New York: St. Martin's Press, London: Macmillan, 1996), p. 64; Benbassa, *The Jews of France*, pp. 60, 70, 97; Rosenswaike, *Edge of Greatness*, pp 35–36; Zosa Szajowski, "The Demographic Aspects of Jewish. Emancipation in France During the French Revolution," *Historia Judaica* 21 (April 1959): 20–21, 26.

74. For references see fn. 71.

75. Jacob R. Marcus, *Studies in American Jewish History: Studies and Addresses* (Cincinnati: Hebrew Union College Press, 1969), pp. 55, 76–82; Goodman, "German Mercenary": 227; Rebecca Samuel to Mr. and Mrs. Aaron Alexander, 12 January 1791 and another letter, date unknown, both in Marcus, *American Jewry: Documents*, pp. 52–53.

76. Marcus, *To Count*, pp. 147, 204; Jaher, *Scapegoat*, pp. 125–26; Rosenswaike, "Estimate and Analysis": 28, 32, 34–35; idem, "Jewish Population": 136, 152; and idem, *Edge of Greatness*, p. 4.

77. Benbassa, *The Jews of France*, pp. 66, 98–99; Szajowski, "Demographic Aspects": 7, 16–17, 21.

78. The numbers for London and Paris are, respectively, in B. R. Mitchell, *British Historical Statistics* (Cambridge and New York: Cambridge University Press, 1988), p. 30, and *International Historical Statistics; Europe 1750–1993* (New York: Stockdon, 1998), p. 75; Szajowski, "Demographic Aspects": 8, 16.

79. For an analysis of American Jewry along these lines see Elazar, *Community and Polity*, pp. 169–75, 181, 190–91, 194–95, 205–7, 259–60.

80. Moses M. Hays to the General Assembly of the Province of Rhode Island, 17 July 1776, in *Jews and American Revolution*, ed. Marcus, pp, 121–22.

81. The Rabbi, President, and Council of Mikveh Israel to the Pennsylvania Council of Censors, December 1783, in Marcus, *Early*, 2: 257–58. Four years later, another Philadelphia Jew addressed similar objections to the federal Constitutional Convention in the mistaken belief that it could amend state constitutions. See Jonas Phillips to the U.S. Constitutional Convention of 1787, 7 September 1787, in *Jews and American Revolution*, ed. Marcus, pp. 242–43.

82. Jacob Henry, Address to the House of Commons of North Carolina, 1809, in *A Documentary History of the Jews in the United States: 1654–1875*, ed. Morris U. Schappes (New York: Schocken Books, 1971), pp. 122–25.

83. Rev. Ezra Stiles, "The United States Elevated to Glory and Honor," 8 May 1783, in *The Pulpit of the American Revolution: or, the Political Sermons of the Period of 1776*, ed. John Wingate Thornton (Boston: Gould and Lincoln, 1860), pp. 467–68.

84. Charles Pinckney speech at the U.S. Constitutional Convention, 25 June 1787, in *Records*, ed. Farrand, 3: 402.

85. "Centinel," 8, 29 December 1787, in *Complete*, ed. Storing, 2: 176.

86. In the colonial era, naturalization meant full economic, not political, rights. Thereafter, it meant citizenship for the foreign-born.

87. *Narratives of Early Carolina: 1650–1708*, ed. Alexander S. Salley, Jr. (New York: Barnes and Noble, 1911), pp. 347–48.

88. James H. Kettner, *The Development of American Citizenship, 1608–1870* (Chapel Hill: University of North Carolina Press, 1978), pp. 74–128; Jaher, *Scapegoat*, pp. 90, 103–6.

89. *Federal and State Constitutions*, ed. Thorpe, 5: 2367–68, 3091, 6: 3748; Kettner, *Development*, pp. 126–27, 215–19, 746–48.

90. *Documents Illustrative*, ed. Tansill, pp. 492, 504, 524–25, 528, 988–99.

91. Ibid., pp. 505, 508 (quote), 523.

92. Benjamin Franklin to unknown recipient, 1783; to William Stranan, 19 August 1784, in *The Writings of Benjamin Franklin*, ed. Albert Henry Smyth (New York: Macmillan, 1906–7), 9 vols., 9: 150, 263; *Documents Illustrative*, ed. Tansill, p. 506.

93. *Documents Illustrative*, ed. Tansill, p. 524.

94. Ibid., p. 524.

95. Ibid., pp. 236–50; Frank George Franklin, *The Legislative History of Naturalization in the United States: from the Revolutionary War to 1857* (Chicago: University of Chicago Press, 1906), pp. 48, 70–108.

96. First Annual Message to Congress, 8 December 1801, in *The Writings of Thomas Jefferson*, ed. Paul Leicester Ford (New York and London: The Knickerbocker Press, 1897), 14 vols, 8: 124. Unofficially, Jefferson expressed reservations about immigrants. His thoughts on the foreign-born in "Notes on Virginia" (1782) resemble Hamilton's public sentiments, ibid., 3: 188–90.

97. ."Lucius Crassus" (Alexander Hamilton), no. 8, 12 January 1801, in *The Works of Alexander Hamilton*, ed. Henry Cabot Lodge (New York: G. P. Putnam's Sons, 1885), 12 vols., 8: 289.

98. Ibid., pp. 290–91.

99. *The Autobiography of Benjamin Franklin* (New York: Vintage Books, 1990), p. 78; Franklin to Joseph Priestly, 21 August 1784, in *Writings of Benjamin Franklin*, ed. Smyth, 9: 266.

100. *The Works of Alexander Hamilton*, ed. John C. Hamilton (New York: John F. Trow, 1850), 7 vols., 7: 345, 351.

101. James Madison to Jacob De La Motta, August 1820, in *Madison on Religious Liberty*, ed. Alley, p. 81; cf. Madison to Mordicai [sic] Noah, 15 May 1818, p. 80. Madison's views on religious freedom are most conveniently consulted in ibid.

102. Thomas Jefferson to Mordecai Noah, 28 May 1818, in *Jewish Experience*, ed. Karp, p. 359.

103. John Adams to F. A. Vanderkemp, 16 February 1809, in *The Works of John Adams*, ed. Charles Francis Adams (Boston: Little, Brown, 1854), 10 vols., 9: 609; and to Mordecai Noah, 31 July 1808, in *Jewish Experience*, ed. Karp, p. 361.

104. The most convenient reference for Washington's religious opinions is Paul F. Boller, Jr., *George Washington & Religion* (Dallas: Southern Methodist University Press, 1963), especially reprints of Washington's remarks on pp, 165, 167, 173, 175, 179–82, 192–94.

105. George Washington to the Hebrew Congregation in Newport, Rhode Island, 17 August 1790, in *Jews and American Revolution*, ed. Marcus, pp. 256–57; cf. Washington's Reply to the Hebrew Congregations in the Cities of Philadelphia, New York, Charleston and Richmond, 1790, in *The Jews in the United States, 1790–1840: A Documentary History*, ed. Joseph L. Blau and Salo W. Baron (New York: Columbia University Press; Philadelphia: Jewish Publication Society of America, 1963), 3 vols., 1: 10; Washington's Reply to the Hebrew Congregation of the City of Savannah (1790), in ibid., 1: 11.

106. Anson Phelps Stokes, *Church and State in the United States* (New York: Harper and Row, 1950), 3 vols., 1: 467–68.

107. Memorial of the Trustees of the Congregation Shearith Israel to the New York State Legislature, drawn up by DeWitt Clinton (1811), in *Jews in the United States*, ed. Blau and Baron, vol. 2, pp. 445–46; cf. *Documentary History of the Jews*, ed. Schappes, pp. 126–27. See also, *Jews in the United States*, ed. Blau and Baron, vol. 2, pp. 443–46; Jacob Hartstein, "The Polonies Talmud Torah of New York," in *Jewish Experience*, ed. Karp, vol. 2, pp. 45–63; Pool and Pool, *Old Faith*, pp. 218–19.

108. For the impact of the Enlightenment on French Jews, see Hertzberg, *French Enlightenment*, pp. 280–86, 309–12; Leon Poliakov, *The History of Anti-Semitism*, 3: 88–99, 108–15; Jacob Katz, *From Prejudice to Destruction: Anti-Semitism, 1700–1833* (Cambridge: Harvard University Press, 1980), pp. 33–47, and *Out of the Ghetto: The Social Background of Jewish Emancipation, 1770–1870* (Cambridge: Harvard University Press, 1973), pp. 80–103; Charles C. Lehrmann, *The Jewish Element in French Literature* (Rutherford, NJ: Fairleigh Dickinson University Press, 1971), pp. 116–28. For the influence of the Enlightenment in America, see Henry F. May, *The Enlightenment in America* (New York: Oxford University Press, 1976). For Deism in Franklin and Washington, see Alfred Owen

Aldrige, *Benjamin Franklin and Nature's God* (Durham: Duke University Press, 1967), pp. 3, 13, 41, 83, 139, 172–73, 190–91, 211, 251–52, 269–71; Boller, Jr., *George Washington*, pp. 80–97, 121.

109. Voltaire, *Philosophy of History* (New York: Philosophical Library, 1965), pp. 17–18, 115, 131, 145, 158, 163–65, 172–203, 206–7, 215–16, 218–19, 225–28, 233, 242, and idem, *The Philosophical Dictionary: The Works of Voltaire*, ed. John Morley (Akron: Werner, 1905), 43 vols., 5: 50; 10: 264, 266, 278, 280–86, 292–94, 313; 38: 161; Denis Diderot, "Philosophic Thoughts" (1746), in *Diderot's Philosophical Works*, ed. Margaret Jourdain (New York: Burt Franklin, 1972), pp. 296–98, 320–21; Paul Henry Thiery d'Holbach, *Good Sense; or Natural Ideas Opposed to Supernature* (New York: Wright & Owen, 1831), pp. 77, 105; idem, *Superstition in all Ages* (New York: Truth Seeker, 1950), pp. 32, 123–24, 171, 216, 273–74, 291–96, 319–24, 329; and idem, *Ecce Homo; or, A Critical Enquiry, Into the History of Jesus Christ; Being A Rational History of the Gospels* (London: D. I. Eaton, 1913), pp. 23–29.

110. Rush to Julia Rush, 27 June 1787, and Rush to Elhanan Winchester, 11 May 1791, both in *Letters of Benjamin Rush*, ed. Butterfield, 1: 431, 581–82.

111. Jefferson to Rush, 21 April 1803, "Syllabus of an Estimation of the Merit of the Doctrines of Jesus, Compared with Those of Others," in *Writings of Thomas Jefferson*, ed. Ford, 8: 226, and to Marquis de Lafayette, 14 May 1807, ibid., 10: 83–84. Other examples of Jefferson's negative attitude toward Jews are: Jefferson to Joseph B. Priestly, 9 April 1803, ibid., 8: 229n, and to John Adams, 13 November 1813, in *The Writings of Thomas Jefferson*, ed. Albert E. Bergh (Washington, D.C.: Thomas Jefferson Memorial Association of the United States, 1903), 20 vols., 13: 388–89, and to Ezra Stiles, 15 June 1819, ibid., 15: 203.

112. *Autobiography, Correspondence, Etc., of Lyman Beecher*, ed. Charles Beecher (New York: Harper & Bros., 1864), 2 vols., 1: 43; Lester Douglas Joyce, *Church and Clergy in the American Revolution* (New York: Exposition Press, 1966), pp. 148–52; William Warren Sweet, *The Story of Religion in America* (New York: Harper & Bros., 1950), pp. 5, 223, 225–26; Martin Marty, *Righteous Empire: The Protestant Experience in America* (New York: Dial Press, 1970), pp. 35–381; Loren P. Beth, *The American Theory of Church and State* (Gainesville: University of Florida Press, 1958), p. 73; *Documents Illustrative*, ed. Tansill, pp. 295–97; Phelps, *Church and State*, 1: 457, 523, 654; Leo Pfeffer, *Church, State and Freedom* (Boston: Beacon Press, 1967), pp. 121–22.

113. Sweet, *Story of Religion*, pp. 225–26; Marty, *Righteous Empire*, p. 39; Phelps, *Church and State*, 1: 654–55.

Chapter 6
The Argument

1. Sudhir Hazareesingh, *Political Traditions in Modern France*, p. 69, and *From Subject to Citizen*, pp. 27, 72–73, 239, 266–70; Michel Winock, *Nationalism, Anti-Semitism*, pp. 101–2; Michael Graetz, *The Jews in Nineteenth-Century France*, p. 45; Chilton Williamson, *American Suffrage from Property to Democ-*

racy: 1760–1860 (Princeton: Princeton University Press, 1960), pp. 92–117, 123–24, 131–35, 146–57, 190, 205, 208, 213–14, 218–22, 265–66.

2. Iris Marion Young, "Polity and Group Difference: A Critique of Universal Citizenship," *Theorizing Citizenship*, ed. Ronald Beiner, pp. 175, 180–83.

3. Tocqueville, *Democracy*, 1: 370–97, 418–20; 2, 270.

4. Louis Hartz, *The Liberal Tradition in America*, pp. 145–200.

5. Tocqueville, *Democracy*, 1: 348–70, quote on p. 354.

6. Ibid., 1: 343–97.

7. Louis Hartz, *The Founding of New Societies*. Hartz's discussions of Indians, African-Americans, and racism are on pp. 16–20, 40–44, 49–65.

8. Tocqueville, *Democracy*, 2: 209–24, quotes on pp. 209, 211.

9. *The Statistical History of the United States from Colonial Times to the Present* (Stamford, CT: Fairfield Publishers, 1965), p. 9; Robin Blackburn, *The Overthrow of Colonial Slavery, 1776–1848* (London and New York: Virso, 1988), p. 165; David Geggus, "Racial Equality, Slavery, and Colonial Secession during the Constituent Assembly," *The American Historical Review* 94 (December 1989): 1291; Shelby T. McCloy, *The Negro in France* (New York: Haskell House, 1973), pp. 52–53; Susan Peabody, " 'There are no Slaves in France": The Political Culture of Race and Slavery in the Ancien Regime* (New York and London: Oxford University Press, 1996), p. 3.

10. Geggus, "Racial Equality": 1291; McCloy, *Negro in France*, pp. 83–111, 124. William B. Cohen, *The French Encounters with Africans: With Response to Blacks, 1530–1880* (Bloomington and London: Indiana University Press, 1980), pp. 117–18; David Brion Davis, *The Problem of Slavery in the Age of Revolution* (Ithaca and London: Cornell University Press, 1975), p. 29.

11. Geggus, "Racial Equality": 1294–1303; Cohen, *French Encounters*, pp. 114–16, 119, 181, 190–204; Blackburn, *Overthrow*, pp. 187–90, 224–29, 280–81; Davis, *Problem of Slavery*, pp. 27–31, 137–45, McCloy, *Negro in France*, pp. 75, 117, 122.

12. McCloy, *Negro in France*, pp. 47–48, 142; Blackburn, *Overthrow*, pp. 494–98 ; C. Duncan Rice, *The Rise and Fall of Black Slavery* (New York and London: Harper & Row, 1975), pp. 247–48, 252–58, 261–62.

13. Shapiro and Markoff, *Revolutionary Demands*, pp. 438, 443; Beatrice Fry Hyslop, *French Nationalism in 1789*, pp. 142, 244, 276–77; Blackburn, *Overthrow*, pp. 170–76, 224; Cohen, *French Encounters*, pp. 139–40; Davis, *Problem of Slavery*, pp. 26–27, 95–101; McCloy, *Negro in France*, pp. 67, 75, 117, 122, 124; Pierre H. Boulle, "In Defense of Slavery: Eighteenth-Century Opposition to Abolition and the Origins of a Racist Ideology in France," in *History from Below: Studies in Popular Protest and Popular Ideology*, ed. Frederick Krantz (New York and Oxford: Basil Blackwell, 1988), pp. 222–46; Lawrence C. Jennings, *French Anti-Slavery: The Movement for Abolition of Slavery in France, 1802–1848* (Cambridge: Cambridge University Press, 2000), pp. 1–3.

14. Blackburn, *Overthrow*, pp. 245–52, 258–60, 475–76; Davis, *Problem of Slavery*, p. 33; Cohen; idem, *French Encounters*, pp. 185–91; Michael Kiestra, *The Politics of Slave Trade Suppression in Britain and France, 1814–48: Diplomacy, Morality and Economics* (New York and London: St. Martin's Press and Macmillan Press, 2000).

15. Charles Pinckney, 21 August 1787, *The Records of the Federal Convention of 1787*, 2: 371.

16. Tench Cox to James Madison, 31 March 1790, in ibid., 3: 361; Davis, *Problem of Slavery*, p. 100.

17. Rice, *Rise and Fall*, pp. 186–87; Blackburn, *Overthrow*, pp. 114–15; Davis, *Problem of Slavery*, p. 24.

18. Blackburn, *Overthrow*, pp. 120–21, 272–73; Rice, *Rise and Fall*, pp. 207–8; Davis, *Problem of Slavery*, pp. 26–28.

19. Rice, *Rise and Fall*, p. 196; Blackburn, *Overthrow*, pp. 120–21; Davis, *Problem of Slavery*, pp. 25–28.

20. Davis, *Problem of Slavery*, pp. 23–25, 78–80, 87, 119, 312–13; Blackburn, *Overthrow*, pp. 112–18.

21. Davis, *Problem of Slavery*, pp. 25–27, 30–31, 312–13; Blackburn, *Overthrow*, pp. 112, 118–21, 273–74; Rice, *Rise and Fall*, pp. 210–11.

22. Rice, *Rise and Fall*, pp. 215–16, 221, 225, 232–38, 248; Blackburn, *Overthrow*, pp. 124–26, 286; Davis, *Problem of Slavery*, pp. 32, 122, 125–27; *Slavery and Freedom in the Age of the American Revolution*, ed. Ira Berlin and Ronald Hoffman (Urbana: The University of Illinois Press, 1986), p. 256.

23. Davis, *Problem of Slavery*, pp. 24, 26, 29–31, 100–7, 125–27, 133–34; Blackburn, *Overthrow*, pp. 124–26.

24. Davis, *Problem of Slavery*, pp. 153, 156–58; Blackburn, *Overthrow*, p. 284.

25. Davis, *Problem of Slavery*, pp. 25–26, 29, 32.

26. Thomas Jefferson, *Notes on the State of Virginia*, ed. William Peden (Chapel Hill: The University of North Carolina Press, 1955), pp. 139, 141, cf. pp. 140–42.

27. Jennings, *French Anti-Slavery*, pp. 3–4, 6.

28. Patrice Higonnet, *Goodness Beyond Virtue*, pp. 57, 98.

29. Jennings, *French Anti-Slavery*; Kiestra, *Politics of Slave Trade*; Geggus, "Racial Equality, Slavery": 1304–8; Seymour Drescher, "Two Variants of Anti-Slavery: Religious Organization and Social Mobilization in Britain and France, 1780–1870," in Drescher, *From Slavery to Freedom: Comparative Studies in the Rise and Fall of Atlantic Slavery* (New York: New York University Press, 1999), pp. 35–56; and idem, "British Way, French Way: Opinion Building and Revolution in the Second French Slave Emancipation," ibid., pp. 158–95.

30. Geggus, "Racial Equality": 1292; Jennings, *French Anti-Slavery*, pp. 1–3, 8–10, 13, 16–17, 21–29, 38–39, 51–61, 73–74, 86–87, 133, 278–89; Drescher, "Two Variants," pp. 36, 41–45; idem, "British Way," pp. 160, 162–69, 170–80; and idem, "The Ending of the Slave Trade and the Evolution of European Scientific Racism," Drescher, *From Slavery to Freedom*, pp. 281, 289; Kielstra, *Politics of Slave Trade*, pp. 43, 114–15, 161.

31. Drescher, "British Way," p. 160; Jennings, *French Anti-Slavery*, pp. 9, 239–40, 278–89; Kielstra, *Politics of Slave Trade*, pp. 114–15.

32. Jennings, *French Anti-Slavery*, pp. 278–89; Drescher, "British Way," pp. 179–80.

33. Drescher, "British Way," pp. 158–95, and "Ending of the Slave Trade," pp. 280–82; Dwight Lowell Dumond, *Anti-Slavery: The Crusade for Freedom*

(Ann Arbor: University of Michigan Press, 1961), pp. 158, 175–90, 245–49, 264–94, 298–304, 308–9, 316–19, 348–49.

34. *Concise Dictionary of American History*, ed. Wayne Andrews (New York: Charles Scribner's Sons, 1962), pp. 33, 382; Dumond, *Anti-Slavery*, pp. 245–49, 264–74.

35. It could be argued that Father Charles E. Coughlin emerged in the 1930s as an equivalent of Drumont, but his popularity was much briefer. This issue will be discussed in chapter 7.

36. For a discussion of scientific racism in France and England and the slave trade see Drescher, "The Ending of the Slave Trade," pp. 275–311.

37. Blackburn, *Overthrow*, pp. 188, 195, 224–25, 229; Cohen, *French Encounters*, pp. 117–18, 188–90, 202; McCloy, *Negro in France*, pp. 82–85, 124; Higonnet, *Goodness*, pp. 98–99.

38. Michael R. Marrus and Robert O. Paxton, *Vichy France And the Jews* (New York: Basic Books, 1981), pp. 367–68; Robert O. Paxton, *Vichy France: Old Guard and New Order, 1940–1944* (New York: Alfred A. Knopf, 1972), pp. 174–75.

39. Cohen, *French Encounters*, pp. 118–20; McCloy, *Negro in France*, p. 124.

40. Frédérick Charles-Heitz, *Les Sociétiés Politiques De Strasbourg Pendant les Années* 1790 à 1795: *Extraits De Leurs Procès-Verbaux* (Strasbourg: Frédérick-Charles Heitz, 1865), p. 141.

41. Higonnet, *Goodness*, pp. 98–99; Michael L. Kennedy, *The Jacobin Clubs in the French Revolution: 1793–1795* (New York and Oxford: Berghahn Books, 2000), pp. 204–8.

42. Blackburn, *Overthrow*, pp. 482–86, 494–95; Cohen, *French Encounters*, pp. 188–90, 200, 202, 204; McCloy, *Negro in France*, pp. 142–44.

43. Desmond King, *In the Name of Liberalism*; Rogers Smith, *Civic Ideals*, p. 714.

44. Tocqueville, *Democracy*, 2: 270.

45. An excellent discussion of these aspects of American liberty and slavery in the Revolution is in Davis, *Problem of Slavery*, pp. 257–76.

46. William O'Neill, *Everyone Was Brave: The Rise and Fall of Feminism in America* (Chicago: Quadrangle Books, 1969), pp. 11–18; William H. Chafe, *The American Woman: Her Changing Social, Economic, and Political Roles, 1920–1970* (New York: Oxford University Press, 1972), pp. 3–4.

47. *Historical Dictionary*, ed. Scott and Rothaus; *Critical Dictionary*, ed. Furet and Ozouf.

48. Hannelore Schroder, "The Declaration of Human and Civil Rights for Women (Paris, 1791) by Olympe De Gouges," *History of European Ideas* 11 (1989): 265–70; Jane Abray, "Feminism in the French Revolution," *The American Historical Review* 80 (February 1975): 48–49.

49. R. B. Rose, *The Enragés: Socialists of the French Revolution?* (Melbourne, Australia: Melbourne University Press, 1965), pp. 11–13, 20, 54–61, 65–70, 72, 73–80, 88; idem, *The Making of Sans-Culottes: Democratic Ideas and Institutions in Paris, 1789–92* (Manchester: Manchester University Press, 1983), pp. 98–107, 110, 112–14, 132, 150; Scott H. Lyle, "The Second Sex (September

1793)," *The Journal of Modern History* 27 (March 1955): 14–26; Richard Cobb, *A Second Identity: Essays on France and French History* (London and New York: Oxford University Press, 1969), pp. 168–76, 221–36; Dominque Godineau, "Masculine and Feminine Political Practice during the French Revolution, 1793–Year III," in *Women and Politics in the Age of Democratic Revolution*, ed. Harriet B. Applewhite and Darlene G. Levy (Ann Arbor: University of Michigan Press, 1990), pp. 61–63, 65–66, 70–71; Applewhite and Levy, "Women, Radicalization and the Fall of the French Monarchy," in ibid., pp. 81–104; Gary Kates, " 'The Powers of Husband and Wife Must Be Equal and Separate': The Cercle Social and the Rights of Women, 1790–91," in ibid., pp. 163, 172–74; Singham, "Betwixt Cattle and Men," in *The French Idea of Freedom*, ed. Dale Van Kley, pp. 143–48; Abray, "Feminism": 44–50, 59–62; Joan B. Landes, *Women and the Public Sphere in the Age of the French Revolution* (Ithaca and London: Cornell University Press, 1988), pp. 93, 109–12, 117–18, 139–42; Olwen H. Hufton, *Women and the Limits of Citizenship in the French Revolution* (Toronto, Buffalo, and London: University of Toronto Press, 1992), pp. 7–18, 25–50; idem, "Women in Revolution," *Past and Present* 53 (November 1971): 100–11; Ruth Graham, "Loaves and Liberty: Women in the French Revolution," in *Becoming Visible: Women in European History*, ed. Renate Bridenthal and Claudia Koonz (Boston: Houghton Mifflin, 1977), pp, 239–46; Woloch, *The New Regime*, pp. 89–90; Darlene Gay Levy, "Women's Revolutionary Citizenship in Action, 1791: Setting the Boundaries," in *The French Revolution and the Meaning of Citizenship*, ed. Renée Waldinger, Philip Dawson, and Isser Woloch (Westport, CT and London: Greenwood Press, 1993), pp. 171–83; Simon Schama, *Citizens*, pp. 324, 458, 460–64, 529–30, 548–49, 605, 611, 749; Higonnet, *Goodness*, pp. 93, 95, 133; Suzanne Desan, " 'Constitutional Amazons' ": Jacobin Women's Clubs in the French Revolution," *Re-Creating Authority in Revolutionary France.* ed. Bryant T. Ragan, Jr. and Elizabeth Williams (New Brunswick, NJ: Rutgers University Press, 1992), pp. 12–13.

50. Hufton, "Women in Revolution": 106–8; idem, "The Reconstruction of a Church, 1796–1801," in *Beyond the Terror*, ed. Gwynne Lewis and Colin Lucas (Cambridge: Cambridge University Press, 1983), pp. 21–52; and idem, *Women and Limits*, pp. 94–130, 133–36, 141–44.

51. Cobb, *Second Identity*, pp. 224–25; James F. McMillan, *Housewife or Harlot: The Place of Women in French Society 1870–1940* (New York: St. Martin's Press, 1981), p. 78; R. B. Rose, "Feminism, Women and the French Revolution," *Historical Reflections* 21 (Winter 1995): 198; Landes, *Women and the Public Sphere*, pp. 122–23, 139; Lynn Hunt, "The Unstable Boundaries of the French Revolution," in *A History of Private Life*, ed. Michelle Perrot (Cambridge: Harvard University Press, 1990), 4 vols., 4: 30–31; Abray, "Feminism": 58–59; Singham, "Betwixt," pp. 149–50; Kates, "Powers," pp. 165–69; Graham, "Loaves and Liberty," p. 245; Higonnet, *Goodness*, pp. 25, 94–95, 196.

52. Abray, "Feminism in the French Revolution": 54; Singham, "Betwixt," pp. 149–50; Rose, "Feminism, Women": 193; Godineau, "Masculine and Feminine," pp. 62–63; Joan Wallach Scott, *Only Paradoxes to Offer: French Feminists and the Rights of Man* (Cambridge: Harvard University Press, 1996), pp. 34–36; Graham, "Loaves and Liberty," pp. 244, 248–49; Levy, "Women's Revolutionary

Leadership," pp. 169–82; Madelyn Gutwirth, "*Citoyens, Citoyennes*: Cultural Repression and the Subversion of Female Citizenship in the French Revolution," in *French Revolution and the Meaning of Citizenship*, ed. Waldinger, Dawson, and Woloch, pp. 17–29; *levée en masse* quoted in John A. Lynn, *The Bayonets of the Republic: Motivation and Tactics in the Army of Revolutionary France* (Urbana and Chicago: University of Illinois Press, 1984), p. 6. I am indebted to Prof. Lynn for pointing out the antifeminist implications of the levée.

53. Landes, *Women*, pp. 122–23; James F. McMillan., *France and Women 1789–1914: Gender, Society and Politics* (London and New York: Routledge, 2001), pp. 33–34.

54. McMillan, *France and Women*, pp. 33–35.

55. Higonnet, *Goodness*, pp. 93–95, 99, 196; Desan, " 'Constitutional Amazons,' " p. 15.

56. Graham, "Loaves and Liberty," p. 244.

57. *The Code Napoleon*, pp. 12, 59–60, 73–74, 103–7, 330, 391–94, 426–28, 439, 432; *The Civil Laws of France to the Present Time*, ed. David Mitchell Aird (London: Longmans Green, 1875), pp. 40, 42–43; *Le Moniteur Universel*, no. 40 (30 October 1793), reprinted in *Reimpression de l'Ancien Moniteur* (Paris: Bureau Central, 1841), vol. 18: 300; Landes, *Women and the Public Sphere*, pp. 93, 145–46, 170; Hunt, "Unstable Boundaries," pp. 18–19, 33; Scott, *Only Paradoxes*, pp. 47–51; Abray, "Feminism in the French Revolution": 56–58; Singham, "Betwixt Cattle and Men," pp. 148, 150; Rose, "Feminism, Women": 193–94, 199; idem, *Enragés*, pp. 62–63; and idem, *Making of Sans-Culottes*, pp. 110–11; Lyle, "Second Sex": 25–26; Hufton, *Women and Limits of Citizenship*, pp. 35–36, 40–50; Graham, "Loaves and Liberty," pp. 248–49, Gutwirth, "*Citoyens*," pp. 23–26; McMillan, *France and Women*, pp. 35–44; Claire Goldberg Moses, *French Feminism in the Nineteenth Century* (Albany: State University of New York Press, 1984), pp. 18–20.

58. For Napoleon's personal view of women and policy toward their education, see D. M. G. Sutherland, *France 1789–1815: Revolution and Counterrevolution* (Oxford and New York: Oxford University Press, 1985), p. 369; Napoleon quoted in Schom, *Napoleon Bonaparte*, pp. 178, 706; McMillan, *France and Women*, pp. 35–36; Graham, "Loaves and Liberty," p. 253.

59. Abray, "Feminism in the French Revolution": 44, 54.

60. Graham, "Loaves and Liberty, p. 248; Rose, *Enragés*, pp. 61–62, Cobb, *Second Identity*, pp. 173–74, 224–25; Lyle, "Second Sex": 14–16; Schama, *Citizens*, pp. 800–803.

61. Desan, " 'Constitutional Amazons,' " pp. 12, 17–19, 25–27; Higonnet, *Goodness*, p. 94.

62. *Réponse de la citoyenne Blandin-Desmoulins de Dijon au citoyen Prudhomme*, 10 February 1793, *Révolutions de Paris*, no. 189 (16–23 February 1793): 369; Desan, " 'Constitutional Amazons,' " pp. 22–25.

63. *Historical Dictionary*, ed. Scott and Rothaus, 1: 440–41; *Feuillant de salut public*, in *Moniteur*, no. 59 (17 November 1793), reprinted in *Reimpression*, 18: 450; Gérard Walter, *La Révolution française: vue par ses journaux* (Paris: Tardy, 1948), p. 304; Graham, "Loaves and Liberty," pp. 241–44, 246; Rose,

Making of Sans-Culottes, pp. 104, 110, 112–14, 150; idem, *Enragés*, pp. 12, 60, 66; Lyle, "Second Sex": 16; Schama, *Citizens*, pp. 801–3.

64. *Historical Dictionary*, ed. Scott and Rothaus, 2: 533–34, 585–86, Lyle, "Second Sex": 14–16; Cobb, *Second Identity*, pp. 173–74, 224–25; Rose, *Enragés*, pp. 56–72; idem, *Making of* Sans-Culottes, pp. 110–14; Graham, "Loaves and Liberties," pp. 243–44, 247–48; Higonnet, *Goodness*, p. 55; Desan, " 'Constitutional Amazons,' " p. 30.

65. *Historical Dictionary*, ed. Scott and Rothaus, 1: 179–80; Lyle, "Second Sex": 25; Rose, *Making of Sans-Culottes*, pp. 110–11; Cobb, *Second Identity*, pp. 224–25; Hunt, "Unstable Boundaries," pp. 19–20, 45.

66. See footnote 67, below.

67. *Moniteur*, no. 40 (31 October 1793), reprinted in *Reimpression*, 18: 299–300; *Historical Dictionary*, ed. Scott and Rothaus, 1: 9–10; Lyle, "Second Sex": 22–26; Cobb, *Second Identity*, pp. 224–25; Rose, *Making of* Sans-Culottes, pp. 110–11.

68. 115. Graham, "Loaves and Liberty," pp. 248–49; Higonnet., *Goodness*, pp. 92–93; Hunt, "Unstable Boundaries," pp. 19–20, 45; Rose, *Enragés*, pp. 61–63.

69. "*Aux Republicaines*," *Feuille de Salut Public*, appearing in *Le Moniteur Universel*, no. 59 (17 November 1793), *Reimpression*, 18: 450.

70. Ibid.: 450.

71. Ibid.: 450.

72. Michael Kennedy, *Jacobin Clubs in the French Revolution: 1793–1795*, pp. 105–6; Higonnet, *Goodness*, pp. 92, 95, Richard Cobb, *The French and their Revolution*, p. 16; Desan, " 'Constitutional Amazons,' " pp. 14, 20–22, 31–34.

73. Desan, " 'Constitutional Amazons,' " pp. 28–30.

74. Ibid., pp. 31, 33–34.

75. Landes, *Women and the Public Sphere*, pp. 51, 146–47, 160–62, 167–69; Hufton, *Women and Limits of Citizenship*, pp. 3–4; Graham, "Loaves and Liberty," pp. 251–52; Abray, *Feminism in the French Revolution*, pp. 58–62; Rose, "Feminism, Women": 189–93; Schroder, "Declaration": 263–65; Joan Hoff Wilson, "The Illusion of Change: Women and the American Revolution," in *The American Revolution: Explorations in the History of American Radicalism*, ed. Alfred D. Young (Dekalb: Northern Illinois University Press, 1976), pp. 386–87, 414–19, 426–31; Linda K. Kerber, " 'History Can Do It No Justice': Women and the Reinterpretation of the American Revolution," in *Women in the Age of the American Revolution*, ed. Ronald Hoffman and Peter J. Albert (Charlottesville: United States Capitol Historical Society, by University Press of Virginia, 1989), pp. 41–42; idem, *Women of the Republic: Intellect and Ideology in Revolutionary America* (Chapel Hill: University of North Carolina Press, 1980), pp. 8–12; idem, "The Paradox of Women's Citizenship in the Early Republic: The Case of Martin vs. Massachusetts, 1850," *The American Historical Review* 97 (April 1992): 351–56, 376–78; idem, " 'I have Don . . . much to Carrey on the Warr': Women and the Shaping of the Republican Ideology After the American Revolution," in *Women and Politics*, ed. Applewhite and Levy, pp. 232–35, 250–51; Carole Shammas, "Early American Women and Control Over Capital," in *Women in the Age of the American Revolution*, ed. Hoffman and Albert, pp. 150–52; Mary Beth

Norton, *Liberty's Daughters: The Revolutionary Experience of American Women, 1750–1800* (Boston and Toronto: Little, Brown, 1980), pp. 191, 235. For comparisons of women in the French and American Revolutions, see Kerber, " 'I Have Don," pp. 223–30.

76. Wilson, "Illusion of Change," pp. 397–98, 417, 420–21; Norton, *Liberty's Daughters*, pp. 163–88, 191; Kerber, " 'History Can Do It No Justice,' " pp. 11–16, 19, 23; Laurel Thatcher Ulrich, " 'Daughters of Liberty': Religious Women in Revolutionary New England," in *Women in the Age of the American Revolution*, ed. Hoffman and Albert, pp. 215–28; Alfred Young, "The Women of Boston: 'Persons of Consequence' in the Making of the American Revolution, 1765–76," in *Women and Politics*, ed. Applewhite and Levy, pp. 194–207, 216–17; Marylynn Salmon, *Women and the Law of Property in Early America* (Chapel Hill: University of North Carolina Press, 1986), pp. 5, 7, 10–11, 59–80, 86–87, 92, 99–100, 125, 129, 134–35, 141–42, 152–53, 157–58, 187, 189–90.

77. Kerber, *Women of the Republic*, pp. 120–55; idem, " 'History Can Do It No Justice,' " pp. 35–36, 39, 41–44; idem, "Paradox": 351–56, 374–78; idem, " 'I Have Don,' " pp. 228–30; Norton, *Liberty's Daughters*, p. 191; Shammas, "Early American Women," pp. 151–52; Wilson, "Illusion of Change," pp. 408–19, 426–31; Salmon, "Republican Sentiment," p. 447; Norma Basch, "Invisible Women: The Legal Fiction of Marital Unity in Nineteenth-Century America," *Feminist Studies* 5 (Summer 1979): 346–66; Carole Shammas, "Re-Assessing the Married Women's Property Acts," *Journal of Women's History* 6 (Spring 1994): 9–30.

78. John Adams to James Sullivan, 26 May 1776, *The Works of John Adams*, ed. Charles Francis Adams, 10 vols., 9: 376.

79. Same to Same, ibid., 9: 375–78; Thomas Jefferson to Anne Willing Bingham, 11 May 1788, *The Papers of Thomas Jefferson*, ed. Julian P. Boyd, et. al. (Princeton and Oxford: Princeton University Press, 1950–2000), 28 vols., 13: 151; same to Angelica Schuyler Church, 21 September 1788, 13: 623.

80. Kerber, "Paradox": 351–56, 374–78; idem, *Women of the Republic*, pp. 209–22, 227–31, 235, 283–88; idem, " 'History Can Do It No Justice,' " pp. 29–33, 35–36, 38–39, 41–42; idem, " 'I Have Don,' " pp. 232–35, 250–51; Wilson, "Illusion of Change, pp. 386–87, 408–10, 416–17; Norton, *Liberty's Daughters*, p. 191.

81. An interesting discussion of Indian captivity literature is in Tom Engelhardt, *The End of Victory Culture: Cold War America and the Disillusioning of a Generation* (Amherst: University of Massachusetts Press, 1998), pp. 22–28.

82. Candace Lewis Bredbrenner, *A Nationality of Her Own: Women, Marriage and the Law of Citizenship* (Berkeley, Los Angeles, London: University of California Press, 1998), pp. 5–14, 45–79, 241–45; *Code Napoleon*, p. 6; *The French Civil Code (As Amended up to 1906)*, ed. E. Blackwood Wright (London: Stevens and Sons, 1908), p. 8; Maria Verone, *La femme et la loi* (Paris: Larousse, 1920), pp. 7–11; Marc Ancel, *Traite De La Capacité Civile De La Femme Mariée D'Après La Loi Du 18 Fevrier 1938* (Paris: Librarie Du Recueil Sirey, 1938), pp. 10–167; McMillan, *Housewife or Harlot*, p. 129.

83. Carl N. Degler, *At Odds: Women and the Family in America from the Revolution to the Present* (New York and London: Oxford University Press,

1980), p. 438; Christine Bolt, *The Women's Movements in the United States and Britain from the 1790s to the 1920s* (Amherst: University of Massachusetts Press, 1993), pp, 148–49, 152, 193–94.

84. Suzanne Daley, "France's Most Courted: Women to Join the Ticket," *New York Times*, February 4, 2001, [section 1], pp. 1, 8. For the American statistics, see the internet: for the senate: http://www.senate.gov/learning/stat_14.htm/; for the House of Representatives: http://bioguide.congress.gov/congresswomen/state.asp

85. Marie-France Toinet, "Women's Political Participation in France," *Social Science Working Papers* (Irvine, CA: University of California, School of Social Sciences), 79 (August 1975): 1; McMillan, *Housewife*, pp., 50–53; idem, *France and Women*, pp. 59–60, 147–48; Moses, *French Feminism*, pp. 32–33; William L. O'Neill, *Everyone*, p. 305; Chafe, *American Woman*, pp. 58, 91; Nancy E. McGlen and Karen O'Connor, *Women's Rights: The Struggle for Equality in the Nineteenth and Twentieth Centuries* (New York: Praeger, 1983), p. 160; Bolt, *Women's Movements*, pp. 156–59.

86. *Civil Laws*, ed. Aird, pp. 40, 43, 51; McMillan, *Housewife*, pp. 25–26.

87. McGlen and O'Connor, *Women's Rights*, pp. 272–73; Shammas, "Re-Assessing": 11, 21; Degler, *At Odds*, p. 332.

88. *Civil Laws*, ed. Aird, pp. 40; *The French Civil Code: With the Various Amendments Thereto as in Force March 15, 1895*, ed. Henry Cachard (London: Stevens and Sons, 1895), pp. 50, 59–60, 62; McMillan, *Housewife*, p. 26.

89. Shammas, "Re-Assessing," 14–23; Basch, "Invisible Women": 346–66; McMillan, *Housewife*, p. 129.

90. *Code Napoleon*, pp. 64–85; *Civil Laws*, ed. Aird, pp. 42–43; *French Civil Code*, ed. Cachard, pp. 62–81; McMillan, *Housewife*, pp. 26–27; Degler, *At Odds*, pp. 166–69.

91. Michel Martin, "From Periphery to Center: Women in the French Military," *Armed Forces and Society* 8 (Winter 1982): 304, 307–11; Sandra Carson Stanley and Mady Wechsler Segal, "Military Women in NATO: An Update," ibid., 14 (Summer 1988): 563; Jean Bolègue, " 'Feminization' and the French Military: An Anthropological Approach," ibid., 17 (Spring 1991): 344.

92. "Gender-related Development Index," *Human Development Report 2001, United Nations Development Programme*, on the internet at http://www.undp.org/hdr2001/indicator.

93. Degler, *At Odds*, pp. 417, 426; Toinet, "Women's Political Participation": 3.

94. Bolt, *Women's Movements*, pp. 80–84, 195.

95. McMillan, *France and Women*, pp. 84–89, 131–32, 145, 190–95; Moses, *French Feminism*, pp. 209–10, 233, quote on p. 236.

96. McMillan, *France and Women*, p. 190; Bolt, *Women's Movements*, p. 97.

97. McMillan, *France and Women*, p. 212; Bolt, *Women's Movements*, p. 196.

98. Rodgers, "Republicanism": 11–38; idem, "Exceptionalism," in *Imagined Histories*, ed. Anthony Molho and Gordon S. Wood, pp. 21–40.

Chapter 7
The Outcome

1. p. 212; Yankelovich, Skelly and Wright, Inc. Poll (1981) in Nathan and Ruth Perlmutter, *The Real Anti-Semitism in America* (New York: Arbor House, 1982), p. 75; ABC News/Washington Post Race Relations Poll, 2–3 February 1981, James G. Gimpel and James R. Edwards, Jr., *The Congressional Politics of Immigration Reform* (Boston and London: Allyn and Bacon, 1999), p. 33.

2. The present comparison of American and French Jewry is informed by texts cited in the footnotes to chapters 3–5.

3. Hyman, *Jews of Modern France*, pp. 190, 196; Arnold Schwartz, "Intermarriage in the United States," *The Jew in American Society*, ed. Marshall Sklar (New York: Behrman House, 1974), pp. 311, 319; C. Bezalel Sherman, *The Jew Within American Society: A Study in Ethnic Individuality* (Detroit: Wayne State University Press, 1965), p. 184; Dinnerstein, *Antisemitism in America*, p. 341.

4. Jaher, *Scapegoat*, p. 122; Marcus, *United States Jewry*, 1: 113, 117, 410–11.

5. Graetz, *Jews in Nineteen-Century France*, pp. 43–62; Berkovitz, *Shaping*, p. 126; Benbassa, *Jews of France*, pp. 115–19; Birnbaum, "Between Social and Political Assimilation," pp. 114–25; Hyman, *Jews of Modern France*, pp. 90–100; Marrus, *Politics of Assimilation*, pp. 36–38, 41, 123–24; Eugen Weber, "Reflections on the Jews of France," *Jews in Modern France*, ed. Malino and Wasserstein, pp. 9, 13, 22n, 33;

6. Marcus, *United States Jewry*, 2: 192, 197–208; Jaher, *Scapegoat*, pp. 177, 181, 189–90.

7. Marrus, *Politics of Assimilation*, pp. 66–68; Berkovitz, *Shaping*, p. 126; Benbassa, *Jews of France*, p. 127; Birnbaum, "Between Social and Political Assimilation," p. 121; Rodrigue, *French Jews, Turkish Jews*, p. 22.

8. Jaher, *Scapegoat*, pp. 170–248; Dinnerstein, *Antisemitism in America*, pp. 35–196; Oscar Handlin, *Race and Nationality in American Life* (Garden City, NY: Doubleday Anchor Books, 1957), pp. 3–164.

9. Hyman, *Emancipation*, pp. 22–26.

10. The references to this and the preceding paragraph are: John Higham, *Strangers in the Land: Patterns of American Nativism 1860–1925* (New York: Atheneum, 1963); sales figures for *Passing of the Great Race* on p, 271; Wallace Evan Davies, *Patriotism on Parade: The Story of Veterans and Hereditary Organizations in America, 1783–1900* (Cambridge: Harvard University Press, 1955); Barbara Miller Solomon, *Ancestors and Immigrants: A Changing New England Tradition* (Cambridge: Harvard University Press, 1956); Oscar Handlin, *Race and Nationality*; Robert A. Divine, *American Immigration Policy, 1924–1952* (New Haven: Yale University Press, 1957); Thomas F. Gossett, *Race: The History of an Idea in America* (Dallas: Southern Methodist University, 1963); Mark H. Haller, *Eugenics: Hereditarian Attitudes in American Thought* (New Brunswick, NJ: Rutgers University Press, 1984); Donald K. Pickens, *Eugenics and the Progressives* (Nashville: Vanderbilt University Press, 1968); Kenneth M. Ludmerer, *Genetics and American Society* (Baltimore: The Johns Hopkins University Press, 1972); Allen Chase, *The Legacy of Malthus: The Social Costs of the New Scientific Rac-*

ism (Urbana: University of Illinois Press, 1980); Hamilton Cravens, *The Triumph of Evolution: American Scientists and the Heredity-Environment Controversy 1900–1941* (Philadelphia: University of Pennsylvania Press, 1978); Sheldon Morris Neuringer, *American Jewry and United States Immigration Policy 1881–1952* (New York: Arno Press, 1980); Stephen Jay Gould, *The Mismeasure of Man* (New York, London: W. W. Norton, 1981), pp. 25, 43, 51–63, 116–94; Daniel J. Kevles, *In the Name of Eugenics: Genetics and the Uses of Human Heredity* (New York: Alfred A. Knopf, 1985).

11. The references for this and the previous paragraph are: Benbassa, *Jews of France*, pp. 135, 138–41; Marrus, *Politics of Assimilation*, pp. 53, 125, 128–32, 135–36, 206–8; Weber, "Reflections," pp. 21, 23; Zeev Sternhell, "The Roots of Popular Anti-Semitism in the Third Republic," *Jews in Modern France*, ed. Malino and Wasserstein, pp. 103–8; idem, *Neither Right Nor Left: Fascist Ideology in France* (Berkeley, Los Angeles, and London: University of California Press, 1986), pp. 38–40; Hyman, *Jews of Modern France* 95–96; idem, *From Dreyfus to Vichy*; pp. 10, 14–16; Winock, *Nationalism*, pp. 6, 11–13, 84, 75–78, 98, 115–16, 120, 136, 153–54; Robert F. Byrnes, *Anti-Semitism in Modern France: The Prologue to the Dreyfus Affair* (New Brunswick, NJ: Rutgers University Press, 1950), 1: 110–14, 128–35, 181–82, 302–4.

12. Byrnes, *Anti-Semitism in Modern France*, 1: 137–55, 253–61; Hyman, *Jews of Modern France*, pp. 95–102, 110–16; idem, *From Dreyfus to Vichy*, pp. 12–14, 55–56; Marrus, *Politics of Assimilation*, pp. 125–31, 206–10; Michael R. Marrus and Robert O. Paxton, *Vichy France and the Jews* (New York: Basic Books, 1981), pp. 3, 341; Benbassa, *Jews of France*, pp. 138–45; Sternhell, *Neither Left Nor Right*, pp. 44–46; idem, "Roots," pp. 109–10, 117–18; Winock, *Nationalism*, pp. 11–12, 84, 98, 120, 136, 175–78, 229–33; Frederick Busi, *The Pope of Antisemitism: The Career and Legacy of Edouard-Adolph Drumont* (Lincoln, MD, New York, and London: University Press of America, 1986), pp. 4–5, 33–40, 46, 56–57, 59–60, 92; Birnbaum, *Anti-Semitism in France*, pp. 90–95.

13. Marrus, *Politics of Assimilation*, pp. 128–284; Hyman, *Jews of Modern France*, pp. 109–10.

14. Busi, *Pope*, pp. 145–46; Winock, *Nationalism*, p. 6; Marrus and Paxton, *Vichy France*, pp. 34–35, 321–32; Hyman, *From Dreyfus to Vichy*, pp. 49–54, 65; Gérard Noiriel, *The French Melting Pot*, p. 64.

15. Leonard Dinnerstein, *The Leo Frank Case* (New York: Columbia University Press, 1968), pp. 1–147, 159–60; idem, *Antisemitism in America*, pp. 35–104; C. Vann Woodward, *Tom Watson: Agrarian Rebel* (New York: Oxford University Press, 1963), pp. 434–49, 470–76; Keith Sward, *The Legend of Henry Ford* (New York: Atheneum, 1968), pp. 146–60; Neuringer, *American Jewry*, pp. 127–29, 133–34, 136, 196.

16. Marcus, *United States Jewry*, 3: 145, 184–86; Sward, *Legend*, pp. 157–58.

17. Jaher, *Scapegoat.* pp. 246–47; Leo P. Ribuffo, *The Old Christian Right: The Protestant Right from the Great Depression to the Cold War* (Philadelphia: Temple University Press, 1983), pp. 98, 107–26, 249–50; Ralph Lord Roy, *Apostles of Discord: A Study of Bigotry on the Fringes of Protestantism* (Boston: Beacon Press, 1953), pp. 14, 26–39, 44–45; Donald S. Strong, *Organized Anti-Semi-*

tism in America: The Rise of Group Prejudice During the Decade 1930–1940 (Westport, CT: Greenwood Press, 1979), 71–78, 164–65; Dinnerstein, *Antisemitism in America*, pp. 78–127; Neuringer, *American Jewry*, p. 236.

18. Dinnerstein, *Antisemitism in America*, pp. 115–22, 127.

19. Haller, *Eugenics*, pp. 179–81, 240; Ludmerer, *Genetics*, pp. 63–85, 121–34, 136–38, 158–59, 169; Chase, *Legacy*, p. 352; Cravens, *Triumph*, pp. 176–80, 237–41; Keveles, *Name*, pp. 169–72. 199; Handlin, *Race*, pp. 141–42, 147–54; Pickens, *Eugenics and Progressives*, pp. 98–99.

20. Dinnerstein, *Antisemitism in America*, pp. 128–49.

21. Ibid., pp. 132, 134.

22. For the experience of French Jewry in the 1930s, see Birnbaum, *Anti-Semitism in France*, pp. 1, 15–17, 23–52; Paul J. Kingston, *Anti-Semitism in France During the 1930s: Organizations, Personalities, and Propaganda* (Hull: University of Hull Press, 1983), pp. 1, 6–136; Benbassa, *Jews of France*, pp. 154–55, 166; Marrus and Paxton, *Vichy France*, p. 25, 34–71; Hyman, *From Dreyfus to Vichy*, pp. 31, 68, 199–201, 206–30; 261–66; idem, *Jews of Modern France*, pp. 145–53; Stephen A. Schuker, "Origins of the 'Jewish Problem' in the Later Third Republic," ed. Malino and Wasserstein, *Jews in Modern France*, pp. 156, 160–62, 165; Winock, *Nationalism*, pp. 102–22, 146; Sternhell, *Neither Left nor Right*, p. 263.

23. For Vichy France and the Jews, see Robert O. Paxton, *Vichy France: Old Guard and New Order, 1940–1944* (New York: Alfred A. Knopf, 1976), pp. 136–223; Marrus and Paxton, *Vichy France*, pp. 3–4, 12, 15–16, 85, 98–107, 127–28, 137–44, 152–60, 181–366; Benbassa, *Jews of France*, pp. 168, 170–74; Schucker, "Origins," pp. 137–46; Hyman, *Jews of Modern France*, pp. 165, 167–68, 170–71.

24. Sudhir Hazaressingh, *Political Traditions*, pp. 133–35.

25. These organizations are discussed in Tzvetan Todorov, *On Human Diversity*, p. 190. Hazareesingh, *Political Traditions*, p. 87.

26. This and the previous paragraph are partly based on Birnbaum, *Anti-Semitism in France*, pp. 8–20, 232–52; Hazareesingh, *Political Tradition*, pp. 87, 99–105, 110, 125, 129–30, 137–40.

27. For a discussion of the exclusion of Catholics, women, and workers from full membership in the political community of the Third Republic, see Sudhir Hazareesingh, *From Subject to Citizen*, pp. 26–27.

28. Hyman, *Jews of Modern France*, pp. 186–87, 212; Jean-Philippe Mathy, *French Resistance: The French-American Culture Wars* (Minneapolis and London: University of Minnesota Press, 2000), p. 116; Michael Marrus, "Are the French Antisemitic? Evidence in the 1980s," *Jews in Modern France*, ed. Malino and Wasserstein, pp. 239–40; Dinnerstein, *Antisemitism in America*, pp. 151, 229–31; Gregory Martire and Ruth Clark, *Antisemitism in the United States: A Study of Prejudice in the 1980s* (New York: Praeger, 1982), pp. 5, 17–23.

29. Dinnerstein, *Antisemitism in America*, pp. 228–44.

30. Calvin Trillin, "U.S. Journal: Eureka Springs, Arkansas," *New Yorker* 45 (26 July 1969): 69–79; Hazareesingh, *Political Tradition*, pp. 136, 144; Hyman, *Jews of Modern France*, pp. 209–10.

31. Mathy, *French Resistance*, pp. 115–16.

32. American Jewry's activity on behalf of Israel is so constant, widespread, and well-known that no documentation is needed. For data on French Jews and Zionism, see Benbassa, *Jews of France*, pp. 191–92, Marrus, "Are the French Antisemitic?", pp. 257–81; Hyman, *Jews of Modern France*, pp. 189–90, 197–99, 202–3; Dominque Schnapper, *Jewish Identities*, pp. 68, 86, 104.

33. Hazareesingh, *Political Tradition*, p. 115.

34. Schnapper, *Jewish Identities*, pp. xlix–xlxx, d'Estaing quoted on p. xlix; Hyman, *Jews of Modern France*, pp. 205–9.

35. Hyman, *Jews of Modern France*, pp. 186–87; Hazareesingh, *Political Traditions*, p. 102; Birnbaum, *Anti-Semitism in France*, pp. 2–7, 227–30.

36. Benbassa, *Jews of France*, pp. 185. 192–93, Jacques Chirac quoted on p. 192.

37. *New York Times*, May 6, 2002, pp. 1,8. Despite recent gains in national respect for multiculturalism, this presidential contest reawakened historic French fears of Fascism, reactionary, organic nationalism, political instability, and the future of the republic.

abolition movement. *See* African-Americans; blacks in France; slavery
absolutism, 82, 130–33
Academy of Lyons, 99
acculturation, 129, 148, 152, 157–58. *See also* assimilation
Adams, John, 109–10, 155, 167, 182, 208
Address to the German Nation, 38
Aelders, Etta Palm d', 202
African-Americans, 7, 23–24, 28, 31, 41, 45–46, 164, 175–76, 179–95, 210–11, 228–30, 236, 286; in the American Revolution, 183–85, 187–91; population of, 179–80; in World War II, 230. *See also* slavery
Age of Reason, the. *See* Enlightenment, the
Albert, Phyllis Cohen, 67–68, 129
Alien and Sedition Acts, the. *See* citizenship; naturalization
The Alien in Our Midst or "Selling our Birthright for a Mess of Pottage," 226
Alliance Israélite Universelle, 224
Alsace, 65–66, 73–76, 83, 92, 96–97, 100–1, 104–6, 120, 128, 133, 154, 160, 189, 221, 223
Amar, Jean Baptiste André, 203–4
America First Committee, 40
American exceptionalism, 12. *See also* Hartz, Louis; Tocqueville, Alexis de
American-Israel Public Affairs Committee, 234–35
American Legion, 40, 225
American Party, 40
American Protective Association, 40
American Slavery as It Is, 188
Amies de la Constitution, 202
Amies de la liberté, 202
Amies de la République, 202
Amsterdam, 152–53, 159
ancestral societies: in America, 41
ancien régime. *See* Bourbon regime
Anglicans. *See* Church of England
Anglo/American model of change and state formation, 149
Anglo-Saxon, 26

Anthony, Susan B., 216
anti-Semitism, 24, 64, 96, 147; in America, 194, 221, 224–31, 233–34; in England, 64; in France, 55, 66, 69–70, 72, 74–75, 82–83, 85–87, 101, 104–5, 109, 120–21, 127–28, 133, 135–36, 190, 194, 217, 221, 224, 228–29; in Germany, 225; racial, 189; and World War II, 229
Army of the Coast of Brest, 34
Army of France: Jewish officers in, 223–24. *See also* women
Army of the Rhine, 37
Army of the United States: in the War For Independence, 128–29. *See also* women
ARTFL database, 4
Aryans, 134, 227
Asian-Americans, 28, 211, 336
Assembly of Notables, 61, 73, 91, 103, 105–6, 122–24, 126, 132; Napoleon's twelve questions of, 108–13, 115, 121, 124, 126, 155; of Rhin-et-Moselle, 119–20
assimilation, 116, 130, 134, 150, 153, 156. *See also* acculturation; conversion of Jews
Association pour le Droit des Femmes, 215
Australia, 179
Austria, 39, 132, 204
Authoritarian Personality, The, 236
Authoritarianism, in France, 217, 219
autocracy. *See* absolutism
"Aux Républicaines," 204–5
Avignon, 66, 72–73, 93

Backus, Isaac, 146
Baltimore, 37
Bank of France, 105
Baptist General Committee of, Virginia, 185
Baptists, 146, 182
Barlow, Joel, 100
Bastille, 40, 81, 99
Bayonne, France, 72

Beardian-Progressive history, 6–7. *See also* historiography
Belgium, 82, 130
Belmont, August, 224
Benjamin, Judah P., 224
Berlin, 38
Berr, Isaac Berr, 90–93, 95, 98, 107, 116, 159
Bible, 92, 133
blacks: in America (*see* African-Americans; slavery); in France, 192, 196; —, emancipation of, 191, 198; —, and final abolition of slavery in 1848, 180; —, and National Assembly Law of 4 April, 1792, 190; —, and National Convention decree of 4 February, 1793, 180, 186, 190–92
Bloch, Maurice, 81
Blum, Léon, 231, 237
Bonaparte, Napoleon, 38, 45, 52, 60–62, 72, 76, 79, 82, 88–89, 94, 96, 99, 155, 165, 185–86; and blacks, 190–91, 194; Civil Code of, 105, 108–9, 122, 125, 211; and Jews, 103–34, 225, 233 and women, 200, 208. Decrees: decree of May 30, 1806, 105–6; decree on the "the Regulation of Commercial Transactions and Residence of Jews," 127–28; decree on the "Organic Regulation of the Mosaic Religion," 127; decree on the "Organization of the Mosaic Religion," 118–20, 122–23; decree "Relative to the Names of Jews," 129
Bonapartism, 99
Bordeaux, 66, 70–73, 96–97, 127, 159–60
Boston, 143
"Bostonian, A," 144
Bourbon regime, 14, 16, 42, 44, 59, 61, 63, 78, 85, 88, 90, 99, 101, 116, 121, 131, 135, 140, 169; restoration of, 16, 209, 217, 233; and women, 200–1
Bowling Alone, 29
Bressole, Peicam de, 190
Broglie, Charles Victor de, 74–76
Buchanan, Pat, 234, 236
Butler, Pierce, 164

cahiers de doléances, 3, 33–34, 64–66, 181, 196
Canada, 179

capitalism, 9, 29, 71, 89
Catherine II, 132
Catholicism, 40, 43, 62–63, 77, 105, 110, 121, 133; in America, 141, 143, 145, 155, 169, 227, 229; in France, 59, 70, 82, 100, 102, 140, 196, 226–27, 231, 233, 235; in the French Revolution, 84–85, 87–88, 93, 116, 197–98, 201; and women, 197–98, 201, 206–7. *See also* Christianity
"Cato," 144
centralized state: in France, 5, 89, 101, 175–76
"*Certificat De Civism Épuré*," 35
Chamber of Deputies, 100, 222, 227–28
Champagny, Jean Bapiste de, 106, 115, 124, 128
Chapelier, Le, Law, 116
Charleston, SC, 154, 156–57, 160–61
Chaumette, Pierre Gaspard, 203–4
China, 10, 12
Chirac, Jacques, 236
"Chosen People," 148
Christendom. *See* Christianity
Christian American Patriots, 229. *See also* Pelley, William
Christianity, 5, 15, 18, 24, 39, 43, 51, 60–62, 88, 96–97, 105, 134, 145, 149, 168–69, 229; anti-Semitism of, 225; —, in America, 143–44, 150–51, 163, 169, 171; —, in France, 82, 225; triumphalism of, 170. *See also* Catholicism; Protestantism
Church, the. *See* Catholicism
church establishment in America, 144–45
Church of England, 151–52
citizenship, 35, 41–44, 46–48, 51–52, 56, 62, 64, 101–3, 108, 134–35, 139, 144, 147, 153, 164, 169, 237; and African-Americans, 179; and Alien and Sedition Acts, 45, 165–66; in America, 67, 83–85, 139, 142, 144, 147, 164, 169, 209–11; in France, 92, 112, 176, 192, 198, 201, 232–33; in Germany, 52; and Jews, 49, 149, 155, 158, 195; and women, 198, 201, 209–11. *See also* naturalization; suffrage
civic community, 232
civic equality, 71, 79, 84
Civic Ideals, 29–32, 192
civic morality: of Jews, 4
civic oath: in France, 75–76, 83, 91

civic religion: in America, 81, 86, 168; in the French Revolution, 81, 86

civic rights, 77, 90, 145, 148

civic titles, 59–60. *See also* dechristianization campaign

Civil Code of France, 53, 85, 96, 105, 200, 207, 212

Civil Constitution of the Clergy, 69, 72, 85, 87

Civil Judaism, 154–56

civil society, 24, 26, 49, 130. *See also* Tocqueville, Alexis de

Civil War, 49, 175, 177, 183, 193, 195, 218–19, 221

class, 9, 44, 62, 194. *See also* middle class

Clermont-Tonnerre, Stanislaus de, 66–69

Clinton, De Witt, 168

Clinton, George, 154–55

Clinton, William Jefferson, 212, 236

Club Massaic, 181

Clubs: women's in the French Revolution, 197, 199–201, 204–7

Code Napoleon. *See* Civil Code of France

Cohen, Jacob, 158

Cold War, 10

Colmar, France, 101

Colon, 186. *See also* slavery, abolition of: in France

Colonial America, 163–64, 169

colonialism, 39

Colrain, MA, 146, 152–53, 158

Columbia College, 166, 184

Comité Juif d' Action, 235

Committee of General Security: and women, 203–4

Committee of Public Safety, 34

Communism, 78, 178, 181. *See also* Russia: Soviet

Comtat, 73

Concordat of 1801, 89, 105

Confederacy, 31, 221. *See also* South, the

Confederation Congress, 184

Congregations, 222; Beth Shalome, 152; Mickva Israel, 154, 156–57; Mikveh Israel, 139, 152–53, 158; Shearith Israel, 140, 150–54, 156–58, 168–69

Congress. *See* Confederation Congress; Continental Congress; U.S. Congress; U.S. House of Representatives; U.S. Senate

Congress of Vienna, 181

Connecticut, 145–46, 160, 163, 182–83

consistories, 117–21, 123, 128, 133, 162, 222, 224

constitution: of 1791, 44, 52, 59, 75, 85, 88, 90, 198; of 1793, 51–52, 80, 190, 192, 197, 199; of 1795, 52, 176; of 1799, 52; of Massachusetts, 144, 166; of New Jersey, 208; of New York, 154–55; of North Carolina, 162, of Pennsylvania, 98, 162, 166; U.S., 21, 35, 38–42, 47–49, 141–46, 162, 165, 162, 170, 182–84, 193, 219, 250n.6

Constitutional Convention: of states to ratify the U.S. Constitution, 144; of the U.S. Constitution, 78, 143, 163–64, 170, 182, 183; of Virginia, 98

Continental Congress, 35–36, 168, 183–84

conversion of Jews, 5–6, 97, 130, 159–60. *See also* assimilation

corporate state and society, 71, 77, 83, 91, 93, 101, 112, 135, 147, 152

cosmopolitanism, 95–96, 164–65

Coughlin, Charles E., 227, 229–30

Council of Five Hundred, the 199–200

Council of State, 103–6, 125

Counter-Reformation, 63

counter-revolution in France, 197–98, 201

"court Jews," 132

Coxe, Tench, 143

Crémieux, Adolph, 224

Critical Dictionary of the French Revolution, A, 196;

Cult of Reason, 95, 190, 203

Cult of the Supreme Being, 88, 100. *See also* civic religion: in the French Revolution; dechristianization campaign

"Curtiopolis," 144

Darwinism, 285

"daughters of the revolution," 207, 210

Davison, Charles Stewart, 226

Dearborn *Independent*, 229. *See also* Ford, Henry

dechristianization campaign, 86–87. *See also* civic religion: in the French Revolution

Declaration of Independence, 35–36, 40–42, 46–48, 56, 138–39, 184, 196

"Declaration of Repentance," 235–36

Declaration of Rights for Women and Female Citizens, 196

Declaration of the Rights of Man and the Citizen, 40, 42–44, 46–48, 59, 66–67, 75–76, 80–81, 85, 134–35, 140, 196

Décret Infame. *See* Bonaparte, Napoleon.

Decrees: decree on the "Regulation of Commercial Transactions and Residence of Jews"

De Gaulle, Charles, 217

Deism. *See* Enlightenment, the

Deity of Liberty, 88. *See also* civic religion: in the French Revolution

Delaware, 145–46, 152–53

Democracy in America. See Tocqueville, Alexis de

Democratic Party, 220, 224, 230, 250

Democratic-Republicans, 166–67

Demos, John, 8

Derrida, Jacques, 7

Desan, Suzanne, 206–7

diaspora, 156–57

Dictionairre de la Langue Française, 38

Diderot, Denis, 170

divorce, 197–99, 207–8, 214. *See also* women's rights

Doctrinaires, 100

Drancy internment camp, 236

Drescher, Seymour, 186

Dreyfus Affair, 189, 226–28, 232–33, 235; and Alfred Dreyfus, 227, 232; and anti-Dreyfusards, 228, 232, 234. *See also* Drumont, Édouard; anti-Semitism: in France

Drumont, Édouard, 40, 189, 227–31. *See also* anti-Semitism: in France; Dreyfus Affair: and anti-Dreyfusards

Du Port, Adrien-Jean-François, 68–69, 75–76

Dutch. *See* Holland

Eastern Europe, 97, 228

École Normale, 133

Edict Concerning the Civil Conditions of Jews in the Prussian State, 131–32

Edict of Nantes, 63

Edict of Toleration, 84, 131. *See also* Joseph II

egalitarianism. *See* equal rights/equality

Egypt, 114

Eisenhower, Dwight David, 10, 12

Ellis Island, 55

Ellsworth, Oliver, 143

England, 25, 38, 42, 48, 77–78, 134, 147–48, 154–57, 161, 187–88, 193, 217; empire of, 76; and invasion of West Indies, 180–81; and Jews, 66, 147, 149, 159

English Common Law: doctrine of coverture in, 28, 211. *See also* women: property of; women's rights: and property

Enlightenment, 1, 51, 61, 74, 81, 88, 93, 95–96, 131, 134, 158, 169–70, 177, 185, 193

enragés, 197, 201–2. *See also* women

e pluribus unum, 164

equal rights/equality, 5, 78, 84, 101, 162; and the French Revolution, 81; and Jews, 147

eschatology: in Christianity, 79; and the French Revolution, 79; in Judaism, 156

Essay on the Physical, Moral and Political Regeneration of the Jews, 64, 68. *See also* Grégoire, Henri

Estaing, Valéry Giscard d', 235

Estates General, 3, 38, 40, 66, 68, 200

ethnic/ethnicity, 50, 135, 164, 178, 219; and composition of Jews in America, 219, 221; and France, 219, 221

Etienne, Paul Rabaut de Satin, 98

eugenics, 225, 230

Exclusion Act of 1882, 225

Expatriation Act of 1907, 211–212. *See also* naturalization

Faber, Eli, 155

Fairchild, Henry Pratt, 226

Fair Employment Commission, 230

Fare, Anne-Louis-Henry de la, 69

fascism, 95, 190

fatherland, 134

federalism, 24, 59

Federalist Party/Federalism, 52, 166–67; anti-Federalists, 144, 155

feminism. *See* women's rights

Fête Américaine, 190

feudalism, 12, 14–15, 44, 59, 70, 78, 141, 193

Feuille de salut public, 204

Fichte, Johann Gottlieb, 38

flags, American, 36

food riots, in the French Revolution, 202
Ford, Henry, 228–29
Fort McHenry, 37
Foucault, Michel, 7–8
Founding of New Societies, The. See Hartz, Louis
"*France aux Française, La,*" 40
France Juive, La, 227
Franco Prussian War, 217
Frank, Leo, 228
Franklin, Benjamin, 88, 97–100, 165–66, 169
Franks, David S., 140
Free Soil Party, 188
French Academy, 9
French and Russian model of social change: and state formation, 149
Furtado, Abraham, 73, 107, 109–10, 116, 126–28

gays/lesbians, 195, 236
Gellner, Ernest, 88
gender, 9, 24, 44. *See also* women
general will, 46
genocide, 141. *See also* Holocaust
Genovese, Eugene, 55
George III, 184
Georgia, 145–46, 156, 183, 228
German-American Jews, 94
German/Germany, 4, 25, 41–42, 52, 64, 91, 93, 95–96, 104, 131–34, 158; 228; and Jews, 62, 149, 226, 229; and Rhineland, 124; and the Third Reich, 41, 191; and Vichy France, 231–32. *See also* Hitler, Adolf; Nazism.
ghettoes, Jewish, 35
Gironde/Girondins, 98, 100, 181, 187
Glotzer, Scott, 119
Gobineau, Arthur de, 14
Goddess of Reason, 88
Good Friday, 151
Gore, Albert, 220
Gospels, 127
Gouges, Olympe de, 196–97, 200, 202–5
Grant, Madison, 226
Great Depression, 229
Great Seal of the United States, the 164, 168

Grégoire, Henri, 64, 68, 128
Guadeloupe, 191

Habsburg Empire, 62
Halakah, 108, 120
Hamilton, Alexander, 45, 100, 105–7, 182
Handlin, Oscar, 11, 55
Hartz, Louis, 6, 9–11, 28, 39, 44, 60, 99, 157, 175, 188, 192, 195, 211, 216, 218–19, 221, 225; and American exceptionalism, 12–13; and American national character, 20, 27–28; and the American Revolution, 14–15, 17–18, 20–21, 147–48; and equality in America, 13–15; and the French Revolution, 15–16, 147–48; and lack of classes in America, 14–15; and lack of feudalism in America, 15; and the middle class, 17–18, 22–23; and Native-Americans, 178; and property, 17–18; and racism, 31; and religion, 15, 18, 20, 89; and slavery, 177
Haskalah, 61, 93, 120
Hays, Moses M., 162
Hazareesingh, Sudhir, 79
Hébert, Jacques-Rene, 190
Hébertists, 190
Hebrew, 61, 86, 112
Hebrew Bible, 151
Hebrew calendar, 158
Hebrew language, 96, 130, 132, 151, 153, 159
hederim, 50, 92, 96
Henry, Jacob, 162–63
Higham, John, 11, 35
Higonnet, Patrice, 186
Historical Dictionary of the French Revolution 1789–1799, 196
historiography: American, 6–12; French, 8
Hitler, Adolf, 191
Hobsbawm, E. J., 34–35
Hofstadter, Richard, 11
Holbach, Baron d', 170
Holland, 42, 48, 118, 202, 224; and Jews, 25, 147, 152–53, 159
Hollywood, 236
Holocaust, 234, 236–37; Museum in Paris, 236
Holy Trinity, 81

Hopkinson, Francis, 139
Hyman, Paula E., 97
Hyslop, Beatrice Fry, 33, 196

Idéologues, 99
immigrants/immigration: and America, 49, 54–55, 217, 225–26, 234; 228–30; and France, 54–55, 226, 228–29, 231, 234. *See also* anti-Semitism; citizenship; Exclusion Act of 1882; Ku Klux Klan; National Origins Acts of 1921 and 1924; naturalization; xenophobia
Imprimeur ou la Fete de Franlin, L', 99
Indians. *See* Native-Americans
intermarriage of Jews, 95–96, 110, 124–25; in America, 159–60, 222; in England, 159–60; in France, 130, 159–60; in Germany, 159–60; in New York City, 110, 124–25
"International Jew, The," 229. *See also* Dearborn *Independent*; Ford, Henry
In the Name of Liberalism, 192
Iredell, James, 142
Irish-Americans, 164
Israel: ancient, 118, 122–24, 152, 156, 167–68; and the Six Day War of 1967, 234; State of, 218, 236; and the War of Independence of 1948, 218
israélites-française, 71
Italian-Americans, 230
Italy, 82, 117–18, 120, 131

Jacobins, 3, 44–45, 77, 80, 86, 89, 99–100, 130, 186, 190–92, 199; clubs of, 101, 181, 189–92, 197, 199; clubs of, Chatroux, 205; —, Grenade, 205; —, Toul, 205; and emancipation of slaves, 202; and women, 197–99, 201–6
Jacobs, Hart, 130
Japanese-Americans, 230
Jefferson, Thomas, 45, 52–53, 98, 166–68, 182, 184–85, 208–9, 270n.6
Jerusalem, 81, 112, 118, 156
Jesus Christ, 71–72, 105, 127, 145–46, 170
Jewish bible, the, 167
Jewish law, 110, 153
Jewish liturgy, 150
Jewish name changes, 222–23

Jewish question, 136, 140. *See also* Mosaic Code/Law
Jewry, French: cohesiveness, 158
Johnson Acts. *See* immigrants/immigration; National Origins Acts of 1921 and 1924
Joseph II, 131–32
July Monarchy, 16, 187, 217
jus sanguinis, 53–55
jus soli, 41, 53

Kahn, Zadoc, 81
Kalm, Peter, 158
Kates, Gary, 4
kehillah/kehillot, 60, 82, 101, 105, 116, 120, 182
Kentucky, 184
Key, Francis Scott, 37
Killing of History, The, 6–8
King, Desmond, 29, 192
Ku Klux Klan, 225, 228–29

Lacan, Jacques, 7
Lacombe, Claire, 202
Ladino, 61
Lafayette, Marie Joseph Paul Yves, Roch. Gilbert Du Motier, Marquis de, 99
Lang, Jack, 235
Latin America, 179
Latinos, 236
Law of the Maximum, 200–1
Lawrence, D. H., 243n.57
League for the French Fatherland, 232
League for the Rights of Man, 232
Léon, Anne-Pauline, 202
Le Pen, Jean-Marie, 40, 234
Lettres Patents, 60
levée en masse, 198
Levi-Strauss, Claude, 7
Levy, Uriah P., 223
Lexington and Concord, Battles of, 37, 40
Louisiana Purchase, 45
Louisiana Territory, 184
liberal era in the French Revolution, 86
liberalism, 4–5
Liberal Tradition, The. *See* Hartz, Louis
Lieberman, Joseph, 154, 220
Ligue Française pour le Droit des Femmes, 215
Lipset, Seymour Martin, 11

London, 152–53, 159
Lorraine, 65–66, 68–70, 73–75, 77, 83, 90, 92, 96, 101, 104–6, 120, 127–28, 159–61, 221, 223
Louis XVI, 16, 37, 40, 44, 61, 69, 81–82, 85–86, 197, 199
Louis XVIII, 72
Lowenstamm, Saul, 152–53
Lower Rhine, Department of, 75–76
Luther, Martin, 143
Lynn, John A. (CV), 227n.52

Madison, James, 98, 142–43, 145–46, 182
Malesherbes, Chrétien Guillaume de La-moignon, 61–62, 73, 84
"Malesherbes Commission," 61–62, 73
"Marianne," 220
Marie-Antoinette, Queen of France, 204–5
Markoff, John, 33, 196
marranos, 63, 226
Married Women's Property Act, 213
"Marseillaise, La," 37, 102
Martinique, 191
Marx, Karl, 194
Marxism, 7, 9, 16, 178
Maryland, 41–42, 141, 143, 145–46, 182
Maskil/maskilim, 92, 116, 131, 156. See also Haskalah
Masonic lodges, 157
Massachusetts, 144–46, 164, 183; Bay Colony, 141, 180; Constitution of ,144, 146
mass society, 24. See also Tocqueville, Alexis de
master narrative, 8–10
Maurras, Charles, 40
Maury, Jean Siffrein, 69–70, 72, 146
Medical Society of New York City, 157
Melting Pot Mistake, The, 226
Mendelssohn, Moses, 93, 95
Méricourt, Théroigne, de, 202
messianic Judaism, 111, 156
messianism: and nationalism, 81–82; and revolution, 80
Metahistory: The Historical Imagination in Nineteenth-Century Europe, 7–8, 242n.35
Methodist Episcopal Church, 182, 184–85

Methodists, 182
Metz, 96, 101–2, 160–61
Middle Ages, 51, 62, 148–49
middle class, 43–44, 59, 65
minihistory, 8
miscegenation, 180
Mississippi, 184, 213
Mitchell, Joshua, 12
Mitterand, François, 235
Molé, Louis-Matthieu, 106–8, 115, 121–22
Montagnards. See Jacobins
more judaico, 133, 223
Morris, Gouverneur, 164–65
Mosaic Code/Law, 71, 92, 103, 108, 110, 112–16, 121–27, 132. See also Jewish law
Moses, 110, 125, 156, 168
Moses, Isaac, 139
Moses, Myer, 156
mulattos, 180–81, 189, 192
multiculturalism. See pluralism

Nancy, France, 68–69, 77, 83, 91, 120, 159, 161
Napoleon. See Bonaparte, Napoleon
Napoleon III, 45
National American Woman Suffrage Association, 216
National Assembly, 4, 38, 44, 64, 100–1, 116, 146, 296, 202–3
National Constituent Assembly, 3, 59, 66–70, 72–78, 84, 98
National Convention, 57, 178–79, 190, 197–99, 204–5
National Council of Regional Languages and Cultures, 235
national culture. See political culture
National Front, 40. See also Le Pen, Jean-Marie
National Guard of France, 35, 86, 100, 199
nationalism, 5–6, 33–56; and authoritari-anism, 41; and exclusivity/organicity, 4, 14, 39–42, 48, 134, 147, 227, 232–33; and inclusiveness/liberalism, 40–43, 48–49, 52, 61, 165–66, 170–71, 216
National Legislative Assembly, 85, 99, 198
National Origins Act: of 1921, 225; of 1924, 225–26

"nation within a nation," 135, 139, 148

Native-Americans, 7, 23, 28, 31, 55, 175, 178–79, 209, 211, 230

naturalization, 52–55, 164–66, 228, 270n.86

Naturalization Act of 1790, 53. *See also* citizenship: and women

natural rights, 73

Nazism, 42, 95, 191, 226, 231. *See also* anti-Semitism: in Germany; Hitler, Adolf

New Amsterdam. *See* New York: City of

New Deal. *See* Roosevelt, Franklin D.

New England, 143, 170

New Hampshire, 145–46, 183

New Jersey, 145–46, 182, 209

Newport, RI, 154, 162, 167–68

New Testament, 162

New York: City of, 107, 140, 151, 153, 160–61, 168, 221, 229; State of, 143–46, 168–69, 182–83, 193–96, 213

New York Manumission Society, 182

Nicholas I, 132

Noailles, Vicomte de, 99

nobility of France, 33–34, 63–65, 181

Noiriel, Gérard, 41

Nordic peoples, 225. *See also* racialism/racism, scientific

North, the, 186–87, 194, 218

North Carolina, 143, 145–46, 162; House of Commons of, 162

Northwest Ordinance, 145, 184

Northwest Territory, 184

Notes on Virginia, 185

Notre Dame, Cathedral of, 81, 88, 190

Old Regime and the French Revolution, The. *See* Tocqueville, Alexis de

Old Testament. *See* Jewish bible, the

Organic Articles of 1802, 105

Orthodox Judaism, 96–97, 110, 120, 134, 136

Oxford English Dictionary, The, 38

Padua, Italy, 35

Palestine, 93

Palladian architecture, 154

Panama scandal, 226

Papal States: in France, 73

Paris, 52, 68, 70, 75, 83, 86–87, 96–97, 99–101, 117, 119, 128–29, 159, 161, 187, 189, 205, 207, 215, 221; and bread riots, 197; Commune of, 74, 87, 190, 197, 201, 203, 207; Constitution of, 98, 162, 166; Department of, 75

Parisian Sanhedrin. *See* Sanhedrin: Great

Parliamentary Oaths Act, 66

Parole, La, 228

particularism, 38–40, 73, 79–80, 177, 230

Pasquin, Etienne Denis, 106–7

Passing of the Great Race: Or the Racial Basis of European History, The, 226

péage corporel, 60–61

Pelley, William, 229–31

Pennsylvania, 141, 145–46, 164, 182–83; Constitution of, 98, 162, 166; Council of Censors of, 162

Periere brothers, 223

Perigord, Charles-Maurice-Talleyrand, 72

Pétain, Henry Philippe, 190–92, 231, 235. *See also* Vichy France

Petersburg, VA, 156–57

Philadelphia, PA, 138–40, 151–52, 157, 163, 168

Philadelphia Abolition Society, 182

Phillips, Jonas, 270n.81

philosophes, 89. *See also* Enlightenment, the

Pinckney, Charles, 147, 163, 182

Pinto, Isaac, 153

Pledge of Allegiance, 36

pluralism, 5, 10, 25, 39, 42, 49–50, 54–56, 118, 136, 146, 161, 163–64, 175–76, 189, 216–17, 219, 235

poissards, 200–1, 203

Poland, 38, 69, 91, 104, 125

political culture, 4–6

Pope, 34, 88–89,

Popular Front, 231, 233

population of France, 96–97

population of Jews: in America, 150, 160, 225; in England, 161; in France, 3, 118, 159–61; in Holland, 159

populism. *See* mass society; Tocqueville, Alexis de

Portalis, Joseph Marie, 106–7

Potter, David, 11

Poujadist movement, 234

Promissory Oaths Act, 66

property, 83; and rights, 210. *See also* women: property of; women's rights: and property
Protestantism, 18, 43, 59, 65, 77, 80, 105, 121, 133; and America, 143–46, 149, 151, 155, 158, 164, 169, 171, 227, 229; and France, 3, 63, 70, 84–85, 87, 90, 93, 98, 116, 169
Protocols of the Elders of Zion, 227–29
Prudhomme, Louis-Marie, 202
Prussia, 35, 131
public opinion polls, 220, 230–31, 234
Putnam, Robert D., 29

Quakers, 141, 182

race, 9, 24, 44, 176, 178–79, 209–10
racialism/racism, 26, 39, 50, 141, 164, 185, 189, 190–91, 211, 217; scientific, 225–26, 230
Randolph, Edmund, 142, 182
Raphael, Jacob, 139
Reconstruction, 45, 217, 230
Reformation, 63
Reform Judaism, 221
"*régénération*," 64–65, 71–72
Reign of Terror, 45, 84, 86, 100, 187, 190, 197, 199. *See also* Jacobins; Robespierre, Maximilien
religion/religious, 43, 50–51; establishments in America, 149; wars of, 148
Renaissance, 38
Renouveau Juif. See Comité Juif d'Action
"republican mothers," 201, 206–10
Republican Party, 188, 234
"Republic of Virtue," 91, 135
Republic: Second, 97, 176, 187, 192, 217, 223, 233; Third, 97, 217, 227–28, 231–33; Fourth, 217; Fifth, 217
"*République Française Une et Indivisible*," 34–36
Reubell, Jean-François, 72, 76, 190–91
Revolt Against Civilization: The Menace of the Under MAN, The, 226
Revolutionary Demands: A Content analysis of the Cahiers De Doléances of 1789, 33
Revolution: of 1830, 217, 225; of 1848, 16, 176, 192, 217, 225
Rhineland, 82, 130

Rhode Island, 145, 162, 164
Richmond, VA, 152, 157, 167
rights of man, 74,
Rising Tide of Color Against White World-Supremacy, The, 226
Robespierre, Maximilien, 68–69, 88, 189–90, 200–1, 203, 206, 208. *See also* Jacobins
Rodgers, Daniel T., 6
Roland, Manon Jeanne Philipson, 202–5
Roland de la Platière, Jean-Marie, 99, 202
Rome, Italy, 87–88, 150, 152, 235
Roosevelt, Franklin D., 230
Rothschild, James, 223
Rothschilds, 223–24
Rousseau, Jean Jacques, 88
Roux, Jacques, 202
Royal Academy of Arts and Sciences of Metz, 64, 68
Royer-Collard, Pierre-Paul, 100
Rush, Benjamin, 138–39, 169–70, 182
Russia, 104, 112–13, 132, 148–49, 169, 191, 221; Orthodox Church of, 147; and the Revolution of 1917, 43, 59, 78, 80, 88–89, 149; Soviet, 56, 105, 147, 149, 163, 169, 191, 194

Saint-Esprit-lès Bayonne, France, 66, 159
Samuel, Rebecca, 156–57
Sanhedrin: ancient, 122, 132, 182; Great, 103, 112, 115, 122–27, 132
sans culottes, 45, 181, 197
Sarna, Jonathan, 156, 267n.41
Savannah, GA, 151, 154, 167
Schecter, Ronald, 4, 114
Schwartzfuchs, Simon, 128
Second Empire, 97, 233
Seixas, Gershom, 129, 140, 150, 153–56, 223
Semites, 227
Shapiro, Gilber, 33, 196
Shays's Rebellion, 45
Shumeli, Efraim, 111
Sièyes, Emmanuel Joseph, 38
Silver Shirts. *See* Christian American Patriots
Sinclair, Anne, 220
slavery, 176–78, 183–95; American, 182–85, 188, 193; French, 180–81; 186–88, 190–91, 196, 199

slavery: abolition of: —, in America, 182, 185–88, 194; —, in England, 186–88; —, in France, 177, 181–82, 185–88, 190, 194, 199, 202
slave trade, 185; American, 182–84; Committee for the Abolition of, 182; English, 182; French, 180–81, 184, 186
Smith, Gerald L. K., 234
Smith, Rogers, 29–32, 192, 230, 236
Smith v. Allwright, 230
socialism, 194
Société de la moral chrétienne, 187
Société des Amis des Noirs, 181–82, 186–87,191–92
Société des deux sexes, 205
Society for Relief of Free Negroes Illegally Held in Bondage. See Philadelphia Abolition Society
Society of Angiers, 192
Society of Friends. See Quakers
Sons of the American Revolution, 40
South, the, 177, 186–87, 194, 218–19
South Africa, 179
South Carolina, 43, 142, 145–46, 164
Southern Europe, 228
Soviet Union. See Russia: Soviet
Spain, 133
Spinoza, Baruch, 93
"Star Spangled Banner, The," 37
Stavisky Affair, 231
St. Domingue, 180, 185, 187, 191, 193
Stiles, Ezra, 163
Stoddard, Lothrop, 226
St. Paul's Episcopal Chapel, 154
Strasbourg, 96–97, 120, 141, 191
Studies in Classical American Literature, 243n.57
suffrage, 31, 198; in America, 176, 212, 216; in France, 80, 190, 196, 199, 212, 216
synagogues, 86, 89, 102, 117–18, 133, 160, 227; in America, 153–54, 157–58, 167–68; in Amsterdam, 153; in France, 97; in London, 153

Talleyrand. See Perigord, Charles-Maurice-Talleyrand
Talmud, 94, 112, 121–22, 158
Telling the Truth About History, 11

"Temples of Reason", 86, 190. See also civic religion: in the French Revolution; dechristianization campaign
test oaths, 98, 250; in America, 144–46. See also, Constitution: U.S.
Thermidor, 45, 52, 199–200
Thiébault, François Martin, 66
Thionville, victory of, 140
Third Estate, 23–24, 85
Tocqueville, Alexis, 6, 9–11, 28, 44, 56, 59, 61, 76, 99–100, 155, 175, 177, 192–93, 211, 216, 218–19, 221, 225; and African-Americans, 31, 177, 185; and American conformity, 23–24; and American democracy, 13–14, 20, 26–27; and American equality, 13–14, 20, 26–27; and American exceptionalism, 12–14; and the American middle class, 17–18; and American national character, 14, 20–21, 24–27; and the American revolution, 13, 17, 21, 147–48; and centralization, 23–24, 27, 83–84, 177, 232; and civil society, 24–26, 49; and despotism, 23; and French national character, 19, 21, 26–27; and the French Revolution, 16, 19–21, 83–84, 147–48; and mass society theory, 10, 24, 26; and Native-Americans, 31, 178; and property, 17–19; and racialism, 26; and religion, 18–19, 21–22; and voluntary association, 24–25, 27, 49, 216, 232; and women, 179
Tocqueville Between Two Worlds: The Making of a Political and Theoretical Life, 243n.57
Torah, 94
totalitarianism, 12, 141
Toul, France, 55
"Tree of Liberty," the, 190
tribunal de famille, 198
Tricolor, 35–36, 90

unifying theory. See master narrative
Union française pour le Suffrage des femmes, 216
United Nations, "Gender-related Development Index," 215
universalism, 38–40, 43–44, 48–49, 78–79, 88, 135, 210
University of Pennsylvania, 223

Unredeemed Captive, The, 8
Upper Rhine, Department of, 76
U.S. Congress, 31, 53, 184, 223
U.S. House of Representatives, 164, 184, 224
U.S. Senate, 224, 228
U.S. Supreme Court, 220, 230
usury, 61, 70–71, 104–6, 108–9, 113, 123–24, 127–28, 148. *See also* Alsace; anti-Semitism; Bonaparte, Napoleon; Lorraine
utopia, 74, 78–81

Vallé de Shénandoah en Virginie, La, 99
Valmy, victory of, 38, 81
Vatican II, 155
Vel d' Hiv, 236
Vendée, 12, 45
Vermont, 145–46, 183
Vernon, Richard, 24
Versailles, 3, 85
Vichy France, 45, 79, 217, 231–32, 234–36, 290; and Jews, 31–33, 226, 235–36;
National Council of, 190. *See also* Pétain, Henri Philippe
Vietnam War, 10
Virginia, 98, 144, 182–83, 185; and Bill for Establishing Religious Freedom, 98, 145, 166
völkisch nationalism. *See* nationalism: and exclusivity/organicity
Voltaire (François-Marie Arouet), 88, 170
voluntary association, 24–25, 27. *See also* Tocqueville, Alexis de

Walzer, Michael, 90
War of 1812, 38, 45, 217
War of the First Coalition, 82
Wars of Religion, 63
Washington, D.C., 213
Washington, George, 36, 99–100, 129, 138, 167–70, 182
Watson, Tom, 228
Weld, Theodore Dwight, 188

Wells, Charlotte C., 62
Western Europe, 134
West Indies, 151–52, 156, 180–81, 187, 190. *See also* Martinique; St. Domingue
West Point, 157, 223
Whiskey Insurrection, 45
White, Hayden, 7–8, 242n.35
White Terror, 46, 199
Wilhelm, Friedrich, 132
Wilson, James, 138
Windschuttle, Keith, 6–8
Winrod, Gerald, 229–31
Winthrop, James, 143
Wolin, Sheldon, 243n.57
women, 179, 194–216; education of, 212–13; employment of, 215; government office holding of, 215; military service of, 201, 210, 214–15; property of, 83
women's rights, 10, 175–76, 179, 194, 206, 211, 215–16, 236; and feminism, 215–16; and marriage, 198, 215; and nationality, 211–12; and property, 208, 213–14
Woodrow Wilson Foundation Award, 9
Woodward, C. Vann, 55
World War I, 39, 214; and America, 228; and France, 217, 228; and Germany, 228
World War II, 9, 95, 215, 221, 235, 237; and France, 221, 230

xenophobia, 4, 225–26, 228–29, 234. *See also* immigrants/immigration; Ku Klux Klan; nationalism; racialism

Yale University, 157, 163, 223
"Yankee Doodle," 37
Yellow Star of David, 231
yeshivot, 86, 92, 96–97
Yiddish, 61, 86, 92–93, 95–97, 131, 153, 159
Yulee, David, 224

Zionism, 81, 93, 234–35; messianic, 94